endpapers

bookplate

half title

The BOOK

ALSO BY

KEITH HOUSTON

Shady Characters: The Secret Life of Punctuation, Symbols, & Other Typographical Marks

title

The BOOK

A COVER-TO-COVER EXPLORATION OF THE MOST POWERFUL OBJECT OF OUR TIME

subtitle

dingbat

Keith Houston

author

W. W. NORTON & COMPANY
Independent Publishers Since 1923
New York London

imprint

Printed in China
First Edition

For information about special discounts for bulk purchases, please contact W. W. Norton Special Sales at specialsales@wwnorton.com or 800-233-4830

Manufacturing by Asia Pacific Offset
Book design by Abbate Design
Production manager: Anna Oler

ISBN 978-0-393-24479-3

W. W. Norton & Company, Inc.
500 Fifth Avenue, New York, N.Y. 10110
www.wwnorton.com

W. W. Norton & Company Ltd.
Castle House, 75/76 Wells Street, London W1T 3QT

1 2 3 4 5 6 7 8 9 0

TO MY PARENTS, LIZ AND JIM

dedication

{ contents page }

Contents

frontmatter head

Introduction *xv*

Part 1 ⇚ The Page

1. A Clean Sheet: the invention of papyrus 3
2. Hidebound: the grisly invention of parchment 18
3. Pulp Fictions: the ambiguous origins of paper in China 35
4. From Silk Road to Paper Trail: paper goes global 50

Part 2 ⇚ The Text

5. Stroke of Genius: the arrival of writing 79
6. The Prints and the Pauper: Johannes Gutenberg and the invention of movable type 102
7. Out of Sorts: typesetting meets the Industrial Revolution 128

Part 3 ⇚ Illustrations

8. Saints and Scriveners: the rise of the illuminated manuscript 155

9. Ex Oriente Lux: woodcut comes to the West 175
10. Etching a Sketch: copperplate printing and the Renaissance 202
11. Better Imaging Through Chemistry: lithography, photography, and modern book printing 219

Part 4 ↞ Form

12. Books Before the Book: papyrus scrolls and wax tablets 241
13. Joining the Folds: the invention of the codex 261
14. Ties That Bind: binding the paged book 283
15. Size Matters: the invention of the modern book 310

Colophon 329
Acknowledgments 333
Further Reading 335
Notes 339
Illustration Credits 403
Index 407

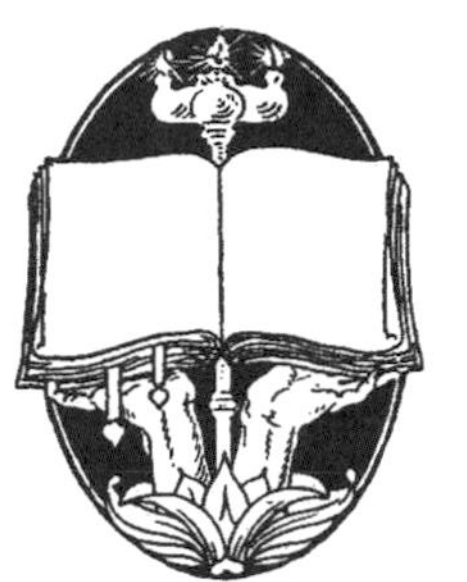

Introduction

frontmatter head

This is a BOOK about books. Until recently, this would have been an unambiguous statement. Whether it was a flimsy paperback or a ponderous coffee-table tome, a book was a book and the word came without caveats. We bought books at bookshops and garage sales; we borrowed them temporarily from libraries and permanently from our friends (and sometimes the other way around); we held them reverently, gingerly, or forced them open until their spines cracked; we filed them neatly on bookshelves or piled them haphazardly at our bedsides. To borrow the words of Supreme Court Justice Potter Stewart, we know a book when we see it.[1]

After more than a thousand years as the world's most important form of written record, the book as we know it faces an unknown future. Just as paper superseded parchment, movable type put scribes out of a job, and the codex, or paged book, overtook the papyrus scroll, so computers and electronic books threaten the very existence of the physical book.* E-books are cheap and convenient, weightless things

*It is worth introducing "codex" as a technical term: it means specifically a paged book, as opposed to a papyrus scroll, clay tablet, or any of the myriad other forms the book has taken

footnote

downloaded at the tap of a touchscreen or the click of a mouse and effortlessly toted around in their hundreds on a phone or tablet. Barring an actual apocalypse, your e-books will be stored safely online forever, duplicated serenely across a host of servers in data centers around the world. It takes a strong will to resist the lure of the e-book.

Yet tiny apocalypses, just not of the physical variety, are happening all the time. In 2009, in an apparent attempt to carry out the world's most ironic act of censorship, Amazon silently deleted certain editions of George Orwell's *1984* from their owners' Kindles as part of a copyright dispute, and news outlets continue to report on the plight of readers whose e-books have vanished without warning.[2] When you click "Buy Now" to get that new title delivered to your account, you are not *buying* anything: the e-book economy is like a housing market where no one is allowed to buy a house and we, the tenants, remain trapped on the wrong side of the divide.

All that set aside, pluck a physical book off your bookshelf now. Find the biggest, grandest hardback you can. Hold it in your hands. Open it and hear the rustle of paper and the crackle of glue. Smell it! Flip through the pages and feel the breeze on your face. An e-book imprisoned behind the glass of a tablet or computer screen is an inert thing by comparison.

This book is not about e-books. This book is about the corporeal ones that came before them, the unrepentantly analog contraptions of paper, ink, cardboard, and glue that we have lived with and depended on for so long. It is about books that have mass and odor, that fall into your hands when you ease them out of a bookcase and that make a *thump* when you put them down. It is about the quiet apex predator that won out over clay tablets, papyrus scrolls, and wax writing boards to carry our history down to us.

It is, admittedly, all too easy to take the existence of physical

---

over the millennia. It is pronounced "code-ex," and its plural is "codices." I have used it where a distinction must be made between a paged book and any other form.

books for granted. The sheer weight of them that surrounds us at all times, in bookcases, libraries, and bookshops, leads to a kind of bibliographic snow blindness. In writing this book I leafed through hundreds more, and even then I gave many of them barely a second glance beyond the text and illustrations on their pages. But every so often I remembered to look again, and I was amazed at what I found. One book fell open to reveal a sheet of handmade papyrus glued onto a blank page. It was the first time I had ever seen or touched a piece of this ancient ancestor of paper. The plastic-seeming material covering the spine of another book turned out to be calfskin vellum, the writing material that saw off papyrus and that was in turn usurped by paper.[3] Some books held elaborate illustrations that had been printed using wooden blocks or copper plates, or even painted by hand; in others, pasted-in color photographs printed on glossy paper were a reminder that the printing of scenes from life has not always been as convenient as it is now. A book's text can tell you something about it too, and it was a treat to come across those old books whose letters were just barely indented on the paper, the ink impressed on the page by the force of a printing press rather than wicked off an eerily flush lithographic plate. Even a humble paperback speaks volumes about bookmaking by the smell of the glue in its spine and the off-white cast of its paper.

This book is about the history and the making and the *bookness* of all those books, the weighty, complicated, inviting artifacts that humanity has been writing, printing, and binding for more than fifteen hundred years. It is about the book that you know when you see it.

Part 1

part number

The PAGE

part title

1

chapter number

A Clean Sheet: the invention of papyrus

chapter title

drop cap

Ever since Napoleon swept into Egypt at the tail end of the eighteenth century, ushering in the modern era of Egyptology, the outside world has thrilled to successive revelations of golden death masks and boy kings; of beautiful queens and matchless libraries; and of million-ton pyramids aligned to the points of the compass with uncanny precision.[1]

In spite of all this, ancient Egypt's most vital commodity is treated nowadays as little more than a souvenir. Papyrus, the paperlike material upon which the ancient world wrote its books and conducted its business, is every bit as Egyptian as the pyramids or mummies that have since eclipsed it—and it was, in its day, considerably more important than either. The intertwined stories of paper, the page, and the book begin not with the glittering wealth of god-kings or their soaring mausoleums but with the weeds that grew abundantly along the Nile's marshy shores.

Cyperus papyrus has always been an interloper in Egypt, if a welcome one. To the south, beyond the country's borders, the banks of the White Nile and the shores of Lake Victoria, its source, are crowded

opener text

by stands of papyrus sedge. Here, triangular, grasslike stems crowned by sprays of fine leaves grow from submerged roots to reach around ten feet in height.[2] Occasionally, a clump of papyrus reeds breaks free from its moorings and drifts off downriver to lodge elsewhere along the river's banks, with some coming to rest in Egypt itself. These temporary islands were (and are) navigational menaces, but ancient Egypt's precious papyrus swamps could not have taken root without them.[3]

The inhabitants of the fertile Nile delta cultivated papyrus for papermaking purposes from the fourth millennium BCE onward, though papyrus reeds were adapted to a bewildering array of other uses too.[4] It was a veritable wonder plant: to the ancient Egyptians, papyrus was an essential part of life, and not only as a writing material.

In a country that was marshy and arid by turns and conspicuously devoid of trees, papyrus reeds provided a convenient alternative to importing timber. The roots of the plant were robust enough to be carved into tools and utensils, and, in the form of charcoal, they burned hot enough to smelt iron and copper, reaching temperatures of 1,650 degrees Fahrenheit (900 degrees Celsius).[5] Early Egyptologists thought papyrus was also burned as a kind of incense: in 1778, a Danish classical scholar named Niels Iversen Schow bought a papyrus scroll from a hoard alleged to have been discovered near the pyramids at Giza, whereupon the "native" sellers reportedly tore up and burned the rest so as to enjoy the pungent smoke.[6] Schow's scroll was later traced not to Giza but instead to an oasis some miles to the south, leading the Victorian scholar F. G. Kenyon to remark sniffily that "the statements of native discoverers as to the provenance of papyri are not valuable as evidence."[7] Kenyon was a prominent member of the first wave of "papyrologists," the name given to scholars who study ancient texts written on papyrus, and the tale of Schow's misattributed scroll has since become a cautionary anecdote for students of the subject. Though it has been told and retold in many papyrological treatises, however, it turns out that burning papyrus is no more or less aromatic than burning paper

↞ An eighteenth-century depiction of the flowering head of a papyrus reed. The triangular section of the stem is visible at bottom.[8]

caption

(both give off an unremarkable campfire aroma, as this author found out), rather undermining claims of its use as incense.[9] The statements of colonial antiquarians, too, are sometimes not valuable as evidence.[10]

Papyrus stood in for wood in ancient Egyptian boatbuilding, especially for the simple, flat-bottomed punts used for hunting and harvesting in the Nile's papyrus swamps. Dried papyrus is around four times more buoyant than balsa wood, and, while it eventually becomes waterlogged and loses that buoyancy, a boat made from sheaves of plentiful papyrus reeds was easily replaced.[11] But papyrus boats were prized for more than just their buoyancy. In Egyptian myth, the goddess Isis sailed the Nile on a papyrus boat to search for fragments of the body of Osiris, her husband (and her brother, so the story goes), and it was said that the river's crocodiles feared to attack any such craft lest they encountered a wrathful deity aboard it instead of a cowering human.[12] Other papyrus vessels, both larger and smaller, plied the Nile alongside the simple rafts of hunters and farmers: papyrus barges may have helped transport the colossal stone blocks used to build the pyramids, while some translations of the Old Testament say that the basket in which Moses was hidden among the reeds of the Nile's shores was made from papyrus, not bulrushes.[13] Moses may have had Isis to thank for preserving him from the Nile's ravening crocodiles as much as he did his mother.

Also in a nautical vein, cords made from papyrus were famously strong and light. The thin green skin of the reed was peeled off in strips and plaited to make rope, while cables up to three inches in diameter could be woven from whole stems.[14] Papyrus rope was so renowned, in fact, that a number of ancient writers mentioned it by name as they recounted near-mythical events of their recent history. Writing in the mid-fifth century BCE, for example, the Greek historian Herodotus described how the Persian king Xerxes, preparing for an invasion of the Greek mainland, ordered the Hellespont strait in northwest Turkey to be bridged with ropes made of Egyptian papyrus and Phoenician flax. The current proved too strong, however, and the bridge's pontoons were

↞ Papyrus harvesting, as shown by a carving on the wall of a tomb belonging to Puyemrê, a priest who lived during the fifteenth century BCE.[15] *Left,* workers load reeds onto a boat made from bundles of dried papyrus; *right,* another worker peels or splits a reed along its length in preparation for plaiting the strips into rope.

swept away. Displaying the sort of theatrical fury that informed his recent reinvention as a comic-book villain, Xerxes ordered the waters of the Hellespont to be whipped three hundred times. The straits now suitably chastised, two more bridges were built—successfully this time, employing four papyrus and two flaxen cables per bridge—and the invasion proceeded.[16]

The papyrus plant was also used in more domestic settings. Herodotus wrote that the Egyptians ate the lowest cubit, or eighteen inches, of the reed's stem, and that "Those who wish to use [papyrus] at its very best, roast it before eating in a red-hot oven."[17] Modern experiments reveal that papyrus contains few calories and is meager in nutrients, though the spongy white pith may have acted as a source of dietary fiber.[18] Aside from its dubious value as a foodstuff, papyrus was a common ingredient in medicinal preparations: papyrus ash healed ulcers; macerated with vinegar, it treated wounds; the pressed juice relieved eye complaints; and, somewhat redundantly, it was mixed with wine to cure insomnia.[19] A patient who imbibed such a draught could sleep it off on a mattress of bundled papyrus reeds, huddled under a blanket woven from papyrus skins.[20]

Papyrus's centrality in the daily lives of Egyptians was a potent symbol of the land, its traditions, and its social strictures. Ancient

Egyptians called the plant *papuro*, or "of the pharaoh"; the hieroglyphic symbol for Lower Egypt, where the Nile delta spreads out to meet the sea, was a clump of papyrus reeds (or); and the sign for a single stem ( ) stood for youth, vigor, and growth.[21] Hapi, god of the yearly flooding of the Nile, which carried essential nutrients into the fields along its banks, was depicted with papyrus growing from his head, and leafy crowns of papyrus reeds were used as decorations at religious services and funerals. Priests were forbidden from wearing sandals made from anything except papyrus, and the temples over which they presided featured columns modeled after the papyrus stem.[22]

For all this, the eponymous writing material is most enduring and widely known of all.

The facts surrounding the invention of papyrus as a writing material are lost. Egyptians had been inscribing hieroglyphs on stone and pottery for some time before the arrival of papyrus, and though they were tight-lipped on the subject of writing materials, they had plenty to say about writing itself. Egyptian tradition, as recounted by the Greek philosopher Plato, told that hieroglyphics had been handed down by the ibis-headed god Thoth, and, for the Egyptians and later the Greeks, Egypt's writing never lost its sacred aura. We still call ancient Egyptian writing by its Greek name of *hieroglyphica*, or "sacred carved [letters]."[23] Thamus, the mythical Egyptian king who received Thoth's gift of writing, was less reverent. Rather than thank his divine benefactor, Thamus complained that hieroglyphics would condemn humanity to absentmindedness and amnesia:

> *This invention will produce forgetfulness in the minds of those who learn to use it, because they will not practice their memory. Their trust in writing, produced by external characters which are*

> *no part of themselves, will discourage the use of their own memory within them.*[24]

Modern-day linguists think that the idea of writing—that visual signs could be used to represent spoken words, sounds, or concepts—came to Egypt from nearby Sumer, in what is now northeastern Iraq. Inspired by the Sumerian system of cuneiform writing, in which angular symbols were pressed into clay with a wedge-shaped stylus, it is thought that the earliest hieroglyphics were created by one person (or a small number of people) over a short period of time, thus explaining their seemingly miraculous appearance in Egypt toward the end of the fourth millennium BCE.[25]

Papyrus as writing material, on the other hand, traces no divine origin, and more than two centuries of archaeological excavations have not revealed a single ancient account of its invention. It may have been inspired by woven papyrus matting, as some papyrologists have proposed, or it may not.[26] The only thing that experts can say for sure is that it was invented around or before the end of the fourth millennium BCE: an extravagant tomb discovered in 1937 and dated to about 3000 BCE gave up a wooden box containing a blank papyrus roll. The thinking behind this particular funeral offering has not been determined (perhaps the high-ranking official buried there planned to record his impressions of the afterlife), but scholars think that this offering was likely a book, or a representation of one at the very least.[27]

However and whenever it was invented, papyrus joined with hieroglyphics to create a self-contained mechanism for the storage and transmission of information—a pairing that endured as the premier information technology of the ancient world even as that world changed and expanded. Dated to around 1100 BCE, for instance, an Egyptian text called the "Report of Wenamun" tells of a voyage to Phoenicia, the coastal region of modern Lebanon, to trade papyrus rolls for timber.[28] The up-and-coming Greeks knew of papyrus by the sixth century BCE, and possibly earlier (Homer had mentioned papyrus rope two hundred years before, in connection with Odysseus's vengeful return home to Ithaca), but he never spoke of papyrus as a writing material.[29] Curiously, the Roman Republic, founded in 509 BCE, and whose citizens generally strove to emulate the Greeks as closely as possible, lagged somewhat.[30] It was not until the third century BCE, by which time Egypt had been invaded by Alexander the Great and colonized by his conquering generals, that the Romans are thought to have obtained a supply of papyrus from Egypt's new rulers.[31]

Thus papyrus flowed out from Egypt and across the Mediterranean for thousands of years, underpinning the workings of the ancient civilization of Egypt, the proud city-states of the Greeks, and the rapacious Roman Republic. And still, in all this time no one thought to write down precisely what this irreplaceable material was or how it was made. Fully three millennia elapsed after the invention of papyrus before a Roman general saw fit to jot down a few notes about the Egyptians' ubiquitous writing material. The description of papyrus penned in the first century CE by Gaius Plinius Secundus, or Pliny, was short, barely a few hundred words in length, but it is the only window we have onto the ancient craft of papyrus making.[32] It is a source of endless contention.

Born in 23 or 24 CE in the far-flung Roman province of Gaul, Gaius Plinius Secundus was a model citizen, serving as a cavalry officer, a lawyer, and later as governor of one of Rome's Spanish provinces. Later still, in 79 CE, while commanding the Roman fleet anchored at Misenum, near Naples, word reached Pliny of a natural disaster unfolding almost on his doorstep. Only a few leagues away from the naval base, Mount Vesuvius had erupted. Pliny immediately took a squadron of ships across the Bay of Naples to aid the beleaguered towns of Herculaneum and Pompeii, but disaster awaited him. In a letter written many years later, Pliny's nephew explained that his brave uncle succumbed to the volcano's noxious fumes after landing on the threatened coast. Given that Pliny's companions survived, the general's asthma and obesity likely hastened his demise.[33]

As remarkable as his life had been, Pliny is best remembered for the writings he left behind. Among the many books he wrote, one work stands apart: his thirty-seven-volume *Naturalis historia*, or "Natural History," is one of the most important surviving records of ancient Roman knowledge and culture.[34] The significance of *Natural History* as a whole has never been doubted, but Pliny's writings were put under fresh scrutiny in the twentieth century by an Egyptian diplomat named Dr. Hassan Ragab. Appointed as Egypt's ambassador to China in 1956, while serving there Ragab had visited the birthplace of the revered Cai Lun, the purported inventor of paper, and began to entertain the idea of resurrecting Egypt's dormant papyrus industry.[35] But though he combed the works of Herodotus, Strabo, and other ancient historians, Pliny's was the only one that contained what he was looking for: tucked away in its thirteenth volume, among stories of exotic trees and unguents, is a passage that remains the only contemporary description of how to make papyrus.[36]

Ragab's resurrection of papyrus was not to be a straightforward task, however. There are ominous clues as to Pliny's reliability (or lack thereof) scattered throughout *Natural History*, where more sober passages are punctuated by lurid tales of cyclopes in the Carpathians, Himalayan tribes whose feet were attached back to front, and one-legged Indians who used their feet as sunshades.[37] These serve as stark reminders of the age in which Pliny lived and wrote, and Ragab and his colleagues approached Pliny's account of papyrus making with a healthy dose of skepticism. This was just as well, because they found themselves tied in knots almost from his first sentence on the subject. The original Latin reads as follows:

> Praeparatur ex eo charta diviso acu in praetenues sed quam latissimas philyras.[38]

This begins plainly enough. Pliny writes that "paper [*charta*] is prepared by dividing, with a needle," and it seems reasonable to assume that the things to be divided are papyrus reeds. The last three words, however, are more opaque. *Quam latissimas* relates to width—"as wide as possible" or "as broad as possible," as two translations have it—while *philyra* translates literally, and unhelpfully, as "linden tree."[39]

Clearly, Pliny did not mean that reeds averaging a scant inch or two in diameter could somehow be "divided" to become as wide as linden trees, but what he did intend to say remains open to interpretation. The reading arrived at by Ragab and most others is that the pith of the reed must be sliced lengthwise into thin strips. With reference to the figure below, one of two methods is employed: either the triangular stem of the reed is peeled face by face, rotating it between each slice, or it is peeled top to bottom without changing its orientation.[40] In both cases a sharp knife is required, rather than Pliny's needle, and both methods produce a series of strips of varying width.

A competing interpretation, proposed by Dutch papyrologist Ignace H. M. Hendriks, is more unexpected. Hendriks took Pliny's mention of a needle at face value and proposed that the triangular pith

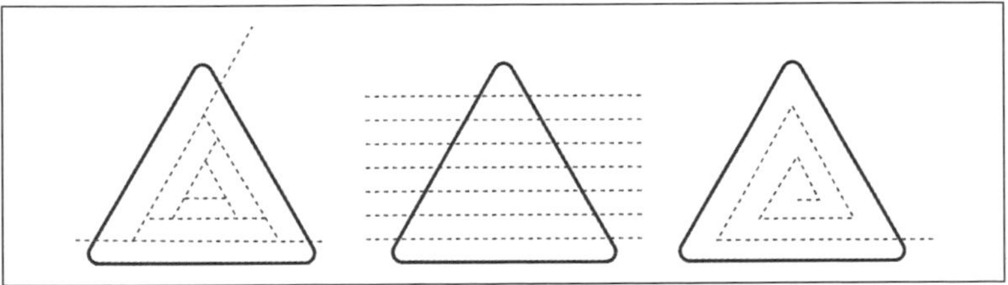

➛ Simplified sections of papyrus reed stems, showing how reeds may have been "divided" before being pressed into sheets. *Left*, a slice is peeled off, the reed is rotated, and the process repeated; *center*, the reed is cut into slices from top to bottom; *right*, Ignace H. M. Hendriks's painstaking "unwinding" of the reed using a needle. Modern examination confirms that all of these methods are compatible with ancient papyrus manufacture.

should be painstakingly unwound, not sliced, to produce a wide, flat sheet with protruding ribs where the needle must change direction at the corners of the stem.[41] As time-consuming and fiddly as this procedure sounds, microscopic comparisons of ancient papyri with modern sheets show that the ancient Egyptians may have both sliced and unwound their papyrus reeds.[42]

With détente reached as to how reeds should be "divided," the next difficulty in parsing Pliny's words lay in working out how these strips or sheets of pith should be assembled into a finished sheet of papyrus. Pliny's description of this next step is more easily translated than the first—there is no incongruous "linden tree" to argue over—but it is not without perplexities. "Various kinds of paper," Pliny writes,

> *are made upon a table, moistened with Nile water; a liquid which, when in a muddy state, has the peculiar qualities of glue. This table being first inclined, the leaves of papyrus are laid upon it lengthwise, as long, indeed, as the papyrus will admit of, the jagged edges being cut off at either end; after which a cross layer is placed over it.*[43]

A sheet of papyrus, in other words, comprises two layers of papyrus pith. The first is made by placing strips of papyrus on a table so that they abut along their long edges, and a second layer running at right angles to the first is laid atop it. Ancient scrolls readily reveal this laminated construction: held up to the light, a crosshatched pattern caused by the two perpendicular layers is easily seen. The reed's vascular bundles, which transport nutrients through the stem, stand out as dark lines against the paler parenchyma, or filler cells.

But what of the need for "Nile water" to glue the layers together? Papyrologists have detected starch between the layers of some early Egyptian papyri, a telltale sign of vegetable-based adhesives such as wheat paste, but the papyrus of Pliny's time is conspicuously free of starch.[44] In the absence of any kind of adhesive, then, the bonding mechanism at work remains mysterious. Hassan Ragab advanced a convoluted theory that ovoid parenchyma cells, bisected by the cutting process, form "dovetail" joints with air pockets in the opposing strips, while botanists at Kew Gardens in London suggested that the reed's sap binds the strips together as it dries.[45] Whatever the truth, a two-ply sheet of papyrus pressed firmly together and left until dry will hold itself together for centuries.[46] Nile water, muddy or not, is not required.

Yet Pliny may not have been entirely incorrect. The waters of the Nile *do* possess a miraculous quality when applied to the papyrus-making process, though it has nothing to do with gluing layers together. Corrado Basile, a papyrologist working in Syracuse, Sicily (one of the few places outside Egypt to possess an indigenous papyrus industry), found that modern papyrus sheets were missing one particular compound found in their ancient counterparts.[47] Aluminum sulfate, the missing compound, is abundant in Nile water, and Basile found that soaking his papyrus strips in aluminum sulfate produced whiter finished sheets.[48] As a bonus, the clay in muddy Nile water may have helped regulate the absorption of ink, a useful property that in modern paper is managed by means of a range of additives—with none other than aluminum sulfate and clay among them.[49] Pliny's cryptic clue about "muddy Nile water" has proven invaluable for modern papyrologists.

The last stage of the papyrus-making process is the least controversial. Having soaked strips of papyrus pith in Nile water (or a solution of aluminum sulfate, depending on one's proximity to that river), Pliny says, "the leaves are pressed close together, and then dried in the sun; after which they are united to one another."[50] The end result is a thin, light sheet perhaps ten or twelve inches on a side, its surfaces textured by the fine lines of the reed's vascular cells.[51] Durable, flexible, and portable, this, at last, is papyrus.

Fortunately, given the sheer necessity of their existence (Pliny could write, without exaggeration, that "all the usages of civilized life depend [...] upon the employment of paper"), papyrus scrolls regularly lived productive lives of hundreds of years. The best scrolls were supple enough to be rolled and unrolled many times, provided that their readers took care to not fray their exposed edges.[52] The books of Aristotle's library, for example, written on papyrus scrolls in the fourth century BCE, were still in use 250 years later when the Roman general Sulla spirited them from Athens to Rome.[53] Even when a papyrus scroll reached the end of its useful life, it might yet live on: Flinders Petrie, an Egyptologist working at the end of the nineteenth century, discovered that many sarcophagi were made from a papier-mâché–like material composed of layers of used papyrus, leading to the recovery of lost works by the philosopher Plato and playwright Euripides.[54] And

⇜ A modern sheet of papyrus trimmed to 5½ by 4½ inches in size.

all this is to say nothing of the countless bookrolls that survived for millennia in tombs, rubbish heaps, and caves, entombed or discarded without thought of preservation or protection, and without which the field of papyrology could not exist.

Papyrus sheets hold together in all but the wettest environments (as long as it is dried under pressure, it is possible to soak a sheet of papyrus in water for days without causing irretrievable damage), though the mold and bacteria that thrive in damp conditions are hazardous to its well-being.[55] The emperor Tacitus, keen to have the works of a favored historian made available in all Roman libraries, had to have ten additional copies made up annually to replace those lost to the soggy weather of Gaul and Germania.[56]

What is it like to work with this fabled writing material? Both Hassan Ragab's "Pharaonic Village" in Cairo and Corrado Basile's Museo del Papiro in Sicily manufacture papyrus according to their founders' instructions, and it is possible to buy sheets of blank papyrus that bear at least a passing resemblance to their ancient ancestors.

Modern papyrus is crackly, rigid, and scratchy in a way that is at odds with the smooth, pliable material described in *Natural History*, and putting pen to paper reinforces the gulf between papyrus ancient and modern. The pens of Pliny's time were made from hollow, dried reeds cut to form a nib like that of a fountain pen, and the meeting of the pen's angular tip with the textured surface of modern papyrus makes for a raspy, shuddering writing process.[57] This writer shivers at the idea that Pliny, or more likely a long-suffering slave, scratched out the 400,000-odd words of *Naturalis historia* with a reed pen on papyrus. Despite their best efforts, papyrologists have not yet cracked Pliny's ancient code.[58]

There is still hope, however. Once cultivated across ancient Lower

Egypt, today's papyrus reeds are grown on a much smaller scale and the reeds themselves have returned to a wild state: papyrus sheets suffer as a result, but at the very least there is room left for improvement.[59] Nor were the ancient Egyptians immune to producing subpar papyrus: Pliny enumerated nine separate grades of papyrus sheet, from *hieratica*, the fine, "sacred" papyrus that Egypt kept for itself, down to the coarse, widely available *emporetica*, or "shop paper," good only for wrapping goods for sale.[60] The enterprising Romans got around the embargo on *hieratica* by purchasing used scrolls and washing off the water-soluble ink; we, of course, cannot take the same shortcut. Perhaps our current level of skill is equal to producing *emporetica* but not *hieratica*, and we should be using it to wrap fish and chips instead of griping about its qualities as a writing surface. Ultimately, even Pliny conceded that papyrus making was not an easy process: "there is so much trickery in the business!" he complained, as if dimly aware of the struggle that would face papyrologists seeking to interpret his words long after they had been divorced from any surviving industry.[61]

Though the contemporary experience of writing on papyrus is a frustrating one, it must not be forgotten that the concept of papyrus itself was momentous: a light, flexible, and durable writing material such as papyrus was an absolute necessity for the existence of the scroll, and without the scroll the book would never have come about. But for the book to live, papyrus had first to die.

2

Hidebound: the grisly invention of parchment

To an ancient Egyptian of the third century BCE, the rolls of papyrus on which the country recorded its history, art, and daily business would have been of all-consuming importance. Scrolls made from papyrus were the medium for hundreds of thousands of books lodged at Alexandria's wondrous library, and blank papyrus sheets were one of the chief exports to Egypt's friends, allies, and trading partners across the Mediterranean. But papyrus's 3,000-year monopoly was about to come under threat. Invented by Egypt's upstart Hellenic neighbors and made from animal hides at great cost in sweat and blood, parchment was smooth, springy, and resilient where papyrus was rough, brittle, and prone to fraying. Its rise at papyrus's expense, however, had little to do with the ergonomics of its use or the economics of its manufacture and everything to do with ambitious pharaohs who ignored the cardinal rule of military leadership: never get involved in a land war in Asia.

The invention of parchment is traditionally ascribed to King Eumenes II of Pergamon, ruler from 197 to 159 BCE of a Greek city-state located in what is now northwestern Turkey. Pergamon comprised only the city itself and a few local towns when Eumenes was crowned as king, but at his death thirty-eight years later it had been transformed into a political, martial, and cultural powerhouse.[1] Chief among his achievements was the founding of a great library to rival that of Alexandria, and Eumenes's institution boasted some 200,000 volumes at its peak.[2] The Pergamenes' book-collecting mania was so notorious that citizens of the nearby town of Scepsis, having inherited Aristotle's library from one of the late philosopher's students, took the extraordinary step of burying its literary treasure to stop it falling into the hands of their acquisitive neighbors.[3] Nor did Eumenes stop at books: in a bid to assemble a staff worthy of his new library he approached Aristophanes, the chief librarian at Alexandria, to offer him a job. The Egyptian king Ptolemy clapped the librarian in irons to ensure his continued loyalty.[4]

The contemporary story of the invention of parchment in Pergamon, as related by Pliny in his compendious but erratic *Natural History*, is a simple one. Writing in the first century CE, Pliny says that King Ptolemy of Egypt—the same Ptolemy, presumably, whom Eumenes had goaded with his importunate headhunting—was so incensed by the rise of Pergamon's library that he banned exports of the papyrus on which it depended. Eumenes responded to the embargo by directing his subjects to find an alternative writing surface; thus, parchment was invented, and Eumenes got the credit.[5]

Pliny's geopolitical parable is not exactly bursting with detail. Dating his story is difficult: exactly which Ptolemy it was (and there were many) who forbade the export of papyrus is not clear, nor was it specified whether it was Eumenes II or his namesake who had invented parchment. And if Pliny's knowledge of royal family trees was shaky, his grasp of history was worse. Writing some five centuries earlier, the Greek writer Herodotus, dubbed the "Father of History" and who would have been required reading for any later scholar, had described how Greeks of the Ionian tribe wrote their books on animal skins when papyrus was scarce.[6] But to hear Pliny tell it, parchment was the spontaneous product of a bibliographic spat—Eumenes's retort to Ptolemy's library envy—that had taken place in more recent, civilized times. Parchment's origins were a good deal more ancient, and its road to prominence much bloodier, than Pliny knew.

As Herodotus had noted back in the fifth century BCE, people of the ancient world had been writing on animal skins long before the tussle between Eumenes and Ptolemy, but the practice was older still. Egyptian texts dated to between 2550 and 2450 BCE mention the use of leather as a writing surface, and the Cairo Museum possesses a fragment of a leather document written shortly after that.[7] A millennium later, the Egyptian "Book of the Dead," a collection of incantations entombed with the dead to help them navigate the afterlife, was commonly written on durable animal skins instead of papyrus.[8] The Sumerians were no strangers to the use of animal skins either; a cuneiform tablet dated to 800 BCE describes how pelts were steeped in baths of flour, beer, and "first quality" wine before being pressed with alum (a mineral salt that causes animal tissues to contract), oak galls (nutlike tree growths caused by burrowing wasp larvae), and "the best fat of a pure ox." A later account of the preparation of goatskin, found in Carchemish in the kingdom of the Hittites (now on the border between Turkey and Syria), is less insistent on fine ingredients. In this recipe, skins were to be soaked in goat's milk and flour, rubbed with oil and cow fat, and finally treated with alum soaked in grape juice and oak galls.[9]

Both recipes describe more or less the same process. First, soaking a pelt in a frothing, enzyme-rich bath of fermenting liquor softens it up, loosens its hairs, and, by means of rising bubbles of carbon dioxide, cleans it. Once the hair has been pushed off by hand or scraped off with a knife, the skin is treated with astringent tannic acids (such as those in alum and oak galls) to "tan" the skin, tightening it up and increasing its durability. The skins of a huge variety of animals were processed according to this basic recipe, and exotic beasts such as lions, leopards, hippos, and hyenas posthumously rubbed shoulders in the tannery with domesticated species such as cattle, sheep, pigs, and donkeys.[10]

The result of all this soaking, scraping, and tanning, however, was not parchment but leather. Tough, flexible, and water resistant, leather was a surprisingly accommodating writing surface, capable of being worked to any desired smoothness and absorbing ink well, but it lacked the rigidity, delicacy, and portability that made papyrus an ideal vehicle for writing.[11] And though the Pergamenes were not the first people to write on leather, they may have discovered the one thing that transforms soft, pliable hide into taut, smooth parchment.

Pergamon's invention might never have left the land of its birth were it not for the war that convulsed Egypt at the midpoint of Eumenes's reign. In 173 BCE, Rome was growing apprehensive about a "cloud in the east"—the predatory Greek king Antiochus IV, head of the Seleucid dynasty, uncle of Egypt's Ptolemy VI Philometor, and ruler of a swath of the ancient world that stretched from the Aegean Sea in the west to the Gulf of Oman in the east.[12] Worried that Antiochus planned to annex his nephew's kingdom, Rome sent a delegation to Philometor at Alexandria under cover of paying tribute to the young king. The envoys' real mission was to monitor the increasingly febrile atmosphere in the region.[13]

It was not long before the situation deteriorated. Philometor, who had ruled with his mother until her death in 176 BCE (his name meant "he who loves his mother"), had fallen under the influence of ambitious advisers and in 170 BCE, still only a teenager, he was persuaded to invade a disputed part of the Seleucid Empire known as Coele-Syria.[14]

The invasion was a disaster.

Forewarned, Antiochus defeated the invading Egyptian army and promptly counterattacked. Within a year he had occupied Egypt and coerced Ptolemy into declaring Antiochus as his "protector," reducing the pharaoh to little more than a puppet king.[15] Only Alexandria eluded Antiochus's grasp: besieged and running out of food, its citizens nevertheless proclaimed Philometor's younger brother—Ptolemy VIII Euergetes,* or "benefactor"—to be Egypt's rightful ruler.[16] With control of Egypt's monarch snatched away, the frustrated Antiochus released Philometor and withdrew, calculating that an Egypt divided between two feuding kings would be easier to subdue.[17]

The Ptolemies did not oblige. Philometor and Euergetes reconciled to face their uncle together. Exasperated, in 168 BCE Antiochus invaded a second time, sweeping aside the remnants of Egyptian opposition as he marched directly to Alexandria. He was drawn up short four miles from the city by a group of men led by a Roman senator: this was Gaius Popilius Laenas, a notoriously short-tempered troubleshooter dispatched by the Senate in response to the Ptolemies' pleas for help.[18] As the invading general approached the Roman deputation with his arm outstretched in greeting, Popilius pressed into Antiochus's hand a tablet bearing the Senate's ultimatum: leave Egypt or suffer the consequences. Before the stunned Antiochus could reply, Popilius drew a circle in the sand around him with his staff and, essentially, dared the conqueror to cross the line. "Before you step out of that circle," Popilius said, "give me a reply to lay before the senate."[19]

Mulling Popilius's demand, and aware of the might of the state on whose behalf it had been issued, Antiochus eventually offered the meek reply, "I will do what the senate thinks right." Popilius accepted his hand

*Eagle-eyed readers will have noticed a Ptolemy VII–shaped hole in proceedings. This unhappy scion of the Ptolemaic dynasty is thought to have been Ptolemy Philometor's son, born long after the war with Antiochus. Ptolemy VII succeeded his father for less than two months before his uncle, Ptolemy Euergetes, had him put to death.

in friendship. The Seleucid king withdrew his forces from Egypt, the Ptolemies were restored to power, and the crisis was averted.[20]

The name of this conflict, the so-called Sixth Syrian War, hardly resounds through history. The Ptolemies and Seleucids had been quarreling over Coele-Syria for a hundred years, and after five earlier conflicts fought by the same dynasties over the same parcel of land, a sixth must have paled into irrelevance.[21] If Antiochus's invasion is mentioned at all outside of academic circles, it is usually because of Popilius's brazen treatment of the invader: according to the author William Safire, the circle that Popilius drew in the desert outside Alexandria has a decent claim to being the origin of the phrase "a line in the sand." (Its main competitor is the story of William B. Travis, lieutenant colonel at the Alamo, who drew a line in the sand with his sabre and said to his men, "Those prepared to die for freedom's cause, come across to me.")[22]

For ancient scribes and scholars, however, the Sixth Syrian War was a watershed. Egypt's economy was wrecked, with papyrus exports driven down and eventually halted altogether, and the literate societies of the ancient world suffered accordingly.[23] Unexpectedly, though, Pergamon's Eumenes II, he of the renowned library, seemed to have the papyrus shortage solved almost before it arose.

In 168 and 167 BCE, as the war in Egypt came to a close, Eumenes's brother Attalus was in Rome on diplomatic business. Among the Pergamene delegation was Crates of Mallus, chief scholar at Pergamon's library, who craved the same approval that the Romans accorded to Aristarchus, his rival at the Library of Alexandria.[24] (Aristarchus had succeeded Aristophanes, the jailbird librarian.) Unfortunately, Crates's visit did not begin well: he fell into an open sewer on the city's Palatine Hill and broke his leg in the process. The librarian made the most of his forced convalescence by delivering lectures to rapt Roman audiences, sparking a renewed interest in grammar and literary criticism as he did so. Though the content of his talks has been lost, the medium on which they were written has not: Crates's books were made of parchment, in the Pergamene fashion, and a Rome starved of papyrus was eager to learn more about this promising replacement. Ever ready to curry favor with his hosts, Crates ordered a shipment to be brought to Rome, and so parchment began its relentless spread across the ancient world.[25]

What, then, elevated the *membrana*, or "skin," with which Crates dazzled Rome above the leather used in centuries past?[26] Today, parchment is often described as untanned leather, but this manages to be an oversimplification and an oxymoron at the same time.[27] An untanned skin is rawhide, not leather; not to mention early parchment often *was* tanned to some degree by the vegetable acids in its preparation baths. But to quibble over this definition misses the point. The innovation that distinguished parchment from leather was not chemical, but mechanical.[28]

Having soaked and unhaired a skin, the Pergamenes discovered that by stretching it on a frame and allowing it to dry before cutting it down, the skin could be made to maintain its tautness and resilience. In mammals the dermis, the middle layer of skin from which leather and parchment are made, is composed of a network of minute collagen fibers.[29] As an unhaired skin soaks in its preparation vat, these fibers absorb and become saturated with the bath's liquid, and this, in turn, mingles with the skin's own secretions to suffuse it with a sticky, adhesive fluid. Stretching the skin causes some of its fibers to break while others are pulled tight, aligning with the plane of the skin, and as the realigned fibers dry out they cause the skin to set in place. (Tanning, by contrast, chemically bonds the collagen fibers together, actively preventing the skin from stretching. The Pergamenes are thought to have modified the ingredients of their preparation baths to minimize this effect.)[30]

The result of this combined stretching and drying process is a taut, flexible material. Whereas leather is soft and limp, a sheet of parchment flexed gently across its surface readily springs back to its original shape and will hold a crease if folded more firmly. More opaque than papyrus, and without the fibrous ridges that made it difficult to write on both sides of a sheet, parchment's physical qualities, the Pergamenes found, made it an almost perfect substrate for writing.[31] Moreover, parchment was stronger than papyrus: a skin gashed by a careless tanner's knife could be safely sewn up, while loose leafs of parchment could be pierced with an awl and tied together without danger of tearing—a property that would be instrumental in shaping the book as we know it.[32]

Tough as it is, parchment is not indestructible. Unlike leather, parchment "breathes," absorbing or releasing moisture to match its environment, and overly damp or dry conditions can eventually damage parchment or its contents. Ink and illustrations may flake off a damp sheet of parchment; it may "cockle," or wrinkle, and lose its stiffness; and it becomes prey to bacteria and mold that can discolor and eventually eat through the parchment entirely.[33] A dry sheet of parchment, on the other hand, will wrinkle, grow brittle, and eventually crack. Fortunately, the temperate climate of Europe, where parchment found greatest use, is relatively benign. Long periods of excessive humidity are rare enough to prevent parchment from becoming too damp, and though parchment can dry out, it requires years in an arid environment—again, a rarity in continental Europe—for it to do so. Parchment is so resistant to dryness, in fact, that it can be heated to 480 degrees Fahrenheit (approximately 250 degrees Celsius) before it begins to shrink and brown. If heated while wet, however, a temperature of only 100 degrees (around 40 Celsius) will shrink a sheet of parchment like a sock left in a hot wash.[34]

In spite of these shortcomings, parchment was an undeniably superior writing material—smooth under a pen's nib, long-lived, and resistant to rough handling. It was perfectly equipped to replace papyrus, in other words, and that is precisely what it did as it was assimilated in turn by each new culture that took it up. The Jewish people of what became modern-day ancient Israel, for instance, were among the earliest

➳ A leather or parchment scroll containing part of the Book of Deuteronomy—specifically, the Ten Commandments. It has been tentatively dated to between 30 BCE and 1 BCE, making it one of the oldest copies in existence.[35]

and most enthusiastic adopters of parchment, as the Dead Sea Scrolls attest. Of the hundreds of documents and fragments found in 1946 in caves near the Dead Sea, more than 90 percent are written on parchment; dated to between 200 BCE and 50–70 CE, the scrolls show how rapidly parchment overtook its Egyptian rival.[36] Even so, ancient Jewish law was strict in its treatment of this new writing material. The tanneries that processed skins, and which often used noisome horse dung to unhair pelts, had to be sited out of town and downwind of prevailing northwesterlies, with one rabbi of special olfactory sensitivity declaring a minimum safe distance of fifty cubits, or seventy-five feet, from the town wall. For ritual documents, only the skins of "clean" animals would do: oxen, sheep, goats, and deer were acceptable, but camels, hares, pigs, and "rock badgers," or hyrax, were not.[37]

Parchment became integral to Jewish tradition. The Mishneh Torah, a fourteen-volume companion to the Torah composed in the twelfth century by Rabbi Moses Maimonides, demands specific forms of parchment for different texts. The Torah, Maimonides wrote, is to

be written only upon *gewil,* or whole parchment, and then only on its hair side. A skin split into two layers yields *kelaf* (flesh side) and *duxustus* (hair side) parchment, which are suitable for tefillin (scrolls contained in small boxes worn on the head and left arm) and mezuzah (scrolls placed on doorposts) respectively. In the cases of *kelaf* and *duxustus,* only the inner surfaces exposed when the parchment is split are suitable for writing. Skins prepared by non-Israelites or Samaritans were prohibited.[38]

Having listed in exhaustive detail the minutiae that governed the ritual use of parchment, Maimonides was considerably more vague as to its manufacture. The few lines the Mishneh Torah devotes to the subject are puzzling, and describe a process that would produce a material more akin to leather than parchment. The crucial stretching process is omitted (though parchment found among the Dead Sea Scrolls does show signs of stretching, rolling, or pressing), and skins are to be finished with "gall-wood or similar materials which contract the pores of the hide," which sounds suspiciously like tanning.[39]

Christianity embraced parchment as eagerly as had its elder sibling, and the spread of the new religion throughout the Western world mirrored the ongoing shift in writing materials. By the fifth century CE, more Christian books were written on parchment than papyrus, and there were more Christian books than any other kind.[40] Oddly enough, the Vatican continued to issue papal edicts, or "bulls," on papyrus until 1022, during the papacy of Benedict VIII.[41] Catholic conservatism may be to blame, but then any pontiff would surely have recalled the words of Revelations 2 in which Pergamon is branded a "seat of Satan."[42] Perhaps Benedict VIII was the first pope who could suppress a reflexive shiver when setting quill to the *pergamena charta*, or "Pergamene paper," that had long been used for more mundane Christian manuscripts.

Like Rabbi Maimonides, medieval Christian writers recorded little interest in how one of the most basic components of their craft was made, and barely a word was written about parchment's manufacture as it took its place as Europe's most important writing material. This indifferent silence was finally broken by a single page tucked away at the back of a fourteenth-century reference book.[43] Following the fashion of its time, this untitled volume was made up of choice extracts from many different works, bound together at its owner's instruction. Now owned by the British Library, today the book goes by its catalogue number (Harley MS 3915, to be precise) and is most often cited for containing a sizeable chunk of a reference work called *De diversis artibus* (The Various Arts), a twelfth-century arts-and-crafts manual attributed to a monk who called himself Theophilus.[44] But though Theophilus holds forth on sundry subjects such as paint mixing, glass blowing, and bookbinding, parchment making is not among them: the page that begins *ad faciendas cartas de pellibus caprinis more bononiense* (on the Bolognese art of making paper from goatskins) is an unattributed orphan.[45] It is worth quoting in its entirety:

> *Take goatskins and stand them in water for a day and a night. Take them and wash them until the water runs clear. Take an entirely new bath and place therein old lime and water, mixing well together to form a thick cloudy liquor. Place the skins in this, folding them on the flesh side. Move them with a pole two or three times each day, leaving them for eight days (and twice as long in winter). Next you must withdraw the skins and unhair them. Pour off the contents of the bath and repeat the process using the same*

⇜ Jost Amman's 1568 woodcut depicting the preparation of parchment. A skin is stretched on a "herse," or drying frame, to be scraped clean with a moon-shaped knife called a *lunellarium*.

quantities, placing the skins in the lime liquor and moving them once each day over eight days as before. Then take them out and wash them well until the water runs quite clean. Place them in another bath with clean water and leave them for two days. Then take them out, attach the cords and tie them to the circular frame. Dry, then shave them with a sharp knife after which leave for two days out of the sun. Moisten with water and rub the flesh side with powdered pumice. After two days wet it again by sprinkling with a little water and fully clean the flesh side with pumice so as to make it quite wet again. Then tighten up the cords, equalise the tension so that the sheet will become permanent. Once the sheets are dry, nothing further remains to be done.[46]

This is a craft transformed. Gone are the ambiguities of ancient soak-scrape-and-stretch methods, now refined into a rigorous multistep program with detail aplenty. Goatskin is explicitly mentioned, hinting at the fact that goats and sheep were more plentiful than cattle, and easier to raise. The fermenting vegetable and animal matter once used to unhair skins has given way to lime, a potent alkaline mineral that burns unprotected skin, and an additional soaking step has been added so that unhaired skins are thoroughly softened. And lastly, an extra-smooth writing surface is achieved by means of an elaborate series of wetting, drying, shaving, and polishing operations.[47]

The driving force behind these advances was the emergence of parchment making as an industry in its own right. Where once a monastery would have raised its own cattle and made parchment from their skins, by the thirteenth century the needs of bookmaking monks were being met by a new breed of professional parchmenters.[48] As the parchment-making industry matured it acquired the inevitable trade jargon: pelts were tied to drying frames, or "herses," by wrapping cords around small pebbles called "pippins" pressed into the skin; shaving of the skin was carried out with a curved, moon-shaped knife, or *lunellarium*, without sharp junctions that might tear the skin; and finished parchment was often "pounced"—polished with powdered pumice, or porous volcanic rock—to improve its color and texture.[49]

Having mastered production of the basic artifact, a skilled parchmenter could branch out into niche varieties and treatments. Parchment was sometimes whitened with liquid chalk in lieu of pouncing, while concoctions made from such things as lime, egg whites, flour, and metal salts were applied to regulate the parchment's moisture content and so stave off environmental damage.[50] Transparent parchment, which was variously used for tracing, windowpanes, and even magnifying glasses, was made by treating the skin with substances such as rotten egg whites, gum arabic (an adhesive made from the sap of the acacia tree), or animal glue, and by deliberately under-tightening the skin on its herse.[51] Richly colored purple parchment, so dark that it demanded the use of reflective gold or silver ink, could be made with dye derived from sea snails called *murex*.[52]

Parchment's name evolved along with advancements in its manufacture. For hundreds of years the Romans called it *membrana*, or "skin," but by the third century a new term had come into vogue, and parchment was referred to as *pergamena charta*, or "Pergamene paper." In time, this led to the Old French *pergamin*, *parcemin*, and *perchemin*, and later a whole host of Middle English variants such as *parchemeyn*, *perchmene*, *parchemynt*, and *pairchment*.[53] The French connection also gave rise to a related term: whereas "parchment" carried connotations of the sheep and goats most commonly farmed in the land of its origin, "vellum," from the Old French *vel*, or "calf," suggested calfskin instead.[54] Calfskin parchment was slightly rougher in texture, making it well suited for painting, and leaves of it were sometimes inserted into sheepskin parchment books where illustrations were required. The distinction between parchment and vellum, however, has always been an uncertain one, and today "vellum" is used to mean any especially fine parchment regardless of the animal from which it was made.[55]

Confronted with an ivory sheet of taut, smooth vellum, it is easy to forget its origins in the flesh. Pens old and new glide effortlessly across it, and parchment invests even a humble rollerball pen with luxury and authority. Whereas an absorbent sheet of paper wicks away ink and blurs lines, the water-based ink found in most modern pens huddles into discrete lines and dots under its own surface tension and dries to a glossy shine atop parchment's impermeable surface. As a writing material—and in stark contrast to papyrus, at least in its modern form—parchment is hard to beat.

For all its preternatural smoothness and seductive appearance, though, parchment cannot escape its provenance. Whether it was made yesterday or a thousand years ago, a sheet of parchment is the end product of a bloody, protracted, and very physical process that begins with the death of a calf, lamb, or kid, and proceeds thereafter through a

series of grimly anatomical steps until parchment emerges at the other end. Like laws and sausages, if you love parchment it is perhaps best not to see it being made.

For the morbidly curious, hints of parchment's provenance are not difficult to see. Tiny hairs still cling to the surface of many a sheet of parchment, and holding it up to the light reveals the delicate tracery of veins—which, if the animal was not properly bled upon its slaughter, are darker and more obvious.[56] Even the best vellum, meticulously scraped and polished so that hair and flesh sides are nigh indistinguishable, cannot obscure its source material: in an ironic reversal of the shape a skin takes while attached to its erstwhile inhabitant, a sheet of parchment left to its own devices will curl toward its less elastic hair side.[57] More unsettling still than these visible reminders, however, is the means by which a very specific form of parchment, called "virgin" vellum, is produced.

Virgin vellum was parchment of the very highest quality, and parchmenters were willing to go to some lengths to make it. It has long been known that the best parchment comes from the skins of the youngest animals, and there is archaeological evidence—specifically, animal bones excavated in the "heel" of Italy—that the proportion of cattle slaughtered at less than twelve months of age grew steadily in line with parchment production.[58] Not only was the skin less likely to be blemished by insect bites, scars, and the like, but the thinner skins of younger animals were easier to work. It follows that if the best parchment is made from the youngest animals, then vellum made from aborted or stillborn calves and lambs must be best of all.[59] Known

↞ (*Opposite top*) A sample of modern vellum cut to approximately 4½ by 3½ inches in size. Visible here on the flesh side of the sheet (the curvature of the parchment is reversed from that of the donor animal's skin) are exsanguinated veins.

↞ (*Opposite bottom*) A sample of modern vellum cut to approximately 4 by 3 inches in size. This is the hair side of the sheet, with some short hairs still present.

less euphemistically as "uterine" or "abortive" vellum, this miraculous material was sought after not only for its qualities as a writing surface but also for its unimpeachable purity, with its donor animal unsullied by life outside the womb. For this reason uterine vellum was prized by the writers of magical charms and grimoires (written with the left, or sinister, hand); ultimately, this association with the occult was so strong that the production of uterine vellum was outlawed in some medieval Italian cities.[60]

This, then, is parchment: the pale, virginal product of a bloody manufacturing process; a delicate writing surface that can withstand desert heat and European chill for centuries or even millennia; the medium upon which ancient and medieval writers set down the most important religious, literary, and scientific tracts of their times. Write with a good pen on a piece of parchment and you may wish you never had to go back to paper again—so why are none of today's books printed on it?

3

Pulp Fictions: the ambiguous origins of paper in China

The world runs on paper. On it we print books, newspapers and magazines, contracts and receipts, certificates of birth and death, posters, maps, ballot papers and passports, banknotes and checks, business cards and greeting cards, playing cards and board games, photographs and paintings. From it we make giftwrap, menus, beer coasters, cigarettes, disposable underwear, coffee filters, sandpaper, wallpaper, paper plates, and throwaway cups. World consumption of paper has doubled since 1980, with each resident of the USA consuming the equivalent of 5.57 forty-foot trees in 2012. That is to say, an average American gets through almost 500 pounds of paper in a year. In Belgium, whose capital, Brussels, is the bureaucratic seat of the European Union, that figure rises to more than 750 pounds per capita; in India, on the other hand, it drops to scarcely more than 20.[1] In the age of email, websites, and e-books, our dependence on paper has grown, not lessened.

Most important here, of course, is the interdependence of paper and books. Of all the pages of all the books in my bookcase, not one is made of anything other than paper, and aside from those few people who study, conserve, or trade in antique books, the vast majority of us will never handle a book that is not made chiefly from paper. Paper, however, was entirely absent from the world in which books first came about. The form of the book was fixed long before paper arrived to meet it, and yet, within a few centuries of that meeting, paper had displaced parchment as surely as parchment had pushed aside papyrus.[2] Without paper, there is no book as we know it today.

The overlapping reigns of papyrus and parchment are plain enough in the archaeological record, with thousands of documents unearthed from tombs and rubbish heaps across Egypt, Europe, and the Near East betraying the slow rise of the one at the expense of the other. The origins of paper are less easily studied. Paper's importance is obvious enough today, but our understanding of who invented it, where, and why, remained hopelessly confused for centuries after the material itself had all but taken over our books.

In the absence of any convincing evidence to the contrary, Western scholars of the nineteenth century constructed a timeline of paper that arced pleasingly upward from modest beginnings and cast a reflected glow back on Western society. The "rag" paper common at the time, the story went, made from discarded linen clothing pounded into discrete fibers, had been invented in Italy or Germany sometime around the thirteenth century. Prior to that glorious Renaissance innovation, heathen Arabs had made do with an inferior sort of paper made from raw cotton, with vague hints that they had learned the secrets of papermaking from the Chinese.[3] The state-of-the-art use of wood pulp, introduced in the 1840s to bolster the waning supply of linen rags, was the brainchild of ingenious Westerners in the form of Friedrich Gottlob Keller, a German, and Charles Fenerty, a Canadian.[4]

At the turn of the century, however, a succession of archaeological discoveries pointed the way to paper's true birthplace. First, between

1878 and 1884, Egyptologists made a series of major finds of manuscripts written on papyrus, parchment, and paper. Collected by Archduke Rainer of Austria, and examined later by scholars at the University of Vienna, the paper manuscripts in the collection, without exception, were made entirely from linen rags. Among them were letters written in Arabic and dated to the late eighth century, showing clearly that Arabs had been making rag paper long before its supposed invention in Europe. Then, in 1900, an enormous cache of paper documents was unearthed near the town of Dunhuang, in China's Gansu Province, and its contents dated to between the fifth and tenth centuries. This paper was made of fibers from tree bark and rags.[5]

All this painstaking excavation, chemical analysis, and historical investigation only hinted at what Chinese scholars, historians, and even schoolchildren had known all along. Paper was invented in China, long ago and far from the cozy Mediterranean stamping grounds of classical scholars, and it had been made variously of tree bark, hempen cloth, linen rags, and worn-out fishing nets a clear millennium before Western papermakers had begun experimenting with similar raw materials.[6] Had those nineteenth-century Westerners thought to ask, the Chinese could even have told them the name of the man who invented it.

Before the invention of paper, books in ancient China were written on whatever material came to hand. Texts have been found inscribed on bones (including, on occasion, those of humans) and tortoise shells; on metal and clay; and on stone, jade, and wood.[7] In the modern Chinese language, however, all ancient books are said to be written on *zhu bo* (竹帛)—literally, bamboo and silk—regardless of what they are made of. More so than any others, these were the materials on which the ancient Chinese wrote.[8]

Bamboo was to China what papyrus was to Egypt. It was used to make mats and baskets; fishing rods and agricultural tools; bows and arrows (and later firearms); scaffolding and buildings; and musical instruments.[9] And, like papyrus, it was an important vehicle for writing: cut into strips as long as a chopstick and as wide as two, bamboo slips had been written upon for ages.[10] Just as papyrus sheets were usually pasted into standard rolls of twenty sheets, so too were individual bamboo slips, or *jian*, bound into matlike rolls of fixed lengths ranging from eight inches to over two feet. Called *jiance* (册, the pictogram for *ce*, or "volume," shows two bamboo slips bound to each other by string), these bamboo scrolls are thought to have led to the development of the distinctive top-to-bottom, right-to-left layout of Chinese writing.[11] The only downside to cheap, plentiful bamboo was its considerable weight: a learned person in ancient China had their knowledge euphemistically measured in cartloads of books read, and one particular emperor was praised for his ability to deal with one *shi*—sixty pounds in weight—of official documents per day.[12]

Airy, woven silk, which absorbed ink well and presented a pleasing surface on which to write with a traditional calligraphic brush, proved to be the perfect complement to weighty bamboo scrolls. Though silk was expensive, its portability made it ideal for letters and other correspondence—and, on occasion, more nefarious communiqués. In the third century BCE, during the last days of the brutal Qin dynasty, a rebel named Chen Sheng stuffed carp with slips of silk bearing the words "Chen Sheng should be emperor," so that the superstitious soldiers who bought the fish would be convinced that his rebellion was blessed.[13] And though silk has since been firmly overtaken by paper, its unique qualities still recommend it. During World War II, captured Allied servicemen relied on silk "escape maps" smuggled into prison camps in Monopoly boxes. Sent by phony charities backed by the British secret service, a red dot on the "Free Parking" space signaled that the game board concealed a hidden silk escape map.[14]

Thus bamboo and silk went well together, each one making up for the deficiencies of the other. Important documents could be drafted on cheap bamboo and transferred to silk once perfected, while a utilitarian bamboo book might be enlivened by the attachment of illustrations painted on pieces of silk.[15] Pleasing though this harmony between *zhu* and *bo* was, bamboo was heavy and silk was expensive; as the demands of literate, bureaucratic China increased, a new writing material was needed.[16]

In the latter part of the first century CE, China was enjoying something of a golden age. The repressive Qin dynasty, which had made a point of burning provocative books and burying uncooperative scholars (alive, to ensure that the regime's point was firmly made), was by now a distant memory, and the later Han period, lasting from 25 to 220 CE, was comparatively serene. The arts thrived: poetry, painting, drama, literature, and dance were encouraged and celebrated, even as the denizens of the imperial court at Luoyang continued their age-old game of scheme and plot.[17]

The story of paper begins in this world of bamboo, silk, art, and intrigue. In 75 CE, a servant named Cai Lun entered the imperial court, and though he merited a short biographical entry in the *Hou Han Shu* (the official chronicle of the later Han period), little is known about him. The date of his birth, for example, remains a mystery, as do the reasons for his admission to the court; Cai was described as possessing "superior qualities and talents," but only one of those qualities was ever spelled out.[18] Cai was a eunuch, a member of the traditional servant caste who traded their manhood for access to the emperor's court. Eunuchs, it was thought, could be trusted to guard the imperial harem or even attend to the emperor himself without fear that they might covet power or wealth for the sake of their offspring.[19] Even knowing this, however, for the most part Cai remains a cipher, a functionary whose life and actions are seen only where they intersect with more exalted characters.

Two years after Cai took up his place at Luoyang, a precocious young courtesan named Dou arrived from Xianyang, 250 miles to the east. The eldest daughter of a wealthy family brought low by a quarrel with the last emperor, Dou was determined to restore her family's station. A year later, at the age of sixteen, Dou was married to Emperor Zhang and set about consolidating her grip on power.[20] Even an empress had her rivals.

First in Dou's path lay one of the emperor's favored consorts, Lady Song. Dou never bore children, and Song's son Liu Qing, the designated heir to the throne, represented an intolerable slight to Dou's authority. When Song fell ill and asked for medicinal herbs to ease her suffering, Dou told Emperor Zhang that the herbs were intended to bewitch him. Song duly confessed to the plot under torture. The enraged emperor stripped the consort and her son of their titles, and Song was said to have "died of worry"—a euphemism for committing suicide—some time later. Her torturer, as noted in the compendious and candid *Hou Han Shu*, was Cai Lun.[21]

Dou next focused her ire on Lady Liang, another of the emperor's favorite wives, and had the obliging Cai Lun write letters accusing Liang's father of "sinister activities." Three generations of the Liang family fell victim to Cai's poison pen: Liang's father was imprisoned for his alleged crimes, dying in jail in 83 CE, while Liang herself "died of worry" the same year. Even worse, Lady Liang's son (and Zhang's newly designated heir), Liu Zhao, fell into Dou's clutches, whereupon she manipulated the boy into believing that she, not Liang, was his mother.[22] The culmination of Dou's campaign came when Emperor Zhang died in 88 CE. The ten-year-old Liu Zhao was enthroned as Emperor He, with Dou to act as his regent until his coming of age. Barely a decade after entering the palace, Dou now dominated it utterly.

Cai Lun was pulled along briskly in the empress's wake. Acting in the name of Emperor He, Dou promoted her obedient eunuch to ever-higher offices. Cai became a private adviser to the emperor and later overseer of the Imperial Workshops, which manufactured weapons, tools, and other instruments for the court.[23] In 105 CE, some years after the death of his malign benefactress, Cai finally stepped out of the shadows. Presenting himself before the imperial court, he displayed the modest results of some backyard experimentation: thin, feltlike sheets made from vegetable fibers that had been pounded, macerated, and sieved in a pool in the grounds of his mansion, then pressed and dried in the sun to a smooth finish. Cai's *zhi*, as the ancient Chinese called it, was the first paper.[24]

In keeping with other ancient inventors, Cai Lun did not document the exact steps—and there were many of them—by which he had made paper. The writers of the *Hou Han Shu* recorded the basic facts of the matter, but from a modern perspective the ancient recipe for paper is perhaps less important than those for papyrus and parchment before it. In the two millennia since Cai first pounded, sieved, and pressed fibers into paper, we have never stopped making it.

The first step in the production of "true" paper, as distinct from laminated materials such as papyrus, is to obtain a source of fiber.[25] Cai's formulation, as the *Hou Han Shu* explained, was a mixture of the inner bark of the *chu*, a mulberry-like tree, along with hemp offcuts, rags, and rope culled from old fishing nets.[26] Paper can be made from a huge variety of materials—asparagus stalks, bark, cactus, cotton, ivory, leather, manure, moss, nettles, papyrus (reeds or sheets), peat, pollen, potatoes, rhubarb, satin, seaweed, straw, sugar cane, tobacco, thistles, wood pulp, wool, and more—but Cai's choices were dictated by the resources and the customs of his native land.[27] Though his recipe has the air of a witch's brew ("bark of *chu* and old fishing nets"!), from Cai's perspective his bill of materials must have seemed as natural as the use of wood pulp today.

Cai's first ingredient, the inner bark of the *chu*, almost chose itself. *Chu* had been used in China for over a thousand years before Cai's time: its fruit was eaten by humans, its leaves fed to silkworms, and its bark used in traditional medicines.[28] Moreover, Cai hailed from a region in which the inner bark of the *chu* was beaten into sheets for use in clothing—sheets that, in a pinch, could serve as an expedient writing surface.[29] From here it is a plausible leap to put the pale, feathery inner bark to work in the manufacture of "true" paper, and so *chu* became synonymous with papermaking. *Broussonetia papyrifera*, the "paper mulberry," is still used in China, Japan, and Korea to make paper in the ancient style.[30]

Before they can be used in papermaking, mature *chu* trees are coppiced, or cut down to a stump, and their bushy regrowth harvested each year. The gathered twigs are steamed, and stripped of their outer bark before the inner bark is scraped off. The inner bark is washed, then boiled with caustic lime or wood ash in order to soften it. A subsequent pounding with mallets tenderizes it yet further. It was an obstinately manual enterprise in Cai's time, and, in the villages that still practice traditional papermaking, it remains one.[31]

The remainder of Cai Lun's fiber mix, too, can be credited to custom and necessity. Hemp was commonly planted as a fiber crop from which ropes, nets, and fabric were made (soothsayers and mediums, especially along China's wilder northern frontier, also made use of its flowers' narcotic effects), and the resultant supply of waste hemp products must have been enticing.[32] And just as Cai Lun had incorporated the *chu* bark of his home state into his papermaking scheme, so another old tradition inspired the use of rags *and* informed the next step in the papermaking process.

A number of ancient Chinese books of Cai's time and before note that rags were washed and beaten in rivers, though the reason for these activities is never made clear. One account, written in the

justified text

A papermaker withdraws a bamboo mold from a vat of pounded fibers suspended in water. This woodcut image, taken from the 1637 book *Tian gong kai wu* (天工開物), usually translated as "The Creations of Nature and Man" or "The Exploitation of the Works of Nature," is the earliest known depiction of a Chinese papermaker at work.[33] The mold shown here is a "laid" mold, with narrow horizontal slats supported on wider reinforcing bamboo strips.

third century BCE, describes a family whose recipe for medicinal hand salve required them to stir and pound rags in water, but this is a rare exception. Adrift from any discernible purpose, the pounding of rags has a certain Sisyphean pathos to it. Nevertheless, Cai Lun took the practice and applied it to papermaking. With his raw materials assembled,

➳ Sheets of paper are "couched," or turned out from the mold.

Cai soaked paper mulberry bark, rags, and other waste fibers in water until they began to break down, and then pounded them thoroughly in a stone mortar to produce a silky, glutinous suspension of fibers.[34]

Next, Cai performed the trick that conjured a sheet of paper out of the vat's murky depths. Taking in hand a bamboo frame supporting a cloth screen, he dipped this makeshift mold vertically into the mixture before turning it flat and then withdrawing it, revealing a layer of tangled, matted fibers. After a shake of the mold to drive off the excess water, Cai would have set the mold and its contents in the sun and waited anxiously for them to dry.[35]

The design of the mold that Cai used to make his paper is necessarily a matter for speculation. The simplest "wove" molds, like the one described above, consist of little more than a cloth screen supported by a rigid bamboo frame and are still used by some traditional papermakers. It is likely that Cai's mold followed the same pattern.[36] Other traditional papermakers use more complex "laid" molds, though complexity is a relative concept here. Laid molds are multipart contraptions of varying design, but the general principle is always the same: a rigid frame supports a removable, flexible mat, which is in turn enclosed by "deckles," or edges, to hold in the fibers. The assembled mold is immersed in and withdrawn from the vat in the same way as a wove mold; after that is

⇜ Wet sheets of paper are pressed onto a brick wall to dry. A fire between the two walls warms the bricks. This seventeenth-century practice is almost certainly more advanced than the earliest efforts; paper made in Cai Lun's time was more likely to be left on its mold to dry in the sun.

done, the deckles are removed, the mat is separated from the frame, and a felted sheet of fibers is "couched," or turned out, onto a drying surface. The mold can be immediately reassembled to make another sheet of paper. Paper made in this way displays a pattern of parallel "laid lines," caused by the bamboo or grass (or, later, wire) of the mat, crossed at intervals by the "chain lines" left by the thread or animal hair with which the mat is bound together. Though laid molds have been in use for some time, paper from Cai Lun's era lacks their distinctive markings, and so we can be relatively sure that he must have used a simple bamboo-and-cloth wove mold to form his paper.[37]

After pounding and beating his bark and rags; after immersing

⇺ A sheet of mulberry-bark paper, approximately 5½ by 4½ inches in size, handmade by the author under the direction of Chrissie Heughan. The paper was made on a fine wire mesh mold.

and drawing out his mold; after draining the water from its saturated fibers; and after setting aside the mold and its burden to dry; finally, Cai Lun would have carefully lifted a sheet of *zhi* off the mold.[38] It is impossible to know exactly how the earliest paper would have responded to a calligrapher's brush or how it withstood being folded, crumpled, or rolled, but we might yet come close. A modern papermaker working with paper mulberry bark and a wove mold can only deviate so far from Cai's method, and in the paper made with these traditional tools and ingredients we can see more than a little of its ancient Chinese counterpart. Paper made this way is heavy, clothlike, and undeniably rough—a reed pen scratches over its surface and a nib pen stutters, though the camel-hair writing brushes of ancient China would have flowed lightly onward—but it is also remarkably robust. With some adjustments to his fiber recipe and a little practice with his mold, Cai Lun's paper would have struck the perfect balance between expensive silk and impractical bamboo.[39]

The imperial court was well pleased with Cai's invention. In 106 CE, a year after he had unveiled his discovery, he was named an "inner palace attendant," becoming an official member of the emperor's retinue and ascending to one of the most coveted posts at court. Though Empress Dou was long dead, Cai had since allied himself with Empress Dowager Deng (another powerful consort who held sway over a docile child emperor), and was further rewarded with the title of marquis and a substantial income.[40]

Cai's fall, when it came, was abrupt. Empress Deng died in the year 121, leaving her ward, the dissolute Emperor An, to take over. This new emperor was the son of one Liu Qing, the deposed crown prince who had been cast from the palace through the machinations of Empress

Dou and Cai, and Emperor An was not ready to forgive and forget.[41] An ordered Cai to give himself up so that he might be punished for his crimes, but Cai never arrived. After bathing and dressing in his finest robes, the inventor of paper, in his turn, "died of worry."[42]

Despite the circumstances of his end, Cai Lun's reputation remained intact. As late as the Tang dynasty of the seventh to tenth centuries, the mortar in which he had pounded his fibers was displayed in the Imperial Museum so that the people might see where the "paper of Marquis Cai" had been made.[43] Later still, during the Song dynasty of the tenth to thirteenth centuries, it was written that a temple had been erected in Chengdu to honor the inventor of paper, to which prominent papermaking families traveled to pay their respects.[44] Alongside gunpowder, the magnetic compass, and printing (of which more in a later chapter) paper has taken its place as one of ancient China's "four great inventions."[45]

Behind this tale of wily eunuchs, power-hungry empresses regent, and miraculous inventions lies another story. Cai Lun, the marquis of paper, did not invent paper at all. Archaeologists have found paper fragments in watchtowers and graves dated to the first and second centuries BCE, indicating that the Chinese had been making rag and hemp paper for at least two centuries before Cai's birth.[46] Historical documents confirm this alternative version of events. A bamboo tablet dated to 217 BCE describes the transformation of hemp into paper (albeit hemp in the form of a shoe) in order to exorcise "evil air" from a person whose hair was standing on end. Later, in 93 BCE, the Han emperor Wu is said to have told a visiting prince to cover his deformed nose with a piece of paper so that the imperial gaze might not be affronted by his disfigurement.[47]

This all invites the question: if Cai Lun demonstrably did not invent paper, why is he associated with its creation? The most probable reason is that he (or an anonymous underling whose ingenuity Cai claimed as his own) advanced the craft in some crucially useful way. He may have pioneered the use of paper mulberry bark, for instance, or improved the design of the molds used to extract sheets of fibers from the vat of pulp.[48] Whatever the specifics of Cai Lun's efforts to advance the art of papermaking, his name is forever attached to the craft. He must have been a past master at the dark arts of public relations, with instincts honed by decades of palace intrigue, and his shadow still looms today.

4

From Silk Road to Paper Trail: paper goes global

Inseparable though they are now, Eastern paper and Western books did not exactly rush into each other's arms. With a vastness of Asian steppe, desert, and mountain between them, it took centuries for the paper of Marquis Cai to reach Europe, and yet more time to inveigle itself into common use. Paper's usefulness in bookmaking, in fact, was only one of the many forces that drove its journey: of equal, if not greater importance, were humanity's parallel obsessions with religion, war, and underpants.

The secret of paper, as with silk before it, was jealously guarded by the ancient Chinese. Traditionally, those who attempted to smuggle out any of the key components of silk production were punished harshly or even executed. Silk cocoons, silkworms, and the mulberry trees on which they fed were prized state secrets. Though there is no suggestion that rogue papermakers were ever subjected to the same extremes of intellectual property enforcement, for centuries papermaking remained the gift of China and a few favored East Asian allies.[1]

It was in this nurturing environment that paper came into its own as a replacement for bamboo and silk. First, its production was updated and streamlined: Cai Lun's bark, hemp, rags, and fishing nets were joined by jute, rattan, grasses, reeds, stalks of rice and wheat, and, fittingly, bamboo, which was both abundant and prized for its long fibers.[2] The simple wove molds of Cai's day were replaced by multipart laid molds, allowing many more sheets to be made each day.[3] Paper's properties as a writing material were improved too: Once removed from the flexible mat of a laid mold, a newly formed sheet of paper was pressed to squeeze out water and to create a more even writing surface. Later, around the eighth century, papermakers experimented with "sizing" their paper—that is, treating it to reduce its absorbency and so prevent unsightly blooms of ink. To size a sheet of paper it had to be lowered into a steaming, odiferous vat of gelatin and carefully withdrawn without being torn, bruised, or dropped into the murk, then firmly pressed to recover any excess gelatin. It was slippery, tricky work, and so many sheets were ruined or lost during the sizing process that Chinese papermakers called the sizing room the "slaughterhouse."[4] Lastly, whether sized or not, paper could then be polished to a lustrous finish with a stone or glassy piece of agate.[5]

It was an involved process. One Chinese papermaker, having counted the operations between the harvesting of paper mulberry twigs and the production of a finished sheet, said that "a sheet of paper does not come easy; it requires seventy-two steps to make."[6] Papermaking held no grand secret that could be traded or sold to a foreign power—there were no silkworms or cocoons to be hidden from prying eyes—but depended instead on a host of little secrets, each of which played an incremental part in the making of this lucrative commodity.

Alongside the changes to its manufacture, the Chinese also confronted the menace of paper-eating insects. There is no such thing as a "bookworm," but there *are* countless species of beetle, cricket, moth, silverfish, and cockroach* that feast on paper and the substances used

* There is one insect whose name is tantalizingly similar to the catchall label of "bookworm"; confusingly, however, the so-called book louse is neither a paper-eater nor a louse. These tiny

to treat it, and that, given a chance, will bore clean through a scroll or a book.[7] Later, when papermaking had made its way farther west, some Arab writers left pleading messages to the "King of the Cockroaches," imploring him to leave their manuscripts unharmed. The Chinese took a more practical view of the problem. In the seventh century it was decreed that all paper should be protected from insects, and Chinese papermakers developed an array of chemical deterrents in response: the bark of the Amur cork tree yielded a toxic yellow dye that kept insects away; or, alternatively, pages could be painted with "litharge" (a concoction of lead, sulfur, and saltpeter that is as noxious as it sounds), to much the same effect.[8] Equally important were the physical precautions that might be taken to preserve paper bookrolls. Jia Sixie, an official who lived during the sixth century, wrote that bookcases should be fumigated with musk and quince to prevent insects from breeding in them, and that scrolls were to be unrolled three times each summer to check for infestations. This should be done on a clear day in a spacious, airy room, Jia said, and care should be taken to avoid the untrammeled rays of the sun lest the paper turn brown and attract insects.[9] Jia Sixie knew, as do modern conservators, that the way we store paper is at least as important as how we make it.

Thus China refined and perfected paper, protecting its secrets all the while. But neither silk nor paper could be protected forever: by the third century silk making had spread to Japan, and by 300 CE it had reached India too. Even the Greeks and Romans, who had constructed an elaborate fantasy of fuzzy "silk trees" in the

insects occasionally attack binding materials but they prefer to eat microscopic mold; as such, a book louse infestation is a sign that conditions are too damp for books rather than a danger to books in itself.

absence of any genuine insight into the silk-making process, were eventually disabused of their collective flight of fancy when the secret of the silkworm was revealed to them.[10] Paper followed silk, almost carelessly. Chinese Buddhist monks were required to learn the arts of paper-, ink-, and brush-making so that they could produce written tracts for their new flocks, and in their missionary zeal they took papermaking to Korea and Japan in the east, Indochina in the south, and India in the west.[11] Beyond China's sphere of influence, however, the spread of paper was checked; to go any farther, it would rely on a new and energetic religion.

By the middle of the eighth century, a little over a hundred years after the death of the prophet Muhammad, a vast Islamic caliphate stretched across North Africa, the Middle East, and Asia. These were the lands of the Umayyad, the first great Muslim dynasty, and they were beset from without and within.[12] Muslim expansion into Europe had been halted at the battle of Poitiers in 732 by Charlemagne's father, Charles Martel, and the caliphate's borders in Central Asia and North Africa were being tested by Turks and Berbers respectively.[13] In the end, it was a tribal rebellion that toppled the Umayyad caliphs. In 750 they were overthrown by Abu al-Abbas as-Saffah, founder of the Abbasid dynasty, who claimed direct lineage from the uncle of the prophet Muhammad. Seeing his ambitions temporarily stymied in Europe, the new caliph turned his attention to the less troublesome east.[14]

A year after as-Saffah's coup, an Arab expedition under the command of one Ziyad ibn Salih departed the city of Samarqand, in modern-day Uzbekistan, and made for Chinese-held lands to the east. Upon reaching the city of Talas, a battle commenced that has since passed into legend: Salih is said to have comprehensively defeated the Chinese army encamped there, with 50,000 enemy soldiers slain upon the field of battle and a further 20,000 taken prisoner. Among those captured was a small cadre of conscripted Chinese papermakers who, according to tradition, instigated the practice of papermaking at Samarqand and so kick-started its diffusion throughout the Arab world.[15]

The stirring details of this anecdote—stupendous armies locked in a noble struggle; prisoners privy to a hitherto forbidden art—are, as might be guessed, a little *too* neat. The story of the battle at Talas was first set down some three hundred years after the fact in the *Lata'if al-ma'arif*—"The Book of Curious and Entertaining Information"—by a poet and writer named Abu Mansur al-Tha'alibi.[16] As the title of his book suggests, al-Tha'alibi was not interested in the general sweep of history: medieval Muslim writers saw the past as a heroic epic, a series of explosive conjunctions of portentous events, notable individuals, and famous places. In truth, neither al-Tha'alibi nor his contemporaries knew how paper had reached Samarqand, but the idea that it had just *arrived*—that some undistinguished artisan had one day walked through the city gates and set up shop—was anathema. If some creative logic was necessary to explain Samarqand's status as a major center for papermaking, then so be it: papermaking was Chinese; a Chinese army was routed at Talas; therefore, paper must have come from Chinese prisoners captured at that battle.[17]

Arabs took to their new writing material with gusto. In 762, over a decade after the battle of Talas, the Abbasid regime moved their capital eastward from Damascus to Baghdad, away from troublesome Europe and closer to their heartland, and there paper thrived.[18] Traditionally, the caliphate's records had been written on papyrus or parchment, but papyrus had to be brought from the far-off land of its manufacture, and parchment, the alternative, was a costly upgrade. Paper, by contrast, could be made anywhere, and cheaply at that. The first paper mill opened in Baghdad during the "golden prime" of Harun al-Rashid, caliph from 786 to 795 and the star of Alfred Lord Tennyson's block-busting Victorian poem, "Recollections of the Arabian Nights," and his grateful government adopted paper almost immediately.[19] The burgeoning caliphal bureaucracy soaked up the new writing material, and the treasury, the post office, the cabinet, the war office, the central bank, and the splendidly euphemistic "office of charity"—the caliphate's tax collectors—all placed increasing demands on the city's papermakers.[20] The new capital became a hive of activity where bureaucrats, scholars, and imams rubbed shoulders in the sprawling *suq al-warraqin*, a stationer's market of a hundred shops, and where a visitor was as likely to find a Christian translator at work in the Bayt al-Hikma (House of Wisdom), the world's first recognizable university, as they were an Islamic theologian.[21]

Arab papermakers refined their product as it spread across the caliphate, and paper, in its turn, subtly changed the peoples whose hands it passed through. By the time papermaking had traversed Iran, Iraq, Syria, Egypt, Morocco, Sicily, and finally Spain, three centuries after the first mills had opened in Baghdad, the Arabs had transformed it from a cottage industry into a bona fide manufacturing enterprise. Rags were no longer pounded by hand, but instead by water-driven hammers; linen and hempen cloth, requiring less beating than raw plant fiber, had replaced exotic Chinese plants; and paper was now sized with simple wheat starch instead of gelatin.[22] Not all such changes were for the better, however; medieval Arab paper was hung up to dry, rather than pressed, and required a healthy application of flour paste sizing to smooth out its uneven surface.[23] Flaws aside, the use of paper suffused Arab life. The notation for mathematical algorithms, named for the Arab mathematician al-Khwarizmi and first used with trays of sand in which figures were drawn by fingertip, was adapted to indelible paper.[24] New genres of literature arose, from cookbooks and popular romances to religious commentary.[25]

For the Muslim Arabs, then, paper ruled. Parchment and papyrus were obsolete, and their anointed successor continued its march across Asia and North Africa with all the might of the Islamic caliphate at its back. Christian Europe watched with unease as this slow tide crept ever closer, and unease turned to horror in the eighth century when the Moors of North Africa crossed the blue waters of the Mediterranean to conquer the fractured Visigothic kingdom of Hispania. There they established an Islamic state called al-'Andalus: Islam had come to Europe, and its favored writing material was not long to follow.[26] For its part, Christian Europe would have preferred that neither one had arrived in the first place.

Papermaking in Europe began in 1150, when a paper mill was established in the city of Xàtiva, halfway up al-'Andalus's eastern coast and near modern València.[27] A paper manuscript found on Sicily and dated to the year 1109 suggests that Europeans already knew of paper, but there were, at that time, no paper mills in Christian Europe. Parchment had long been the writing medium of choice for God-fearing Christians, and they looked askance at the material favored by the infidels who currently occupied a substantial tract of mainland Europe.[28] In 1141, an abbot named Peter the Venerable unfavorably compared paper to parchment and took a swipe at papyrus besides, writing that "God reads the book of Talmud in Heaven. But what kind of a book? Is it the kind we have in daily use made from the skins of rams and goats, or is it from the rags of old cast-off undergarments, or rushes out of Eastern swamps, and some other vile material?"[29] Distrust of Muslim paper intensified to such an extent that in 1221 the Holy Roman Emperor Frederick II, one of Europe's most powerful medieval rulers, declared that any government document henceforth written on paper was invalid.[30]

By the time papermaking arrived in Spain, resentment of the occupiers on Europe's doorstep had boiled over into outright war. Christian crusaders were encroaching on Muslim territory in al-'Andalus even as the mill at Xàtiva was under construction, and the whole future of papermaking in Europe was under threat. Though the Qur'an referred to Christians as "People of the Book," the crusaders burned books as readily as they did heretics, and there was every chance that they

full-page art

↞ Jost Amman's 1568 woodcut depicting a papermaker at work. In the background is a press for squeezing out excess water and an array of water-driven trip hammers to finish the paper.

would visit their wrath upon the factories that turned out Islam's rival to parchment.[31]

Quite the opposite happened. Though Alfonso X, king of the newly liberated central Spanish region of Castile, restricted the use of paper to lesser documents, Spain's paper industry survived the Christian onslaught and thrived in its wake.[32] Given the antipathy with which Europe viewed paper, it is still not clear why this should have been the case. One theory is that moderate Muslim papermakers fled to more tolerant Christian lands in the north as the Moorish rulers of southern al-'Andalus grew increasingly fanatical in their application of Islam. Another suggests that the Christian bureaucracy of newly conquered territories demanded more paper, and supply increased in response.[33]

Xàtiva came under Christian control in 1244, and within a century paper mills like it were dotted across southern Europe. Though abbots, monks, and kings remained leery of this new, heathen writing material, cash-strapped scribes with fewer religious qualms quickly adopted it for books and other documents.[34] Muslim papermakers were overtaken by their European competitors, and, just as the Christian Church muttered about paper's Islamic taint, soon Muslim clerics in the East faced the prospect of imported paper made by wine-swilling, pork-eating Westerners.[35] Even worse, with the art of the watermark perfected in the late thirteenth century, a Muslim scholar holding a sheet of paper up to the light might find it disfigured by a ghostly cross, a crusader's shield, or even the face of Christ.[36] At least one medieval Qur'an was inscribed on paper bearing the sign of the cross, throwing clerics into paroxysms of doubt and leading to a fatwa, or religious judgment, that explained precisely the situations in which non-Muslim paper was safe for use.[37]

Watermarks, depicting anything from geometric shapes to tools, animals, plants, and religious symbols, are imparted to paper by a raised design on the mold. European papermakers had begun to use molds made from wire mesh in the mid-twelfth century, and a design wrought in thicker wire was easily sewn onto the finer mesh of the mold.[38] Today, watermarks are typically used to tie a sheet of paper to its manufacturer,

⁜ A watermarked laid mold (note horizontal laid lines and vertical chain lines) made in England in the late nineteenth century. This mold harks back to an earlier time: the device of a snake eating its tail, or "ouroboros," was commonly used as a watermark by Cathar papermakers. The significance of the bundle of sticks enclosed by the snake is unclear.[39]

but what medieval papermakers meant by them remains unclear. It may be that the illiterate "vatmen" who formed sheets of paper in the mills used watermarks to identify molds of different sizes, or that individual mills trademarked their paper as is done today, but neither of these explanations is entirely convincing.[40] In the early twentieth century an alternative thesis was proposed that would have disturbed Christians and Muslims alike.

For much of the medieval period, European papermaking was confined to a swath of land—northern Spain, southern France, and the Italian provinces of Lombardy and Tuscany—coincident with the haunts of a religious sect that claimed descent from the persecuted Christians of the old Roman Empire.[41] The Cathars, or "pure ones," believed that the "good god" of the Holy Trinity was opposed by a "dark god" who had created the world and filled it with sin. Satan was a deity, real, relevant, and dire, and a direct contradiction of Catholic monotheism.[42] Having failed to talk the Cathars out of their heresy, the murder in 1208 of a Catholic emissary in Cathar lands gave Pope Innocent III the excuse to mount a crusade against the movement, and the Cathars were stamped out.[43]

Much later, in 1909, a writer named Harold Bayley published a catalogue of medieval watermarks entitled *A New Light on the Renaissance* in which he wrote that "watermarks (whatever trade purpose they may subsequently have served), were originally EMBLEMS, and as such possessed very definite meanings that beckon to us for solution."[44] That solution, Bayley proposed, was nothing less than the survival of a Cathar secret society, hidden in plain sight and distributing their heretical symbols throughout Christendom and beyond by means of their industrious papermaking.[45] This subterranean sect, Bayley continued, fostered the Renaissance and fomented the Reformation, communicating their existence all the while with watermarks of pots and jugs (that is, the Holy Grail), unicorns and stags (representing the "pure ones" themselves), and more.[46]

Needless to say, *A New Light* attracted little scholarly attention—and, equally, little criticism. A 1924 article published by the esteemed Royal Geographical Society refers to Bayley's cooking-pot-as-Holy-Grail hypothesis with only the merest hint of incredulity, while Dard Hunter's 1943 book *Papermaking*, an exemplary account of the craft, alludes to Bayley's study but does not pass judgment on it.[47] Esoteric or not, Bayley's book remains one of the few serious attempts to explain watermarks in medieval paper.

Taken separately, the gradual modifications to the papermaking process that helped medieval European papermakers overtake their Arab competitors were simple enough. With the benefit of hindsight, some innovations seem almost comically obvious: the "ass," for instance, was a wooden rest that allowed molds to drain over the vat, relieving the vatman's assistant (the "coucher") of the need to hold them there himself.[48] Lever presses used by the "layman" to compress and dry great stacks of wet paper gave way to screw presses. Lumpy wheat-paste sizing was replaced by gelatin (as the Chinese had used) rendered from scraps of hide and parchment bought from the parchment makers on whose business the papermakers encroached.[49]

By degrees, papermakers came to rely on mechanization. Where once the vat's contents had been mixed by hand with wooden poles resembling giant cocktail muddlers, now the job was done by a mechanically driven "hog," or paddle wheel.[50] Polishing stones were replaced by water-driven "glazing-hammers" that pounded paper to a smooth finish with a single, weighty thwack. (Later still, giant wooden rollers would be employed to even better effect.) And, evoking the raised floors of Roman bathhouses under which slaves lit fires to heat the rooms above, heating flues were built into and under the walls of paper mills to gently evaporate the vats' watery pulp and so help the vatmen form paper more quickly on their molds. This heating system was deficient only from the point of view of the urchin whose job it was to crawl into the workings of the heater, stoke the fire, and avoid choking to death on the fumes.[51]

This newfound efficiency brought with it an unexpected drawback: water wheels, heated vats, and glazing-hammers could not free papermakers from their basic need for linen rags, the founding ingredient of paper.[52] Though linen was used for clothing of all kinds, linen underwear wore out most quickly and so the "rags of old cast-off undergarments" became papermakers' favored raw material (and gave churchmen such as Peter the Venerable something to grumble about in the bargain).[53] Paper was becoming too popular for its own good.

The shortage of linen skivvies was relieved by the arrival in the thirteenth century of the spinning wheel, another Chinese invention.[54] But this was not the end of the saga; rather, the humble spinning wheel was the catalyst for a revolution that would change the face of literate Europe. At the risk of trivializing an epochal change in human history (and without wanting to delve too deeply into the contents of later chapters), for papermakers the centuries following the arrival of the spinning wheel went roughly as follows: More linen rags meant more paper, but this simply pushed the bottleneck in book production onto the army of scribes who copied Europe's books by hand. When Johannes Gutenberg's movable type did away with *that* problem in the 1450s, book production exploded and papermakers found themselves back at square one. They could sell paper as fast as they could make it, but they could make it only as quickly as they could acquire the necessary supply of linen rags.[55]

The situation was reflected in the price of paper, which remained more or less constant even as paper mills sprang up across Europe. The price of parchment, however, suffered dreadfully. When paper arrived the two materials had cost roughly the same, but by the close of the sixteenth century parchment was an order of magnitude more costly and had noticeably worsened in quality.[56] Parchment lingered on as the material of choice for lofty or otherwise important works—as late as 1480, Cambridge University would accept only parchment books as collateral for loans—but paper had won the war. Europeans bought and read more books than ever before; cattle the Old World over looked forward to dramatically longer lifespans; and papermakers cursed anew their difficulty in procuring linen underpants.[57]

The shortage of rags rumbled on into the modern era. In England in 1636, papermakers' rag imports were fingered as the cause of an outbreak of the Black Death, while in 1666, in the teeth of yet another rag shortage, a decree was passed prohibiting the use of linen for burial garments, saving 200,000 tons of rags each year.[58] (As late as the nineteenth century, in both England and Germany it was considered unpatriotic to bury the dead in linen.)[59] Conversely, better postal services and increasing use of paper and cardboard packaging put more pressure on paper supplies, while at the same time cheap cotton and woolen clothes depressed the supply of linen rags, leading to the sight of "rag and bone men"—professional scavengers who gathered rags for papermaking and animal bones to be rendered into grease—plying the streets of London to collect and sell discarded linen to the rag merchants of Petticoat Lane.[60] By 1818, the situation had grown so critical that it was made illegal to publish a newspaper of greater than 22 by 32 inches in size.[61]

The rag shortage was not confined to Europe. North America's first paper mill, established in Philadelphia in 1690, had been operating for less than a century when the Revolutionary War of 1776 saw the newborn United States of America scrabbling to secure enough rags for papermaking. Here, though, it was the need for "weapons grade" paper suitable for packaging gunpowder (for which "cartridge paper" is named), rather than for printing books, that was uppermost in the minds of new American papermakers.[62] The supply of paper had become a matter of national security, and the authorities reacted accordingly. The grandees of the Commonwealth of Massachusetts ordered that every locality establish a "Committee of Safety" to ensure that enough rags were saved for papermaking, while the paper of at least one contemporary Massachusetts mill was watermarked with a bald exhortation to "SAVE RAGS." American papermakers were exempted from military service until at least 1812, and almost every newspaper and periodical of the time, on both sides of the Atlantic, urged their readers to save rags.[63] It seemed that the situation could not get any worse.

And then it did.

The world had barely caught its breath after the United States' departure from its colonial embrace before France, the States' greatest ally during the Revolutionary War, became embroiled in its own revolution. King Louis XVI and his queen Marie-Antoinette had their date with the guillotine, the Republic's "national razor," in 1793, and it was during the decade of relative calm that followed that one Louis-Nicolas Robert, a citizen of the new French Republic, first conceived of the machine that would change papermaking forever.[64]

Robert worked as a clerk at a paper mill owned by Saint-Léger Didot, a scion of the Didot clan who dominated French typesetting and publishing. For years the vatmen, couchers, and laymen who made paper had tussled with their bourgeois bosses over pay and conditions, and Didot eagerly fell upon Robert's scheme for a papermaking engine that could replace his fractious workforce.[65] Robert's proposed machine was deceptively simple: he reimagined the traditional paraphernalia of vat and mold so that the mold became a wire mesh conveyor belt onto which the vat's pulp was gently and continuously deposited. The resultant felted ribbon of paper passed through a pair of rollers to squeeze out excess water, after which it was cut into sheets and hung up to dry.

Work on the machine proceeded slowly, and Didot was not the best of managers. Having disparaged Robert's efforts as "feeble," he banished the glum inventor to a nearby flour mill to recover his enthusiasm. Finally, in 1798, a working model of the machine was finished. Robert wrote to the French government about his device, sheepishly begging the patent office to grant him a patent free of charge: "My fortune does not permit me to pay the tax of this patent [. . .] I implore you to name a number of commissioners to examine my work, and in view of the immense usefulness of my discovery grant me a patent gratuitously."[66]

His impertinence paid off, and the following year the government not only granted his patent but also paid a bounty of 3,000 francs for his troubles.

Monetizing the "endless wire" papermaking machine beyond that first payment turned out to be less easy. Having pledged to buy Robert's patent for 25,000 francs, Didot defaulted on his payments and in 1801 the inventor was forced to recover the patent in the courts. Didot, however, had already sent Robert's plans to London with an English cousin of his named John Gamble. There Gamble sold the drawings to papermaking brothers Henry and Sealy Fourdrinier, and the Fourdriniers gamely set about commercializing the Robert device.[67] When word escaped that the Fourdriniers had installed a prototype machine at a paper mill in Hertfordshire, they discovered that English workers could be every bit as militant as their French comrades: in 1813, at the height of the Luddite movement, threats of a riot forced the Fourdriniers to board up the mill's windows and to stock the roof with jars of sulfuric acid, or vitriol, with which rampaging Luddites might be repelled.[68] It took ten long years and cost more than £60,000 to bring the rechristened "Fourdrinier machine" to commercial readiness, and the brothers emerged with nothing but bankruptcy to show for it.[69]

By now, however, the Fourdrinier (né Robert) machine had taken on a life of its own. By 1830, only two years after Robert died in penury, his machine's offspring had grown to truly monstrous proportions: some were accessorized with wire mesh "dandy rolls" that imparted ersatz laid lines, chain lines, and watermarks to machine-made paper; others were fitted with vacuum devices to suck out excess water from the felted paper on the wire belt. Still others sprouted heated cylinders that sped the drying process—and, inadvertently, made it possible to produce an endless "web" of paper without the need to dry individual sheets—leading to the use of "calendering" rollers to polish and flatten the web to a fine finish.[70] A millennium after humanity had given up pasting sheets of papyrus together to form scrolls, papermakers had finally built a machine that could turn out endless, perfect rolls of paper with nary a join to be seen. But that small irony paled in comparison to the greater contradiction of the Fourdrinier machine. An industry already starved for rags now depended on a device that inhaled them.

By the middle of the nineteenth century only two handmade paper mills still operated in the USA, and the eight hundred Fourdrinier machines that replaced them had a truly appalling hunger for rags. In 1855 alone, America's paper industry consumed 405 million pounds of rags, much of it imported. One fireside story went that the Stanwood and Tower mill of Gardiner, Maine, was so desperate for papermaking fiber that it imported Egyptian mummies solely for the papyrus and linen in their "cartonnage," the layered, papier-mâché–like material used to make sarcophagi, which was then cast into their vats to make coarse brown paper for butchers, grocers, and the like. Workers at the mill, it was said, were stricken with cholera because they had not disinfected their blasphemous raw materials.[71]

Book historians and Egyptologists alike comforted themselves that this was nothing more than a cock-and-bull story, recalling a similarly tall tale told by Mark Twain that for a decade the locomotives of an Egyptian railroad had been fueled by burning mummies.[72] Stanwood and Tower may well have imported rags from Egypt, scholars reasoned, but they were not necessarily wrapped around the honored dead at the time.[73] In 2003, however, an advertisement dated to 1855 came to light when an intrepid librarian named S. J. Wolfe investigated the origins of the persistent rumors. The advertisement Wolfe found had been printed to promote the bicentennial celebrations of the town of Norwich, Connecticut, and at the foot of its single printed sheet was a brief description of its provenance:

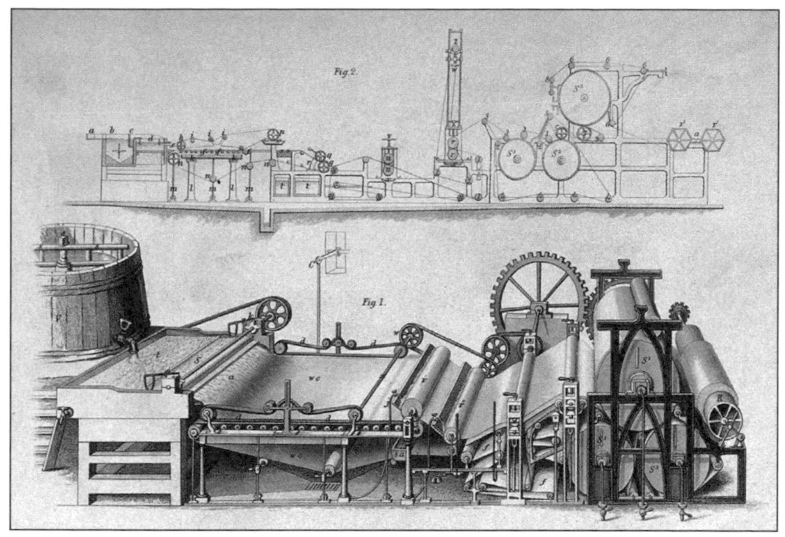

⯪ A contemporary diagram of two Fourdrinier machines, circa 1854. With reference to Fig. 1, pulp flows from a vat, *v*, through a strainer, *s*, and onto the wire mesh conveyor belt, *wc*. Water is squeezed out by rollers r' and r'' and drains into a "save-all," *sa*, to be returned to the vat. The pulp is led onto a felt, *f*, to be further pressed before it is dried by steam-heated rollers S^1, S^2, and S^3. The finished web of paper is wound onto a reel, *R*.[74]

> *This paper is made by the Chelsea Manufacturing Company, Greeneville, Conn., the largest paper manufactory in the world. The material of which it is made, was brought from Egypt. It was taken from the ancient tombs where it had been used in embalming mummies.*[75]

Mummy paper was real. The practice may never have spread beyond Greeneville, Connecticut, but for some unknown period of time workers at the Chelsea Manufacturing Company rendered the funeral garments of ancient Egyptian mummies into fiber from which they made paper.[76]

Appropriately enough, it fell to the wrongly accused mummy despoilers Stanwood and Tower to demonstrate how papermakers might be freed from their dependence on linen rags. In 1863, their Gardiner mill became the first in America to make paper from wood pulp.[77]

The search for an alternative to linen rags had been a long one. As far back as 1684, Edward Lhuyd, a don of Jesus College, Oxford, had theorized that paper could be made from asbestos, a fibrous, naturally occurring mineral now notorious for causing lung disease.[78] Lhuyd enclosed a sample of his brittle asbestos paper with a letter to the journal of the Royal Society of London, but he was soon distracted by other pursuits and his idea went no further.[79] (Not coincidentally, perhaps, Lhuyd was troubled by asthma later in life and eventually died of pleurisy, an inflammation of the lining of the lungs. It is only chance, surely, that has prevented "dead as an asbestos papermaker" from taking its place alongside "mad as a hatter.")[80] Other proposed raw materials were more eccentric than toxic: Robert R. Livingston, one of the Founding Fathers of the United States, obtained a patent on the use of algae called "frog spittle" for papermaking.[81] Livingston's algae was a nonstarter, as were corn husks, seaweed, corn, straw, beach grasses, palm leaves, and the other left-field materials experimented with, patented, and eventually discarded during the search for a replacement for rags.[82]

The inspiration for the use of wood pulp in papermaking was no less unusual than these failed pretenders, nor was it a new idea. Cai Lun and his successors had employed the bark of the paper mulberry, but the idea of using wood itself originated much later, with the French naturalist René Antoine Ferchault de Réaumur. In 1719, de Réaumur regaled the French Royal Academy with an account of his travels to the New World, where he had observed wasps making papery nests out of chewed wood pulp. Might not these industrious insects be emulated in order to make real paper? At his death twenty-eight years later de Réaumur was still waiting for the answer. It would take more than a hundred years for his idea to percolate into the collective consciousness of the papermaking industry and still longer to bring it to fruition.[83]

The eventual breakthrough came in 1844, courtesy of a frustrated German inventor named Friedrich Gottlob Keller. Bored of a provincial life of weaving and bookbinding, and inspired by de Réaumur's idea of wood-pulp paper, Keller built a machine that ground wood against a sandstone roller and successfully made paper from the resultant pulp—rough, brown paper, but paper nonetheless. When it came to reaping the rewards from his invention, Keller was unluckier even than Louis-Nicolas Robert. The German government was not interested in wood-pulp paper, and Keller was forced into partnership with a papermaker named Heinrich Voelter. In 1852, when the time came to renew their joint patent on the grinding machine, Keller could not afford his allotted part of the fee; thus the patent passed to Voelter, who promptly made a killing.[84] Papermakers were free, finally, from their shackles of linen underpants.

As the nineteenth century wore on, papermakers moved away from the brute force of their industrial grinding engines. Instead of being forcibly ground up, wood was now transmuted into pulp by alchemical processes that steamed and cooked wood chips with sulfurous acid or alkaline salts.[85] Pulp was bleached with calcium hypochlorite to turn brown, woody paper into a more pleasant white.[86] And traditional gelatin sizing, which by now cost more than all other raw ingredients combined, was replaced by a combination of aluminum sulfate—"papermaker's alum," the same chemical used to brighten ancient papyrus sheets—and rosin, or pine resin, where the alum caused the rosin to adhere to the pulped fibers and so created a barrier to moisture in the finished sheet. The alum and rosin went straight into the vats of pulp too, further streamlining the assembly line of paper production.[87]

Thus, at the end of the "long" nineteenth century, the protracted spasm of war, revolution, and industrialization that remade the globe, the paper industry was transformed. Books were still books, of course, bound in board and leather and composed of the same old paper, but the book *industry* had grown enormously. The United Kingdom, for instance, had begun the nineteenth century with more than seven hundred vats producing paper by hand and only a handful of papermaking machines, but by the turn of the century the situation was entirely reversed and paper production had increased by an order of magnitude. It was a revolution by any measure.[88] But papermaking's transformation had come at a cost, and trouble was brewing in papermakers' vats.

Back in the early part of the nineteenth century, as consumers became accustomed to the neatness and homogeneity of machine-made products, so the prevailing sense of aesthetics had changed to match the new means of production. Readers wanted their paper to be as bright, white, and smooth as possible, and papermakers adjusted their recipes to match. The difficulties arose when they over-egged the pudding, so to speak: the chlorine with which papermakers bleached their paper degraded the cellulose that held it together, and the more chlorine they added the worse the effect became. This was vastly outweighed, however, by the damage wreaked by papermakers' new sizing chemicals. Aluminum sulfate is extremely acidic, and as printers demanded ever-smoother, less absorbent paper for an improved quality of print, alum-laden paper began to eat itself alive.[89]

As early as 1823, a Scottish science writer and lecturer named John Murray noticed a tendency for newly printed books to turn yellow and brittle almost before his eyes. An amateur chemist, he tested—and tasted—the offending paper to discover that it had a distinctly astringent taste and an acidic pH. He wrote to *Gentleman's Magazine* to describe the phenomenon in no uncertain terms: "I have in my possession a large copy of the Bible printed at Oxford, 1816 (never used), and issued by the British and Foreign Office, crumbling literally into dust. [. . .] I have watched for some years the progress of the evil, and have no hesitation in saying, that if the same ratio of progression is maintained, a century more will not witness the volumes printed within the last twenty years."[90]

There was, admittedly, a touch of the curmudgeon about Murray's complaints. Writers had ever bemoaned the declining quality of paper, and Murray was merely the latest in a long line of illustrious grumblers. In 1594, for example, Shakespeare decried the treacherous paper upon which he wrote:

> *If I could write the beauty of your eyes,*
> *And in fresh numbers number all your graces,*
> *The age to come would say 'This poet lies;*
> *Such heavenly touches ne'er touch'd earthly faces.'*
> *So should my papers, yellow'd with their age,*
> *Be scorn'd, like old men of less truth than tongue.*[91]

In 1750, Ahasverus Fritsch, a German writer of hymns, lamented that "a hundred years ago" paper was "twice as good," and linked the perceived lapse in quality to the increasing demand for paper.[92]

But Murray's point could not be denied: never had paper disintegrated so quickly after its manufacture, though the blame could not be laid solely with the papermakers. The very air of the Industrial Revolution conspired against books, with coal-fired power plants belching out sulfur dioxide that leached into paper, making it even more acidic, while the coal gas with which homes and libraries were heated and lit had similarly deleterious effects. Even the gradual move toward warmer, more comfortable dwellings took its toll, as balmier indoor conditions accelerated the demise of substandard, acid paper.[93] Most insidious of all, in the 1930s it was discovered that wood-pulp paper slowly, inexorably disintegrates even *without* the presence of excess bleach or acid: lignin, a complex molecule found abundantly in wood, reacts to ultraviolet light to destroy the cellulose that binds paper together.[94] In the 1980s, when the Library of Congress first tackled the issue of brittle books, it estimated that 25 percent of books owned by large American research libraries—75 million volumes in all—would crumble to dust if handled. A "slow fire" was consuming books across the world, and something had to be done.[95]

Thus the concept of mass deacidification was born, where

librarians dreamed of treating brittle books in batches of tens or hundreds to halt their decay once and for all.[96] Most such processes rely on the same underlying principle—namely, that acid paper must be impregnated with an alkaline "buffer" to raise its pH to a safe level and then keep it there—but the precise details vary widely. When the Library of Congress first experimented with mass deacidification in 1982, for instance, it recruited NASA and aerospace giant Northrop to gain access to giant vacuum chambers in which it planned to fumigate books with a compound called diethyl zinc, or DEZ.[97] It did not go well.

The books treated with DEZ inexplicably developed an unpleasant odor, and glossy photographic papers were disfigured by iridescent rings. Worse, DEZ reacts violently with water to produce flammable ethane gas and heat, a singularly unhappy combination.[98] Early on, the library's test plant suffered a fire after the accidental mixing of a small amount of DEZ with water; later, several hundred pounds of DEZ were inadvertently inundated with brine from an adjacent system, causing an explosion that blew out the walls of a vacuum chamber. It was suggested that NASA and Northrop stick to spaceships and airplanes, and DEZ was abandoned as too unstable for mass deacidification.[99]

The British Library, on the other hand, has experimented with a system that reads like the origin story of a comic-book superhero. Books were infused overnight with monomers—molecules that can be induced to join with one another to form complex polymers—and then bathed with gamma rays to bind the resultant polymers into the books at a molecular level. This neutralized the acid content of the books' paper and also physically strengthened them, leaving books slightly fatter but much more robust. Though successful, "graft polymerization" has not yet progressed beyond a trial run of a few hundred volumes.[100]

The Library of Congress currently uses a simple process that immerses books for ninety minutes in a solution of magnesium oxide,

The "dry" end of a modern, industrial-scale Fourdrinier machine. Pulp is deposited onto a plastic mesh conveyor belt at the "wet" end and passes onto the drying rollers (enclosed here to reduce energy consumption) before being wound onto a reel for transport.

a chalky, comparatively inert mineral. It is unexciting but effective; at the time of writing, 3.78 million books have been treated in this way, though many millions more remain unprotected.[101]

What are the prospects for a modern book? Once upon a time, it was easy to find out: assuming you hold in your hand a physical copy of this or any other book, find the unnumbered page that follows the title page and precedes the dedication, the one filled with publishing and cataloguing jargon. This is the "copyright page." Note the presence or absence of these magic words: "Printed on acid-free paper." (This incantation may be accompanied with or replaced by the symbol "♾," which denotes conformance to the snappily named international standard Z39.48-1992, "Permanence of Paper for Publications and Documents in Libraries and Archives.")[102] If present, they are signs that you are reading a copy that has benefited from a century-long wrangle to purge destructive chemicals from the papermaking process; if absent, well, either your book will self-destruct sometime within the next couple of decades or its publisher has simply omitted the "acid-free" label in the current fashion of such things. Time will tell.

The first, inadvertent steps toward more permanent paper came in the nineteenth century as papermakers were put under pressure to both improve the quality of their products and reduce costs. In pursuit of ever finer paper, papermakers flocked to new methods of pulping whereby coarse wood chips were cooked in a broth of sulfates, sulfites, or caustic soda to render them into a smoother pulp—a process that destroyed the lignin that causes mechanically pulped paper to degrade and used less energy to boot.[103] Another measure has played an equally important part: Papermakers once used costly titanium oxide as "filler" to bulk out and whiten paper, but they discovered that cheap, abundant chalk did much the same job. Chalk, however, reacts with acidic alum to destroy paper, and so papermakers turned to alkaline sizing agents—available for some time but previously considered unnecessary—as an alternative. The net result of these changes has been a trend toward stable, acid-free paper that brings a host of attendant benefits: alkaline paper drains quickly and so requires less heat (and energy) to dry, while papermaking machines are spared the corrosive effects of acid paper.[104]

But despite its obvious advantages, acid-free paper has not yet succeeded in dispatching its self-destructive predecessor. Due to lower yields, chemically pulped "freesheet" paper (so called because it is free of mechanically pulped wood) continues to be more expensive than its "groundwood" counterpart, though the price differential—usually somewhat less than a dollar per book—remains slim enough so that publishers continue to seesaw back and forth. The size of an expected

⇷ A sheet of modern, machine-produced book paper. This book is printed on acid-free, pH-neutral freesheet paper made by the Yuen Foong Yu Group of Taiwan, produced according to the PREPS sustainability standard and weighing in at eighty-one pounds per ream of 500 sheets at 25 by 38 inches in size.

print run, the printing technologies and paper specifications required to do justice to a book's contents, and the demands of a prospective audience can all sway a publisher's decision to choose longevity over cost or vice versa. That an acid-free copy of this book may last for a hundred years or more owes as much to a balancing act of profit and loss as it does to advancements in papermaking.

Today, then, though paper books masquerade as resolutely old-fashioned artifacts, their production is thoroughly modern. Paper mills crouch near rivers and lakes, pumping water into the vats of their giant Fourdrinier machines. The biggest machines are as long as a row of houses and extend, iceberglike, below the factory floor. Aboveground, their trains of drying rollers are cloaked in heat-retaining shrouds and fed by hissing steam pipes. The web of chemically pulped paper travels through baths of pH-neutral vegetable-starch sizing. The humid air hums with motion and sound. Papermaking today is a sleekly optimized industrial process.

Part 2

The TEXT

5

Stroke of Genius: the arrival of writing

Five thousand years ago, give or take, the inhabitants of the fertile plains between the Euphrates and Tigris Rivers were already one of the oldest settled civilizations in the world when they began to *write*—to convert spoken language into signs scratched on stone and impressed in clay.[1] The wedge-shaped, or "cuneiform," script of the Sumerian people of ancient Mesopotamia was thought given form—concepts and memories abstracted from fallible human brains and recorded for posterity.[2]

Not that anyone realized.

When the first cuneiform inscription was published in 1657 after its discovery by an Italian traveler named Pietro della Valle, contemporary thinkers singularly failed to perceive its significance.[3] Some thought that cuneiform glyphs were random decorations, while the most skeptical refused to believe that humans had had anything to do with them at all—as far as they were concerned, cuneiform's angular indentations were just as likely the footprints of birds that had scurried across fresh clay.[4]

Today, happily, we have a better appreciation of the Sumerians' nascent writing. Thousands of clay cuneiform tablets have been excavated since della Valle's time, some dating as far back as the fourth millennium BCE, with the earliest of them depicting stylized sheep, oxen, and other agricultural commodities.[5] The key to understanding the symbols on these early tablets, in fact, is that they were accompanied by marks intended to convey numbers: the first written document in the history of the world was very probably a farmer's sales receipt.[6]

How it was that the Sumerians invented this system of written accounting has never been quite settled, but in the late 1970s a promising (if still somewhat controversial) theory was put forward by a French-American archaeologist named Denise Schmandt-Besserat. As she catalogued clay artifacts that had been found across the Middle East, Schmandt-Besserat noted the predominance of small, inch-wide clay tokens with no clear purpose. The oldest of them, which took the form of simple discs and cones, had been found at sites dating to the dawn of agriculture in the region, sometime during the early part of the seventh millennium BCE, but Schmandt-Besserat was more interested in a development that occurred much later, around 3300 BCE.[7] Tokens from this later era were incised with line-drawn depictions of sheep, cattle, ears of barley, and other agricultural commodities, and were often unearthed alongside (or even inside) spherical clay "envelopes" called *bullae*. These envelopes, Schmandt-Besserat theorized, were receipts. Ancient farmers trading their produce had been obliged to find some mutually acceptable way of recording their transactions, and, by enclosing one token per sheep, cow, or sheaf of barley within a sealed clay envelope, the subjects of such a transaction were simultaneously recorded and protected from tampering.[8]

It was not a perfect system. Once a clay envelope had been sealed, its contents could only be verified by breaking it open. Some astute farmers, however, had figured out that stamping the surface of their clay envelopes with impressions of the tokens sealed inside let them divine an envelope's contents without having to destroy it. Thus, the tokens themselves became irrelevant: inscribed in hardened, indelible clay, the

↞ A 2-by-2½-inch clay tablet incised with cuneiform characters. This pocket-sized example comes from Anatolia in central Turkey, and was made sometime between 1875 and 1840 BCE.[9]

farmers' decorated tokens were replaced by the symbols they carried.[10] Within a few centuries of the advent of these decorated *bullae*, cuneiform tablets were in evidence at the great city of Uruk in what is now Iraq, and many other places besides. Writing had arrived.[11]

Other advancements followed. The rounded wooden rods used for early Sumerian writing gave way to wedge-shaped styli, creating the angular indentations of cuneiform proper.[12] The lexicon of cuneiform signs expanded. And later, around 2800 BCE, the Sumerians took a great step forward when they began to use their symbols to represent not just words but individual sounds. The cuneiform sign 𒄀, meaning "reed," was pronounced *gi*, as was the word for "reimburse"; thus 𒄀 could be used to mean "reed," "reimburse," or any other word or syllable with the same sound.[13] Cuneiform was not a true alphabet, in which even individual syllables are broken down into abstract letters, but it looked a lot like one.

Across the desert to the west, the ancient Egyptians were intent on creating their own system of writing, and, like the cuneiform of their Mesopotamian neighbors, their earliest hieroglyphs were scratched or carved into hard surfaces such as clay, pottery, and stone.[14] Treasure-hunting Victorian archaeologists were captivated by the grand inscriptions they found on obelisks and temple walls, but the tiny literate minority of ancient Egyptians had been equally happy scribbling on broken pot fragments and slivers of limestone.[15] Ostraca, as these makeshift media are called, after the ancient Greek for "earthenware vessel" or "hard shell," were ubiquitous in Egypt and throughout the ancient world.[16] They served as impromptu notebooks, convenient for laundry lists and other ephemeral documents; they were the vehicles for bawdy sketches and love poems; and they were put to official use as tax receipts and ballot papers.[17] This last practice gave rise to the modern concept of ostracism: once each year, Athenian citizens were

⇜ The earliest known examples of written papyrus sheets, discovered and photographed by Pierre Tallet at Wadi el-Jarf on Egypt's Red Sea coast. They have been dated to around 2600 BCE.[18]

given the chance to banish one of their own by inscribing ostraca with the names of their chosen evictees.[19]

Of course, books as we know them would not exist if the Egyptians had been content to write on stone and pottery. Just as Cai Lun's paper gave China a convenient alternative to weighty bamboo and expensive silk, so the ancient Egyptians hankered for a writing surface more portable than hundred-ton obelisks and possessed of a little more gravitas than sherds* of broken pottery.[20] The solution was the papery sheets the Egyptians made from laminated strips of papyrus reed pith. The earliest written papyrus, a collection of illegible scraps found in 2010 in a silted-up harbor on the Red Sea coast, are a respectable 4,500 years old, but the oldest blank papyrus, in the form of a rolled-up scroll, is a half

*Archaeologists reserve "shard," with an *a*, for fragments of glass. Pottery, on the other hand, breaks into "sherds."

millennium older still. Discovered in a lavish tomb in 1937, it cannot be more than a century younger than hieroglyphs themselves.[21]

As Egyptian scribes moved from clunky clay tablets to portable, delicate papyrus, they were forced to come up with new writing implements to match. Not for them the literal blunt instrument of the Sumerians, a wooden stylus held in a closed fist and pressed into clay like a chopstick pressed into a dumpling; instead, the Egyptians wrote with brush and ink, and they did so with a fluency and grace entirely absent from the writing of their Mesopotamian counterparts.[22]

On the whole, brushes, pens, and ink generate less excitement than headline-grabbing archaeological finds such as tomb carvings and papyrus scrolls. Even so, years of excavation and deduction have given us a remarkably complete picture of the trade and the tools of ancient Egyptian scribes. Between 1911 and 1913, for instance, renowned Egyptologist Flinders Petrie excavated a sprawling graveyard at Tarkhan, near Cairo, whose contents provided a detailed glimpse of life and death in Egypt in the late fourth millennium BCE. Petrie was one of the great characters of his era, a workaholic with a noted disregard for personal hygiene, a disconcertingly ardent belief in eugenics (Petrie's head resides in a jar at the Royal College of Surgeons in London, bequeathed there by the man himself as "a specimen of a typical British skull"), and a predilection for working naked in hot weather.[23] He was, moreover, an excellent archaeologist in his time, and his excavations at Tarkhan uncovered thousands of burials dating to between 3200 and 3000 BCE. Among the burial offerings that were scattered throughout the tombs, Petrie found ceramic jars daubed with crude, inky hieroglyphics, revealing that ink, like papyrus, is very nearly as ancient as writing itself.[24]

Egyptian ink was as simple as it was durable. Chemical analysis of papyrus scrolls, many as sharp and legible as the day they were written, shows that the black pigment of Egyptian ink came from carbon, likely obtained from charcoal or scraped off burnt wooden utensils, and that the ink itself was made by mixing powdered carbon with a solution of gum arabic and water.[25] This is almost exactly the same formulation as that of India ink and of black watercolor paint—the Egyptians hit upon a winning formula, and humanity has been periodically reinventing it ever since.[26]

With the chronology and chemistry of Egyptian ink in hand, the country's ancient art and literature fills in many of the blanks that remain in our understanding of this earliest pen-and-ink writing. Scribes were a celebrated part of Egyptian culture and a popular subject for stonemasons, sculptors, and painters. There are countless depictions of scribes at work with a brush in hand and a spare or two stowed casually behind an ear; some stand, holding a sheet of papyrus in one hand while writing with the other, and others sit cross-legged with a scroll stretched across their lap.[27] The most famous depictions of a scribe comprise a set of wooden panels found in a tomb dating to Egypt's third dynasty (2686–2613 BCE). The tablets declare that the tomb belongs to an official named Hesire, or Hesy-Ra, and they wax lyrical about his station:[28]

Elder of the Qed-hetep; father of Min
Fashioner of the cult image of Mehyt, king's acquaintance
Overseer of the royal scribes
Great one of the 10 of Upper Egypt
Hesyre.[29]

As "overseer of the royal scribes," Hesire was likely more of a manager that a scribe proper, but he is shown nevertheless with the scribe's outfit of his day slung over his shoulder. This scribe's writing kit was so iconic that it gave its form to a very literal hieroglyph—𓏞, meaning "scribe"—comprising a palette for mixing ink attached to a long, thin case for brushes and a pouch for water with which to moisten them.[30]

The palette's circular hollows indicate that ink was formed into cakes to match and this, along with the ink's watercolor-style composition, suggests that ancient Egyptians wrote very much like elementary school students paint, rubbing moistened brushes on circular cakes of tempera paint.

Hesire's eagerness to pose as a scribe was understandable. Egyptians referred to hieroglyphics as 𓏞𓈖𓊹𓌃𓏪, or "writing of the divine words," and, as befitted an art handed down by Thoth himself, hieroglyphics were wielded with respect and humility. Carelessly painted on a tomb wall, for instance, a symbol representing an animal or a human could awaken and consume the food left for the tomb's human occupant, but these specters could be preempted from doing so if their hieroglyphs were deliberately disfigured. Amulets carved in the shape of certain hieroglyphs brought the meaning of those symbols to life: the ankh (☥) granted long life, while the *udjat* (𓂀), or eye of Horus, watched over the amulet's wearer.[31] And lastly, Egypt's water-soluble ink informed the belief that a scroll washed clean of its contents would grant its secrets to whoever drank the resultant inky liquid.[32]

A century or so after Hesire's time, his unwieldy slate-and-rope writing kit had given way to wooden or ivory blocks dimpled with hollows for mixing ink and inset with slots in which to store pens.[33] Archaeologists have unearthed these in the thousands, some still stained with ink or with a complement of brushes in their slots. These finds, in turn, tell us yet more about the habits of Egyptian scribes. The twin inkwells of this later version of the scribe's palette were typically reserved for red and black ink,

↞ (*Opposite*) Carving in wood of Hesire, or Hesy-Ra (his name is spelled out by the leftmost column of hieroglyphs), a high-ranking official of Egypt's third dynasty identified as "overseer of the royal scribes" and "chief tooth physician." Over Hesire's shoulder is slung the equipment of an Egyptian scribe, comprising a palette for mixing red and black inks, a slender pen case, and a pouch for cakes of dried ink (or perhaps water with which to mix ink), tied together with a single cord.

with red employed for important text such as headings, numerical totals, and the like. And the slender brushes with which scribes wrote were made from rushes that grew in the Nile delta, their ends bruised with a rock or chewed until soft, and then shaped into a point with a knife.[34] Scribes wrote like artists paint, holding their brushes perpendicular to the papyrus an inch or two from the tip to produce deliberate, even strokes.[35]

The theory and practice of Egyptian scribal culture—the belief that hieroglyphs possessed magical powers; the palettes, brushes, and handmade ink of the scribes, and their exalted position in society—endured for more than two and a half thousand years. The venerable kingdom of Egypt was not so lucky. In 1070 BCE the country was partitioned into Lower Egypt, ruled over by the pharaoh and comprising the Mediterranean coast and the Nile delta, and Upper Egypt to the south, administered in the pharaoh's name by a high priest. In reality, the arrangement was window dressing for the establishment of two separate states. Over the next seven hundred years a weakened Egypt reeled from a series of civil wars, secessions, and invasions.[36]

Egypt was finally, forcibly integrated into the Hellenic world of the Greeks in 332 BCE, when Alexander the Great liberated the country from Persian occupation only to install himself as pharaoh.[37] Some years later, after Alexander's successors, the Ptolemies, had exhausted themselves through constant strife with their Syrian neighbors, the Romans decided to add an Egyptian conquest to their trophy cabinet. Under Cleopatra VII, the last of the Ptolemies, Egypt allied itself with Mark Antony, one of a triumvirate of Roman leaders whose struggles drove Rome from republic to empire. Only later did she find that she had picked the wrong side. Antony's forces were decisively beaten in 30 BCE by his rival Octavian, later to become the first emperor of Rome, and Cleopatra is said to have committed suicide by pressing a poisonous asp to her breast. Egypt became the Roman province of Aegyptus.[38]

For their parts, the Greeks and Romans viewed Egypt with a mixture of disdain and awe. They saw a hidebound, barbaric culture in free fall, brought low by the righteous strength of their usurpers, and yet they were fascinated by Egypt's ancient monuments and the impenetrable writing inscribed upon them. The Romans in particular were so fond of such treasures that today there are more Egyptian obelisks in the city of Rome than there are in the whole of Egypt.[39] Rome's scholars, however, were stumped as to how to interpret the hieroglyphs on their looted ornaments. Writing in the first century BCE, Diodorus of Sicily hazarded that "their writing does not express the intended concept by means of syllables joined one to another, but by means of the significance of the objects which have been copied," and went on to give some specific examples:

> *Now the hawk signifies to them everything which happens swiftly, since this animal is practically the swiftest of winged creatures. And the concept portrayed is then transferred, by the appropriate metaphorical transfer, to all swift things and to everything to which swiftness is appropriate, very much as if they had been named. And the crocodile is a symbol of all that is evil, and the eye is the warder of justice and the guardian of the entire body.*[40]

It is difficult to be too hard on Diodorus, whose faulty account of hieroglyphics appears in the second of the forty volumes comprising his epic *Bibliotheca historica*, or "Library of History"—evidently, he had a lot of other ground to cover. Nevertheless, his explanation of how Egyptian writing worked reflected the prevailing opinion of his time: the Romans could not believe that hieroglyphics had ever outgrown their pictographic roots and neither, for a very long time, could anyone else.[41]

Finally, in the late eighteenth century, came a breakthrough. Jørgen Zoëga, a Danish archaeologist who had gone to Rome to study the countless archaeological treasures looted by the ancient Romans, wondered if hieroglyphs might be more complex than previously thought. Zoëga proposed that hieroglyphics contained phonetic elements—that somehow the system communicated not just words or concepts but also spoken sounds. But the Dane was frustrated by a lack of data. Even in Rome, which was lousy with Egyptian obelisks, there were not enough texts to develop his theory further.[42]

The impasse was broken in 1799. Napoleonic troops occupying an Egyptian village called Rashid, or Rosetta, located some miles northeast of Alexandria, discovered there a gray stone slab carved with inscriptions in three distinct scripts. Pierre Bouchard, the engineer who excavated the stone, recognized hieroglyphs and Greek letters but could not place the second of the three inscriptions. (It was later determined to be a simplified Egyptian script called "demotic," also untranslated at the time.) Bouchard brought the stone to Jacques-François Menou (later Abdallah de Menou), the commander of the French army in Egypt, who had the stone cleaned and its Greek portion translated—only to find that the text itself declared that all three of the stone's inscriptions were translations of the same text. Menou sent the stone to Cairo's Institut d'Égypte, where scholars copied it by coating the surface with ink and pressing paper against it. Within a year of the stone's discovery, white-on-black prints of its inscriptions were on scholars' desks across Europe.[43]

France's possession of the "Rosetta Stone" lasted barely two years. In 1801, a combined British and Ottoman force seized first Cairo and then Alexandria, where the stone had been sent for safekeeping. Confiscated by the British as war booty, it was shipped to London, where it has been on display in the British Museum ever since.[44] With copies already distributed to Europe's intelligentsia, however, the competition to decrypt the stone's inscriptions raced ahead regardless—and, echoing the colonial struggles in Egypt, its chief protagonists hailed from opposing sides of the Anglo-French divide.[45]

Thomas Young, an English doctor, linguist, and scientist, was first to make a breakthrough. In 1819, in a special article written for the *Encyclopedia Britannica,* Young explained that by comparing repeating patterns of characters, he had deduced that certain demotic characters, used to render Greek names such as Ptolemy and Cleopatra, were employed phonetically, not pictographically. Moreover, he said, many demotic characters corresponded to hieroglyphs with similar shapes, though a complete decipherment eluded him.[46]

A precocious French linguist named Jean-François Champollion read Young's article with interest and incorporated the Englishman's ideas into his own investigation. On September 27, 1822, Champollion took the floor in front of a select audience at the Académie des Inscriptions et Belles-Lettres in Paris to declare that he had succeeded in deciphering hieroglyphics. Champollion revealed to his listeners how he had compared the Rosetta Stone inscriptions to other ancient texts and how he had drawn upon his knowledge of Coptic, the final evolution of the Egyptian tongue, to solve the conundrum. (He chose not to reveal the circumstances of his revelation, at the moment of which he had uttered the words "*Je tiens mon affaire!*"—"I've done it!"—and promptly swooned into a dead faint for five days.)[47] The secret, he explained, was that hieroglyphs could be used phonetically *or* pictographically. The "lion-reclining" hieroglyph (), for instance, could be used to mean "lion" or, depending upon the context, it could stand for an *l* or *r* sound.[48] Champollion's audience, Thomas Young among them, was agog. Thousands of years' worth of cryptic scrolls and inscriptions were now decipherable.

⇝ • ⇜

Philologists, who study the development of language, have long traced a direct line of descent from the writing of the Phoenicians, the Egyptians' trading partners in what is now Lebanon, to the twenty-six letters of our alphabet. Whereas the Egyptians used hieroglyphs to represent both concepts and spoken sounds, by 1000 BCE the Phoenicians had developed an alphabet proper, consisting solely of letters that corresponded to spoken sounds.[49] Phoenician letters are visibly similar to those of the Greek alphabet that came after them, and that were in turn passed on to the Greeks' neighbors to the north, the Etruscans; later still, the Etruscan alphabet was adopted and modified by Rome. Some letters were lost in this process, others gained, and yet more transformed from consonants to vowels. The procession from the Phoenician alphabet to the Roman alphabet had never been much doubted, and the Phoenicians were hailed as the inventors of alphabetic writing.[50] In the wake of the decipherment of hieroglyphics, however, things were set to change.

In 1904 and 1905, some years before his excavations at the vast Tarkhan graveyard outside Cairo, Flinders Petrie had led an expedition to Serabit el-Khadim, a hilltop temple on the Sinai Peninsula at a site where the ancient Egyptians had mined turquoise. Among the many hieroglyphic inscriptions he found, and which were subsequently dated to around 1800 BCE, there were a handful written in a more mysterious script.[51] Petrie could not decipher the new symbols, but he noted that there were far fewer of them—perhaps thirty at most—than would have been expected for a syllabic script such as cuneiform or a pictographic script such as hieroglyphics. There were few enough of them, he thought, to form an alphabet, though a decade would pass before any real sense was made of the so-called Sinaitic script.[52] Finally, in a paper published in 1916, an Egyptologist named Alan H. Gardiner brought the Serabit inscriptions together with a number of other theories to reach a startling conclusion.[53]

The fertile Nile delta, Gardiner knew, had exerted a powerful pull on the ancient inhabitants of Canaan, a loosely defined geographical area encompassing Phoenicia, along with parts of what would later become Lebanon, Syria, Jordan, and Israel. It was the promise of the Nile delta that had persuaded Jacob and the Israelites to make their biblical journey to Egypt, and for centuries the Sinai Peninsula had functioned as the crossroads between Canaan and Egypt.[54] Remarkably, Gardiner knew also what language Egypt's Canaanite visitors had spoken, down to the spelling of individual words; aided by the decipherment of cuneiform, philologists had succeeded in tracing modern Arabic, Hebrew, Maltese, and Amharic all the way back to the "Semitic" languages spoken thousands of years earlier in Canaan, Mesopotamia, and the Arabian Peninsula.[55]

Hieroglyphic texts found at Serabit talked of "interpreters," and Gardiner wondered if there could have been some cross-pollination between Egyptian and Canaanite languages.[56] With this in mind, he selected a sequence of four signs—a word, he hoped—that recurred throughout the mysterious Serabit inscriptions, and subjected them to a little linguistic pattern matching. Noting that his four signs were similar to Egyptian hieroglyphs that depicted a house, an eye, an ox-goad, and a cross respectively, he took a chance. Taking the *Semitic* names for the depicted objects (*bēt*, *ʿaīn*, *lāwī*, and *tāwī*) and discarding all but their initial sounds, Gardiner formed the Semitic word *bʿlt*, or *Baʿalat*. In Hebrew, a descendant of the ancient Semitic language, this meant "the Lady," a title given to local goddesses such as Hathor, the patron deity of the Serabit miners. He had found the key to the Sinaitic script.

Gardiner applied his principle to eleven more symbols, matching symbols to objects and then to the initial sounds of their Semitic names, but the tiny handful of "proto-Sinaitic" texts meant that a full translation was (and still is) impossible.[57] Even so, it was clear that the Phoenician alphabet was no longer the first of its kind, and it is now possible to construct a family tree rooted in hieroglyphics that embraces essentially every alphabetic script ever created. The letters in this book are the offspring of ancient Egyptian writing, filtered through four thousand years of human history.

This welding together of Egyptian symbols and Semitic sounds was the death knell for cuneiform. Philologists still do not know who created the letters found at Serabit el-Khadim—illiterate Canaanite miners, perhaps, appropriating the hieroglyphs they saw around them; Egyptian interpreters managing an international workforce; they may even have originated elsewhere entirely—but whoever it was preferred hieroglyphics' soft curves to cuneiform's hard edges.[58] Soon after, sheets of Egyptian papyrus were being exported across the Mediterranean for use with the new script, and the clay tablets of cuneiform were consigned to history.[59]

All this alphabetic ferment churned onward without any great innovations in the basic technologies of writing. For at least a thousand years after proto-Sinaitic appeared, Egyptian and Semitic scribes continued to dissolve soot in gum arabic to make their ink, and chewed meditatively at the ends of their sea rushes before cutting them to fibrous points.

The first crack in the age-old troika of papyrus, brush, and ink appeared in the sixth century BCE. Alphabetic writing had reached Greece two hundred years earlier, courtesy of the Phoenicians, but when papyrus followed it to the shores of the Hellenic world scribes there chose a radical new writing implement. The ancient Greeks wrote with pens, not brushes, that they called calami after the hollow reeds or canes from which they were carved.[60] Scribes cut reeds to a usable length before shaping, splitting, and sharpening their tips into a recognizably penlike form, and Greek writing took on a more familiar aspect as a result: whereas the Egyptians' rushes made for broad, even strokes, the narrow, flat nib of a calamus on papyrus created the conspicuous variation between thick and thin strokes that characterizes handwritten manuscripts from the Middle Ages until the modern day.[61] If Egyptian brushes were blunt felt-tip markers, Greek calami were neat, precise fountain pens.

Reed pens have been found in abundance, and their use is apparent in the lettering of papyri from Greece, Rome, and Egypt, but scribes themselves barely acknowledged their writing implements.[62] When it came to ink, however, the Greeks and Romans were passionate indeed. Greek writers spoke of experiments with pigments such as cuttlefish ink, or sepia; with the residue left after the fermentation of grapes; and

⇜ Fragment of a papyrus discovered at Oxyrhynchus in Egypt. Dated to between 150 and 250 CE, this 6-by-3-inch scrap of papyrus contains the start of the sixth book of Homer's *Iliad*. Its scribe copied it in the original Greek, almost certainly with a reed pen and carbon ink. The blank area to the left may be a *protokollon* (the first, blank sheet of a roll that protects the rest when rolled up), or it may be a margin separating two portions of the text.[63]

with burnt ivory, which yielded *elefantinon melan*, or "elephant's ink." (Some Greek scribes, lacking in money and morals, robbed graves of cremated bones to make a macabre, economical version of this prized substance.)[64] And though the Romans arrived comparatively late to the literacy party, mostly likely in the third century BCE, they too threw themselves wholeheartedly into the intricacies of ink making.[65] Vitruvius, an architect who lived during the first century BCE, described how to build a special marble furnace in which to burn resinous pinewood for its soot.[66] And Pliny, whose muddled description of papyrus still baffles, explained that adding wormwood to ink helped keep hungry mice away from scrolls.[67]

In spite of all this research and development, neither the Greeks nor the Romans deviated from the old recipe of water, gum arabic, and pigment to create tractable, water-soluble ink. It was almost a point of pride that inky writing was so easily obliterated: Martial, a Roman poet writing in the first century CE, enclosed a sponge with poems sent to his patron so that he could wipe off those he disliked.[68] But as Egypt fell to squabbling with its neighbors to the east and papyrus exports dwindled, things came to a head. Yes, water-based ink could be washed off papyrus if it absolutely had to be erased, but it was perfectly permanent otherwise. The parchment that was set to replace papyrus, however, was more problematic: water-based ink sat precariously on parchment's impenetrable surface, and once dry it flaked off at the slightest provocation. A new writing material demanded a new kind of ink.

The Greeks and Romans shared a long history of sending love letters and military orders alike so as to evade detection. The Greek tyrant Histiaeus tattooed orders onto the shaved scalp of his favored messenger, then waited for the messenger's hair to grow back before dispatching him to deliver the secret message; Demaratus, another Greek, warned the Spartans of Xerxes's oncoming army by hiding a message under the wax of a wooden writing tablet. Ovid, a Roman poet famous for his odes to courtship and forbidden love, recommended writing secret messages with milk instead of ink; these remained invisible until sprinkled with coal dust, whereupon the black dust clung to the milky letters. (For an added frisson, Ovid suggested, such risqué messages could be written upon the skin of a willing go-between.)[69] Predictably, Pliny, too, had something to say about the matter, describing in *Natural History* how the sap of certain plants could be used in the same way.[70]

One particular recipe for invisible ink stood apart from the rest. Writing in the third century BCE, an engineer named Philo from the Greek city of Byzantium described what he called "sympathetic ink."[71]

Ink made from dried tree galls, he wrote, left no trace on papyrus, but when swabbed with a solution of copper sulfate the hidden text would appear as if from nowhere.[72] Philo's is the only description of this cunning technique (the spies of the ancient world generally did not publish tell-all memoirs upon retirement) but it is remarkable how precisely he anticipated the ink that would take scribes into the Middle Ages and beyond. By the second century CE, scribes were using ink that differed from Philo's recipe only in that its two main ingredients were brought together *before* pen met parchment, not after.

The Greeks and Romans made this new ink with tree galls and copper sulfate (*chacantum*, or "blood of copper," as they called it), but scribes had soon replaced copper sulfate with "copperas," or ferrous sulfate.[73] Today we call it "iron gall ink," after this later recipe; it was the perfect complement to papyrus *and* to parchment, and by the twelfth century it had eclipsed traditional carbon ink almost entirely.[74]

Key to iron gall ink's success was its ability to bond with parchment. Out of the bottle and applied to the page, the pale ink leached into the parchment and deepened to a lustrous, permanent blue-black as it reacted with oxygen in the air. Once dry, it was almost impossible to remove.[75] The irony of iron gall ink, in fact, is that the medieval scribe's tool kit contained almost as many implements dedicated to its erasure as to its application in the first place. Quill pens (which replaced reed pens but retained their distinctive split nibs), ink horns, penknives, and straightedges were joined by pumice stones to gently abrade parchment, razors for more radical surgery, and chalk to prepare the erased surface to receive new text.[76] Parchment was so expensive that it would have been unthinkable to discard a book whose contents were no longer necessary or relevant, and so the concept of the "palimpsest" was born: taken from the Greek *palimpsestos*, or "scraped again," a palimpsest is a document that has been erased and then reused.[77] But iron gall ink is nothing if not persistent, and many palimpsests carry the shadows of their former texts. As evidenced by the "Archimedes Palimpsest" unveiled in 2011, a medieval prayer book that concealed two lost works

REGNANTE MAGNIFICO ANGLORUM REGE ETHELSTANO.

hic omittit E

ANNO QUIDEM IMPERII EIUS primo. Aduentus uero anglorum in brittanniam quadringentesimo nonogesimo septimo. cum idem rex hostibus circumquaque subactis pace & concordia regnum tueretur. natus est puer dei DUNSTANUS wessaxoniensium anglie partibus. magnis quidem presculi dignitate parentibus. sed ad religionem quae xpianos decet longe maioribus. Tanta siquidem uirtutis ratione uiuentes animum colebant. tot piis opibus laborantes insudabant. ut communem mortalibus uiam ingressi: angelicis spiritibus mererentur associari. sicut eidem filio suo postmodum diuina reuelatione innotuit. Quod non alienum est diuinitatis consilio factum conicere: ut uidelicet tantus infans tales parentes haberet. qui cum ipsi bene uiuerent. tum bene uiuendi formam nascituro ex se filio tradere possent. Magnum quippe deus illum futurum prouidebat: quem ibi dulcedinis suae benedictionibus preuenerat. ubi omnes filii adam natiuae maledictionis sententiam excipiunt. si non passumptam a filio dei humani habitus formam. ad pristinam reformantur beatitudinem. Magnum inquam deus illum futurum prouidebat: cui tantum muneris donatum est. ut ante mundo signis innotesceret. quam hunc in mundi huius lucem mater fudisset. Atque ut cetera dilucide & ordinate procedant: hinc dicendi initia

The state of the scribe's art at the end of the eleventh century: a parchment page ruled with a lead- or silver-tipped stylus, the text written with iron gall ink, and embellishments added in a variety of colors. Note the translucency of the parchment and the scribe's self-portrait nestled within the decorative capital. The text here is written in a "proto-gothic" form of our familiar roman alphabet, marking the midway point between earliest lowercase letters and the angular, gothic script most often associated with German books.[78]

by the Greek inventor, some of our most prized ancient books have survived *only* as palimpsests, to be revealed by careful examination under ultraviolet lamps.[79]

The manufacture of iron gall ink was a convoluted, alchemical labor. First, globular tree galls were gathered and dried: the oak galls found in Europe's bandit-ridden forests were satisfactory, but those exported from the province of Aleppo in Syria were favored by more discerning ink makers.[80] Copperas occurred natively in Spain in the form of greenish powder or crystals (later, it was manufactured in a drawn-out, protoindustrial process that took four years from start to finish), while gum arabic, like Aleppo galls, came from the Near East.[81] With these ingredients in hand, the medieval scribe settled in for a process that could take from two hours to two months. The dried galls were crushed or pounded, then, depending on the ink maker's proclivities, they were variously soaked, boiled, or fermented in rainwater, wine, or beer, all of which were thought to be purer than drinking water. When the gall infusion was finally ready, it was fortified with powdered copperas and thickened with ground-up gum arabic.[82] The one pitfall in all this was that copperas, one of the main ingredients of iron gall ink, was available in a dehydrated (and more portable) form that was easily mistaken for its regular counterpart. Ink made from dehydrated copperas contained an excess of sulfuric acid, and so conservators today often find parchment manuscripts whose acidic lettering is slowly eating through the page.[83] The nineteenth century gave us brittle books; the medieval period gave us brittle letters.

As befits its convoluted manufacturing process, iron gall ink's permanence was the result of a complex chemical metamorphosis that began as soon as it met the air. Kept in a sealed bottle until needed (scribes learned to breathe into their bottles before closing them, thus replacing oxygen with unreactive carbon dioxide), the pale brown-black ink remained water soluble and was readily absorbed into parchment as it flowed from the writer's pen.[84] As the ink dried, however, the presence of oxygen in the air caused the tannic acids extracted from the tree galls to react with the copperas* to form a darker, insoluble pigment that adhered to the fibers of the parchment, thereby fixing it there for good.[85]

A new formulation for ink is not the most crowd-pleasing of inventions, of course. But the scribe's art was an inherently conservative one and the arrival of iron gall ink set the template for book writing for centuries to come. A split-nib quill pen, a pot of iron gall ink, and a smooth sheet of parchment were the pillars of the scribe's craft from the establishment of the Roman Empire until the height of the Renaissance. For hundreds of years, books were written in the same, comforting way that they had always been written—until one day, a man named Gutenberg pulled and released the lever of a makeshift wine press, and everything changed.

*Specifically, the ink's ferrous sulfate oxidizes in air to a ferric valence state, allowing a ferric-tannate charge-transfer complex to form between iron(III) and catecholic and/or gallate groups of tannins. Contrasted with the action of earlier inks, which can be summarized as "gum sticks soot to the page," it is clear that iron gall ink was quite a different beast.

6

The Prints and the Pauper: Johannes Gutenberg and the invention of movable type

In 1448, a native of the city of Mainz, Germany, returned to his hometown after almost two decades away. For Johannes Gensfleisch zur Laden zum Gutenberg, the occasion of his long-delayed homecoming was bittersweet. His sister Else was dead, and he was to take over the home in which she had lived—the Gutenberghof, or "Jewish Hill house," from which their family took its name.[1] But Gutenberg, a middle-aged man of respectable if not noble birth, was not entirely downhearted. He had a scheme, hatched during his self-imposed exile, to revive his fortunes. All he needed was an injection of capital from a willing investor.[2]

The city to which Gutenberg returned was little changed from the one he had left. Aurea Moguntia—"Golden Mainz"—was a walled town on the banks of the River Main that epitomized the late-medieval urban experience. Its streets were muddy byways, the better of them paved by wooden planks, along which sewage ran in open ditches. Pedestrians had to keep an eye out for the plummeting contents of chamber pots emptied from high windows. Mainz's population, numbering 6,000 souls or thereabouts, had been thinned out over the years by successive outbreaks of the bubonic plague, though the remaining inhabitants could at least find solace in one of the forty churches within the city's walls.[3]

The Mainz of Gutenberg's time was dominated by three distinct forces. One was external: the city's archbishop was an "elector," one of the seven worthies who chose Germany's kings, and Mainz often found itself a pawn in national politics. Two more factions squabbled and wrangled within the city itself: the old families of Mainz, the patricians, were constantly at odds with the up-and-coming guilds of the middle class—the goldsmiths, masons, salt measurers, barber-surgeons (in those days, possession of a good razor was a sufficient qualification for both), and more. Johannes Gutenberg was a patrician by birth but had become a bona fide craftsman during the course of his travels, and his plan upon returning to Mainz depended on its peculiar mix of skilled goldsmiths, a wealthy church, and a pious population.[4]

Gutenberg's initial departure from Mainz seems to have been prompted by the antagonistic atmosphere between the patricians and the guilds. Mainz operated a system of annuities, where wealthy citizens who could afford to loan the city a sizeable lump sum received yearly repayments thereafter of around 5 percent, payable in perpetuity to the annuitant and their heirs. The guilds, whose members were heavily taxed in order to fund this municipal Ponzi scheme, fought the patricians at every turn, and the city was thus locked in a vicious cycle. Periodically, the guilds would gain the upper hand in the city's council, or pack its offices with their sympathizers; in response, the patrician families would retreat in high dudgeon to their out-of-town estates, taking their money with them; and finally, with the city on the brink of financial ruin, the guilds would climb down. In 1429, when one of his annuities was cut in half during a spate of municipal infighting, Johannes Gutenberg vanished from Mainz. He was determined to make a fresh start in a less dysfunctional place.[5]

Gutenberg surfaced again in 1434, named as the plaintiff in a court case heard in Strasbourg, a hundred miles to the south of Mainz. Niklaus von Wörrstadt, the defendant, was one of Mainz's burgomasters, or magistrates, charged with managing the town and its finances. Before leaving Mainz, Johannes had extracted a promise from von Wörrstadt to the effect that the burgomaster was personally liable for Gutenberg's now-diminished annuity, and von Wörrstadt's visit to Strasbourg provided just the opportunity for him to make good on that promise—voluntarily or otherwise. The court found in Gutenberg's favor, and von Wörrstadt was ordered to stump up 310 *Rheingulden*, or Rhenish florins, equivalent to perhaps a year's wages for a skilled craftsman.[6] To this windfall Gutenberg could add his existing income, and an annuity originally paid by the city of Strasbourg to his brother, Friele, but which had been awarded to Johannes after their mother's death some years earlier.[7]

Strasbourg was larger and more crowded than Mainz, but it lacked the other town's crippling debts, internecine strife, and trouble-magnet elector-archbishop.[8] With the court case concluded, Gutenberg, by now in his mid-thirties, found himself in a populous, well-mannered city, and with a disposable income. He took advantage of his tranquil surroundings and comparative riches to establish a house and workshop at St. Arbogast, a nearby village.[9] Settled into a new home and free to pursue his own business, finally some details emerge in the historical record about Johannes Gutenberg's abilities as a craftsman and his instincts as an entrepreneur.

Gutenberg knew, as every God-fearing German would have known, that pilgrims flocked to Aachen Cathedral every seven years to view a quartet of holy relics: the robe Mary wore on the night of Jesus's birth; Christ's swaddling clothes; the cloth used to wrap John the Baptist's itinerant head; and the loincloth worn by Jesus on the cross.[10] There was, at the time, a fad for pilgrims to brandish tiny framed mirrors as they took in the spectacle of the relics; by gathering the "rays" emitted by the relics, it was said that a mirror might become charged with their power and so confer blessings on those who later looked upon it.[11] With the 1439 pilgrimage approaching, Gutenberg maneuvered to take advantage of this religious craze. He would manufacture these "holy mirrors" in his workshop, and he would sell them to the hordes of pilgrims due to descend on Aachen.[12]

Why it is that the unremarkable scion of an upper-middle-class family would have known anything about making mirrors has occupied Gutenberg scholars since the first books on the subject. It is an important question—the rest of Gutenberg's career hinges on it—but the man himself left no records of his education or work experience. The accepted answer, such as it is, runs as follows. Back in Mainz, Gutenberg's father had held the position of "Companion of the Mint," or overseer of the city's mint, one of three in Germany with the dispensation to coin Rheingulden and that also made jewelry and regalia for the city fathers.[13] It is supposed that the young Johannes would have been exposed to the technologies of minting and goldsmithing from an early age—that he would have seen how the mint's artisans sculpted letters and images onto steel punches that were then struck into molds for minting coins, and that he would have learned how molten metals could be blended into alloys with varying properties.[14] When it came to making tiny metal pilgrim mirrors, it is conceivable that Gutenberg would have known where to begin.

The business of the mirrors was short-lived. An outbreak of plague in 1438 caused the pilgrimage planned for the following year to be postponed, and the partnership that Gutenberg had formed with three Strasbourgeoise investors was dissolved acrimoniously that same year. Statements given during the resulting court case hint at some shared, hidden project: there was talk of a press involved in the mirror-making, while Gutenberg required that certain *Formen*, or "forms," be melted down to prevent them from falling into the wrong hands.[15] Most intriguing of all are mentions of some unnamed device that consisted of four parts joined by two screws, and which was to be dismantled so that its intent and operation were obscured.[16] Gutenberg's former partners were bought off with generous settlements; little more is heard of them after the court case, and the man himself drifts out of the written record after 1444.[17]

It is not until four years later that the erstwhile mirror maker crops up again. Defeated in Strasbourg, Gutenberg returned to the town of his birth.

In 1450 a revitalized Johannes Gutenberg entered into an agreement with one Johann Fust (sometimes spelled "Faust"), a Mainzer goldsmith and guildsman, to borrow a staggering 800 Rheingulden at 6 percent interest.[18] Gutenberg's sales pitch must have been convincing, for Fust would later testify that he himself had borrowed money in order to fund the loan. Gutenberg sank the money into his new workshop and promptly defaulted upon the interest payments.[19] Fust must have been incandescent in his rage, and yet, two years later, as recorded in the inevitable court judgment, he would go on to lend Gutenberg *another* 800 Rheingulden on the condition that Gutenberg take on Fust's adopted son, Peter Schöffer, as his foreman. Gutenberg assented, Schöffer was hired, and Fust paid out the second loan.[20]

Why was Fust so ready to throw good money after bad? The prize that Gutenberg had dangled in front of his financier was, of course, the invention of movable type: the promise that a book could be replicated over and over again with minimal effort. In an era when a handwritten Bible commanded a price equivalent to a laborer's yearly wage, the ability to print an endless run of books must have appeared as a license to mint Rheingulden.[21] And so Fust was content, if not entirely happy, to leave Gutenberg to tinker with the devices that littered his printing workshop in anticipation of the truly colossal profits that lay ahead if the process could be perfected.

For his part, Gutenberg was faced with a difficult decision: what should he print first? The scholarly consensus is that he settled on a Latin schoolbook called the *Ars grammatica*, written by a Roman grammarian named Aelius Donatus in the waning days of the Roman Empire, and which by Gutenberg's time had become the standard beginners' text.[22] It was a sensible place to start; to attend church, school, or university meant being exposed to Latin as an ancient but living tongue, and Gutenberg himself would have learned the language as a child and occasionally spoken it as an adult.[23]

Gutenberg's first book survives only as parchment scraps pasted into the bindings of other works, but the fifty or so partial copies that do exist reveal what must have been a truly radical item, even as it did its best to appear entirely ordinary.[24] Gutenberg's Donatus was a short book, its twenty-eight pages written in the dense Gothic *textura*, or "woven" letters, common to continental books of the time.[25] The otherwise monotonous column of text is relieved by the occasional red flourish; scribes known as rubricators were often called upon to decorate capital letters and to add paragraphs marks (¶) in this way.[26] In closer review the text is a little *too* neat. Though the letters vary slightly in form—one *a* is subtly different from the next *a*, as would be expected of a practiced but human hand—eventually, different instances of the same letter reveal themselves to be not similar but identical. There are not an infinity of *a*'s in Gutenberg's Donatus, for example, but rather ten concrete versions. Paleographers, who study historical handwriting and printed texts, agree that by 1450, Gutenberg had printed this, his first book.[27]

Gutenberg was soon ready to move beyond this run-of-the-mill Latin textbook. Around the same time that the first copies of the *Ars grammatica* issued forth from Gutenberg's workshop, Mainz was graced by an important visitor. The renowned cardinal Nicholas of Kues—Cusanus, to his learned friends—was engaged on a "grand legation," a tour of Germany ordered by the pope so that his favored troubleshooter could resolve disputes, bolster the Church's influence, and raise a little money.[28] It was not Cusanus's first visit to Mainz. That had come a quarter century earlier, when Nicholas had participated in a court case in the city—and when he may have made the acquaintance of one Johannes Gutenberg. Historians have long wondered if Cusanus and Gutenberg ever met; as near-contemporaries, and as ambitious commoners in a society that favored those of noble birth, they would have had much to discuss if ever their paths had crossed. As with everything in Gutenberg's life, however, concrete proof of this hoped-for meeting of minds is sorely lacking. If Gutenberg and Cusanus met, neither one mentioned it.[29]

What is certain is that Nicholas's grand legation brought him to Mainz in 1451. Uppermost in the cardinal's mind during this particular visit were ongoing negotiations over the text of the Church's daily manual, or "missal." The Church was riven by theological disputes and Cusanus hoped that a single, authorized missal—*his* missal—might rein in the heretical tendencies on display from some of its flock.[30] Here academic speculation about any hypothetical friendship between Gutenberg and Cusanus runs riot. Had he known of Gutenberg's invention, historians say, Cusanus would have jumped at the chance to print an endless stream of missals, each one free from human error and conforming to his preferred manuscript. But whether or not the two connived to print a new missal, Mainz's intransigent archbishop had other ideas. He backed a different version of the missal, the dispute rumbled on, and Gutenberg's guaranteed bestseller evaporated.[31]

Frustrating though this setback must have been, Cusanus could not afford to dwell on it. The Christian island of Cyprus was under threat from the Ottoman Turks, and the Church needed money for its defense. To raise the necessary funds, Pope Nicolas V had authorized Cusanus to sell ecumenical instruments called "indulgences" that could be purchased by the faithful to help commute their sins. The granting of an indulgence was recorded by a simple written contract, and Cusanus asked the prior of St. Jakob's, in Mainz, to prepare 2,000 such contracts in readiness for a concentrated sales offensive.[32] But the prior did not have his in-house scribes carry out the work, as might have been expected. Instead, the 2,000 indulgences were commissioned from Gutenberg, who printed them over the course of 1454 and 1455 with lettering that matched that of his *Ars grammatica*.[33]

The surviving Mainz indulgences have been a vital source of evidence for historians, but for the man who printed them they were little more than a distraction. Inspired by Nicholas's religious fervor—or, at least, awakened to the commercial possibilities presented by a rich, omnipresent Church—Gutenberg had been working on a much grander project calculated to find an audience among the monasteries and abbeys that dotted the Holy Roman Empire. In 1452, Gutenberg convinced Johann Fust to lend him a second sum of 800 Rheingulden, and let his benefactor in on the plan. They would print the holiest book of all.[34]

But wait. It bears mentioning that Johannes Gutenberg, the "father of printing," was most definitely not the *inventor* of printing.[35] "The action of making an impression, indentation, etc.," predates Gutenberg and his Bible by a huge margin, and if the *Oxford English Dictionary* is to be believed then humanity has been printing for far longer than it has been writing books. In Iraq, for instance, archaeologists have unearthed 8,500-year-old stone seals with which the ancient Mesopotamians made marks on clay jars and boxes.[36] (Proving that the human psyche has changed very little in the intervening millennia, one of these very earliest seals is engraved with a stylized penis.)[37] Even if we narrow our definition to the printing of written texts, Gutenberg was still a latecomer. The ancient Egyptians used wooden stamps to impress hieroglyphics on clay tiles within tombs, while the so-called Phaistos Disk, a mysterious artifact found on Crete and tentatively dated to the second millennium BCE, bears a series of distinctly letterlike indentations on its clay surface.[38]

But if Gutenberg did not invent printing, surely he can be given the credit for pioneering movable type, where individual letters and characters can be rearranged to print an infinite variety of texts?

Well, no. Four hundred years before Gutenberg, a Chinese

commoner named Bi Sheng preempted the German. As told by Shen Kuo, a contemporary Chinese historian:

> *During the reign of Qingli [1041–1048 AD], Bi Sheng, a man of unofficial position, made movable type. His method was as follows: he took sticky clay and cut in it characters as thin as the edge of a coin. Each character formed, as it were, a single type. He baked them in the fire to make them hard. He had previously prepared an iron plate and he had covered his plate with a mixture of pine resin, wax, and paper ashes. When he wished to print, he took an iron frame and set it on the iron plate. In this he placed the types, set close together. When the frame was full, the whole made one solid block of type. He then placed it near the fire to warm it. When the paste [at the back] was slightly melted, he took a smooth board and pressed it over the surface, so that the block of type became as even as a whetstone. [. . .] For each character there were several types, and for certain common characters there were twenty or more types each, in order to be prepared for the repetition of characters on the same page. When the characters were not in use he had them arranged with paper labels, one label for each rhyme-group, and kept them in wooden cases.*[39]

This is movable type, almost to its dictionary definition: the printing of a text from symbols on discrete blocks that can be rearranged and reused as necessary.[40] Unfortunately, this passage contains all that is known of Bi Sheng's invention.[41] Did he cut his letters into the surfaces of clay blocks, for example, or did he sculpt them in relief? The Chinese had a tradition of taking rubbings from engravings in stone and another of printing from wooden blocks carved in relief, leaving this most basic question unanswered.[42] Worse, although Shen Kuo's account of Bi Sheng's system has the confident tone of an eyewitness account, no physical evidence survives to corroborate it. We have no texts printed by this method, and neither, despite Shen Kuo's claim that

"[Bi Sheng's] font of type passed into the possession of my nephews" in the manner of a treasured heirloom, has any physical trace been found of the equipment itself.[43] All that can be said with confidence is that in the middle of the eleventh century a man named Bi Sheng developed a form of movable type that used earthenware letters, and that his invention faded away before it made any lasting impact.[44]

But China was not finished with movable type. Two and a half centuries after Bi Sheng's experiments with earthenware type, and many years yet before Gutenberg would address himself to the subject, a government apparatchik named Wang Zhen approached the problem of movable type from a new angle. Books in China at the time were often printed from carved wooden blocks, each one cut to the size of two facing pages and incised with a mix of text and illustrations.[45] This was immovable type, so to speak: each block could be used to print only its specific pair of pages, and each new book required the manufacture of a complete new set of blocks. Wang Zhen, however, saw an opportunity to meld the simplicity of woodblock printing with the flexibility of Bi Sheng's method. Accordingly, in an appendix to his celebrated *Book of Agriculture*, written in 1313, Wang Zhen summarized Bi Sheng's invention of earthenware type before explaining how he had improved upon it to create the new and intricate system of wooden type with which he had printed the book.[46]

First, a block of wood was cut square and planed flat. Next, a calligrapher painted the characters to be cut onto a sheet of waxed paper and laid that paper onto the block; when the paper was peeled off, the wet ink left behind a perfect mirror image of the hand-drawn characters. From there, it was a simple matter for a practiced woodworker to carve out the characters and saw them into separate blocks.[47] And there were many, many blocks. In the course of printing one particular history book, Wang Zhen used more than 60,000 individual characters. Arranging this enormous battery of symbols in some intuitive manner must have taxed his ingenuity. In the end, he settled upon a system composed of two revolving tables not unlike lazy Susans, with each one divided into a series of discrete compartments. On one table were arranged the bulk of the words, numbered and organized according to rhyme; on the other were placed a selection of the most common words, along with special characters such as numerals. One worker stood between these seven-foot spinning tables and retrieved characters as a second read them out in sequence.[48]

With the required characters in hand, each page was assembled, inked, and printed. Characters were wedged into a wooden frame with slivers of bamboo; ink was applied with a brush, column by column; and lastly, an impression was taken by placing a sheet of paper onto the inked page and rubbing it lightly to transfer the ink. Wang Zhen had successfully designed and implemented China's second complete system of movable type—and this one too failed to last.[49] As the years passed, Chinese (and later Korean) printers resorted to ever more esoteric materials in an attempt to find a workable system. To Bi Sheng's earthenware type and Wang Zhen's wooden blocks were added bronze, tin, and copper types; later, in the eighteenth century, porcelain was tried and rejected.[50] There is no suggestion that ancient Chinese craftspeople, engineers, or scientists were any less astute than their Western counterparts, and yet Chinese movable type never reached critical mass. So what *were* the problems? Put simply, high standards and an unwieldy written language.

Chinese ink was one of the main culprits. Although their ink was essentially the same as that of the ancient Egyptians, Greeks, and Romans, the Chinese had refined it to a new level of sophistication. Black pigment was obtained from pinewood from which all resin had been removed ("a small hole is cut near the root of the tree, into which a lamp is placed and allowed to burn slowly [. . .] the resin in the entire tree will gather at the warm spot and flow out," as one writer explained), which was then burned in a bamboo tunnel to capture the purified soot.[51] The soot was mixed with animal glue and sundry other substances such as musk, mother-of-pearl, egg whites, cinnabar, black beans, and camphor in order to achieve the desired consistency, fragrance, and color.[52]

Finally, the gummy suspension was poured into a mold—decorated with delicate, sculpted designs, ink molds were works of art in their own right—to produce a cake of solid ink for safekeeping.[53]

The end result was a peerless calligraphic ink. When Pliny compared the "India ink" exported from the port of Barbaricum to the best inks made in Rome, he was unwittingly singing the praises of Chinese ink, which first made its way to the West via this bustling subcontinental shipping hub. Even as late as the eighteenth century, European writers lamented the failure of their indigenous inks to match the deep black color and permanence of their favored "India ink."[54] The Chinese themselves may have started to believe the hype: by the tenth century, ink was being mixed with substances such as turnip, foxglove juice, and bile for use as a medicine to stop bleeding.[55] But as enticing as Chinese ink was to calligraphers and doctors, it was a stumbling block for Chinese printers who tried to move beyond simple woodblock printing. Their water-based ink did not adhere well to metal, earthenware, or porcelain and produced blotchy, indistinct images.[56]

Another famed Chinese invention bound up with books and bookmaking also proved to be an obstacle to the wider adoption of movable type. Chinese paper was too delicate to withstand the pressure needed to form a crisp impression, requiring that printers use handheld brushes rather than firm mechanical presses to impress their paper onto their type. Not only that, China's water-based ink tended to seep through the paper and made it impossible to print on both sides of a sheet.[57]

In the end, however, Chinese movable type was undone as much by economics as by anything else. As Wang Zhen had found to his cost, a font representing a usable fraction of the 50,000 or so extant Chinese characters could run to tens of thousands of individual types. (Others told of vast fonts of 200,000 types or more.)[58] Wooden type had to be cut character by character, and there is no evidence that Chinese printers ever tried to expedite the process by casting type from metal or other malleable substances. Moreover, the mechanics of movable type weighed against it: printers found that it was often faster to cut entire pages in wood, as had been done since time immemorial, than it was to set, print from, and distribute movable type on a page-by-page basis.[59] China's printers were hamstrung by the writing they sought to reproduce.

Back to Johannes Gutenberg and his ambition, in the mid-1450s, to print and sell a Bible. Though he had not invented the idea of movable type, if Gutenberg is to be credited with anything it must be that he made it *work*—that he systematically tackled each aspect of a finicky, delicate process until he had perfected it. If calligraphic ink did not meet his needs, he would look elsewhere; if embossed characters were too costly to cut individually, he would find a way to produce them in bulk; and if a firm hand was necessary to get the best impression of the printed page, he would choose tools and materials that could withstand that pressure. Gutenberg was not the father of printing so much as its midwife.

The first stage of the process to which Gutenberg addressed himself was the creation of the letters and other characters with which the Bible was to be printed. Gutenberg would almost certainly have encountered the woodcut prints then in vogue with contemporary artists, but his intuition would have told him that wooden stamps would be both too time-consuming to produce in bulk and too crude to reproduce the detailed Renaissance handwriting he had in mind.[60] In collaboration with a Strasbourgeoise goldsmith named Hans Dünne, then, Gutenberg began by making a series of delicate steel punches, each one of which was tipped by a tiny, embossed letter or mark of punctuation around seven millimeters in height.[61] To make each punch, a letter or other character (all were traced from the work of some unknown scribe) was lightly incised in reverse on the tip of a rod of mild steel before Gutenberg or Dünne took up hardened

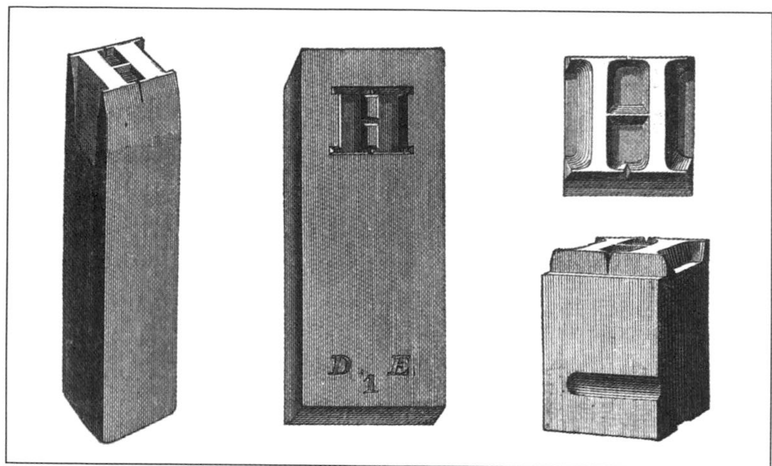

⇷ *Left*, a letter punch; *center*, a matrix struck with that punch; and *right*, front and oblique views of a sort cast from the matrix, slightly enlarged. The "nick" in the bottom of the sort allows the compositor to orient it by touch alone.[62]

steel gravers and files* to sculpt the letter in relief in infinitesimally small increments.[63] Fred Smeijers, a modern Dutch type designer, describes the operation as like sculpting cold butter; even so, with 290 separate characters counted in Gutenberg's finished Bible, that is a lot of butter to sculpt, and two more workers had to be drafted to help finish the process.[64]

Punch-cutting like this would have been familiar work to any jeweler who had made a punch with which to brand their work, or to the engravers at Mainz's mint who used letter punches to add inscriptions to coin molds. (Jewelers' punches were carved in reverse, like Gutenberg's, so that they created a readable imprint when driven into a piece of jewelry; the punches used at the mint, however, were carved "right-side

*The name of the counterpunch, another type-cutting tool, lives on even though the tool itself is long since obsolete. Counterpunches were used to hollow out the bowls of O's, R's, D's, and so on, and today any enclosed space in a letter is termed a "counter."

up" to give a reversed impression in the coin mold. Striking a coin from the mold reversed the letter again so that it faced the right direction.) From here on, however, Gutenberg's method diverged.

He, or Dünne, would have taken up their completed letter punch and driven it into a small piece of brass or copper with a careful whack from a mallet. This produced a *matrix* (from the Latin for "mother") carrying an indented, forward-facing impression of the character.[65] The most critical part of the procedure was the creation of matrices whose sunken letters were all the same depth; with no way to accurately gauge how hard to strike his punch, Gutenberg would likely have given each punch a slightly more forceful tap than necessary and later filed down the face of each matrix to obtain letters of the same depth.[66] The positioning of the punch had to be perfect too: it had to be precisely square to the edges of the matrix, and the distance from the bottom edge of the matrix to the baseline of the letter (the imaginary floor on which an *x* or *m* would sit) had to be absolutely identical in all matrices for the printed text to line up.[67]

Matrix in hand, it was time for Gutenberg to deploy his secret weapon. The device alluded to in the Strasbourg court case, the four-part contraption that was so sensitive it had to be dismantled in case someone might discover its use, was a mold for casting metal characters.[68] No examples of Gutenberg's original design have survived, but if later molds are representative (and they almost certainly are), then we can see why one witness in the Strasbourg case said that "nobody would then be able to see or work out what [it was] for."[69] Gutenberg's mold must have rivaled a cryptic crossword in the intricacy of its construction.

Conceptually, however, Gutenberg's hand mold was nothing more than a cavity of adjustable width closed off by a matrix at its foot. With a matrix slotted into place at the bottom of the mold and its width adjusted appropriately (an *l* or *i*, for instance, is narrower than an *x* or *m*), it was a relatively simple matter to pour some molten metal into the mold, give it a firm shake to drive the metal into the recesses of the matrix, and then crack it open to reveal a pristine piece of type.[70] Ultimately, the hand mold was the key to the entire scheme; without this groundbreaking device, Gutenberg could never have produced enough type.

By examining how paper from differing batches is distributed throughout the surviving printed Bibles, and by tracking idiosyncrasies of spelling, spacing, and other typographical quirks, experts

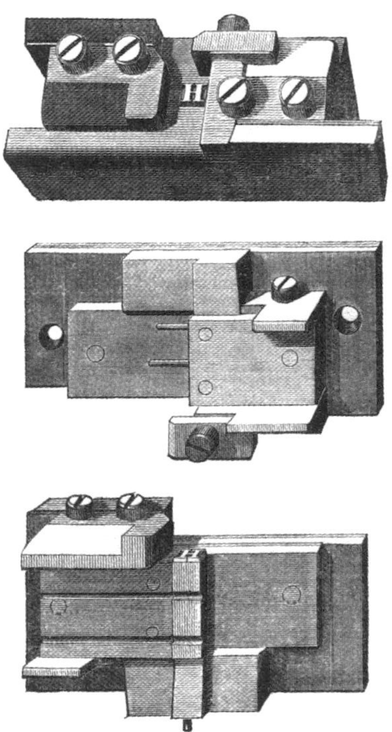

↞ Three views of a type mold. *Top,* a view of the underside of the mold with the matrix removed. A cast lead sort shows where the matrix is placed in normal operation. *Middle,* one half of the disassembled mold, this time with both the sort and matrix removed. *Bottom,* a view of the inner surface of the other half of the mold, with a cast sort in place. The "tang" of excess type metal attached to the sort illustrates the path of the molten metal as it flows into the mold's cavity.[71] None of Gutenberg's molds have survived, but the construction and operating principles of more recent molds are unlikely to have changed a great deal.

have concluded that four workers (later six) were engaged in assembling pages, or "composing" them, at once. Each page carried around 500 words and required around 2,600 characters and if, as is usually assumed to be the case, each compositor had a working set of three pages (the first being composed, the second being printed, and a third waiting to be broken up and its letters distributed back into the type case), then Gutenberg would have needed to cast some 46,000 individual sorts.[72] His mold, with which a practiced operator could cast around 600 characters per day, was essential.[73]

What metal Gutenberg or his employees poured into their molds is yet another unanswered question. The composition of his "type metal" was likely to have been arrived at through trial, error, and informed guesswork, and historians have been forced to look to other early printers for guidance. Analysis of type cast around a century after Gutenberg printed his Bible shows that lead predominated, at 82 percent, with tin making up a further 9 percent, the soft, metallic element antimony 6 percent, and trace amounts of copper among the remainder.[74] Given that type foundries still use variations on this same basic recipe, we can be reasonably sure that Gutenberg must have arrived at a similar formula.[75] Gutenberg would have found that lead made for an economical and accommodating base metal, while the addition of tin helped the molten alloy flow more easily into the mold and antimony made the resultant type harder and more durable. Not only that, but antimony shrinks less than other metals as it cools; a character cast in pure lead pulls away from the niches and edges in the matrix and produces a noticeably inferior printed letter.[76] (This formula was not perfect. Antimony in particular is a noxious substance, and two centuries after Gutenberg, workers in English type foundries would customarily end their day by drinking half a pint of red wine mixed with vegetable oil "intended for an Antidote againſt the Poyſonous Fumes of the *Antimony*.")[77]

And so, with some 46,000 sorts arranged into wooden cases and a cadre of workers trained in his mysterious new art, Gutenberg embarked on the composition and printing of the Bible. What we know

↞ Jost Amman's woodcut of *Der Schriftgiesser* (The Typecaster) of 1568, depicting a worker pouring molten type metal into a mold.

about the operation of Gutenberg's workshop is gleaned from a host of woodcut illustrations, such as Jost Amman's *Der Buchdrucker* (The Printer) of 1568, printed over the following years and decades as movable type took Europe by storm.[78] And what these woodcuts tell us, in the main, is that printing by means of movable type is an intensely traditional craft: any one of the workers depicted by Amman would feel instantly at home in a modern letterpress workshop.

The first part of the printing process was to assemble the type for a single page. We can only speculate as to the method employed by Gutenberg's four "compositors," but Amman's woodcut depicts a scene familiar to printers in which a compositor plucks sorts from a wooden case and places them onto a wooden or metal "composing stick" that holds up to a few lines at a time.[79] Whereas Wang Zhen had constructed a pair of elaborate rotating tables to organize his type, Gutenberg and his successors found the Latin alphabet easier to manage: printers placed their capital letters in one case, arranged according to the frequency of their use, while lowercase letters were placed into, well, a *lower* case below the first, from which they take their name.[80] The composing stick, a handheld tray into which type is placed, was the

➳ Jost Amman's 1568 woodcut depicting a printer's workshop. *At back,* compositors pluck sorts from type cases. *Left,* a printer removes a printed sheet of paper from the press's "tympan." Hinged to the tympan is the "frisket," a frame that holds the paper in place.[81] (Amman has depicted the frisket as a solid piece; in reality, it would have been pierced by a series of apertures corresponding to the printed areas of the page.) *Right,* the type is inked with a pair of "dabbers" or "ink balls."

compositor's main tool in all this, and its sheer simplicity means that it has received scant attention relative to the fabled hand mold or the printing press itself. *Disquisition on the Composing Stick*, the one book that examines this tool in depth, was written in 1971 by a New York advertising executive named Martin K. Speckter.[82] This noble work of inquiry, however, pales next to Speckter's other labor of love—the 1962 invention of the "interrobang," or "‽," a mark of punctuation intended to signal a confused, excited, or rhetorical question.[83] Sadly, and not a little unjustly, both the composing stick and the interrobang remain obscure.

Once their composing stick was full of sorts, arranged upside down and left to right, a compositor would gingerly slide its contents onto a tray called a galley. Line by line, a page of type took shape upon the galley, and after proofreading the type was locked tightly into a frame, or "chase," by means of wooden wedges named "quoins."[84] Printers nowadays call this completed unit of chase, type, and quoins a "forme"—and there is a suggestion that Johannes Gutenberg also knew it as such, given the naming of the so-called *Formen* that he insisted were to be destroyed as part of his scorched-earth campaign to protect trade secrets in Strasbourg.[85] Whatever he called this mirror-image-in-lead, however, the next step was to apply ink to it in preparation for printing.

Ink was crucial to Gutenberg's success. As Chinese printers had found to their cost, water-based ink was unsuited to metal type, and analysis of the surviving Bibles has shown that Gutenberg used instead something closer to the vivid, viscid oil paints popular in the art world of his day.[86] Popularized by Dutch painters such as Jan van Eyck, oil paint made from boiled linseed oil* had the right viscosity for printing.[87] Gutenberg went further still, experimenting with pigment recipes until he hit upon a color to his liking, and chemical analysis of the ink from

*Until the Industrial Revolution made ink a mass-produced commodity, most printers made their own by boiling linseed oil and then mixing in pigment. The staff of a print shop would gather around the cauldron of boiling oil and fry bread in it. These impromptu picnickers would have kept a keen eye on the temperature of the oil, which would boil over if it got too hot: "a stream of liquid fire run all over the place," as one writer put it, would ruin anyone's lunch.

surviving Bibles shows that along with carbon his ink contained copper, lead, and other metallic compounds that lent it a lustrous, reflective sheen.[88] Gutenberg also recommended specific pigments—cinnabar for red and lapis lazuli for blue—to the rubricators who would later fill in the spaces he had left blank for the addition of hand-drawn capitals and other decorations.[89]

As Jost Amman's illustration shows, formes were inked while on the bed of the press by a worker bearing a pair of "ink balls," or "dabbers." Each of these mushroom-shaped implements consisted of a short wooden handle attached to a sheepskin bag padded with wool or animal hair. One ball was dipped into the ink, and worked together with the other to smear ink evenly across both; then, as their name implies, the forme was inked by dabbing it with the balls in a rolling motion.[90]

Gutenberg would have directed a worker to peel a blank sheet of paper (wet down the night before so as to better hold ink) from one of the huge bales procured in readiness for printing the Bible, and bid them fasten it to the "tympan," a flat, padded membrane that evened out the force of the press's platen, or driving plate.[91] But what form did this legendary press take? Hand presses driven by screws or levers were common enough, used for winemaking or pressing olives, and bookbinders used a variety of screw-driven presses in the course of their work, but these were blunt instruments.[92] The force of Gutenberg's press had to be carefully calibrated: too little and the paper would receive only a patchy impression; too strong and the fragile lead type would be crushed. At the same time, the forme and the paper had to be precisely aligned, or "registered," so that the text was printed in the right position on the page.

Unfortunately, we know as little about how Gutenberg overcame these difficulties as we do about the precise form of his hand mold, or the composition of his type metal. Plainly, though, he solved them. With a page of metal type composed, locked up, and inked; with a piece of paper fastened to the tympan and positioned over the waiting forme; finally, then, the platen of the press would have been driven home and then raised back up. Gutenberg would have freed the paper from the tympan and held it up to the light, and heaved a sigh of relief as he took in the finished article.

The finished product was spectacular. Though Gutenberg had deliberately aped the Gothic handwriting favored by the Church, and though the text was organized in an entirely conventional manner, each page of the Bible that came off the press was a revolution writ small. Contemporary observers unaware of Gutenberg's art were dumbfounded by the evenness of the individual letters, the exacting alignment of the text as a whole, and the unwavering perfection of the margins. As befitted the Word of God, Gutenberg's Bible was as close to perfect as human hands could make it.[93]

On a temporal level, however, not all was well. Scholars think that Gutenberg printed around 30 Bibles on vellum and about 150 on paper, and, at a handsome 17 by 24½ inches when opened flat, he would have needed some 5,000 calfskins yielding two double-page spreads each for the vellum copies alone. The paper editions would have required the importation from Italy of ten times as many sheets of paper.[94] The Bibles themselves betray the precise point at which their creator's financial worries overcame his sense of aesthetics: the first nine pages of each copy have a relaxed forty lines of text; page ten has forty-one so as to cram in a little more, and each of the more than twelve hundred pages that follow bear forty-two lines each, giving rise to the common nickname of the "42-line Bible."[95]

Gutenberg sent his worries to the back of his mind and pushed on. By the autumn of 1454, enough was done so that a few sample pages could be sent to the Frankfurt Book Fair (an annual gathering that continues to this day) to drum up interest.[96] A year later and the work on the books was complete. Gutenberg's compositors had typeset more

EXO

⤛ Facing pages from Gutenberg's 42-line Bible, comprising Exodus 14:27–16:22. These two leaves, owned by Boston Public Library, display a minimal approach to decoration and rubrication: "EXO" and "DUS" are used as running heads; verse numbers and versals (decorative capitals) have been

Fugientibusq; egipciis occurrerunt a-
que: ⁊ inuoluit eos dn̄s ī medijs flu-
ctibȝ. Reuerseq; sunt aque: ⁊ operuerūt
currus et equites cūcti exercitus pharaonis · qui sequētes ingressi fuerāt mare: nec unus quidē supfuit ex eis. Filij
autē isrl̄ · perrexerūt p mediū sicci maris:
⁊ aque eis erāt quasi pro muro · a dex-
tris et a sinistris. Liberauitq; domin⁹
ī die illo isrl̄ de manu egiptiorū: ⁊ vide-
runt egiptios mortuos sup litus maris: ⁊ manū magnā quam exercuerat
dn̄s cōtra eos. Timuitq; pp̄ls dn̄m: et
crediderūt dn̄o · ⁊ moysi suo ei⁹. XV
Tunc cecinit moyses ⁊ filij isrl̄ · car-
men hoc dn̄o: et dixerūt. Cante-
mus domino. Gloriose eni magnifi-
catus est: equū et ascensorem deiecit in
mare. Fortitudo mea ⁊ laus mea domin⁹: ⁊ factus est michi in salutē. Iste
deus meus et glorificabo eū · deus pa-
tris mei: ⁊ exaltabo eū. Domin⁹ quasi
vir pugnator · omīpotens nomen ei⁹:
currus pharaonis · et exercitū eius pie-
cit ī mare. Electi principes ei⁹ submersi sunt ī mari rubro: abissi operuerūt
eos: descenderūt in pfundū quasi lapis.
Dextera tua dn̄e magnificata ē in fortitudine: dextera tua dn̄e pcussit inimi-
cum: et ī multitudine glorie tue depo-
suisti adūsarios meos. Misisti iram
tuā · que deuorauit eos sicut stipulā:
et in spiritu furoris tui cōgregate sunt
aque. Stetit unda fluens: congregate
sūt abissi in medio mari. Dixit inimi-
cus. Persequar ⁊ cōprehendā: diuidā
spolia: implebit̄ aīa mea. Euaginabo
gladiū meū: interficiet eos man⁹ mea.
Flauit spirit⁹ tu⁹ · ⁊ operuit eos mare:
submersi sūt quasi plūbū ī aquis ve-
hemētibȝ. Quis silis tui ī fortibȝ dn̄e?
Quis silis tui magnific⁹ ī sanctitate:
t̄ribilis atq; laudabilis · ⁊ faciēs mira-
bilia? Extendisti manū tuā: ⁊ deuorauit eos t̄ra. Dux fuisti in misericordia
tua: pplo quē redemisti. Et portasti eū
in fortitudine tua: ad habitaculū san-
ctū tuū. Ascenderūt ppli ⁊ irati sūt: dolo-
res obtinuerūt habitatores philistijm.
Tunc cōturbati sunt principes edom:
robustos moab obtinuit tremor: ob-
riguerūt omēs habitatores chanaan.
Irruat super eos formido et pauor in
magnitudine brachij tui. Fiant im-
mobiles quasi lapis · donec ptrāseat
ppls tuus dn̄e: donec pertranseat po-
pulus tu⁹ iste quē possedisti. Introduces eos · et plantabis in monte heredi-
tatis tue: firmissimo habitaculo tuo qd̄
operatus es domine. Sanctuarium
tuū domine: qd̄ firmauerūt man⁹ tue.
Dn̄s regnabit in eternum ⁊ ultra. In-
gressus ē eni eques pharao cū curribȝ
et equitibȝ eius in mare: ⁊ reduxit sup
eos domin⁹ aquas maris. Filij autē
isrl̄ ambulauerūt p siccū: in medio ei⁹.
Sumpsit ergo maria pphetissa · soror
aaron · timpanū ī manu sua: egresseq;
sunt omēs mulieres post eā cū timpa-
nis et choris: quibus p̄cinebat dicēs.
Cantem⁹ dn̄o. Gloriose eni magnifi-
catus est: equū et ascensorē eius deiecit
in mare. Tulit autē moyses isrl̄ de mari rubro: ⁊ egressi sunt in desertum sur.
Ambulaueruntq; tribȝ diebȝ per solitu-
dinē: et nō inueniebāt aquā. Et vene-
runt in marath: nec poterant bibere a-
quas de marath · eo q essent amare.
Unde ⁊ congruū loco nomē imposu-
it: vocans illū marath id ē amaritu-
dinē. Et murmurauit ppls cotra moy-
sen dicēs. Quid bibem⁹? At ille clama-
uit ad dn̄m. Qui ostendit ei lignum:
qd̄ cū misisset ī aquas · in dulcedinem

added; and capital letters have been accessorized with a splash of red ink.[97] Decoration was carried out according to the buyer's whim, and other copies are more heavily illustrated.

than 3 million characters to make up the Bible's 1,282 pages; the workshop's press had been driven home some 237,170 times to print almost 60,000 leaves of vellum and paper; and the 180-odd resultant Bibles were all spoken for, if not yet paid for in full.[98] It was an incredible achievement, and it was snatched away from its chief architect almost immediately.

Gutenberg's fall is related in a clinical manner by the so-called Helmasperger Notarial Instrument, a legal document dated November 6, 1455. On that day, in the refectory of a Franciscan friary in Mainz, Johann Fust presented himself to a notary named Ulrich Helmasperger to demand repayment of his delinquent loans and of five years' unpaid interest. Perhaps aware that the game was up, Gutenberg stayed away, trusting to a motley delegation of his parish priest, valet, and house servant to argue on his behalf.[99]

They lost.

The sum total owed to Fust (Gutenberg must by now have preferred to spell his creditor's name with the optional *a*) was 2,020 Rheingulden.[100] It is not known whether Gutenberg ever found the money to repay this enormous debt, but it is obvious that his reckless business dealings had ruined him: the precious presses, molds, matrices, and type of Gutenberg's shop passed into Fust's hands, along with the entire stock of 42-line Bibles.[101]

Barely two years after the Helmasperger judgment a new run of handsomely printed religious books emanated from Mainz. The so-called Mainz Psalters of 1457 and 1459 were glorious books: hymns were printed in small black type with important words picked out in red; psalms were printed in larger black letters with red capitals; and decorative initial capitals, larger still, were printed in blue and red. Typographic experts think that all three colors were printed *at once*: the intricately interlocking blue and red portions of each decorative capital were inked separately, then assembled and slotted into place with the rest of the black- and red-inked forme. The entire page was then printed with a single pull of the press. Gutenberg must have pioneered this delicate process, but it was the two men whose combined coat of arms was printed on the final page of each of the psalters who took the credit: the firm of Fust & Schöffer. Johann Fust may have been a Machiavellian businessman and Peter Schöffer little better than a sleeper agent in the Gutenberg workshop, but it is difficult to despise this devious pair when the books they printed were every bit as beautiful as the Gutenberg Bible itself.[102]

There was little time for the pair to enjoy their newfound success. In June 1462, Adolf von Nassau, the pope's chosen candidate for Mainz's archbishopric, arrived at the city at the head of an army of mercenaries and robber barons. Diether von Isenburg, the incumbent, was unhappy at the prospect of his enforced retirement and promised the townspeople that he would resist the depredations of the pope's men. When von Nassau's forces scaled the walls, however, and after the few hundred citizens loyal to their archbishop had been overcome, he found that von Isenburg had fled. Always a borderline ungovernable bunch, Mainz's populace was expelled from the city for supporting von Isenburg—and the city's nascent printing industry, comprising perhaps a dozen men who had learned their trade in Gutenberg's workshop (or, later, that of Fust and Schöffer), was evicted along with them.[103] Like seeds blown before a forest fire, Mainz's printers were scattered across the Continent: within fifteen years of the publication of Gutenberg's 42-line Bible there was a printing press in every country in Europe, and the making of books had changed forever.

7

Out of Sorts: typesetting meets the Industrial Revolution

Johannes Gutenberg's system of steel punches and brass matrices, of hand mold and lead type, of chase, forme, quoins, and press—collectively, the printing press—blew apart the insular world of Europe's scholars, scribes, and clergy. More books were made in the first half century after Gutenberg's Bible than in the preceding thousand years put together, and book production only accelerated from there: 12.6 million *incunabula* were printed between 1454 and 1500 (these earliest books are known by the Latin word for "cradle" or "swaddling clothes"), and book production subsequently more than tripled every hundred years. In the second half of the eighteenth century, western Europe alone had printed more than 600 million books.[1]

Not everyone was happy about the new development. From the very first days of printing, the penning of tirades against the process became a favorite pastime among the intelligentsia, and particularly among those who saw a moral value in the patient copying-out of texts. In Venice, for example, one of the foremost centers of early printing, a Benedictine monk named Filippo de Strata railed against the racy classical poetry favored by printers seeking a popular market: "*Est virgo haec penna: meretrix est stampificata,*" he wrote toward the end of the fifteenth century, "[Writing] is a maiden with a pen, a harlot in print." Filippo's agitation was bolstered by a general dislike for the underclasses (as he saw it) who printed books—the lowly craftsmen, rebellious servants, and foreign drunkards who found work in the new industry. At least, he mused, tax receipts from the sale of wine might rise as a result.[2]

Regardless of the displeasure emanating from Filippo de Strata and his ilk, the spread of printing could not be stopped. Books are a narcotic, as Franz Kafka wrote centuries later, and an ever-growing community of readers needed their fix.[3] By the nineteenth century, however, demand was outstripping supply, and Gutenberg's centuries-old system was in dire need of an upgrade.

The world of the late nineteenth century was in the throes of a new Iron Age. The belching funnels of steam engines were sprouting up from factories all over Britain, with America close behind, and traditional wooden devices of all kinds were being replaced by larger and more robust counterparts wrought in iron and steel.[4] Even the hidebound printing industry, a holdout that had advanced little from its fifteenth-century origins, was finally encouraged to take a few halting steps into a more modern age.

Those first steps were tentative indeed. A number of attempts to reinforce wooden presses with iron components had been tried and abandoned over the years until finally, in 1772, a Swiss typefounder (that is, a maker of metal type) named Wilhelm Haas designed an all-metal screw press. His use of iron and brass in place of wood let Haas print much larger sheets than traditional presses, but the local printers' guild was not about to let a typefounder muscle in on their business. The guild told Haas to choose between typefounding and printing; Haas duly gave up his foray into the design of printing presses and went back to typefounding.[5]

Nevertheless, news of Haas's experiments percolated through the printing grapevine. More iron presses followed, culminating in 1803 with the "Stanhope" press, designed in London by a notoriously obsessive politician, inventor, and aristocrat named Charles Stanhope.[6] Stanhope's sturdy iron press was the first notable example of its kind: rather than simply replicating a wooden press in iron, he designed a system of levers that multiplied the operator's strength so that, for the first time, an impression could be made with a single pull of a lever rather than the laborious tightening and loosening of a screw.[7] The Stanhope press spawned a wave of imitations, some of which survive to this day: the baroque American "Columbian" press, famous for the cast-iron eagle that perches vigilantly atop it, and the more restrained English "Albion" press are still common fixtures in letterpress print shops.

In truth, Stanhope's press and those it inspired were little different from those that had been used since Gutenberg's time. A sheet of paper and a forme of type were fitted to a sliding "coffin" on the base of the press, the type was inked by hand, and the coffin slid into position under the platen to be impressed by the pull of a lever.[8] There were more gears, levers, and decorations to marvel at, certainly, and it was physically much easier to print a page of type, but they remained painfully manual devices. For all that they advanced the operating principles of the printing press, the first wave of iron presses were technological oxymora—the print-shop equivalent of carbon-fiber chopsticks or a titanium abacus.

The first glimmers of the presses' exit appeared in 1790, when an English chemist and science writer named William Nicholson filed a patent for "A Machine or Instrument on a New Construction for the Purpose of Printing on Paper, Linen, Cotton, Woolen and other Articles in a more Neat, Cheap, and Accurate Manner than is effected by the Machines now in use."[9] As with all good patents, Nicholson's title spoke to his aspirations more than it did his ability to deliver on

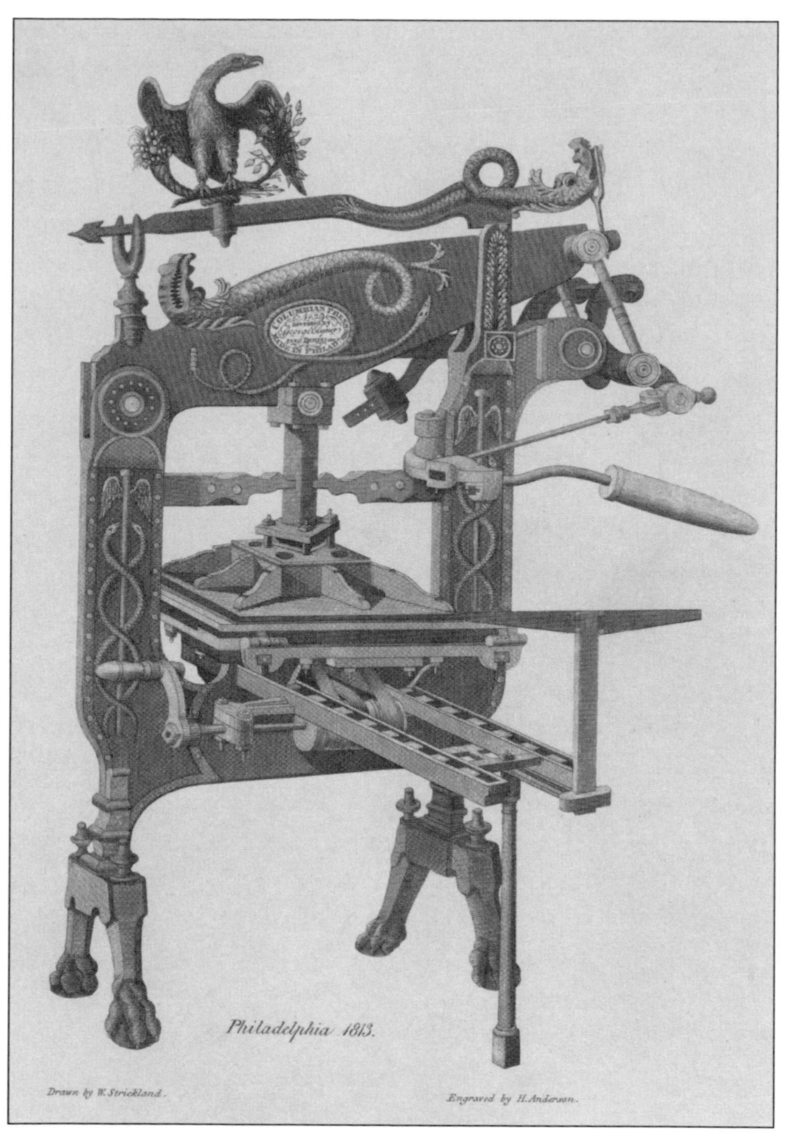

George E. Clymer's "Columbian" press of 1813. The eagle, "with extended wings and grasping in his talons Jove's thunderbolts combined with the olive branch of Peace and cornucopia of Plenty, all handsomely bronzed and gilt," acted as a counterweight to raise the platen after each impression.[10]

them. With no especial mechanical nous, nor any great affinity for printing, Nicholson set out the basics of a radical new printing press: in place of the familiar vertical action of platen and bed, he envisioned a machine composed of cylinders smoothly rotating against one another. One cylinder was to carry a curved forme of type; a second, covered in leather, spread ink onto the first; and a third pressed a sheet of paper against the inked, rotating forme to receive an impression of the type. It was an ingenious, clean-sheet rethink of an ancient design—and it was never built. Lacking in money and motivation, Nicholson moved on to other things even as his idea assumed a life of its own.[11]

Twenty-five years later, Friedrich Koenig took up Nicholson's legacy. Koenig had been apprenticed to a printer at the age of fifteen, and after a stint at Leipzig University he found work with a man named Friedrich Riedel, who dreamed of establishing himself as a bookseller and printer. Koenig threw himself into the printing side of the business but became frustrated by the "horse-work" it involved, the manual labor of fixing the paper in place, pulling an impression, and removing the printed page. There had to be a better way.[12] With William Nicholson's hypothetical cylinder press at the back of his mind, Koenig put together a sales pitch for a new kind of press and shopped it around Germany's leading printers. He was greeted by polite indifference. Forced to look farther afield, he traveled to Russia in search of willing partners only to be stymied by tsarist bureaucracy; finally, he decided to try his luck in England. Things went better in Britain than they had on the Continent, and by November 1814—on the morning of the twenty-ninth, to be exact—Koenig was on the cusp of realizing his ambitions.[13]

That morning, as they did every morning, the printers of the *Times* newspaper awaited the formes they would load into their Stanhope presses to print the day's paper. They waited and waited, but no formes were forthcoming. Word arrived that developments on the Continent, where the Napoleonic wars raged, were expected to delay the day's edition, and the printers settled in to wait. But they had been deceived: earlier that morning the completed formes had been delivered to an adjacent building in which Friedrich Koenig's radical new press awaited.[14] For John Walter, proprietor of the *Times*, the subterfuge was necessary. Just as the Fourdrinier brothers' contraption was raising hackles among traditional papermakers, so Friedrich Koenig's experiments with mechanically driven presses had not endeared him to London's legions of printers. Walter worried that installing a powered press at the newspaper would invite mischief and sabotage, and so Koenig's press had been assembled next door to the newspaper's offices by workers kept silent by the threat of a £100 fine should any rumors leak out.

The controversial press itself consisted of a flat base on which the forme was placed, and that shuttled back and forth beneath two paper-bearing cylinders and a built-in inking mechanism. It was a halfway house between a traditional hand press and William Nicholson's fully "rotary" design, and, in truth, it was not entirely automated—it required constant attention to place sheets of paper on the cylinders as they rotated and to remove the printed pages—but Walter did not trust the *Times*'s printers and assistants to see the distinction.[15]

So it was that John Walter oversaw the smuggling of the day's formes to Koenig. By the time the printers realized that they had been duped, the print run was already complete, the day's newspapers churned out by Koenig's press at a rate of more than 1,100 double-sided sheets per hour. (On a good day, the *Times*'s printers might have managed 200 single-sided sheets in an hour on each of their manual Stanhope presses.)[16] Walter himself wrote the issue's leading article, which praised the new press in fulsome terms, and it is thought that he may have even set the article's text himself, letter by halting letter, so that his compositors were kept as oblivious as his printers. In doing so, Walter would have appreciated yet another benefit of Koenig's machine: previously, the only way to print enough copies to meet demand was to typeset each page a number of times so that it could be printed simultaneously on a number of Stanhope presses, but, with a speedy mechanized press at hand, each page had only to be typeset once. Had the compositors at the *Times* realized what their employer was up to, they too would have recoiled at the implications.

In any case, the revelation of the day's events to the *Times*'s employees went off without a hitch, the shock of the new printing press ameliorated by Walter's declaration that redundant workers would be paid a full wage until they could find employment elsewhere. The overturning of the old order had been a bloodless coup.[17]

As the century rumbled on, the trickle of improvements to the printing process grew into a flood. Two years after Friedrich Koenig's press was put to work at the *Times*, an English printer named Edward Cowper patented a method for making "stereotypes"—thin metal casts of an entire forme of movable type—that could be wrapped around a cylinder, thus paving the way for presses composed entirely of rollers.[18] In America, in 1838, David Bruce devised a machine for casting type

➻ Friedrich Koenig's double cylinder press of 1814, as clandestinely installed next to the *Times*'s existing print shop. Paper was placed onto the cylinders sheet by sheet, to be printed by a forme that shuttled back and forth in the bed of the press.

more quickly and reliably than by hand. And nine years later, in New York, an inventor named Richard M. Hoe built the first practical rotary press, albeit one that relied on a precarious system of fixing movable type (rather than the more robust stereotype) to a rotating cylinder.[19]

These separate developments were brought together in 1863. In that year a Pennsylvania newsman named William Bullock filed a patent describing a Frankenstein's monster of a press that combined seemingly all of the advances that had gone before. Bullock's steam-powered rotary press was fed by the rolls of paper now being produced in bulk by Fourdrinier machines, with the web of paper led around a series of cylinders carrying curved stereotype plates and out through a mechanism that sliced the paper—printed on both sides—into individual sheets.[20] It was capable of producing 12,000 complete newspapers every hour.[21] Unfortunately, today William Bullock is remembered for the manner of his demise as much as for his invention. In 1867, Bullock's leg was caught and mangled by one of his own presses; gangrene set in, and he died during the subsequent botched attempt at amputation. (Some versions of the tale say that Bullock was injured when he tried to kick a recalcitrant drive belt back onto a pulley.)[22]

Bullock's gory and permanent retirement aside, the nineteenth century's continuous innovation in printing technology helped newspapers grow from four-page weeklies in the 1820s to sixteen-page dailies by the 1880s—and put an alarming strain on the surrounding publication pipeline.[23] Just as Louis-Nicolas Robert's "endless wire" papermaking machine had exposed a chronic shortage of rags, so did the mechanized presses of Friedrich Koenig and William Bullock throw an unforgiving spotlight on the human compositors who typeset the newspapers, advertisements, and books to be printed on them. The composing stick could not match a steam-driven press.

Still, the nineteenth century was hopping with inventors and entrepreneurs. And if printers had been reluctant to embrace mechanized presses, the race to automate the composition of type would be an entirely more cutthroat contest.

The first typesetting machine to intrude into the public consciousness was the so-called Paige Compositor. In development since the early 1870s, this ill-starred device was the brainchild of James W. Paige, a charming, devious ex-oilman blessed with a talent for self-promotion and cursed with a pathological inability to see projects to their conclusions.[24] Supporting Paige's endless tinkering was an increasingly bitter Samuel Clemens—better known as the author Mark Twain—whose expenditure on the project would crest $170,000 before the 1880s were out and leave the writer in perilous financial straits.[25]

Clemens and Paige's entanglement began in 1880, when a mutual acquaintance took the writer to see Paige's embryonic typesetting device. Having worked for years as a journeyman printer and compositor, Clemens was much taken with the charismatic inventor and his miraculous machine.[26] Flush with the success (and the proceeds) of *The Adventures of Tom Sawyer,* Clemens gamely invested $2,000 in Paige's enterprise, though he was realistic about his prospects of getting it back. As he wrote in a later account of the affair, "I was always taking little chances like that; and almost always losing by it, too."[27]

The machine that Paige demonstrated to Clemens solved two-thirds of the problem of mechanical composition. Where a human compositor would pluck characters from a wooden type case and place them on a composing stick, Paige's machine sported an alphabetic keyboard that released characters from channels arrayed along the top of the machine and assembled them into a line. Separately, a distribution mechanism accepted "dead matter"—pages that had already been set and printed—and sorted the characters back into the appropriate channels. The only thing missing was the ability to "justify" the type, to tweak the spaces between words so that each line perfectly abutted the margins of the page, as they have done in most printed books since Gutenberg's time.[28] By 1886, Paige had completed a new version that could reliably set and distribute type many times faster than a human, though justification was still beyond it. Clemens implored the inventor to put the device on sale as it was, but Paige argued that a justification mechanism was a necessity. Clemens conceded, against his better judgment, and Paige began work on an entirely *new* machine that would integrate setting, justification, and distribution.

Even as Clemens chafed at Paige's endless delays, he continued to funnel money into the project. The writer's weakness was that he knew too much about the business of printing: he had seen firsthand how cantankerous human workers could get and was obsessed with the notion that printers would welcome Paige's device with open arms. It was, as Clemens saw it, a perfect mechanical employee that would never get drunk, that would work as diligently at three o'clock in the morning as it would at three in the afternoon, and that was immune to unionization.[29] Having assured Clemens at the outset that the work could be done in a few months and would cost no more than $9,000, Paige nevertheless labored on for four more years and spent another $150,000 of the writer's money—some $4,000,000 today—before finally completing the machine.[30]

The Paige Compositor, in its final form, was a machine of breathtaking complexity. Assembled from more than 18,000 separate parts, its single operator could set, justify, and distribute type six times faster than was possible by hand, with the machine automatically rejecting broken or cracked sorts as they arrived for distribution.[31] The patent describing the machine ran to fifty-nine pages and languished in patent examination purgatory for eight years, suffering the death of one examiner, the insanity of a second, and the committal to a mental asylum of the attorney who prepared it.[32] The Paige Compositor was a masterpiece of mechanical engineering, and a true marvel. It was also fatally flawed.

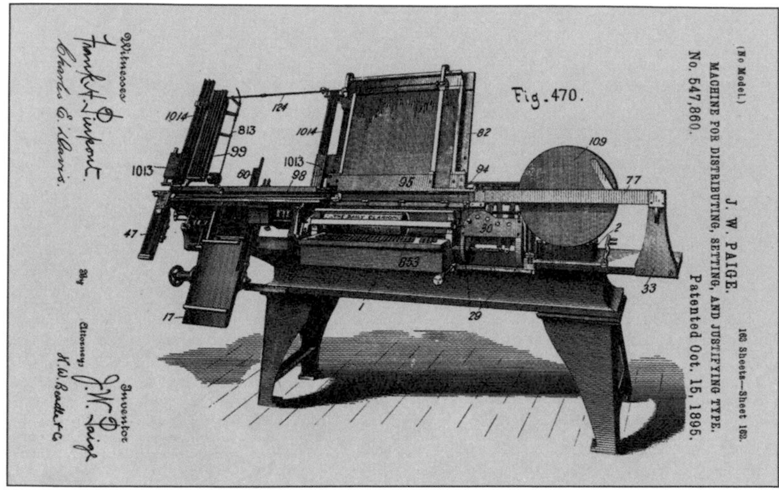

Patent image of the Paige Compositor designed by J. W. Paige and funded by Samuel Clemens. The device, which set foundry type and distributed it afterward, comprised more than 18,000 parts and was prone to breaking down. Paige spent fourteen years perfecting his machine, by which time competing devices such as Ottmar Mergenthaler's "Linotype" had proven that it was far easier to cast new type than it was to distribute it.[33]

By attempting to replicate the human actions required to set type—the composition, justification, and distribution of individual letters—Paige had doomed his machine. There was no denying that it could set type at a prodigious rate, but Paige had built a high-strung thoroughbred rather than a dependable draft horse and the newspapers to which he tried to sell the device balked at its unreliability. By 1894 the success of other, simpler devices had exposed the Paige Compositor as the elaborate folly it was; Clemens was almost bankrupt, and Paige died broke and forgotten.[34] The writer's venomous biographical account of "The Machine Episode" concluded thusly: "Paige and I always meet on effusively affectionate terms; and yet he knows perfectly well that if I had his nuts in a steel-trap I would shut out all human succor and watch that trap till he died."[35]

James Paige might have avoided his travails entirely had he read through the burgeoning stack of patents on typesetting devices. In 1822, fifty years before Paige embarked on his quest, an American inventor named William Church had filed a patent in England for "An Improved Apparatus for Printing" comprising a trio of machines that did exactly what Paige aimed to do.[36] Church's keyboard-driven typesetter was very likely the first such device ever patented; his automated type caster *may* have been the first of its kind; and his press, by comparison, seems to have been mostly similar to existing devices.[37] In the end, the relative merits of his "apparatus for printing" mattered little to Church. He was afflicted by an unhelpfully short attention span, a malady common to inventors, and none of his devices progressed beyond an experimental stage.[38] Within a decade Church had forgotten all thoughts of typesetting in favor of steam-driven coaches that took nervous passengers (nervous, because they sat near a boiler at a time when such things still exploded with regularity) between London and Birmingham.[39]

More enduring than any of Church's typesetting machines was a concept he articulated in his patent for them: why bother to disassemble and distribute a page of type when one might simply melt it down and cast the type again as needed? "Church's principle," as one writer called it, was the imaginative leap that would propel typesetting into the Industrial Age.[40]

The first person to successfully apply Church's principle was Ottmar Mergenthaler. Born in 1854 in Hachtel, Germany, as a boy Ottmar tinkered with the village clock and as a young man he was apprenticed to a watchmaker in nearby Bietigheim.[41] With the German job market clogged by soldiers returning from the Franco-Prussian War, in 1872 Mergenthaler emigrated to the United States, where he found employment at an electrical workshop in Baltimore, Maryland, owned by his cousin August Hahl. There he might have stayed had not a frustrated inventor named Charles T. Moore come calling in the summer of 1876.[42]

Moore had designed a kind of typewriter that printed words onto a long, thin paper tape, which was then cut up and pasted onto a regular piece of paper to form a complete page of text.[43] The trick was that the machine printed using "lithographic" ink, a greasy concoction more often used to print works of art, and Moore intended to use the assembled pages of text as masters from which to print further copies. Moore's prototype was temperamental, but where Moore saw only shoddy workmanship, Hahl's precocious cousin Mergenthaler pointed out defects in the underlying design. Within days, he had proposed a number of improvements, though Moore's backers, among them a court recorder, secretary, and technophile investor named James O. Clephane, would not shoulder the cost of the work.[44] Hahl took the job anyway on a no-fix, no-fee basis, swayed by Mergenthaler's conviction that the machine could be made to work.[45]

As work progressed, it became clear that Clephane was the true innovator. In years past he had been a bugbear of Christopher Latham Sholes, the inventor of the first commercially successful typewriter, whose prototypes Clephane had throttled into submission in grueling tests. Sholes, his patience exhausted, thundered to his business partner James Densmore: "I am through with Clephane!" The canny Densmore replied,

> *This candid fault-finding is just what we need. We had better have it now than after we begin manufacturing. Where Clephane points out a weak lever or rod let us make it strong. Where a spacer or an inker works stiffly, let us make it work smoothly. Then, depend upon Clephane for all the praise we deserve.*[46]

James O. Clephane had good reason to be exacting. He was famous, if such a thing is possible, for the speed and accuracy of his court recordings and was obsessed with having them printed as soon as possible.[47] Clephane saw as clearly as Samuel Clemens that composition was the major bottleneck in the printing process, and he wished, more than anything, that he could "bridge the gap between the typewriter and the printed page."[48] It was Clephane who had first contracted Moore to design the lithographic typewriter, and, as Mergenthaler worked to address its malfunctions, it was Clephane who urged him onward.

However Mergenthaler finessed Moore's device, its output remained too imprecise for the finicky processes of lithographic printing.[49] Clephane proposed a second machine that would strike characters into papier-mâché, from which a metal stereotype of an entire page could be cast. Mergenthaler was unconvinced. To indent a *W* to the same depth as a ".", for example, requires a much greater shove; tiny variations in letter height wreak havoc on the resultant printed page, and Mergenthaler thought that the papier-mâché machine was doomed.[50] He persisted with it at Clephane's behest, but the completed device, ready late in 1878, was not a success: the cast-metal stereotypes clung stubbornly to their papier-mâché molds and the resultant printing surfaces were often wildly uneven, as Mergenthaler had predicted. Mergenthaler abandoned the machine, but Clephane would not be swayed, and he took his business to a machine shop in Washington, DC, to carry on the work. Five fruitless years later and no closer to his goal, a chastened Clephane returned to Mergenthaler in Baltimore.[51] This time they would do things the German's way.

The machine that Mergenthaler proposed to Clephane in 1883 was not a typesetter but a type *caster*. Having watched Moore and Clephane struggle with complex printing methods such as lithography and stereography, Mergenthaler fell back on the oldest printing technology of all: his machine was a hopped-up hand mold—a keyboard-controlled contraption that arranged brass matrices in a line and then cast them en bloc in type metal. After printing, these "slugs" of type were tossed back into the cauldron of molten metal that fed the machine. It was William Church's principle made real, seventy years after the fact.

Mergenthaler built a bewildering series of prototypes over the years from 1883 to 1890.[52] His earliest machines were the simplest, and the clumsiest, employing a series of parallel brass rods, or "bands," each of which was engraved with the letters of the alphabet along its length. To cast a line of type, the operator slid the rods up or down to place the appropriate letters in front of the mold, as if selecting numbers on a briefcase's rotary combination lock, before molten metal was pumped into the completed line. Each band had to be of a uniform width along its entire length, so that the molten type metal could not escape between them, but this meant that narrow letters such as *i* and *l* were marooned within islands of white space while wider letters such as *m* and *Q* sat snugly against one another. The "monospaced" fonts used in typewriters and computer programming are carefully designed to hide this limitation, but applying fixed spacing to a proportional font such as this one looks odd by comparison.[53]

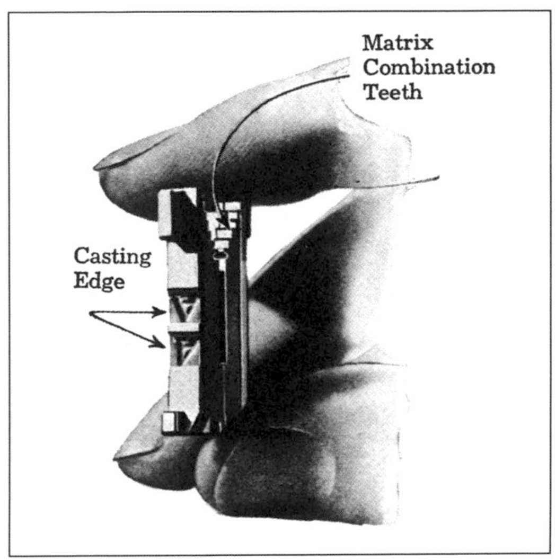

➳ Linotype matrices (some of which carried two letters, selected via a "shift" mechanism like that of a typewriter) were identified by the toothed patterns along their *V*-shaped upper edges. Each pattern encoded a binary number, with the presence of a tooth representing the digit *1* and the absence of a tooth the digit *0*.

Mergenthaler's second design did away with the vertical bands. In their place, he engraved tiny brass matrices with individual letters, just as Gutenberg had done, but rather than place them in a mold one by one he devised a kind of rack, or magazine, from which individual letters were released at the press of a key to be pushed into a line in front of the mold by blasts of compressed air. In its final incarnation, his "square base" machine replaced compressed air with a more civilized conveyor-belt mechanism on which matrices trundled from the magazine to the mold and back again.[54]

The product of Mergenthaler's work was a tall, monolithic machine with a distinct steampunk air about it. To cast a line of type—a sentence, perhaps, or a single line of a newspaper column—an operator sat at the keyboard attached to the front of the machine, which was linked by rods to the rows of matrices in the magazine suspended above, and typed out the text. With every lettered key that was pressed, a single brass matrix bearing the corresponding character was released from the magazine and onto the conveyor belt that ran above the keyboard. Once the line was complete (a bell rang when the current line was almost full), the operator pulled the "casting lever" to swing the row of matrices in front of the mold, where hydraulic rams clamped them tightly together, to be pumped full of molten type metal. The result was a slug of lead, the line of type embossed upon it.[55] After casting, the matrices were distributed back into the appropriate channels in the magazine. This last operation was perhaps the most futuristic aspect of the machine: as shown in the figure opposite, each of Mergenthaler's brass matrices was identified by a toothed pattern, corresponding to a binary number, that caused the matrix to drop straight back into its destination channel.[56]

With setting and distribution thus dispatched, Mergenthaler dealt with justification, that other bête noire of mechanical typesetting, by means of an ingeniously simple mechanism. Word spaces were represented by long, vertical wedge-shaped "spacebands" assembled into the line between matrices. When the current line was complete, a hydraulic ram forced these spacing wedges up and so pushed the words apart until

➳ A Model 31 Linotype, circa 1940. All Linotypes after 1890 were designed according to the same basic arrangement of keyboard, magazine, mold, and distribution mechanism.

the ends of the line hit the limits of a preset guide.[57] It was an elegant solution to a vexing puzzle.

Mergenthaler demonstrated his machine at the offices of the *Chicago Tribune* in 1886 to a rapturous reception. Upon seeing a shiny slug of type emitted from the machine the newspaper baron Whitelaw Reid exclaimed, "You have done it, Ottmar, you have done it, you have produced a line o' type," and the name stuck.[58] No longer would a compositor ever run out of type; no longer could a carefully set forme be scattered by a stray hand; and the tedious job of distributing used type (traditionally delegated to a hapless assistant called the "printer's devil," as the young Mark Twain had once been) was done away with entirely.[59] Typesetting in the fast-moving newspaper industry was transformed in the Linotype's wake, with Thomas Edison declaring it to be "the eighth wonder of the world"—even if book printers remained to be convinced.[60]

Johannes Gutenberg had set a high bar for book printers. The text of his 42-line Bible was preternaturally neat and abutted the margins perfectly to present, as the famed twentieth-century type designer Hermann Zapf put it, a "perfect grey type area without the rivers and holes of too-wide word spacing."[61] For all its speed and convenience, the Linotype was not great when it came to producing such precise text: almost as soon as the first Linotypes had gone on sale, a British printer named James Southward lambasted the fragility of the device itself, its inflexible justification mechanism, and the uneven lines it produced.[62] Moreover, the Linotype positively rebelled against any attempts to set complex material such as tables, mathematical equations, and chemical formulae. A dime novel or penny dreadful might survive being typeset by a Linotype machine, but the printers of more rarefied material wanted nothing to do with Mergenthaler's brash, noisy invention.[63] A different kind of machine was needed—and appropriately enough, it would come not from the world of letters and type but instead from that of numbers, math, and statistics.

Col. Charles W. Seaton, chief clerk for the 1880 US census, had a problem. A veteran of the 1870 national census and the 1875 New York State census, Seaton found his department faced with an unprecedented mountain of paper describing more than 50 million Americans.[64] The traditional approach to compiling census data, where demographic data such as ethnicity, age, and employment were tallied by hand, was woefully inadequate. And with the population expected to balloon by 15 million or more over the coming decade, it was possible the tabulation of the 1880 census would be incomplete when the next one began.

Seaton had already moved to solve the problem of manual tabulation. Back in 1872, he had patented a contraption comprised of a series of rollers that simplified data entry on long rolls of paper.[65] A contemporary account claimed that the "Seaton device" increased the speed of tabulation fivefold, and certainly, the government of the day was sufficiently impressed to pass an Act of Congress releasing $15,000 for the purchase of Seaton's patent. A twentieth-century reappraisal of the machine was a little more circumspect, guessing that Seaton's device could have increased efficiency by 33 percent at best—and, tellingly, Seaton was reluctant to rely on his own device. For the 1880 census the harried chief clerk turned to a mechanically minded acquaintance, a Mr. Tolbert Lanston over at the Pension Office, and entreated him to develop an adding machine that might expedite the tabulation process.[66]

A twenty-one-year-old veteran of the Civil War at its close in 1865, Tolbert Lanston took a job at the Pension Office in Washington, DC, to help deal with the surge of ex-servicemen left unemployed or injured in the wake of the conflict, and there he stayed for twenty-two unremarkable years.[67] But Charles Seaton did not want this career civil servant for his expertise in pensions—quite the opposite. Because during those twenty-two years of toil in Washington, DC, Tolbert Lanston had used his spare time well. Without any formal training in engineering, he had designed and patented a hydraulic dumbwaiter, an adjustable horseshoe, a mailbag lock, a railway car coupler, a sewing machine, a water faucet, and a window sash.[68] It was little wonder that Charles W. Seaton sought him out. In the early 1880s, at Seaton's request, Lanston began work on a mechanical adding device that might avert the looming crisis at the Census Office.[69]

Seaton was not the only census officer suffering under the weight of paperwork. Elsewhere in the department, a doctor named John Shaw Billings was making slow progress evaluating the "vital statistics" gathered during the census—the gender, age, ethnicity, and other physical characteristics of the surveyed population.[70] At dinner with one of his underlings, a recent graduate of Columbia Mining College named Herman Hollerith, Dr. Billings mused, "There ought to be a machine for doing the purely mechanical work of tabulating population and similar statistics."[71] Hollerith, though nominally qualified as a mining engineer, and despite having only narrowly scraped through his classes in bookkeeping and machinery, was convinced that Billings's suggestion could be made to work.[72] Unable to persuade the older man to join him in working on the project, Hollerith left the Census Office in 1882 for a teaching position at the Massachusetts Institute of Technology and threw himself into work on tabulating machines in his spare time.[73]

As processing of the 1880 census dragged on, Lanston and Hollerith were pulled into Charles W. Seaton's orbit for a meeting of minds, if not persons, that would prove pivotal for both men. First, sometime during 1882, Seaton demonstrated Lanston's mechanical adding machine to the young Herman Hollerith. Hollerith was impressed; so much so, in fact, that he later bought the rights to Lanston's device, drawing inspiration from it when he came to work on statistics requiring addition, rather than simple counting.[74] A few years later, Seaton invited Lanston to the Census Office to view a prototype of Hollerith's electromechanical tabulator.[75] It was Lanston's turn to be intrigued, most of all by the tabulator's method of data entry.

Writing later about his invention, Hollerith recalled watching a railroad conductor carefully punch tickets to record a passenger's eye color, gender, or other identifying feature, and he borrowed the concept to encode a person's vital statistics as holes punched on a rectangular card. As the card was fed into his tabulator, each hole allowed a steel-sprung pin to complete an electrical circuit and so increment the count on an odometer-like dial.[76] As Charles Seaton demonstrated all this to Tolbert Lanston, the germ of an idea was planted: Hollerith's punched cards, Lanston thought, could be applied to mechanical typesetting. Composing machines were not a new idea, of course—the very public misadventures of Samuel Clemens and James Paige had seen to that—but in the mid-1880s Ottmar Mergenthaler's revolutionary Linotype was still more of an aspiration than a reality, and Lanston perceived a gap in the market.[77]

Charles Seaton's death in 1885 jolted Tolbert Lanston into action.[78] Lanston's patent filings, always a reliable indicator of his favored projects, turned from adding machines to automated typesetting and in 1887 he quit the Pension Office to found the Lanston Monotype Machine Company.[79] The very first Monotype system emerged from the company's workshops that same year, and it was every bit as marvelous as Ottmar Mergenthaler's "eighth wonder of the world."[80]

On the face of it, the new device had much in common with Mergenthaler's feted Linotype. An operator tapped away at a keyboard, causing type to be cast from captive brass matrices, and, like the Linotype, the problem of distributing loose sorts was sidestepped entirely, with used type tossed back into the melting pot to be cast again. Beyond these superficial similarities, however, almost everything about the Monotype was different from its competitor. Most noticeable of all, it was not one machine, but two.

The first part of the Monotype system was a keyboard that resembled a typewriter grown fat with multiple alphabets. Paying tribute to Herman Hollerith's use of punched cards, the Monotype keyboard punched holes through paper instead of printing letters upon it: as the operator entered the text, the keyboard consumed, punched, and spat out a spool of paper on which the words were encoded. Completed spools were taken to a separate, desk-sized casting machine that decoded their punched patterns with blasts of compressed air to produce a stream of shining, newly cast type that marched in regimented lines across an attached galley. Like Ottmar Mergenthaler's machine, the Monotype used captive brass matrices to cast its letters; unlike the Linotype, it cast sorts individually so that mistakes could be corrected by rearranging or inserting extra type as required.[81]

The Monotype's modular configuration made itself useful in a

⇚ *Left*, a Monotype keyboard and *right*, a Monotype caster, circa 1916. Paper tape punched by the keyboard was fed into the caster to be decoded by blasts of compressed air.

variety of ways. The caster, which racketed away at up to 140 characters per minute, could process paper tape far more rapidly than a single keyboardist could punch it, and so it was common for Monotype's customers to employ a number of typists for each of their casters to keep them running at full speed. The caster was so fast, in fact, that the Monotype owner's manual boasted that "it does not pay to pick up dropped letters from the floor"—it was quicker to cast the whole page again.[82] Spools could be keyed in a different building or even a different city and dispatched by mail to a printer for casting, and mistakes in the keyed text could be corrected by patching holes (or punching new ones) in the tape itself. In many ways, the Monotype's paper tape was a precursor to magnetic tapes and floppy disks: in the same way that a computer stores data in memory and reads it back when it is required, so a caster's human operators might prioritize rush jobs or file away punched spools for future use.[83]

The Monotype's justification mechanism too was a remarkably prescient piece of work. If Ottmar Mergenthaler's use of wedges smacked of engineering pragmatism, Lanston's solution spoke eloquently of its inventor's mathematical proclivities. Each character on the Monotype keyboard was assigned a width of between five and eighteen "units." An uppercase *W*, for instance, might be a full eighteen units in width while the narrowest characters, such as *i* or ".", were the minimum five units wide. Using a series of toothed racks and gears, as the user typed in a line of text the keyboard maintained a running total of the width of all letters *and* the number of word spaces. As with the Linotype, a bell rang when the line was almost full, giving the user an opportunity to hyphenate the final word if required. Finally, when the user pressed a key to signal that the line was finished, the keyboard mechanically computed the width of word space required to justify the line.* A cylindrical gauge atop the keyboard displayed the computed width to the user, who duly punched it on the tape via a set of special keys. This meant that punched spools had to be fed to the caster tail-first so that it could select the width of a line's spaces before casting them. When the gleaming type emerged from the caster, it came out bottom to top and right to left.

The Monotype Company was justifiably proud of this mechanical marvel. The owner's manual crowed, "The printer who for the first time sees examples of [Monotype] justification [. . .] ought not to be blamed for believing that such results can be produced only by a system of justification both complicated and mysterious, a system that requires the operator to make intricate and brain-racking calculations."[84] Sophisticated and cerebral, the Monotype was the typesetting machine of choice for the discerning book printer.

*If l is the desired width of the line, or "measure"; s is the number of spaces; and c is the cumulative width of all non-space characters, then the size of the word space, w, required to justify that line, is computed to be $w = (l-c)/s$. The Monotype keyboard was essentially a mechanical calculator that could perform this one operation.

⇻ • ⇷

Neither the Linotype nor the Monotype could displace the other. The Linotype was cheaper and easier to operate, but the Monotype was more versatile (its individual sorts could be set by hand so that a Monotype caster became a self-contained type foundry) and, arguably, produced a higher-quality product. But there was room for both machines. Newspapers preferred Linotypes, while bookmakers favored Monotypes, and their respective creators profited from their inventions in a way that James W. Paige and Samuel Clemens could only have dreamed. Though he endured a number of commercial disputes with the company he founded, Ottmar Mergenthaler made a handsome living from his device; weakened by tuberculosis, he died young but wealthy in 1899.[85] And Tolbert Lanston, the consummate inventor, continued to work on his device as long as he was able. He suffered a stroke in 1910, just after his final Monotype patent was granted, and died three years later at the age of seventy.[86] Unlike Paige and Clemens, the two men's machines outlasted them both by decades: almost every book printed between 1900 and 1950 was the product of a Linotype, a Monotype, or one of their many clones.

By the mid-twentieth century, relief printing was running out of steam. The method of printing that had been used for more than a thousand years—the inking of a raised surface sculpted into letters and other characters—was being supplanted by sophisticated photographic and "lithographic" techniques, where flat plates were sensitized to attract or repel ink to form letters and illustrations alike. Linotypes, Monotypes, and their clones were hastily retrofitted to expose letters onto photographic paper rather than cast them in lead, but this only delayed the inevitable. "Phototypesetting" was mechanical typesetting's last gasp.

In the end, a bit player in the drama of Monotype versus Linotype cast the longest shadow over the printing of books. As Mergenthaler and Lanston toiled over their respective machines in the late 1880s, Herman Hollerith's business was ascendant. Renting out his electromechanical tabulators to the Census Office, the 1890 census was processed two years faster than its predecessor, with the attendant savings estimated at $5 million. In the years that followed, Hollerith founded a business empire that would become synonymous with computing: International Business Machines, or IBM.[87] Nowadays it is the personal computer, the descendant of Herman Hollerith's tabulating machine, that has replaced the mechanical drama of the Linotype and Monotype. Text and images are shuffled around silently and electronically, prepared for printing without ever coming into contact with the physical world. The printed book may be a stolidly analog artifact, but its making is an unerringly digital matter.

Part 3

ILLUSTRATIONS

8

Saints and Scriveners: the rise of the illuminated manuscript

The writing of books evolved in fits and starts. If we could plot a line tracing that history, it would be punctuated with abrupt spikes announcing the invention of hieroglyphs, papyrus, movable type, and any one of a hundred other innovations, large and small. The story of book illustration is a similar one, and one of the key inflection points on our hypothetical graph—a skyrocketing discontinuity that dwarfs what came before and paved the way for what followed—marks the arrival, in medieval times, of the illuminated manuscript.

The birth of the illuminated manuscript was set into motion by a ruction in the broader history of the world. In the fourth century CE, the Roman Empire was sliding into chaos. Though nominally a single political entity, in reality the empire had long since fractured into eastern and western regions, its two halves administered by bickering imperial courts at Constantinople and Rome.[1] The western Empire in particular was in a parlous state: the citizens on its fringes were going native, identifying themselves with indigenous tribes in preference to the remote Roman elite, and nationalism was on the rise. Rome's writers, orators, and politicians called them "barbarians," but the ascendant Goths, Vandals, Huns, Angles, Saxons, and Franks would have disagreed. They were the new face of things, and the tired western Empire could do little about it.[2]

Things came to a head in the latter part of the fourth century CE. In 376, a huge influx of Goths settled in the Balkans, then controlled by the Romans; a decade later, a civil war with the eastern Empire saw both Huns and Goths fight against the west; and in 410 an army of Goths sacked Rome itself. All the while, Roman influence waned across the empire and its borders retreated before the encroaching tribes. Its North African provinces were conquered by the Vandals; in Gaul, the Franks took control, and in Britain the Angles and Saxons rose to power. Finally, in 476, the sixteen-year-old puppet emperor Romulus Augustulus was forced to abdicate by Odoacer, a Germanic military leader, and the western Roman Empire was no more.[3]

A thousand miles from beleaguered Rome, the island of Ireland on Europe's western edge had escaped the worst of the turmoil. Ireland had always been a rural backwater by Roman standards, lacking roads, cities, and even towns of any great size, and yet it was here that the first flickers of a new kind of bookmaking arose in the wake of Rome's fall. The catalyst was the arrival of a new religion among the pagan *túatha*, the Irish tribes: Christianity came to Ireland in 431, introduced there by a bishop named Palladius and reinforced by the ministry of a Roman Briton named Patricius.[4]

Patricius—or Saint Patrick, as he is called today—had a fraught relationship with his adopted country. Kidnapped at the age of sixteen, he spent six years in captivity on the island before escaping back to Britain at the urging of a disembodied voice in his head.[5] On returning as an evangelical cleric some years later, he was met at every turn by distrustful druids and murderous bandits, and it was only by bribing the tribal kings and retaining their sons as bodyguards that he saved himself from untimely martyrdom. Eventually, his efforts paid off. Patrick came to Ireland in the fifth century; the island was studded with monasteries by the sixth, and by the seventh the scribes of these centers of religious life were experimenting with new forms of decoration and bookmaking, the better to reflect God's glory in the written word. The adherents of the old pagan religions might have *illustrated* their religious books, but the monks of the Middle Ages aspired to *illuminate* their meticulously copied Bibles, hymnals, and prayer books.[6] Though the term has since come to mean any lavishly decorated manuscript, for the pedant (or the paleographer), an illuminated manuscript is worthy of the name only if it is embellished by radiant gold or stately silver.[7] A new age of lavish illustration was at hand.

Before we delve into the gilded world of the illuminated manuscript, there remains the matter of what came before it.

From the middle of the second millennium BCE, more and more Egyptians chose to be buried with copies of what early archaeologists thought was a religious text—an untranslated tract presumed to be akin to the Bible or the Qur'an. But when one such scroll was deciphered in the nineteenth century it transpired that this "Book of Going Forth by Day," as the text called itself, focused less on how to behave in this life than it did the next. The purpose of the book was to help its reader to reach the afterlife, whether they were a pharaoh, an aristocrat, or a commoner, and to tip the scales of the final judgment in their favor. Its translator, a Prussian named Karl Richard Lepsius, nicknamed it *das Todtenbuch*—"the Book of the Dead"—and his plainspoken shorthand title caught the popular imagination.[8]

Narrated in the first person, the Book of the Dead offered a kind of positive visualization of the journey to come, including spells to transform the spirit of the deceased into powerful animals, to gain access to higher levels of the afterlife, and to call upon the protection of the gods. It would not be inaccurate to call it the *Guidebook* of the Dead. If everything went according to plan, the decedent would eventually come face-to-face with the jackal-headed god Anubis, who balanced their heart against a feather to determine what would become of them. (On hand to witness the verdict was Thoth, the god who was said to have given writing to the ancient Egyptians.) A fortunate soul could look forward to eternity in the Elysian paradise of the "Fields of Peace"; they might travel the sky with Ra in his sun-boat, or even rule the underworld with Osiris. Those found wanting were cast into the slavering jaws of Ammit the soul-eater, an ungainly but ferocious chimera of crocodile, lion, and hippo.[9]

All this was written out in the Book of the Dead, and, as time went by, it was increasingly illustrated to match. The earliest scrolls were prepared by scribes who left blank spaces for subsequent illustration, but gradually this was turned on its head: in later copies, illustrators painted their vignettes as they pleased and scribes were forced to write the text in the white space left around them. A wealthy buyer could pick and choose from almost two hundred spells to build a portfolio appropriate to their preferred route through the afterlife, while the less prosperous had to make do with off-the-shelf copies written and illustrated in advance, and with blank lines left for their names to be filled in when the end drew near.[10] However costly a given *Todtenbuch* had been in life, its fate in death was the same as all the others: to be entombed with its erstwhile owner, and, perhaps, to be disinterred millennia later by inquisitive archaeologists or grave robbers.

A desert tomb, it turns out, is a very good place in which to preserve a papyrus scroll. One of the main reasons that the Book of the Dead is so well studied is because so many copies have survived, their colorful illustrations intact for Egyptologists to pore over endlessly.[11] And though their subject matter may have been a little monotonous, it is clear that the ancient Egyptians were past masters at the art of

⇜ A facsimile of the Book of the Dead of Hunefer. The original is dated to around 1275 BCE. In life, Hunefer was a high-ranking official with the titles "Royal Scribe" and "Scribe of Divine Offerings." Thoth, the divine creator of hieroglyphics, stands to the right of the scales with a palette and brush in hand, ready to record Anubis's verdict.[12]

illustrating books. Surely their inheritors in Greece and Rome, those two other beacons of ancient civilization, would carry on the tradition?

Therein lies the rub. The wetter weather to the north of the Mediterranean is less conducive to papyrus's continued survival than the dry cocoons of Egypt's tombs, and only a literal handful of illustrated papyrus fragments have come down to us from the classical heyday of Greece and Rome. Moreover, they all come from the "Hellenized" Egypt of the Ptolemies rather than from Europe itself, preserved there by Egypt's accommodating climate, and they are all frustratingly incomplete.[13] That the Greeks and Romans were prodigious artists is not in dispute—our museums are full of painted vases and classical sculptures, and our cities are littered with buildings that emulate the columns and porticoes of ancient Rome and Athens—but our understanding of how they illustrated those books is woefully incomplete. The craft and the

⯬ A fourth-century CE papyrus fragment depicting Briseis's abduction from Achilles's tent. This scene from Homer's *Iliad* is one of the few that survive in classical Greek manuscripts.

aesthetic of the illuminated medieval manuscript did not come out of nowhere, but we have very little understanding of where they *did* come from.

Appropriately, the first examples of this medieval scribal renaissance were modest, and the oldest known Irish manuscript, a book of psalms called *An Cathach,* hints but coyly at the glorious books that were to follow. Dated to as early as 560, the *Cathach* was written in black and red ink, with the latter reserved for enlarged initial letters and occasional embellishments such as dots and spirals. The text itself is a little shaky, though this could only have reinforced the legend that the book had been hurriedly copied one night by Saint Columba himself, another of Ireland's founding saints, aided by a "miraculous light" of apparently less-than-optimal brightness.[14]

Columba was much more than a middling scribe. Before his death at the end of the sixth century, he had founded a string of important monasteries in Ireland and abroad, including one on rugged Iona, off the west coast of Scotland, that helped bring Christianity to the pagan Picts and Gaels.[15] A hundred years after Columba had dashed off the *Cathach* by night, many more monasteries inspired by his mission had been established across northern Britain. Behind their walls, monastic scribes were laboring over some of the most iconic books ever produced.[16]

The upward course of "insular" bookmaking (that is, the bookmaking of the British Isles) is charted by a series of remarkable works. The Book of Durrow, for instance, rescued in the seventeenth century from a farmer who used it like a sacred teabag to produce holy water for his ailing cattle, is thought to have been written between 650 and 700. Its pagan-inflected designs and intermittently wavering lines of text mark the midpoint between Columba's austere *Cathach* and the masterworks that were to follow.[17] The makers of the Lindisfarne Gospels, produced around the year 715 at a monastery off the coast of Northumberland, were more confident still, venturing to full-page illustrations of Matthew, Mark, Luke, and John and amplifying initial letters into sprawling, abstract shapes.[18] Surpassing all these was the celebrated Book of Kells. Completed sometime around the year 800, it was the vehicle for all that had been learned since Columba's time. It may be the most famous single book in the Western world.

Named for the monastery at Kells, northeast of Dublin, Ireland, where it spent much of its life, the Book of Kells was both the pinnacle of the Irish monastic scribes' art and their last great work before the ugliness of the outside world intruded upon their cloistered lives.

Comprising 680 vellum pages, the visual impact of this edition of the Gospels of Matthew, Mark, Luke, and John stands in stark contrast to the silent, gloomy scriptoria in which such books were written. Images erupt across the parchment in the form of grandly decorative initial letters, stylized representations of the Four Evangelists, and intricate "carpet" pages of geometric designs that resemble later Islamic art.[19] All these are rendered in red, yellow, purple, and black inks that shine almost as brightly today as they must have done twelve hundred years ago. It is only very recently, in fact, that the ink has shown any sign of its age; flown to Australia for an exhibition in 2000, one of the four volumes in which the book is currently bound suffered "minor" pigment damage from the vibrations of the aircraft carrying it.

The text of the Book of Kells, which had been inscribed with almost mechanical precision, was framed by borders of interwoven ribbons and depictions of sinuous, contorted animals, many of which echoed Pliny's fast-and-loose approach to natural history. Another characteristic feature was the extensive use of "diminuendo," a metrical approach to linking large, decorative capitals to small, unadorned body text. From the capital onward, each letter or group of letters was drawn successively smaller and with less adornment, until the eye had been led to the body of the page's text.[20] And for all their relative insignificance, even the unadorned letters of the text itself tell a story of innovation and evolution: Irish scribes had developed a rounded "insular" style of handwriting that was quite different from the angular roman letters favored on the Continent.[21] (Insular script can still be seen today, although it has since come down from its throne of monastic manuscripts to the less sacred environs of the typical IRISH PUB.)

Equally as important as the Book of Kells's glorious imagery and careful script was the measured *absence* of text. Roman writers had never much cared to separate words (a brief dalliance with PLACING·DOTS·BETWEEN·WORDS was over and done with by the second century CE) but their traditional *scriptio continua*, THERUNNINGTOGETHEROFWORDS, made for difficult

A decorative "chi rho," occupying an entire page of the Book of Kells. This early Christian symbol was derived from the Greek letters *chi* (χ) and *rho* (ρ), used together as an abbreviation for the word "Christ."[22]

reading. And so, in addition to softening Rome's abrupt capital letters, Irish monks began to add spaces between words to make their writing duties less onerous.[23] The Book of Kells and its contemporaries are as important for what they tell us about the state of the art in writing practices as what they reveal about art itself.

The blossoming of bookmaking in Ireland ended when marauding Vikings first hauled their longships onto the Emerald Isle's charmed shores—and onto the beaches of its remote monastic outposts.[24] Lindisfarne, famed for its lavish Gospels, was sacked in 793; Iona, where the Book of Kells is thought to have been written, was targeted in 795, 802, and again in 806, when sixty-eight monks were slain. An attack in 825, during which the abbot was killed, was the final straw, and the island's religious treasures—including, it is thought, the Book of Kells and Saint Columba's relics—were evacuated over the following decades to a new monastery at Kells, established safely inland from Ireland's hazardous coastal waters.[25] The Dark Ages had come to Ireland.

Even as Scandinavia's roving delinquents made life a misery for the Scots and the Irish, on the Continent the hangover from the fall of Rome was finally ebbing. The souls who escaped from Ireland to mainland Europe took their scribal skills and their sense of aesthetics with them, and the illuminated manuscript was not long to follow.[26]

The rumors from Rome of a "barbarian invasion" turned out to be greatly exaggerated. There was, no doubt, a sporadically violent rebalancing of power in the old western Empire, but historians have wavered on how to interpret events. Was it the inevitable overthrow of a decadent, decaying empire by vital, disciplined northern Europeans? Or had a sophisticated, civilized state been unjustly smashed to bits by brutish, warlike tribespeople?

For a start, the roving Germanic tribes that supplanted Rome's incumbent elite were far outnumbered by the urban populations they found themselves ruling. And having settled among their new charges, the tribes' laissez-faire paganism withered in the face of a thoroughly Christianized Roman society: within a century or two of their arrival, the incomers had largely converted to the religion of their vassals.[27] Moreover, faced with the challenges of governing such a massive territory, Rome's new tribal rulers were more or less forced to learn Latin, its lingua franca, ensuring that it carried on across Europe as the preferred language of scholars, priests, lawyers, and civil servants.[28] At the coronation in 800 of Charles the Great, the ruler of the (forcibly) united barbarian states that had formed in the ashes of the Roman Empire, an obliging Pope Leo III styled the new king "Charles, most serene Augustus, crowned by God, great and pacific emperor, governing the Roman empire."[29] The new boss was a lot like the old boss.

Politics, religion, and art flourished under Charlemagne's Holy Roman Empire, as the man and his kingdom are now called.[30] Finding his Frankish compatriots lacking in intellectual vigor, the new emperor established a court of noted foreign scholars and tasked them with the modernization of his creaking realm—and the members of the clergy, variously corrupt, illiterate, and ignorant, were not spared from Charlemagne's reforms.[31] Back in the sixth century, an influential Roman Christian named Benedict of Nursia had renounced his inherited wealth and developed a series of rules by which the righteous man might live.[32] Along with admonishments on the value of honest work and the temptations of material wealth, Saint Benedict's rules prescribed daily readings of religious texts (three hours in summer and two in winter); recommended the cover-to-cover reading of a worthy book during Lent; and specified that a book should be carried at all times while traveling.[33] Charlemagne firmly reminded his priests of these obligations, decreeing that all monasteries should keep their books correct and free from error, and made it clear that his clerical subjects would no longer be permitted to rest on their laurels.[34]

And so, at the stern urging of the Carolingian dynasty's greatest son, the monasteries of Europe became the last refuge of the book on a largely illiterate continent. Monks filled their libraries with tens or even hundreds of volumes (enough, at any rate, to supply their Lenten reading binge); they borrowed and copied books to expand their holdings and occasionally to sell to wealthy laypeople; and they made and circulated ad-hoc catalogues to make intermonastery borrowing easier to manage.[35] As they did all this, the monks who wrote and collected books came to realize that it was important to *illustrate* them too. Two hundred years before Charlemagne, Pope Gregory had declared that "pictures are books for the illiterate," and, in a society where barely 1 in 7 laypeople could write their own name, he had a point. (Some hapless souls could not even hold a pen to mark their names with an *X*, and were invited to touch the parchment of a contract or deed to "sign" it.)[36] Ironically, Charlemagne himself could not read or write—on sleepless nights he sat up with parchment and pen, trying over and over to master the letters of his name—but he could at least gaze in satisfaction upon the magnificently illuminated manuscripts that now issued from monasteries across Europe.[37]

For a body of men who prized silence so highly, the monks responsible for the survival of Europe's written history were vocal in complaining about their lot.[38] Banned from speaking aloud while at work, the margins of the pages on which they wrote became outlets for endless grousing about physical maladies and working conditions. "Writing is excessive drudgery," wrote one broken scribe. "It crooks your back, it dims your sight, it twists your stomach, and your sides." "Thank God, it will soon be dark," said another, eager for the gathering dusk to put an end to his day's work.[39]

The dismal chambers in which scribes toiled were called *scriptoria*, or writing rooms. Other than the church itself, the scriptorium was one of the most important features of a medieval monastery and yet contemporary plans, letters, and books paint scriptoria as much the same as the other rooms in which a monk might pass his days. The "Plan of St. Gall," for instance, a parchment blueprint that depicts an idealized eighth-century monastery, details forty-odd buildings subdivided into innumerable rooms, including a "dwelling for the keeper of the geese," a "dwelling for the keeper of the chickens," an infirmary, a brewer's granary, and an ominously named "house for bleeding"—and, nestled in the angle of the church's crossed nave and transept, a two-story scriptorium and library.[40] The upstairs library at this hypothetical monastery was furnished with cupboards for its books, while the scriptorium on the lower floor contained seven writing desks aligned under seven windows and a central cabinet in which to store works in progress.[41] The Plan of St. Gall made no provision for heating the scriptorium, and neither did many of its real-world counterparts; these would have been chilly rooms at best and almost uninhabitable in winter.

Some monasteries in England went without dedicated scriptoria. Instead, monks lined up their writing desks under the pillared arcades, or cloisters, surrounding the courtyard. More fortunate scribes laboring in these alfresco scriptoria might have luxuriated in a window of oiled paper to block the wind or a straw mat to keep their feet off the freezing flagstones of the floor, but the cloisters were rarely an agreeable workplace. "The book which you now see was written in the outer seats," wrote one unhappy monk, "while I wrote I froze, and what I could not write by the beams of the sun I finished by candlelight."[42] Certainly, a scribe's eyesight would have benefited from working outside, but the slightest whisper of wind would have ruffled pages and a single drop of rain could ruin hours of work in an instant. God gaveth a little to the scribe in the cloisters, but mostly He took away. Elsewhere in the famously inclement British Isles, a few monasteries displayed signs of humane architects: some indoor scriptoria in Ireland were sited next to the monastery's kitchen or its fire-heated "calefactory," or warming room.[43]

These variously dark, frigid, windy, or stuffy factories for bookmaking typically accommodated between three and twenty scribes.

➻ A lay scribe and a monk in a scriptorium. This image, taken from a German manuscript of the eleventh century, is one of the few medieval illustrations that show more than one scribe at work.

Twelve was thought to be a happy number, although some larger monasteries juggled staffs of up to a hundred scribes and auxiliaries who worked in shifts to maximize productivity.[44] Discipline in the scriptorium was strict. Forbidden from speaking aloud, monks signaled to one another in a rudimentary sign language or passed notes like naughty schoolchildren. Supervisors hovered vigilantly at scribes' shoulders, and workers could leave only with the permission of the abbot.[45] Reluctant scribes of the Carthusians, a monastic order founded in France in the eleventh century, were subjected to a very French punishment: a text dated to the thirteenth century describes how wine was withheld from any monk unwilling to submit to their scribal duties.[46]

When they could be persuaded to man their desks, scribes formed a kind of production line. Parchment, quills, ink, and gold were fed in at one end, and from the other emerged manuscripts of carefully regimented text set off by images leaping out from shining fields of gold. Thanks to the many medieval manuscripts that have been found in a half-finished state, the details of that production line are plain to see.[47]

After the relevant supplies had been procured, the first stage in creating an illuminated manuscript was to rule its pages in preparation for writing. A scribe "pricked" the parchment at regular intervals down both sides of each page using either an awl or a tiny spiked wheel, like a surveyor's wheel scaled for pages instead of roads. Next, a straightedge was used to rule lines between opposing pairs of holes: the earliest manuscripts were scored with the back of the scribe's penknife or a piece of bone whittled to a point, but from the eleventh century onward a pointed lead "plummet," a distant ancestor to the graphite pencil, was sometimes used to draw in gray lines.[48] And just as Johannes Gutenberg deliberately mimicked the handwriting of his era, so did many of the earliest printed books faithfully replicate the faint guidelines found in the best medieval manuscripts.[49]

With a sheet of ruled parchment propped on his angled wooden desk, a quill taken firmly in one hand and a penknife in the other, the scribe proceeded to copy out the text.[50] Monasteries employed both skilled *antiquarii,* who specialized in careful, "antique" writing, and *scriptores,* less practiced scribes entrusted with more mundane tasks.[51] *Scriptores* were not expected be able to read the words they copied, and even the scribes who produced the celebrated Book of Kells were not immune to failures in reading comprehension: this most famous of illustrated manuscripts is rife with spelling mistakes and other textual errors.[52] It would have benefited from the keen eye of a *corrector*, an experienced scribe engaged by more exacting scriptoria to proofread newly copied manuscripts.[53]

Whether or not a scribe understood a word of the text he was copying, progress was slow and methodical. Each letter was constructed stroke by stroke in iron gall ink, and a conscientious scribe would pause to sharpen his quill tens of times each day to maintain an even line. The penknife with which he did that, in fact, was every bit as important as his pen: with it, he could prick holes for guidelines; scrape off a mistake before its ink soaked into the page; or hold springy parchment flat so as to write upon it more easily.[54] At the end of all this he would have picked up the completed page, cast an expert eye over its neatly ruled lines and disciplined text, and then passed it on to a colleague practiced in the graphic arts.

Transforming a written text into an all-singing, all-dancing illuminated manuscript was a complex process, considerably costlier and more involved than the writing of the text itself, and fewer than one in a hundred surviving Carolingian manuscripts are illustrated in any meaningful way. Even in the fifteenth century, at the very height of the craft, less than one manuscript in every ten was illuminated. This sort of embellishment was reserved for the most revered texts, and later, for the wealthiest clients.

The illumination of a manuscript began straightforwardly enough. An illustrator—a monk, in the early days; as time went on, professional artists were increasingly drafted in—used a plummet or a silver-tipped stylus to sketch images in the blank spaces left for decorative initials and other illustrations.[55] To speed things along, symmetrical decorations such as borders were traced from the other side of the thin, translucent parchment.[56] Now the illumination proper could begin.

The illustrator first spread a base coat over the areas to be gilded, using anything from egg white to gum arabic, animal glue, or gelatin to provide a suitable ground. In some cases a thick, chalk-based paint called gesso was used to build up a three-dimensional base for a miniature, multifaceted gold relief.[57] Once the ground had dried, the illustrator breathed lightly onto the page, moistening the tacky or roughened areas of the base coat, before laying down an impossibly light sheet of gold or silver leaf. The moisture from their breath was enough to hold the leaf in place as they burnished it to a bright finish with a smooth, semiprecious stone such as a sapphire, garnet, or amethyst.[58] (Scribes of more modest means had other options: one fifteenth-century artist's manual advised that "the teeth of dogs, lions, wolves, cats, leopards, and of all clean flesh-feeding animals are also good.")[59]

So light that an unattended sheet could be borne aloft by a stray breeze, gold leaf was made by interleaving solid gold ingots between sheets of very fine parchment called "goldbeater's skin" and then hammering the completed stack until the gold had been beaten out to the desired thinness. Honoring the parchment industry's tradition of stomach-churning raw materials and noxious manufacturing processes, goldbeater's skin was made from ox intestine—taken, ideally, from undernourished cattle, since the organs of well-fed oxen were too fatty—that were subsequently degreased, peeled apart, stretched, and dried.[60] The end product was a durable, flexible form of parchment about a thousandth of an inch thick.[61] Goldbeater's skin has proved so useful that it has outlasted illuminated manuscripts by several centuries: goldsmiths continued to use it until the 1960s; book conservators use it to repair damaged parchment; and for a few brief, glorious years between the First and Second World Wars, it took to the air in enormous quantities as the material of choice for the gas bags of airships such as the Graf Zeppelin.[62]

Once the gold leaf (or, more rarely, silver leaf) had been applied and burnished onto the page, the illustrator proceeded to paint the image. Designs were first outlined in black ink, like a comic-book panel; next, colored areas were treated with a neutral undercoat and then filled in with a variety of inks.[63] The inks used were similar to modern tempera paints, consisting of a pigment suspended in a binding medium such as egg white, but they were adulterated with additives such as urine and earwax to achieve the desired consistency, color, and opacity.[64] The pigments themselves spoke of a world well accustomed to international trade: ultramarine was made from lapis lazuli mined in Afghanistan; vermilion came from cinnabar, a mineral native to Spain; and the crocuses that yielded saffron yellow were brought from Asia to Europe by Muslim merchants.[65] Of all the colors an illustrator might use, however, a pigment named *minium*, or "orange lead," was the one most indelibly associated with the art and craft of illuminated manuscripts.

Minium was made by roasting a pigment called "white lead" in air and then scraping off and grinding up the burnt-orange crust that formed upon its surface.[66] (White lead was made by burying pots of lead and vinegar in warm, fermenting animal dung.)[67] The resultant orange-red coloring was eminently affordable in comparison to exotic pigments such as ultramarine and vermilion, and it was commonly used both for textual flourishes such as contrasting letters and for more elaborate illustrations. Cheap, ubiquitous minium gave rise to a whole lexicon of terms that persist to this day: Scribes who used *rubrica*, or red ink pigmented with minium, to decorate letters and symbols became known as "rubricators," and their contrasting headings became "rubrics." Illustrators who painted with minium were called "miniators," and their illustrations—their little book-bound paintings—became "miniatures."[68]

At the end of all this, having ruled, written, illuminated, and painted a book, the monks in the scriptorium's production line would have been excused for being happy to see the back of it. As an anonymous scribe noted on the final page of one particular manuscript: "Now I've written the whole thing: for Christ's sake give me a drink."[69]

➳ • ➳

bouure · ꝛ garder si de touibles
ꝛ de salces ꝛ dautres manieres
asses se ce nest por remouoir
maladies · mais se user les
estuet si les amendent selon
les ensegnemens que nous
desimes en le premiere partie ·
car por les ensegnemens que
nous desimes desimes la si nos
en passerons briement. de vin
ins si
se deu
se fie
en ma
tes m
nieres
se lotu
se sus
tance
ꝛ selo
ce quil est nouiaus ꝛ vies ·

↞ A thirsty monk—a scribe, perhaps?—avails himself of the contents of his monastery's cellars. The illuminated initial capitals of this late-thirteenth-century manuscript are typical of the Gothic style of the time.[70]

The technology of the illuminated manuscript went unchallenged for centuries even as the medieval world changed around it. The Holy Roman Empire rumbled on as Europe's main political power, but society within the empire was transformed. Skilled peasants were leaving their rural homes for towns and cities, while the cities themselves, such as Johannes Gutenberg's hometown of Mainz, fought to eke out some measure of independence from the old feudal aristocracy. Money was assuming a progressively larger role, and it spoke louder than an inherited title.[71]

Always a reflection of the societies that had made them, books were changing in response. Once the preserve of monasteries and churches, they made their way out into the wider world, coveted as status symbols by wealthy private citizens. In response, a burgeoning class of professional scribes and illustrators sprang up who created lavish, illuminated books that spoke persuasively of their owners' wealth.[72] In particular, illustrated versions of the "Book of Hours," a devotional text containing calendars of religious observance and prayers to be said at different times, were featured in the collections of wealthy bibliophiles. One example in particular outshone all the rest: painstakingly written, illustrated, and bound between 1412 and 1416, *Les tres riches heures du duc de Berry*—the aptly named "Very rich hours of the Duke of Berry"—was the pinnacle of the illuminated manuscript, boasting realistic images drawn in perspective and painted with ten vibrantly colored inks. It was a movable feast for the eyes.[73]

But the Duke of Berry's celebrated Book of Hours was the end of a fading genre. Gutenberg's printing press, which churned out books too rapidly for them to be illustrated by hand, is often blamed for killing off the illuminated manuscript, but that is only part of the story. It was a different form of printing, one that had been brought to Europe a century before Gutenberg's time by a new breed of world traveler, that was the illuminated manuscript's true nemesis.

9

Ex Oriente Lux: woodcut comes to the West

At the tail end of the thirteenth century, the notorious Genoese prison of the Palazzo di San Giorgio was clogged with Venetian prisoners. Renowned city-states both, Genoa and Venice had always been archrivals in war and trade; in 1298, the Genoese held the upper hand, having recently won a decisive naval battle against their Venetian counterparts. So devastating was the defeat that Andrea Dandolo, the Venetian admiral, was said to have tied himself to the mast of his flagship and battered his head against the timber until he lolled lifeless in his bonds. Some eight thousand Venetian sailors were captured and jailed.[1]

The inmates of the Palazzo di San Giorgio were permitted to roam around the building (though not to leave it, of course), and life there was not squalid or cruel. Wealthy prisoners slept in four-poster beds with curtains for privacy and sent requests to their relatives for gifts and supplies to make their incarceration more bearable.[2] Among those well-to-do captives were two who sought to make the most of their temporary misfortune: one, a Pisan named Rustichello, was the author of Arthurian novels of dubious literary value; the other was a merchant from Venice named Marco after that city's patron saint. His surname was Polo.[3]

Rustichello listened agog as his fellow prisoner recounted the story of a seventeen-year sojourn in the lands of the great Mongol khans far to the east. Polo told the writer of a three-year trek that he had taken in the Holy Land, Turkey, Persia, and Afghanistan. He explained how he, his father, and his uncle had reached the court of Kublai Khan in stately Xanadu; and how, at the khan's bidding, they had journeyed to the far corners of the Mongol Empire as emissaries of the court.[4] The merchant also described the many differences between daily life in China and Europe, such as China's distinctive copper coins, each one punched with a hole so that a stack could be conveniently strung together. Moreover, Polo remarked on the *paper* money that circulated widely throughout the Mongol domains. Each slip of paper was redeemable for a specified sum of hard currency kept in the government's coffers and individual slips could be saved, traded, and transported in exactly the same manner as coins.[5]

The merchant (or, perhaps, the writer; it is difficult to tell where Polo's voice ends and Rustichello's begins) made much of China's paper money, incorporating it into a kind of shorthand by which he described the cities he had visited. "Cacanfu [Heijan] is a noble city," he explained. "The people are Idolators [Buddhists], and burn their dead; they have paper-money, and live by trade and handicrafts." Only a few lines later, Polo describes "a town called Changlu [Zhang lu zhen]. This is another great city belonging to the Great Kaan, and to the province of Cathay. The people have paper-money, and are Idolators and burn their dead."[6] Polo explained that this paper money, made from a familiar substance he described as "a certain fine white bast or skin which lies between the wood of the tree and the thick outer bark," was decorated with characters denoting its worth and stamped with the vermilion seal of the khan.[7] But there was something else too. China's paper banknotes, in their millions, had been printed.

⇝ • ⇜

The China that Marco Polo visited during the thirteenth century—Cathay, he called it, from the name of a Uighur dynasty that had ruled some centuries earlier—was a technological superpower.[8] Gunpowder, invented in China sometime during the fifth or sixth century, had still not made it to Europe; the magnetic compass, in its infancy when Polo arrived, promised to revolutionize travel at sea; and the use of paper money whose value was determined by the state rather than being inherent in some precious substance—"fiat money," as it is known—was perhaps the greatest financial innovation the world had ever seen.[9]

More vital than these technical and financial advances was the information revolution that had begun more than a thousand years earlier with the invention of paper. Barely 1 in 20 Western manuscripts of Polo's time were written upon paper (to a European scribe, paper would have been scarcely less exotic than parchment is today), but in China the "paper of Marquis Cai" had long since replaced bamboo and silk as the writing material of choice.[10] Polo told Rustichello of a stopover in the city of Chengdu, though he did not mention its shrine dedicated to the patron saint of Chinese paper, Cai Lun.[11] But paper, though necessary to make the banknotes that Polo lauded so highly, was not all that was required. Polo would have known, as would any literate Westerner, that it would have been nigh impossible to produce the innumerable banknotes issued in China each year (37 million annually in Polo's time, and more as depreciation took hold) without some miraculous advancement in the technology of writing.[12] Here, again, China had outdone the West. The miracle in question was called *yin* (印), or printing, and the Chinese had been using it for centuries.[13]

The origins of printing in China are mired in uncertainty. Unlike papermaking, the craft had no Cai Lun to lay claim to it. And unlike the later development of movable type in Europe, there was no Johannes Gutenberg to leave a trail of legal summons and delinquent loans for later discovery. Instead, the key to the invention of printing lies in its name: *yin*, in its original sense, referred to the act of authenticating a document with the impression of a seal in clay, and the tradition runs deep in Chinese history.[14]

In 221 BCE, Qin Shi Huang, the eponymous First Emperor of the Qin dynasty, ascended to the throne of a China he had united through espionage, bribery, and overwhelming force of arms.[15] Qin was a pitiless ruler: he ordered dissenting scholars to be buried alive and their scrolls burned; he set out standards for everything from units of weight to cart axle width, and brooked no deviation from them; and he directed criminals and prisoners of war to be castrated in their hundreds of thousands and set to work making an army of terracotta warriors that would protect him in the afterlife.[16] And so, enthroned as the absolute ruler of this nation he had cajoled, intimidated, and wrestled into being, Qin Shi Huang literally stamped his authority on official documents with a magnificent jade seal. Qin had not invented the idea of an embossed seal any more than Cai Lun had invented paper, but in embracing *yin* he conferred upon it a great and terrible pedigree. Ever after, successive emperors and empresses of China vested their authority in similar seals, wrought in stone or metal, and *yin* percolated into every layer of Chinese society. Ancient seals have been found made out of everything from copper to gold, soapstone, jade, ivory, and rhinoceros horn, and surviving wooden and bamboo documents, sealed with telltale impressions in clay, show how widely those seals were used.[17]

But here we reach the perplexing part of the story of printing in China. Like the ancient Sumerians and their clay tablets, China's scribes and bureaucrats relied on a deformable medium—dabs of wet clay—with which to seal their bamboo documents. Around 300 BCE, however, silk entered use as a writing material, followed by paper a century or so later, and these new materials required a different approach. It is not hard to guess what that approach was: rather than stamp their seals into wet clay, the Chinese now daubed them with ink and pressed them onto paper and silk. *Yin*, "to seal," took on a new meaning, "to print." The curious thing is that all this happened with no fanfare whatsoever—a fragment of silk printed by means of a seal has been dated to the first century, for example, and paper documents sealed in vermilion ink have been dated to the fifth century, but in all those centuries no one claimed credit for this innovation.[18] We know how printing started in China, but precious little else.

In 1900, paleographers trying to piece together the fragmentary history of early Chinese writing and printing received exciting news. Word had arrived from remote Dunhuang, a town perched on the edge of the Gobi desert in China's northerly Gansu Province, that tens of thousands of documents had been discovered in cave dwellings first occupied in the year 366.[19] Found behind a false wall by a Taoist priest named Wang Yuanlu, a cuboidal chamber just ten feet on each side was piled floor to ceiling with stacks of books, paintings, and other documents, with barely enough floor space remaining for two adults to stand side by side.[20] There were books written in Chinese, Tibetan, Sanskrit, Eastern Iranian, Uighur, and even Old Testament Hebrew, and the handiwork of China's modest scribes could finally speak for itself.[21]

One document in particular, a scrap of what had once been a larger work, provided a perfect snapshot of the development of printing from simple inked seals into something much more elaborate. Rendered in stark white characters against a black background, the text was called the *Wenquan ming* (温泉銘)—"The Eulogy on the Hot Springs"—and it appeared to be a near-perfect replica of an inscription attributed to the Emperor Taizong, China's ruler from 626 to 649.[22] China had long carved its most important texts and images in stone to preserve them for posterity, but this sliver of paper showed that these stones were not simply monuments but also master copies that could be duplicated over and over again by means of an "inked squeeze," or rubbing.[23] Dated to no later than the year 654, the *Wenquan ming* found at Dunhuang was one of the best examples yet of this process, called *ta* (拓, derived from the symbols 扌手, or "rolling hand," and 石, or "rock"), which formed an important stepping stone on the way to printing proper.[24]

A rubbing was made as follows: First, a sheet of paper was

moistened (water or rice water would serve, but the juice of the *pai chi*, a variety of orchid, was best) and then placed on the inscription to be reproduced. With a brush, the paper was worked into the lines and hollows of the engraving so that it took on the three-dimensional shape of the stone beneath. Next, when the paper was almost dry, the engraved, indented design was picked out against a dark background by dabbing a rounded pad dipped in ink across the surface of the paper.[25] The ink was dabbed on cautiously at first, so that the characters stood out in white from a pale-colored background; if the rubbing was sufficiently legible at this point, it was considered to be complete and said to be "as light as the cicada's wings." If more definition was required, a coat of lustrous dark ink was added to bring out the details, yielding a "black-golden rubbing." Finally, the paper was peeled off to liberate the copy from its master.

The making of rubbings in this way was a skilled task, and the best rubbings were sought after as much for the craft of their making as for the works they copied. A whole class of experts who specialized in rubbings arose in the wake of Emperor Taizong's famous carving, and today the fruits of their labor—*hei laohu* (黑老虎), or "black tigers," as rubbings are known—are noted for devouring art collectors' bank balances.[26]

But this was not how China's banknotes were produced. The making of an inked squeeze was a laborious process, entirely too time-consuming to have been of use in the printing of China's millions of banknotes—banknotes that, tellingly, were rendered in the black-on-white of relief printing rather than the ghostly white-on-black of the average rubbing.[27] *Yin* had one more evolutionary step yet to take.

China's fabled Han period came to an end in the year 220 with the country fractured into three warring states, and until the short-lived Sui dynasty put things together again in 589 (only for Emperor Taizong to seize control in 626), China suffered through its own Dark Age of squabbling kingdoms, civil wars, and invasions from without.[28] The Chinese people turned to a new religion to help make sense of their predicament and, as in the West, their monks and monasteries became the guardians of literary traditions. Buddhism had come to China, brought there by itinerant priests following the Silk Road from India, and with them had come a vast body of religious texts.[29]

Unlike Christianity and Islam, Buddhism had no God whose Word had to be preserved at all costs, but its adherents on this earthly plane were voluble all the same. By the time Taizong was in power, the monks of a temple at Fangshan, near Beijing, had decorated the walls of a cave with a hundred square meters of inscriptions detailing the Buddha's teachings and the commentaries of his followers. They would add another eight such cave chambers in the years to come.[30] Nor was theirs an isolated case; the Chinese Buddhist canon, the *Dazangjing* or "Great Treasury of Sutras," continued to grow as scholars returned from India with new texts and translations.[31] Comforting as it must have been to have such a comprehensive body of wisdom, preserving and communicating it was another matter entirely.

Ancient Japan adopted many cultural tics from China, its older, larger neighbor. If the Chinese imperial palace was painted red, then so too would be its counterpart in Japan; if the Chinese gentry amused themselves with the sport of *cuju*, or football, then the Japanese upper classes would play it too; and if Chinese emperors and empresses used seals to stamp their authority onto official documents, then Japanese rulers would have their own seals carved in emulation.[32]

In 694, as was traditional in the wake of an emperor's death, Japan's capital was moved to a new site, the city of Fujiwara, modeled on China's then-capital Luoyang, and then again, in 710, to Nara a few miles to the north and which in turn was laid out to match China's new capital at Chang'an.[33] And with Buddhism now installed as China's official faith, Japan's rulers were eager to make their own devotion to the same religion plain for all to see.[34] In 732, a giant, forty-nine-ton bell was cast for the main Buddhist temple at Nara, while a few years later the same temple would see construction begin on a fifty-foot, five-hundred-ton statue of the Buddha to be finished with fifty pounds of gold. Fully 10 percent of the Japanese population was involved in this monumental commission, from metalworkers to carpenters, and more than 100,000 Buddhist priests witnessed the eventual dedication ceremony in 752.[35]

The Empress Shōtoku, born in 717 in a Japan obsessed with Buddhism, was always going to look favorably upon the faith.[36] Her fondness for one particular Buddhist practitioner, however, stirred suspicion among the ruling classes: in 762 Shōtoku moved her court to Nara's Buddhist temple to spend more time in the company of a monk named Dōkyō. Rumors swirled of an affair between the two, with one account written in the ninth century stating that the priest and the empress had "shared a pillow" even as it tactfully declined to say anything more.[37] Infatuated as she was with Dōkyō, the empress was even more obsessed with her own mortality, and her lover's spiritual teachings seemed to offer her a way out. Mindful of a smallpox epidemic that had racked Japan in her youth, Shōtoku retained 116 priests to exorcise the demons that were thought to cause disease, and, in 767, in her fifth decade, she embarked on a project she felt sure would immunize her against the illness for good.

There is a Buddhist sutra, or sermon, that speaks of an Indian Buddhist who is told by a seer that he has only seven days left to live. The Buddha himself, upon receiving this startled disciple, is more sanguine. To prolong his life, the Buddha tells the man, he must copy out a prayer seventy-seven times and place the copies within seventy-seven pagodas. Only then will his sins be forgiven and his life preserved. The Empress Shōtoku seized upon this parable as the means of her salvation and, erring on the side of caution, she ordered a *million* such prayers to be copied out and placed within miniature pagodas a few inches in height.

The official annals record that the feat was completed in 770. Transliterated from the original Sanskrit and spelled out in Chinese characters, the instruments of the empress's deliverance took the form of slips of paper around eighteen inches long and two inches wide covered in incantatory text—text that had been printed, not written. The characters of the few surviving copies are rendered in dark ink against the lighter paper, suggesting a relief printing surface, and the consensus among experts is that the prayer in its entirety had been carved onto monolithic wooden blocks before being inked and printed.[38] Though there are other early examples of printed documents from Korea and China, their dating is uncertain, and the Empress Shōtoku's million-charm offensive represents the first datable mass production of woodcut printings.[39] Alas, it was all for naught; a million prayers or no, the empress died the same year her project was completed.[40]

The Empress Shōtoku's million-prayer print run may be the earliest attested use of woodcut printing blocks, but archaeologists cataloguing the papers discovered at Dunhuang soon discovered that the Chinese had been equally industrious in applying this new technique. Among the many handwritten documents, rubbings, and seals found there was a sixteen-foot-long scroll pasted together from seven sheets of paper, tinted yellow by Amur cork dye, and prefaced with a startlingly detailed illustration of the Buddha in conversation with a kneeling disciple, the pair of them surrounded by monks, officials, and supernatural beings.[41] At the end of the scroll is a message from its maker, or perhaps its sponsor: "Reverently made for universal free distribution by Wang Jie on behalf of his two parents on the fifteenth of the fourth moon of the ninth yeạr of *Xian tong*"—that is, May 11, 868.[42] The so-called Diamond Sutra, British Library manuscript Or.8210/P.2, is the oldest dated, printed book *and* the first book to contain a printed image.[43]

This printed edition of the Diamond Sutra was one of twenty

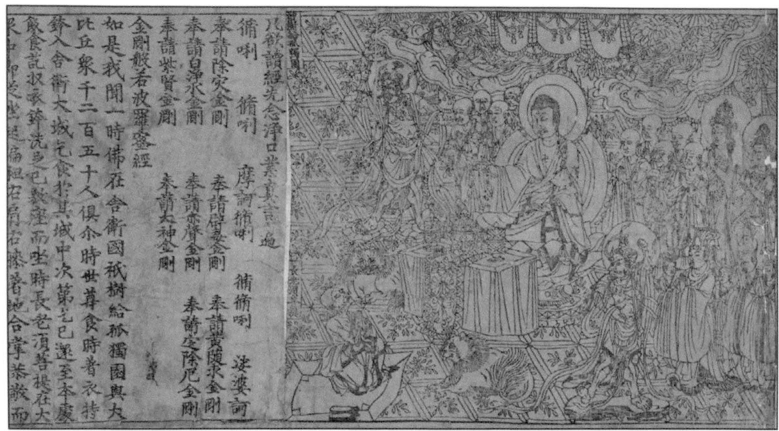

凡欲讀經先念淨口業真言一遍
脩唎 脩唎 摩訶脩唎 脩脩唎 娑婆訶
奉請除災金剛 奉請辟毒金剛 奉請黃隨求金剛
奉請白淨水金剛 奉請赤聲金剛 奉請定除災金剛
奉請紫賢金剛 奉請大神金剛
金剛般若波羅蜜經
如是我聞一時佛在舍衛國祇樹給孤獨園與大
比丘衆千二百五十人俱尒時世尊食時著衣持
鉢入舍衛大城乞食於其城中次第乞已還至本處
飯食訖收衣鉢洗足已敷座而坐時長老須菩提在大
衆中即從座起偏袒右肩右膝著地合掌恭敬而

⁂ Frontispiece and opening text of the Diamond Sutra, the earliest dated, printed book. The Buddha receives Subhuti, his disciple.

printed documents found in Dunhuang's "library cave" (by contrast, there were five hundred handwritten copies of the Diamond Sutra alone), and together they formed a motley collection of texts.[44] There were single-sheet prayers, each one presided over by an illustration of the Buddha, to be presented as temple offerings similar to Gutenberg's indulgences. There were farmers' almanacs, illustrated with stylized figures of people and animals and augmented by minutely rendered maps. There were lengthy sutras devoid of imagery. And among all these, there were a handful of paper slips bearing nothing more than repeated images of the Buddha, silent and inscrutable, and devoid of explanatory text.[45] Whether a document saved your soul or helped run your farm, it could and would be printed: *yin*, finally, had attained its modern meaning.

These treasures and others were sealed into Dunhuang's library cave in the early years of the eleventh century. The nearby Buddhist kingdom of Khotan had been sacked by Muslim invaders in 1006 and the monks at Dunhuang feared the same fate, so to protect their precious library they deposited it in a cave then concealed the entrance with mud and plaster. Sure enough, Dunhuang was overrun in 1035—only the invaders were not Muslims but Buddhists, hailing from the Xi Xia Empire to the east.[46] As important as the Dunhuang library has turned out to be for modern scholars, however, its loss in the eleventh century would have been of little consequence to China at large. By then, woodblock printing had thoroughly permeated Chinese life.

The man credited with kick-starting China's woodcut printing renaissance was a slippery tenth-century politician named Feng Dao. Born only a few years after the printing of the Diamond Sutra, Feng rose from lowly stock to become a senior adviser to seven successive emperors. Contemporary Chinese historians cast him as a silver-tongued flatterer of deplorably plastic morals.[47] In 932, Feng announced the printing of the entire set of Confucian "classics," the canon of China's *other* ancient religion, amounting to 150 volumes in all. This mammoth project took more than twenty years to complete, and, though Feng acted more as project manager than printer, in recent times he has rightly acquired a reputation as China's Gutenberg.[48] Printing spread dramatically in Feng's wake, and in the centuries that followed, China printed works on astrology, the interpretation of dreams, alchemy, biography, religion, history, poetry, and more. Illustrations kept pace with printed text: there were medicinal treatises depicting therapeutic herbs; there were architectural drawings detailing beams, columns, and joints; there were forensic anatomical charts; and there were schematic diagrams of astronomical clocks and star maps.[49] While scribes in Europe toiled away with their quills, Chinese printers were printing comprehensively illustrated books by the hundreds and thousands.

As had been the case with the inventions of papyrus, parchment, and movable type—all the main ingredients of pre-modern bookmaking, basically—Chinese woodcut printers were tight-lipped about their craft. Scribes did not write about it and woodcutters did not print pictures of it. But like parchment and movable type, woodcut printing never really went away; the specifics of ancient woodblock printing may be unknown but the craft itself has endured.

It begins with a block of wood. Blocks that have survived from ancient times show that pear, jujube, and catalpa woods were favored in the past; today's printers prefer boxwood, gingko, and the Chinese honey locust tree. Having been roughly cut to size, each block is checked for knots and other imperfections and then left to soak in water for about a month. The soaked wood is then cut square and planed flat, and the softened surface is polished to a smooth finish. Next, with brush and ink, a calligrapher draws whatever is to be printed onto a sheet of waxed paper, so that the ink sits on its surface, and the paper is laid facedown on the block to transfer the design. The block is now ready to be cut: with a sharp cutting tool (woodcutters nowadays use knives, chisels, and *U*-shaped gouges), the wood curls or chips effortlessly off the block's surface. The design is thus sculpted in reverse, the non-printing areas carved out as hollows in the wood, and the block is ready for printing.[50]

(Attentive readers may have found the previous paragraph a little repetitious, and so it is; when Wang Zhen experimented with wooden movable type in the early fourteenth century, he proceeded exactly as though he were making a traditional wooden printing block, only to cut the engraved block into chunks before printing. But as Wang Zhen found out, movable type could not capture the human touch behind the letters of an expert calligrapher. Woodblock printing agreed with China's sense of aesthetics but movable type did not.)

Printing with an engraved block was simple and fast. With a pot of China's famous "India ink" at the ready, the printer inked the surface of the carved block with a horsehair brush before laying a sheet of paper onto it. A soft pad was pressed over the paper to ensure that the ink was taken up evenly, and the paper was peeled back to reveal the printed page. Working like this, a veteran printer could make perhaps 2,000 impressions a day—a figure even Gutenberg in his heyday, directing a cadre of workmen at a clutch of presses, likely never got near.[51]

⇝ • ⇜

Marco Polo took in China's ancient tradition of printing, its myriad printed texts and images, and was unmoved. At least, that is the impression given in his memoir; aside from a few oblique references to printing in connection with paper money, woodblock printing is not discussed.[52] Paper money itself, on the other hand, fascinated the Venetian merchant.

For more than two millennia, from the second century BCE onward, China's economy had been well served by the familiar round, pierced copper coins called *tongqian* (铜钱).[53] In the early ninth century, however, this traditional monetary system found itself up against a quite unforeseen difficulty: China's burgeoning Buddhist community had cast so many copper statues of the Buddha that the country was beginning to run out of the raw material from which to mint its coins. In desperation, in 807 and again in 809, the government issued certificates of indebtedness they called *feiqian* (飞钱), or "flying money." Merchants trading in Chang'an, the capital, purchased *feiqian* with coins before traveling home, where they could exchange their certificates at local government offices for cash.[54] It was a boon for all concerned: merchants no longer had to transport bulky, heavy, and untraceable coins, ripe for the stealing; Chang'an gained a ready supply of copper currency; and provincial governments effectively gave themselves interest-free loans, lasting from the purchase of a note until it reached its destination.[55]

In the centuries that followed China resorted to paper currency on an ever-grander scale. As Polo related to Rustichello some five hundred years later, "The Kaan causes every year to be made such a vast quantity of this money, which costs him nothing, that it must equal in amount all the treasure in the world." Each of the Khan's "vast quantity" of banknotes were bedecked with Chinese characters that declaimed their purpose and denomination, offered rewards for informing on forgers, and warned those same forgers that they ran the risk of beheading if caught.[56] They also sported a host of images: strings of coins, stylized dragons, horses, and phoenixes were framed by decorative borders of

A sealed Chinese banknote from the Ming dynasty, printed on a sheet of mulberry bark paper and dated to the latter part of the fourteenth century. "Counterfeiters will be decapitated," warns the text.[57]

honeysuckle, lotus, and chrysanthemum.[58] The technology behind each and every Chinese banknote would have dumbfounded a contemporary Western scribe or artist.

Venice and Genoa settled their feud in 1299, releasing Polo and his compatriots from the Palazzo di San Giorgio, and the wandering merchant returned to his home city to stay. His father and uncle had managed the family's wealth ably in his absence (the trio had returned from Asia with a small fortune in precious stones) and Marco, by all accounts, lived out the rest of his days as a well-to-do but otherwise unexceptional merchant. He died in 1324.[59]

Copies of Rustichello's record of Polo's travels circulated widely among scholars and historians during the century that followed Polo's death, and for many years the text stood as Europe's primary source of knowledge on the lands and peoples of the mysterious East. Legend has it that a manuscript copy was chained to Venice's Ponte di Rialto so that the traders and customers who thronged the bridge could lose themselves in Rustichello's excitable account of Polo's journey.[60] Even saddled with the nickname "*il Milione*," after the million lies it was said to contain, Polo's narrative was translated and retranslated, copied and recopied, and finally, when Western technology had caught up with the China of Polo's memory, printed and reprinted.[61] The cult of Marco Polo, world traveler, had taken root.

In 1854, in the journal of the Philobiblon Society of Great Britain, Robert Curzon published a six-page account of his own modest travels, during which he had visited "some of the most celebrated libraries in Italy."[62] Curzon, the fourteenth Baron Zouche of Harringworth, had been in turn a failed student, a limp Member of Parliament, and a reluctant diplomat before admitting that perhaps public service was not his métier. Beginning in 1833, he embarked on a series of journeys across

Europe and the Near East, publishing accounts of his travels to some acclaim, and it was during a tour of Italy that he had visited libraries in Naples, Siena, the Vatican, and more.[63]

Curzon prefaced his article with an anecdote about the origins of printing that he had come across in an Italian newspaper. An Italian scribe named Panfilo Castaldi, Curzon said, who lived from 1398 to 1490, had been employed in copying legal documents for the town of Feltre, near Venice. Castaldi was said to have eased his workload by means of glass seals or stamps, made on the Venetian island of Murano, which he used to print outlines of elaborate capital letters before further embellishing them with quill and ink. Sometime before 1426, Castaldi allegedly got wind of books brought back from Asia by the late Marco Polo, which had been neatly printed with wooden blocks. Seizing on this information (and perhaps having seen the books firsthand), Castaldi "caused movable wooden types to be made, each block containing a single letter."[64]

Stop the presses! a historian might have thought. Was this really true? Had Marco Polo introduced Europe to printing in general and to woodblock printing in particular? It was not a revolutionary idea—as early as the sixteenth century, European writers had theorized that traders could have encountered printed banknotes in the Mongol colony of Russia, or that woodblocks, banknotes, or stories of printing could have traveled west by sea from "the Indies"—but this was the first time that Marco Polo, the original celebrity travel writer, had been linked to the arrival of printing in the West.[65]

The newspaper article to which Curzon referred had been written by a Feltre native named Dr. Jacopo Facen. Facen was a well-respected physician and a prolific writer, having published books on subjects as diverse as poetry, archaeology, geology, mining, entomology, and religion, but it was the history of the town of Feltre that held his interest most keenly. Located in the shadow of the Dolomites, the Feltre of Facen's time languished as a pawn of the great southern European powers (in his lifetime, Facen witnessed control of the town pass from

France to Austria and finally to Italy) and the doctor made it his personal mission to revive the town's fortunes.[66] With this in mind, in 1843 Facen set down the story of Panfilo Castaldi in a book of local songs and history.[67] The town duly erected a monument to Castaldi, their rediscovered local hero, but Facen's tale attracted precious few believers outside Feltre. Curzon remained carefully neutral as he related Facen's newspaper article, and lamented that he had not been able to inspect the printed documents allegedly filed away in Feltre's archives. "I must leave it to others to produce proofs of the authenticity of this curious story," wrote the English lord.[68]

Curzon's hoped-for proof did not appear. Nor, most likely, does it exist at all. There is no evidence that Marco Polo brought woodblocks back from China or that he ever explicitly referred to the process of printing except as it related to the use of seals on banknotes. Even then, Polo was hardly unique in his admiration for China's paper money: at least seven other European travelers of his era mentioned it, and, to a man, the Venetian and his contemporaries were more concerned with the financial possibilities of this radical form of currency than they were with the methods of its production.[69]

What seems to have happened is an almost exact parallel to Abu Mansur al-Tha'alibi's idealized story of how paper had come to the Islamic caliphate seven hundred years earlier. Al-Tha'alibi had massaged the facts available to him into a pleasing narrative—China had paper; the Arabs had taken Chinese prisoners at the battle of Talas; thus, there must have been papermakers among those prisoners—and Facen, in his turn, constructed a tidy history of glass stamps and wooden type with a seductive ring of truth and a convenient lack of evidence. Too credulous of a local legend, perhaps, or desperate to see his hometown lifted out of its nineteenth-century gloom, he wrote down what he thought—or hoped—to be true.[70] The last word must go to Henry Yule, the nineteenth century's preeminent translator of *il Milione*. Introducing his 1875 translation of Polo's travelogue, the Scotsman was witheringly skeptical of Facen's claims: "Seriously; if anybody in Feltre cares for the real reputation of his native city, let him do his best to have that preposterous and discreditable fiction removed from the base of the statue. If Castaldi has deserved a statue on other and truer grounds let him stand; if not, let him be burnt into honest lime!"[71]

No; if Castaldi or anyone else had laid eyes on Chinese printing blocks in the years before Gutenberg printed his 42-line Bible, their encounter almost certainly came courtesy of someone too insignificant to have been memorialized. A merchant, perhaps, traversing the Silk Road on a swaying camel's back; a trader visiting the "Cathay" quarter of the Mongol trading outpost at Nizhny Novgorod in Russia; or a sailor aboard a cargo ship hugging India's coast—any one of the adventurous souls who braved the journey into the East could have brought home a wooden printing block, and with it sparked a revolution among Europe's bookmakers.

The Catholic Church was first to exploit this new artistic medium. Pilgrims, the Church knew, were gold mines. Visitors to monasteries, cathedrals, and other important religious sites liked to commemorate their trips with souvenirs, and the Church was happy to oblige them in exchange for an appropriate offering. Chief among the mementos available to the faithful as they exited via the proto–gift shop were so-called *Andachtsbilder*, devotional images that depicted scenes and figures from Christian tradition.[72] Buyers installed these single-sheet illustrations in makeshift shrines in their homes, the better to receive their blessings, and the relative potency of such a shrine depended on the position of its subject on the Catholic corporate ladder. An image of Saint Appolonia was said to ward off toothache, for instance, while Saint Roche kept the plague at bay; Saint Sebastian prevented injury, and perennial favorite Saint Christopher protected travelers.[73] The personalities at the top of the sacred hierarchy were best of all: in 1428, one image of the Virgin Mary and the infant Jesus was said to have survived a fire that destroyed its owner's house.[74] Pilgrims were happy with their souvenirs, and the Church was happy with the money they brought in; the only real problem was that each *Andachtsbild* had to be drawn by hand, and they were correspondingly expensive both to produce and to buy.

One of the earliest clues that some new art might yet save the day came in 1412, as the Dominican Order of preachers pursued the canonization of a lay member of their order named Catherine of Siena. As part of the Dominicans' campaign, a friar named Tommaso d'Antonio gave a deposition in Venice in which he mentioned that devotional images of Catherine had been "*de facili multiplicabilis*," or "easily multiplied"—a first for any kind of image, in the West at least.[75] Concrete proof that woodcut had arrived in Europe appeared soon after in the form of a devotional image of the Madonna and Child attended by four martyred saints, tentatively dated to 1418, and unmistakably the product of a printed wooden block.[76]

Experts will admit that the timing of all this is a little shaky. Some historians think that the "Brussels Madonna" is a copy, printed as late as 1450, of a 1418 original.[77] But then another early woodcut image, a picture of Saint Christopher carrying the infant Jesus across a river, bears a more generally accepted date of 1423; therefore woodcut printing debuted on European soil at least that early. Taken together, these prints and the mess of circumstantial evidence that surrounds them suggest an even earlier date. By the year 1400 or thereabouts, half a century before Gutenberg printed his first book, the ancient Chinese art of woodcut printing had begun its quiet overthrow of Europe's laboring ranks of scribes.[78]

These early prints were modest things. The Brussels Madonna, for instance, and the Saint Christopher that followed it five years later were printed in the Chinese style: a thin, water-based ink was dabbed onto the printing block with a mushroom-shaped ink ball and transferred to a sheet of paper by rubbing or burnishing to achieve a (mostly)

⫷ A facsimile of the "Buxheim Saint Christopher" of 1423, the earliest dated European woodcut print. The only surviving original copy was colored by hand.

even finish.[79] Their designs were simple and direct—one might even say childlike, so much do they resemble coloring books with their thick, dark lines and expanses of uncolored paper. This was partly due to the inexperience of the first woodcutters and printers (a thicker line was more likely to survive the engraving process and, subsequently, the many impressions that might be taken from it) but it was also an aesthetic choice. Early prints were expected to be "colored in" by hand, to the extent that some printers provided stencils to guide the illustrator's brush as they applied blocks of color to their black-and-white prints.[80]

As they grew in confidence, Europe's woodcut printers began to push back the boundaries of their medium. In the mid-sixteenth century, for instance, a French printer and anatomist named Charles Estienne took old, disused woodblocks depicting nude human figures and inserted blank wooden plugs on which he engraved organs, bones, and other bodily details. Published in 1545 in his book *De dissectione partium corporis humani libri tres* (On dissection of the human body), the resultant anatomical diagrams are famed for their artistry and for their novel construction. A male figure carved in front of some ancient Roman basilica was apt to have his chiseled torso replaced with a diagram of the heart and lungs; equally, a book of erotica might supply an image of a woman in a compromising position whose abdomen could be excised in favor of the female reproductive organs. These were mash-ups by another name.[81]

The artistry of woodcuts themselves accelerated, and by the turn of the fifteenth century the "easily multiplied" woodcut print had attracted a host of virtuoso artists. In 1498, an up-and-coming German illustrator named Albrecht Dürer published a set of astonishingly detailed woodcuts depicting the events of the Book of Revelation.[82] Dürer's *Apocalypse*, as the prints were called, displayed both artistic flair and business acumen. Though his medium was effectively a binary surface—each area of a print was either inked or blank, "on" or "off"—Dürer conjured up an incredible range of shadings and texture. Surfaces and shadows were defined with contoured lines or dimpled with flicks of a chisel-like tool called the graver; his work transcended woodcut's coloring-book roots so completely that the famed Renaissance scholar Erasmus wrote that to add color would "injure the work."[83] *Apocalypse* was a canny marketing ploy too, simultaneously stoking and benefiting from the midmillennial hysteria that gripped Europe in the last years of the fifteenth century.[84] When preachers called out from their pulpits that the Last Judgment was nigh, Dürer's woodcuts could be relied upon to

Albrecht Dürer's 1498 woodcut of the four horsemen of the apocalypse.[85]

demonstrate in exquisite and terrifying detail just how the end times were going to play out.

As Dürer pushed the limits of what was possible with simple black-and-white prints, another German sought to free woodcut from its monochrome rut: Hans Burgkmair is credited with pioneering the multiblock technique that came to be known as *chiaroscuro*, or "light-dark" printing.[86] His cheerily entitled print of 1510, *Lovers Surprised by Death*, in which the arrival of a bewinged Grim Reaper turns a lovers' tryst

⇜ Hans Burgkmair's grisly *Lovers Surprised by Death*, a *chiaroscuro* woodcut executed using a black "line block" and two colored "tone blocks" in different shades of red.[87]

into a carnival of terror, was the first known image in which woodcut's traditional black lines were augmented by blocks of color. To achieve this effect, Burgkmair carved three separate woodblocks and applied them in turn to a single sheet of paper to produce deep black lines and shadows, paper-white highlights, and two distinct swaths of colored "tone." No one of the blocks alone would have produced a comprehensible image, but together they created a striking, rich picture.[88]

The sheer size of woodcut images increased as the years went by. The Venetian artist Tiziano Vecelli (Titian, we call him now, esteeming him with a single name) had a number of his drawings transformed into woodcut prints, culminating in 1514 or 1515 with a massive, seven-foot-by-four rendering of the *Destruction of Pharaoh's Host in the Red Sea.* The print was so large it had to be carved onto twelve separate blocks.[89] A few years later, at the behest of the Holy Roman Emperor Maximilian I, Albrecht Dürer countered with his *Triumphal Arch*, a fanciful interpretation of Maximilian's family tree etched onto the sides of a fabulous Romanesque arch. It was over a hundred square feet in size and was composed of no fewer than 192 individual blocks.[90] The artist grumbled that he had worked for Maximilian "at my own expense" for three years, but he need not have worried; upon completion of the print the emperor granted Dürer a stipend of one hundred florins per year for life, only to die before he could sign the order. Dürer, ever a robust businessman, fought and won his case in the courts.[91] If the money, fame, and legal wrangling it engendered were anything to go by, by the early sixteenth century woodcut printing had well and truly arrived.

Before Titian, Dürer, and their ilk propelled woodcut printing into the realm of fine art, however, it had already made a disproportionate impression on Europe's scribes and bookmakers. It was the easiest thing in the world to embellish a handwritten manuscript with a few woodcut prints—books illustrated this way date to 1433—but things changed when woodcutters realized that they could replicate text as easily as images.[92] Thus, for the briefest of interludes, spanning perhaps twenty years from the 1430s onward, the so-called blockbook lived and died a mayfly existence, replaced within a generation by Johannes Gutenberg's all-conquering movable type.[93]

Blockbooks were books printed from wooden blocks that bore *only* text. A mere handful were printed—thirty-six editions are known of, all from the Low Countries or southern Germany—and the dating of this tiny body of work is as contentious as it is important. Some experts place them as early as the 1430s; others, relying upon analysis of the paper stock, propose instead the early 1450s.[94] A twenty-year sliver of printing's five-century history should not matter a jot, but Gutenberg's printing of the 42-line Bible in 1454 brings the matter into focus. Do we take at face value the claim advanced by one of Cologne's printers, writing in 1490, that Gutenberg had been inspired by these early blockbooks? And what about the blockbook that mimics Gutenberg's own *Ars grammatica*, its typeset letters carefully traced over and cut into wood in a blatant act of literary piracy?[95] The relationship between woodcut printing and movable type is an unsolved question of chicken and egg.

Whatever happened during those embryonic years of European printing, the eventual outcome was plain. Movable type emerged as the preferred way to print text; woodcut, however, was too useful to be discarded, and as the century wore on one printer brought the two together to create the prototype for the book of the future.[96]

On Saint Valentine's Day in 1461, a printer named Albrecht Pfister, resident in the town of Bamberg, Germany, published a collection of fables entitled *Der Edelstein*, or "The Precious Stone," that had been written a century earlier by a Swiss author named Ulrich Boner.[97] This much is known because Pfister printed his name at the back of the book, along with the date and place of his endeavors; almost everything else about him, however, is speculation. Like Gutenberg, he is glimpsed only in the official records of his city and diocese, and rarely

leit · wer liep hat das sein nicht ist · Billich ist das
ym das geschicht · Geitikeit wirt nymer gut · Sie
betreuget mäches mēschen mut · Das freunt freun-
den wirt gehas · Dasselbe thut nymer pas · Geitikeit stifft grosen zorn · Von geitikeit wirt mäch se-
le verlorn · Geitikeit gemeī hat · In dorffern in pur-
gen unde in der stat · Der voit der schultheis der pau-
er · der richter · Der knecht der pot torwarter · Pfaffē
iūg unde alt · Mūch nūnē manigfalt · Der pischof
und der caplan · Der apt und der techan · was man
singet oder seit · Sie leben alle in geitikeit ·

Auff einē hohē perge stat · Ein paum der mich
el wunder hat · Er ist gros lang unde preit ·
Mit schonen esten wol becleit · Mit leubern ist er ge-

↞ A page from Albrecht Pfister's *Biblia pauperum* of 1461. The woodcut image and movable type of the text were locked up in a single chase and printed with one pull of the printing press.

at that. Pfister seems to have begun his career as a priest before being appointed secretary to Bamberg's bishop; his foray into printing came later and is attested almost exclusively by his surviving books.[98] Those books, though, tell a story all of their own.

Der Edelstein was Pfister's first effort, and it was clear that the priest-turned-printer harbored lofty ambitions. Its hundred and seventy-six pages are neatly set in type somehow acquired from Johannes Gutenberg himself (it was the same type that Gutenberg had used for his earliest work, the *Ars grammatica* of 1450), but, more intriguing still, the text was interspersed with a series of pictures rendered in the line-art, comic-book style of early woodcuts. The crooked, unevenly inked images appear to have been stamped in place by hand after the text had been printed in a press, but with this tentative step Pfister had overturned millennia of tradition. The printed, illustrated book was at hand.[99]

Emboldened, Pfister sought to tighten up his makeshift printing process. His next work was to be a *Biblia pauperum*, a new entry in a crowded genre of short, illustrated "Bibles of the poor" that brought the Christian message to those incapable of reading the Word of God or unable to afford it in its unabridged form.[100] For this book, published at the end of 1461, Pfister had considerably improved his method. This time around his woodcuts were locked up along with the type so that each page was inked as a single unit (the oily inks employed by Johannes Gutenberg and his disciples suited woodcut printing every bit as well as lead type) and printed with a single pull of the press's lever.[101] It was a modest improvement, but it stuck. Woodcuts were the perfect way to print those things that were impossible to put into words—the beauty of a human face, the workings of a clock, the curl of a plant's leaf—and within a century woodcut images were found on the pages of books on architecture, botany, engineering, anatomy, zoology, clothing, archaeology, and numismatics.[102] Gutenberg's lead soldiers would rule the world of books for the next four hundred years, but they could not do it without pulling woodcut printing along with them.

10

Etching a Sketch: copperplate printing and the Renaissance

Albrecht Pfister, dead by the mid-1460s, did not live to see his neat dovetailing of woodblock printing and movable type take over the world.[1] Fewer than 1 in 10 handwritten books had ever been illustrated, even at the height of the illuminated manuscript's dominance, but by 1550, less than a century after Pfister's first woodcut-illustrated book, more than half of all printed books were illustrated in one way or another. For woodblock printing, however, it was to be a short-lived triumph.

Woodblock's foibles became apparent soon after it came into common use. Engraved blocks of even the hardest woods wore away after extended use, their lines made indistinct by repeated impressions.[2] This had never much troubled Chinese printers, whose blocks were used for small print runs separated by years, decades, and sometimes centuries, but Gutenberg's system of movable type, where a finite supply of letters and characters had to be reused every few pages, encouraged longer print runs and punished the wooden illustrations bound up with its robust lead type.[3] In itself, this was not an insurmountable problem—it seems that some printers took casts of their wooden blocks to save them from repeated use—but woodcut prints suffered from a more fundamental limitation.[4] Dürer, Titian, and company had pushed the woodcutter's craft as far as it could go, and prints made from wooden blocks simply could not reproduce the level of detail their creators desired.[5] To borrow a modern term, woodcut was too low-res.

In 1476, Colard Mansion, a bookmaker from Bruges, in Flanders, printed a new edition of an old book entitled *De casibus virorum illustrium* (On the Fates of Famous Men), whose cautionary tales taught that prideful men are destined for precipitous falls.[6] Mansion's career straddled the advent of both movable type and woodcut printing, and he was aware that his wealthy customers remained unconvinced by the merits of the printed book. It was only a few years since Filippo de Strata, the hectoring Benedictine monk, had characterized writing as "a maiden with a pen, a harlot in print," and Mansion was careful to present his workshop as a traditional, hand-copying scriptorium even as he turned to printing to reduce his costs.[7] Chiefly, this meant limiting print runs to a handful of copies, but it was in the same spirit that he peppered *De casibus* with empty spaces so that his clients could have their copies illustrated by hand. There would be no low-rent woodcuts in his books.

Mansion's elitist business model could not last. A number of hand-illustrated copies of *De casibus* survive today to bear witness to his scheme, but in later editions he gave in and decided to fill the blanks with printed images.[8] The odd thing about these later images is not their style, nor their content (they are indistinguishable from contemporary woodcuts), but that they were printed on separate sheets of paper and pasted into the book. The obvious explanation for this—that Mansion had lost his nerve and was trying to entice buyers for a batch of unsold books—is belied by the fact that he had substantially reworked the text, reflowing it to accommodate the newly added images. The pasted-in prints had to have been deliberate additions. If they were woodcuts, Mansion could have slotted them directly into his formes of type—so why did he not?[9]

They were not woodcuts. Mansion was the first book printer to deploy Europe's next great printing technology: engraved copper plates, minutely carved with jewelers' tools so as to inlay images into the metal itself.

Printing with copperplate engravings was an exacting business. Liberally inked to drive pigment into all their lines and hollows and wiped down to remove the excess, copperplate images had to be printed with special roller presses strong enough to force a wetted sheet of paper into the plate's incised outlines. This was the simple reason for Mansion's scrapbook assembly of *De casibus*: it was impossible to print movable type and copperplate images at the same time, on the same press. A standard printing press driven by a lever or screw would have failed to extract much of an impression from an engraved copper plate, while the tons of pressure imparted by a roller press would have crushed a forme of lead type.[10] In comparison to cozy old woodcut blocks, the "intaglio," or engraved print, was a different beast.[11]

Credit for the earliest printed engravings was claimed for Italy by the sixteenth-century polymath Giorgio Vasari, a writer, artist, and architect devoted to his adoptive hometown of Florence. In an unashamedly partisan survey of Renaissance artists entitled *Lives of the Most Eminent Painters, Sculptors, and Architects*, Vasari explained that a Florentine goldsmith, Maso Finiguerra, had invented copperplate printing a century earlier.[12] Finiguerra was already a recognized master of the art of *niello*, where engraved silver objects such as knife hilts, cups, and belt buckles were inlaid with a contrasting black metal alloy, and he and others often recorded their designs by rubbing them with ink and "printing" them onto pieces of paper.[13] None of this was especially controversial—some of Finiguerra's niello prints still exist—but Vasari also anointed his fellow Florentine as the inventor of intaglio printing.[14] Unfortunately for Vasari's story, prints have since been found

Cy commence Jehan bocace
de Certald son liure intitule
de la Ruyne des nobles hom
mes et femmes. Lequel con
tient ensemble .ix. liures par
ticuliers comme il apperra
ou proces de ce present volu:
me. Et premierement le pro
logue du premier liure.

Diu strennue miles
et cetera. Bocace
commence ici son
premier prohesme
q̃ est de la intitulation de son
liure et dit ainsi. O cheua
lier prens ceste oeuure empraĩ
te de mon engin en quoy sont
traittez les maleureuses for

↞ One of nine pasted-in copperplate prints from the 1476 edition of Colard Mansion's *De casibus virorum illustrium*. Like contemporary woodcut prints, the engraving has been colored by hand.[15] (Photograph © 2015 Museum of Fine Arts, Boston.)

that place the first copperplate engravings in Germany's Rhine valley, sometime during the 1430s; Maso Finiguerra, born in Florence in 1426, would have had to have been a child prodigy in order to have had any influence on his German counterparts.[16]

Even so, the basic premise of Vasari's account is likely true. Engraving was a venerable practice, with roots in metalworking and jewelry that stretched back to ancient times. Both the Greeks and Romans had decorated the backs of handheld bronze vanity mirrors in this way, and medieval jewelers carried on the tradition by engraving silver and gold pieces with decorative patterns—and, like Maso Finiguerra, they had recorded their best work with a hasty smear of ink and a blank sheet of paper.[17] Within a few decades of the arrival of woodcut printing and inspired, perhaps, by the effortless reduplication of their carved designs, some anonymous German goldsmith or printer brought engraving and printing together to take the next leap forward in bookmaking.[18]

Engraving did not endear itself, at first, to those printers who tried it out. The first step in what was a lengthy, rigorous process was to transfer the design to be printed to a copper plate a millimeter or two thick. Some artists drew freehand on the plate with a sharpened stylus, scratching their design into the copper with the original work propped up next to a mirror so as to reverse it for the printing plate. Others sketched in chalk on paper before laying their drawing facedown on the copper and burnishing it thoroughly to transfer its chalky outlines onto the plate.

With the design transferred to the plate, the engraver took up a jeweler's "burin," a sharp metal tool capped with a wooden pommel that rested against the heel of the hand, and proceeded to engrave the plate. Slowly and with infinite care they pushed their burin along the lines of the design, biting out curls of copper as they went and leaving behind shallow channels and reservoirs in the metal.[19] It was a difficult task. Tracing even a straight line was difficult, and an engraver's heart must have sunk whenever their burin veered off its intended path. The only way to repair an error was to flip the plate over, hammer out the offending area, then turn it back over to be scraped and polished flat once more.[20]

Nor did the difficulties stop once the plate was engraved. Because the design is sunk into the plate's surface rather than being raised above it, the straightforward slathering-on of ink typical of relief printing was

⭠ Jost Amman's 1568 woodcut depicting an engraver at work. He is described as a "designer" in the accompanying verse and boasts that he can reproduce "Images of men and animals / Also plants of various kinds, / Script and capital letters, / Historical scenes and anything else that is requested." And, helpfully, "I can also engrave all of this on copper."[21]

out of the question. First, the plate had to be warmed to help the sticky, tacky ink flow into the smallest nooks and crannies; next, the plate was liberally daubed with ink, and the ink firmly rubbed into the hollows of the design; and finally, excess ink was wiped off with a series of increasingly fine rags.[22] The inked copper plate was placed onto the sliding bed of a mangle-like roller press, a sheet of dampened paper and several protective blankets laid atop it, and then the whole assemblage driven through the press with the turn of a handle.[23] As the sandwich of plate, paper, and blankets passed through the press, the moistened paper was forced into the hollows of the engraved plate to pick up its ink, along with a characteristic indentation—a "plate mark"—left by the edge of the plate itself.[24]

In short, intaglio printing was a slow and fussy process. It took minutes to ink, clean, and print a plate, which must have seemed like an eternity for woodcut printers used to churning out a page or more per minute. Moreover, printing from a copper plate was intrinsically, unavoidably *difficult*: amateurish intaglio printers produced faint, blotchy, and indistinct images, and clumsy handling could shorten a plate's useful life by subjecting it to unnecessarily severe pressures in an ill-adjusted press. By the eighteenth century, artists anxious to have their works faithfully reproduced often stipulated by name the printer who was to be entrusted with the job.[25]

In spite of all this, fifteenth-century printers such as Colard Mansion plowed on with the delicate, slow-moving method of intaglio printing. And of course, they all faced the same obstacle: how best to reconcile copperplate engravings with relief-printed movable type? In 1481, Nicolò di Lorenzo della Magna tackled the problem when he decided to illustrate a printed edition of Dante's *Divine Comedy* with engravings patterned after drawings by Botticelli.[26] Four years earlier, Colard Mansion had sidestepped the issue by printing engravings separately and pasting them into his books, but Nicolò della Magna—"Nicolò the Great," as the printer styled himself—was not a man to back down. Having printed the first few pages of the *Divine Comedy* with movable type, Nicolò proceeded to print the first of his knockoff Botticellis directly into the blank space left for that very purpose. He inked and wiped clean the engraved copper plate, aligned it with the blank space on his printed page of text, made ready with his roller press, and gingerly turned the handle.

The image was askew.

Frustrated, Nicolò tried again, only for the same thing to happen. No surviving copy of his *Divine Comedy* has printed images on more than its first two pages; the rest of the book's nineteen illustrations are all pasted into place. Each one was a tacit admission of defeat.[27]

Colard Mansion, for his part, fell back on woodcut illustrations for his follow-up to *De casibus*, a sumptuous, annotated edition of Ovid's *Metamorphoses*. *Ovide moralisé* took Mansion headlong into bankruptcy and was his last book.[28] The same pattern repeated all across Europe: bookmakers experimented with engravings only to revert to wooden blocks when the limitations of the new medium became apparent. More damning yet, woodcut tended to win out even when engraving had a head start: in the early twentieth century, a German academic named Erich von Rath identified nine European cities in which the first illustrated printed books all used copperplate engravings—and yet, many later works published in those same cities were unceremoniously downgraded to woodcut illustrations instead.[29] As far as the average letterpress printer was concerned, copperplate engraving was an almighty pain in the ass.

Artists, though, loved it. For printmakers such as Albrecht Dürer, intaglio printing offered a precision entirely absent from woodcut, an ability to faithfully reproduce fine details and subtle variations in tone with cross-hatching and lines of varying width.[30] Any competent engraver could inscribe a plate to a far higher level of detail than a comparable woodcutter, and for a skilled practitioner the advantages were substantial: a Dutch engraver named Lambert Suavius was said to have used a diamond-tipped stylus in his quest to create ever-finer lines.[31]

As engraving gained momentum in the art world, bookmakers

were forced to pay heed. By degrees they submitted to the indignity of placing copperplate engravings on separate pages, giving rise to the concept of the "plate" as a standalone illustration, and toyed with engraved title pages that married text and images in the form of decorative borders, their logo or coat of arms, and the title and author of the book.[32] (The florid handwriting of these nascent title pages came to be known as "copperplate," after the material on which it was inscribed.)[33] And though engraved plates were still agonizingly slow to produce, help soon arrived from an unexpected source.

The Renaissance is remembered as a buoyant tide of science, literature, and culture that carried Europe out of the Middle Ages and into the modern era. But progress toward a more intellectual way of life did not dampen the Continent's enthusiasm for robustly traditional pursuits such as jousting, territorial disputes, and outright war, and military technology advanced as steadily as did the arts. By the sixteenth century, knights, mercenaries, and martially inclined princes were marching into battle clad in iron-plate armor designed to repel arrows, swords, and lances.[34] But no armor yet had been invented that could protect a warrior from the needling gaze of his fashion-conscious peers, and armorers became couturiers too. Some suits made in Germany came complete with a rigid iron "skirt" that mimicked similar cloth garments, while others sported swelling, segmented upper-arm plates in the style of the puffed sleeves popular at the time.[35] Later, English knights could look forward to donning breastplates that bulged out and down toward the groin in imitation of the fashionable (and brazenly suggestive) "peascod" doublet.[36]

To satisfy their increasingly demanding customers, German armorers turned to a new metalworking technique that allowed them to engrave iron plates with honorific titles, intricate scenes of battle, and other fashionable motifs. But if copper was difficult to work with, iron was worse, and cunning German armorers looked to bend the subtle arts of chemistry to their purpose.[37]

Taking a cue from swordsmiths, who had been engraving steel blades for centuries, the armorers' new technique proceeded as follows.[38] First, a breastplate, helmet, or other component was coated with a protective "resist" such as a thin layer of paint or beeswax. Next, the armorer drew the desired design in the resist with a needle, scratching it away to reveal the naked iron beneath. Once the design was complete, the area was washed with a mildly acidic solution (the specific recipe varied from practitioner to practitioner), and when the remainder of the resist was removed the design had been etched into the metal surface.[39] Where a jeweler's burin would have skated harmlessly across the iron, a solution of ammonium chloride or nitric acid was more than capable of biting clearly defined channels and depressions into an iron plate, and, with this done, it was a simple matter to rub some lampblack, or soot, into the etched lines to bring out the design in sharp relief.[40]

Soon after its introduction, a German armorer named Daniel Hopfer of the town of Augsburg, Germany, took the craft of iron plate etching in a novel direction. The designs he etched into breastplates and gauntlets, he noticed, were reminiscent of the lines and hollows of an engraved printing plate, and sometime around the year 1490 he graduated from the fluted, curved surfaces of armor plating to rectangular iron plates etched in emulation of the copperplate prints of his time.[41] Tentatively dated to 1503 or 1504, Hopfer's print of *Conrad von der Rosen*, a surly jester-adviser at the court of Emperor Maximilian I, etched by an acid wash on an iron plate, marks the moment that intaglio printing transcended its manual roots.[42]

Iron, however, was too durable for its own good. Though an iron plate would yield to a blacksmith's hammer or an alchemist's acidic potions, its resistance to puny goldsmithing tools made correcting mistakes difficult. A solution emerged within the decade, when a Dutch

❧ Daniel Hopfer's 1503 or 1504 etching of Kunz (Conrad) von der Rosen, an adviser and alleged jester at the court of Emperor Maximilian I.

printer named Lucas van Leyden took Hopfer's acid-etching technique and applied it to conventional copper printing plates to stunning effect.[43] Van Leyden's scheme rapidly matured into a craft in its own right. First, a copper or zinc plate was heated on a stove or in an oven before an acid-resistant substance such as gum, wax, or resin was spread evenly across its surface. Once the resist had cooled and hardened, the design to be etched was transferred to the plate in the same way that armorers had always done it, with a sharp stylus, or "etching needle," drawn across the resist like a pencil across a page. Artists loved etching for just this reason: rather than trust a woodcutter or engraver to interpret their work, with a "grounded," or coated, copper plate before them and an etching needle in their hand artists such as

Lucas van Leyden and Albrecht Dürer were free to set down exactly the scenes they envisioned.[44]

Though artists found etching easier than engraving, it still took considerable skill to "bite" a design into a grounded copper plate. (Not coincidentally, "etch" comes from the old German *ezjan*, or *azjan*, "to be eaten.")[45] Some printers built a dam of wax around their plates and poured acid into the resulting basin; others stood their plates at an angle and repeatedly poured acid over them to etch out their lines bit by bit. The depth to which lines were bitten out was dependent upon how long the acid was in contact with the plate—deeper lines held more ink, and so printed with a richer color—and an accomplished etcher would sometimes fill in lines with varnish to prevent them from being etched too deeply. Worn plates could also be re-etched in order to deepen lines as they grew shallow after multiple impressions.[46] It was a challenging process, with ample opportunity to ruin the image. Writing in the nineteenth century, the landscape artist Samuel Palmer captured the contradictions of this expressive and occasionally frustrating medium:

> *[Etching is] an elegant mixture of the manual, chemical and calculative, so that its very mishaps and blunders (usually remediable) are a constant amusement. The tickling sometimes amounts to torture, but, on the whole, it raises and keeps alive a speculative curiosity—it has something of the excitement of gambling, without its guilt and its ruin.*[47]

By the start of seventeenth century, a hundred years after Daniel Hopfer had first branched out from armor to art, the most pressing wrinkles in his "manual, chemical and calculative" craft had been worked out, and by the end of the eighteenth century etching had supplanted woodcuts as the default medium for book illustration. As if celebrating its newfound ubiquity, the early decades of the nineteenth century saw etching put to work in producing what may be the most famous illustrated book in the English-speaking world: John James Audubon's fabled *The Birds of America*.[48]

⋙ • ⋘

Born in Haiti (then Saint-Domingue) in 1785, the son of a French slaver, plantation owner, and ship's captain, young John James Audubon appeared mostly average.[49] Spirited to France in 1789 in order to escape an imminent slave revolt, Audubon was a creative, physically adept child—he fenced, danced, and played music well, and later claimed to have studied art in Paris—but he chafed at the strictures of formal education.[50] Audubon returned to the Americas in 1803, sent to the family's Pennsylvania estate to avoid conscription into Napoleon's army, and there he settled into a comfortable routine of walking in the woods, sketching birds or shooting them as the mood took him, and neglecting the management of the estate.[51] After four years in Pennsylvania, the amateur naturalist decided to start a business, though he lacked his father's steely commercial instincts. In 1819, after presiding over a string of failed ventures, the state of Kentucky declared Audubon bankrupt and sent him to debtor's prison.[52]

As the calamity faded, Audubon's mind returned to his carefree days in the Pennsylvanian woods and he began to entertain the idea that his hobby could deliver him from penury. Thus it was that in 1820, and again in 1821, he and an acolyte named Joseph Mason spent months traveling the Ohio and Mississippi Rivers with rifles in one hand and paintbrushes in the other. When the pair returned to civilization, they had an unparalleled collection of watercolors in which Audubon's birds frolicked, fought, and preened in front of Mason's detailed backgrounds.

An attempt to publish the collection in Philadelphia came to nothing. The city's natural historians were still in thrall to Alexander Wilson, an immigrant Scot credited with founding American ornithology, and they did not want him dethroned even years after his death. And so, in 1826, Audubon sailed to Britain to seek a publisher.[53] He found one in Edinburgh, Scotland, in the form of an engraver named William Home Lizars, and together they hashed out a business plan:

Audubon would exhibit dramatic oil paintings of wildlife ("potboilers," he called them, referring to their deliberately arresting subject matter; one early painting depicted a trapped otter chewing off its own leg) to drum up interest while Lizars would at the same time engrave copperplate copies of Audubon's bird portraits for sale to the public. The printed, hand-colored plates would be sold by subscription, with five issues containing five plates each to be published each year.[54] A single issue cost two guineas—the equivalent of $10 then, and around $200 in today's money—and Audubon envisaged a run of eighty issues in total, encompassing more than four hundred separate plates divided among four volumes.[55] Subscribers could buy one issue or many, investing as much money as they pleased; *The Birds of America*, in other words, was crowdfunded.

Things did not start well. Audubon and Lizars disbanded their partnership after a colorists' strike halted work on the second issue, but the American found a new engraving firm in London and work soon began again.[56] For the next thirteen years, Audubon divided his time between Europe and America, wooing subscribers, stalking the woods, and painting in his studio, where he propped freshly shot birds into lifelike poses with taxidermy wire. And all the while, from the London offices of Robert Havell and son, engravers, the constituent issues of the masterpiece that was *The Birds of America* issued like clockwork.

Subscribers with the financial means and the patience to last out the print run were rewarded with an unprecedented work of art, printing, and bookmaking. As Audubon had promised, the 435 plates of *The Birds of America* came printed on sheets of "double elephant folio," the largest paper then available, with each page measuring 26 by 40 inches, or ten times the area of today's standard letter paper.[57] (It is tempting to call it the first coffee-table book, if only because it was large enough to physically serve as a coffee table.) Each sheet was given over to a life-size illustration of one or more birds, accompanied by a short engraved caption listing the species, sex, and age of the birds depicted. This simple arrangement was as much a product of Audubon's budding commercial sense as aesthetics: By law, certain of Britain's libraries had the right to demand a copy of all textual works published in the country, and Audubon could ill afford to donate even a single set of *The Birds of America.* Thus he banished his written observations of avian physiology, habits, and habitats to a modest companion work called *Ornithological Biography,* copies of which he magnanimously provided to the libraries at Oxford, Cambridge, Edinburgh, and more.[58] If a library wanted *The Birds of America,* it would have to pay for it like everyone else.

Each of the prints made by Robert Havell Jr. and his army of colorists, modeled after Audubon's original paintings, was a work of art in itself. Where William Lizars had engraved his plates in the old-fashioned manner, Havell both engraved *and* etched his, employing a time-consuming technique called "aquatint" to create subtle gradations of light and dark.[59] Having first engraved a plate to define its basic outlines, Havell next dusted it with powdered resin and heated it so that the resin's tiny granules melted and adhered to the plate's surface, mottling it with acid-resistant dots. Havell then varnished and etched the plate over and over again to define successively darker areas of tone. Each bath in nitric acid deepened the channels between the tiny resinous islands to create a microscopic stippling effect. It was a counterintuitive process, like painting in reverse: the first coat of varnish was applied to the brightest highlights so that they were not etched at all, and each subsequent coat of varnish expanded to cover darker and darker tones. When the varnish was removed and the plate was inked, the deepest channels (which had been exposed to the full course of acid washes) held the most ink, and so printed as the darkest tones; the shallowest channels, having been protected by the stopping-out varnish, held very little.[60]

Havell's prints were markedly better than Lizars's. Both men had employed painters to "color in" their prints, but Lizars's stark, black-and-white line engravings depended on the ability of those painters to suggest tone and contrast. Audubon scorned Lizars's efforts as "scarcely colored at all," even after the naturalist had provided detailed written instructions as to how the colors should be added. Havell's aquatints,

↞ Robert Havell's hand-colored aquatint print of the Columbia Jay, after John James Audubon's hand-drawn original. This reproduction is necessarily reduced from the 26-by-40-inch original.[61]

on the other hand, their shades of gray built in from the start, required only a simple wash of each color to achieve a rich variety of tones, and Audubon declared them "so greatly superior to the first two [issues] that I am told by all those who see it that I will do well altogether."[62]

His subscribers agreed. Audubon was feted by learned societies, affluent clients, and royalty across Europe and America, and Havell's prints were instrumental in persuading between 175 and 200 subscribers to see it through to the end, their sets of *The Birds of America* finally completed in 1839. Considerably more than half of all complete sets survive to this day; in 2010, an immaculate set bound in leather and housed in a dedicated mahogany cabinet sold for £7.3 million ($11.3 million), making it, for a time, the world's most expensive printed book.[63]

The Birds of America was also the swan song for copperplate printing. The chemical revolution that had begun when Daniel Hopfer first etched an iron plate was gathering pace—but more than that, the very role of the human artist was being called into question. The next hundred years would see the way that books were illustrated change beyond recognition.

11

Better Imaging Through Chemistry: lithography, photography, and modern book printing

Alois Senefelder, the man whose invention would change the way books are illustrated and later how they were printed in their entirety, was born in 1771 in the Bohemian capital, Prague.[1] Peter, Alois's father, was an actor by trade, whose outlook on life had been jaundiced by a career spent looking behind the curtain, and he was determined that his son should not similarly waste his life. Thus the adolescent Alois was packed off to Ingolstadt to study law, only to fall in with a crowd of precisely the kind of people that his father had warned him against. By 1789, having written, produced, and acted in a play entitled *Die Mädchenkenner,* or "The Connoisseurs of Girls," Alois Senefelder was obsessed with the stage.[2]

Peter died in 1791, before he could disabuse his son of his theatrical inclinations, and before long Alois had thrown himself wholeheartedly into the world of acting.[3] For two years he trod the boards in a variety of provincial theaters to little acclaim, eventually accepting that acting was not the best way to make a living. He turned instead to a series of plays he had written during his time away and decided to self-publish.[4] Senefelder had gained a passable knowledge of printing during the publication of *Die Mädchenkenner*, when he had watched his manuscript transformed into a printed book, though he had neither the equipment to print his plays nor any money to buy said equipment. Rather than abandon his plan, however, he set about creating his own unique method of printing.[5] It was an unorthodox thing to do—as if E. L. James, in possession of a manuscript entitled *Fifty Shades of Grey* but without a publisher, had decided to invent the Kindle.

Over the next few years, Senefelder tried out almost every known method of printing. He began his odyssey in a relatively conventional manner, engraving intaglio letters into metal plates in the Renaissance fashion, but gave up in frustration after failing to master the intricacies of the process. Next, he investigated movable type. Having somehow acquired a few lines' worth of type, Senefelder arranged his lead sorts into short passages before taking casts of them with a mixture of sand, clay, flour, and coal dust, and so built up a series of casts that represented a complete page of text. He poured sealing wax into each cast, producing waxy replicas of the original type, and successfully printed the resultant "stereotypes" using a small press.[6]

By now, though, Senefelder had been distracted by yet another kind of printing, and his experiments with sealing wax waned. On a grounded copper plate he was making good progress teaching himself to write backward with an etcher's needle. But here his lack of formal training weighed against him. He did not know how to correct the errors he made as he scratched out his writing-in-reverse, and so he created a kind of Wite-Out for etching, a greasy, acid-resistant concoction of wax, soap, and lampblack that allowed him to fill in mistakes before continuing.[7]

Senefelder quickly wore out his single copper plate and, as broke as ever, he looked for a more economical practice material. Glancing over at the slab of limestone he used as a mixing palette, he wondered: if he coated the stone with his waxy correcting fluid, might it not stand in for a grounded copper plate for the purposes of his writing practice? And if that were the case, who was to say he could not etch his writing into the stone itself? It took a little finessing, and tested Senefelder's patchy knowledge of chemistry, but he eventually succeeded in grounding, etching, and printing with his stone palette as if it were an engraved copper plate.[8] For the first time, his goal of printing was within reach.

Soon after this, one day in 1796, Senefelder's mother appeared at the door of his workshop to ask for a piece of paper on which to write a laundry list. "My own supply had been used up by pulling proofs," Senefelder wrote—had the perpetually penniless printer looted the house of all his mother's paper too?—and anyway, his writing ink had dried out, so he grabbed a cake of his waxy correcting ink and, wielding it like a crayon, used it to take his mother's dictation on a polished printing stone. The locally quarried limestone had exactly the right degree of porosity to take the ink well, and later, after the laundry crisis had been dealt with, Senefelder's curiosity went to work. He built a retaining wall of wax around the perimeter of the stone, poured in etching acid, waited five minutes, and then poured it off. His mother's laundry list stood proud of the stone's surface by about a playing card's thickness. Spreading ink across it with a makeshift squeegee in the form of a piece of cloth wrapped around a stiff board, he laid a piece of paper onto the stone and took a passable impression from it. First intaglio printing and now, less than a year later, printing in relief; perhaps, mused Senefelder, there was something in this use of stones for printing.[9]

But still he was stymied by a lack of cash. Senefelder applied to join the Bavarian army, where, he hoped, he might earn enough money to revive his dreams of self-publishing, but he was dismissed after a single night in the barracks because of his foreign birthplace. At his lowest ebb, Senefelder traveled to Munich with the intention of selling his inventions to a music printer who worked there, only to bump into an old theater acquaintance, a composer named Gleissner, who had recently had some of his own music engraved and printed. Sensing a potential business partner, Senefelder pleaded first with Gleissner's wife and subsequently the composer himself, telling them that his "stone-printing" was the future of music publishing. Gleissner was persuaded to establish a print shop in which Senefelder could work, and for a time the two men navigated the middle ground between riches and penury, oscillating between success and failure almost with each successive print job they took on. Senefelder found it difficult to train others in his stone-printing methods, whether they were jobbing printers or discharged soldiers, and tried to engineer out as many of the process's variables as possible. His efforts met with varying degrees of success—one of his experimental presses employed a three-hundred-pound counterweight that often detached from its ten-foot-high perch—and the quality of the pair's print jobs inevitably declined whenever Senefelder was called away from the presses.[10]

Neither did the printer's fortunes improve when he spent time away from the shop. In or about 1793, he presented prints made by his stone-etching method to the learned fellows of Bavaria's Academy of Sciences, stressing the frugality of his process and explaining, to appreciative noises from his audience, that the press on which he had pulled these impressions had cost a mere six gulden. Later, he received a letter from the vice president of the academy, who declared that its members had voted in favor of Senefelder's invention, and who offered, in light of his expenses, a prize of twelve gulden—less than a month's salary. The academy's polite indifference was also a rebuke.[11]

Five years later, something very close to magic happened in Gleissner and Senefelder's modest print shop. By now Gleissner had taken charge of penciling music directly onto the printing stones, whereupon Senefelder would trace Gleissner's draft with his waxy correcting fluid (he now thought of it as "stone ink") before washing the stones with acid to leave the music standing out in relief. Senefelder's own penmanship was not up to writing music in reverse, and so when Gleissner was indisposed Senefelder would pencil out a draft on paper, wet it, and press it onto a printing stone. A mirror-image ghost of the music, perceptible enough to trace over, would transfer itself to the stone. With the same persistent logic that had brought him this far, Senefelder asked himself:

was there some way to write out music on paper—the right way 'round, so to speak—and then transfer it directly to the stone, with no need to trace over it afterward?[12]

As part of his attempts to transfer ink to a printing stone, Senefelder had cause to dip a sheet of paper bearing his waxy stone ink into a bath of water. The water had a few rainbow drops of oil floating on its surface, and he saw that the oil clung to the writing on the paper as he removed it. Tearing a page out of an old printed book, he soaked it in a solution of gum arabic—a known oleophobic, or oil-repelling, substance—and waited impatiently for the paper to dry. He laid the gummed page flat on a handy stone and dabbed it with diluted printing ink, made up according to Gutenberg's traditional recipe of pigment suspended in oil, and watched with glee as the ink shrank from the white spaces of the paper's surface and onto the printed letters. He laid a clean sheet of paper atop it, ran the lot through his engraving press, and pulled the top sheet back to reveal a "very good transfer, in reverse, of course," of the original printed page.[13]

The principle of the thing was simple. The torn-out original page had been printed with traditional, greasy printing ink, and so the oil-hating gum solution leached into the page everywhere *except* the printed lettering. Senefelder's own ink, with its oily pigment suspended in water, separated upon touching the page so that the pigment fled to the oleophilic lettering and the water retreated to the oleophobic gummed areas. To a chemist, it would have been an unremarkable observation; to Senefelder, it was an epiphany. He found that he could make only fifty or so impressions using his stack of stone, gummed paper, and printing paper before the original page disintegrated, but that if he drew directly onto a stone with a crayon of his trusty stone ink he could print as many copies as he liked.[14] Though the word had yet to be coined, he had invented lithography, from the Greek *lithos*, for "stone," and *graphein*, for "writing."[15]

In its final form, the lithographic process combined all that Senefelder had learned during his years of experimentation. First, a slab of Bavarian limestone was polished flat and an image drawn upon it with Senefelder's greasy stone ink, which was absorbed into the limestone's pores. Next, the stone was cleaned with dilute nitric acid—not to etch it but instead to remove all stray traces of grease from its surface—before being "desensitized" to any further contamination with a wash of oleophobic gum arabic. To print the image, the stone was washed with water before a layer of greasy ink was applied with a roller. The two substances retreated to their preferred areas of the stone—the ink to the waxy writing, the water to the gummed white space—and an impression was taken.[16]

To Senefelder's eyes, lithography was patently superior to the old regime of woodcut carvings and engraved copper. Drawing an image on a stone was child's play in comparison to etching or engraving a copper plate, while the stone itself was far more robust than a wooden block. And lithography was fast too: Senefelder could print 150 impressions per hour when conventional copperplate printers would struggle to complete a handful of prints in the same time.[17] Because the printing surface was perfectly flat, without ridges or troughs to be gradually worn flat, a lithographic stone could theoretically produce a near-unlimited number of impressions; in practice, however, it more often happened that a stone would be ground down and polished for reuse, or outright "cancelled"—that is, deliberately defaced to increase the value of surviving prints—long before its usability became an issue.[18]

Over the next twenty years, Alois Senefelder developed an arsenal of techniques for applying designs to his limestone slabs and parlayed his innovation into a veritable empire of lithographic printing. A calligrapher such as Herr Gleissner could write directly on a stone (albeit backward) with a steel pen dipped in greasy lithographic ink, while for artists a paintbrush sufficed.[19] (As discovered by Henri Toulouse-Lautrec, the French painter, printer, and absinthe fanatic, even a humble toothbrush could be pressed into service to spatter a stone with a hazy spray of ink.)[20] For the less artistically gifted, an existing drawing, map, or blueprint could be copied onto a stone by means of a pantograph—a contraption of levers and joints that mirrored a user's movements from left to right while preserving vertical motions.[21]

These were ancillary benefits when compared to lithography's unique ability to reproduce *any* two-dimensional image, whether a manuscript, a printed text, or an engraving, as long as it could be rendered in Senefelder's waxy "chemical ink." The inventor described how one could print a traditional, engraved copper plate prepared with his chemical ink before impressing the resultant print, its ink still wet, onto a lithographic stone from which further copies could be taken. The same technique could be applied to a forme of movable type, a woodcut block, or even handwritten text—anything that could be printed with lithographic ink was a candidate for Senefelder's copying process. Senefelder boasted of how Munich's city clerk took down minutes with a pen dipped in lithographic ink, and how, with his notes transferred to a litho stone, copies could be delivered to council members within the hour.[22] Newspaper printers later worked out how to speed up printing even further by transferring a printed proof of the day's edition onto multiple stones so that it could be churned out on many presses at once.[23] And of course, there remained Senefelder's trumpeted ability to replicate any existing printed book simply by treating its pages with gum before "printing" them onto lithographic stones and then printing new copies from the mirror images on the prepared stones.[24]

Lithography, then, was miraculous. And unlike Johannes Gutenberg, who had been unceremoniously relieved of his own miracle in the courts of medieval Mainz, Alois Senefelder was determined to cling to his invention. In 1799 he was granted an exclusive license to carry out "chemical printing" in Bavaria, and he successfully patented the lithographic process in London a year later.[25] He established lithographic printing houses across Germany, England, and France (where the Teutonically direct *chemische Druckerei*, or "chemical printing," was supplanted by the more picturesque *lithographie*); and in 1819 he wrote and published what remains the definitive text on lithographic printing.[26]

Senefelder's invention only grew in stature. When *The Birds*

⇜ A "chromolithograph" made using a series of lithographic stones printed with colored ink. *Left,* in this depiction of a lithography studio, a lithographic stone is sanded flat; *center,* an artist copies an image onto a prepared stone; and *right,* a printer tends to a lithographic press. Louis Prang, whose studio produced this print, is considered to be the father of the modern American Christmas card; by the 1880s, his company was printing in excess of five million cards each year using the lithographic process.[27]

of America was reissued between 1840 and 1844, a few years after Senefelder's death, its copperplate engravings were replaced by lithographs modeled after Audubon's original paintings.[28] Color lithography arrived, in which a series of stones were used to print a different color each.[29] And lithography fired the imaginations of a succession of artists too: like the fibers on the surface of a sheet of paper, the minute pores of a limestone slab took up more or less pigment as a crayon of Senefelder's waxy ink swept across them, creating the illusion of smooth shifts from light to dark like aquatint etchings. Lithographic prints from masters such as Goya, Manet, Degas, and Picasso became sought-after works of art.[30]

Not bad for a failed playwright from small-town Bavaria.

Today, virtually all books are printed using the lithographic process, the paper version of this one included. But lithography did not have things all its own way. Toward the end of the eighteenth century, as Alois Senefelder toiled in his Munich workshop, an Englishman named Thomas Bewick was busy bringing the long-dead technique of woodblock printing back to life. Bewick found that by cutting against the grain of the wood with an engraver's burin (rather than with it, as his medieval predecessors had done) he could create a durable and long-lived printing surface, and so "wood engraving" was born.[31] Bewick's technique was a great success: wood was cheap and skilled engravers were ten a penny, while the engravings they produced on wood rivaled those on copper in terms of detail and handily outlasted them on the press. Even better, wood engraving was a relief printing method, like movable type; illustrations and text could be locked into a forme together and printed with a single pull of the press.[32]

Wood engraving, though, was the least of lithography's worries. Developed separately on both sides of the English Channel, by Louis-Jacques-Mandé Daguerre and William Henry Fox Talbot respectively, and unveiled near-simultaneously by both men in 1839, the new art of photography was as futuristic as wood engraving was old-fashioned. It shook the world of printing to its very foundations.[33]

Fundamentally, both the "daguerreotype" and "talbotype" processes (neither Daguerre nor Talbot labored under an excess of modesty) depended on chemical compounds that reacted to light, though they differed in the details. Daguerre's method produced one-off "positive" images: each of his silvered copper plates, having been exposed to light in a camera, was then treated to develop an image that faithfully reproduced the light and dark tones of the photographed scene. Talbot's camera, on the other hand, produced reusable paper negatives that could be used to make as many positive copies as desired.[34] Daguerreotypes were crisp and detailed in comparison to talbotypes, which were often marred by shadows of the negative's paper fibers, but there was room for both systems to flourish. It became the fashionable thing to carry about a daguerreotype of one's family, while Talbot's infinitely reproducible negatives promised to revolutionize book illustration.[35]

In 1844, Talbot published the first volume of *The Pencil of Nature*, an illustrated tour of art, architecture, and nature—and the first

➛ A view of the boulevards of Paris. This was the second plate from William Henry Fox Talbot's *The Pencil of Nature*. His "talbotype" process required only a comparatively short exposure, but even so, the pedestrians and carriages that traversed the camera's field of view did not linger long enough to be captured.[36]

mass-produced book to be photographically illustrated. It was a critical and technical triumph, worthy of mention in the same breath as Gutenberg's 42-line Bible or Audubon's *Birds of America*, but it was a financial disaster. Every illustration in every copy was a photograph that had to be developed on costly silver-treated paper and then "tipped in," or pasted onto the page. This, combined with Talbot's lack of business acumen and a haphazard approach to marketing, ensured that the profits were marginal.[37] Worse still, talbotypes faded with alarming rapidity: photographs at one exhibition of Talbot's work were declared to be "fading before the eyes of the nations assembled."[38]

With the photographic genie out of the bottle, Talbot and his competitors raced to pin it to the page. The problem they faced was that printing had always been an obstinately binary craft: either there was an embossed surface, a recessed line, or a speck of waxy crayon to collect ink, or there was not. Technically speaking, photographs were binary too—every sensitized molecule of silver nitrate formed a single pixel, switched on or passed over by incoming photons—but these molecular pixels were too small for the naked eye to see, and photographs had a subtlety of tone that was at odds with printing's blunt, on-off nature. To truly marry books and photographs, printers needed to convert analog photography to digital print.

In 1839, the same year that Daguerre and Talbot had revealed their respective inventions to the world, a Scottish lawyer-turned-scientist named Mungo Ponton discovered that paper coated with potassium dichromate, a compound often used to tan leather, changed color on exposure to light.[39] Others found that the effect was strongest in paper that had been sized with organic substances such as gelatin, and so "dichromated gelatin" was born—a miraculous material that hardened and became insoluble when exposed to light.[40]

Talbot saw dichromated gelatin as the solution to his problem. Taking a cue from aquatint etching, whose tiny resin islands were too small for the eye to see, he realized that if he could print a black-and-white image made up of small enough dots of ink then the human eye would obligingly smooth out the gaps between them. As such, in 1852, he patented the use of a "photographic veil" to break an image into a field of discrete dots. His idea was simple, though its execution was not: Having coated a copper plate with photosensitive gelatin, he placed a sheet of fine gauze over it before exposing it to a light source so that it partially hardened into a regular pattern of dots. Next, he replaced the gauze with a paper photographic negative and again shone light through it and onto the partially exposed copper plate.[41] The result was that the gelatin on the plate hardened into minuscule dots that were located according to the weave of the gauze and sized according to the brightness of the negative. Once etched in the manner of an aquatint plate, the little moats around the hardened gelatin dots trapped more or less ink accordingly, and the inked "halftone" image could be printed like a copperplate engraving.[42]

With time, Talbot's idea was expanded and improved upon—it was discovered that exposing a positive image onto the gelatin-treated plate, rather than a negative, allowed the creation of a relief image—and by the end of the nineteenth century halftoning had become the de facto standard for the mass reproduction of printed photographs.[43] Relief halftone images could be fixed in a forme along with movable type, letting words and photographs coexist on a single page, and they could survive any number of trips through a conventional printing press. The "resolution" of printed halftones could be varied by using coarser or finer screens to accommodate rough newsprint or smooth, shiny art paper. (Ironically, halftone illustrations were often banished to separate

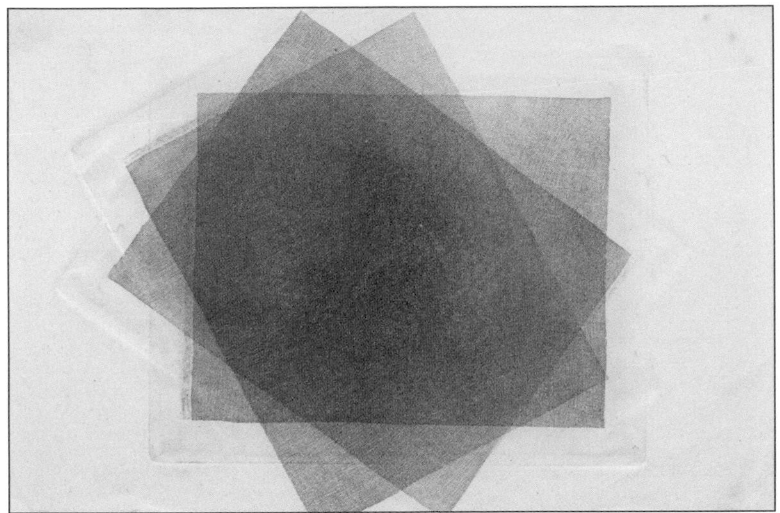

⇜ An image of Talbot's "photographic veils," the overlapping sheets of gauze with which he made halftone prints. Although this is a photograph of a set of halftone screens, it is *not* a halftone print; instead, Talbot printed this image with a time-consuming etching method called "photogravure" that was usually confined to expensive artistic prints.[44]

leaves of expensive photographic paper, leaving a book's text to slum it on cheaper stock. The standalone illustration, or "plate," was a tough beast to kill.)[45] If you have read an illustrated book, newspaper, or magazine printed between 1880 and 1960, then you have almost certainly seen halftone relief printing at work.[46]

Thus lithography's thunder was stolen for a third time: first wood engraving, then photography, and now halftone relief printing. But not all was lost. In 1853, almost in passing, William Henry Fox Talbot discovered that the same dichromated gelatin that

hardened with exposure to light also repelled water—and so, conversely, attracted greasy lithographic ink. A French chemist named Alphonse-Louis Poitevin built on Talbot's discovery to patent what he called "photolithograpy" in 1855, where a gelatin-treated sheet of tissue paper was exposed to a photographic negative. Once the unhardened gelatin was washed away, the tissue could be laid on a supporting surface, inked with greasy ink, and printed from. Poitevin's was a modest innovation, capable of reproducing only high-contrast, line-drawn originals before the tissue was damaged beyond repair, but he had succeeded in bringing photography and lithography together for the first time.[47]

In 1860, Col. Henry James of the Ordnance Survey, Britain's state mapping agency, gave photolithography its first big break. Tasked with printing copies of the OS's maps, James employed Poitevin's photolithography but added a twist of his own. To duplicate a given map, James first photographed it before exposing the negative onto a dichromated gelatin tissue. But rather than print directly from the fragile tissue, as Poitevin had done, James inked it with greasy lithographic ink, laid it on top of a zinc plate (hence "photozincography," as he called his system), and ran the lot through a lithographic press. The ink clung to the minute graining on the surface of the plate to create, in effect, a lithographic stone without the stone, from which many more copies could be printed.[48] At first, James confined his attentions to maps, but the lure of more famous works led him to print an astonishingly faithful reproduction of the Domesday Book, England's medieval register of land ownership, and soon other printers adopted his "zinco" process. A facsimile edition of Shakespeare's First Folio arrived in 1866, to be followed by other rare manuscripts and books.[49] Halftone lithographed images arrived the same year.[50]

⧼ (*Opposite*) A halftone photograph published in a newspaper before 1913. Halftone printing was crude in comparison to photogravure and other more involved methods of reproducing photographs. Its saving grace was that it worked with, not against, movable type.

It was James's introduction of metal plates—the ironic removal of the "litho" from "lithography"—that sparked the first real change in lithography's fortunes. As well as being lighter and more robust than stone, zinc (and later aluminum) made it possible for the first time to print lithographic images with the newfangled rotary presses that were gradually replacing traditional flatbed models. The one problem that remained was the tendency for the images on those metal plates to wear away after repeated impressions, and so rotary lithographic printing remained a niche occupation into the twentieth century.[51]

Thus it was that in the early twentieth century many books were still produced using well-worn methods such as wood engraving and movable type, even if rotary presses and automated typecasting machines had rather advanced things since Gutenberg's time. In 1904, however, one of the few lithographic believers, a New Jersey printer named Ira Rubel, was about to make a discovery that would overturn the old order.

Rubel was supervising the operation of his rotary lithographic press when a worker sheepishly brought him a misprinted sheet of paper. Rubel's press, like many lithographic presses of its time, was a partly automated hybrid of flatbed and rotary designs. Sheets of paper were pressed against the lithographic stone in the bed of the press by a cylinder that rolled along it like a rolling pin over pastry dough.[52] Paper was fed in manually, sheet by sheet, and an inattentive operator would occasionally miss a beat. When this happened, as it just had, the inked litho stone would leave its print on the cushioning rubber surface of the impression cylinder—the "blanket," as it was called—so that the *next* sheet of paper to be fed through the press would be printed on both sides: once by the litho stone, as usual, and again by the ink left on the blanket cylinder. As he scolded his assistant for the mistake, Rubel inspected the double-printed sheet. It was printed on both sides, as was to be expected, but what he had not anticipated was that the

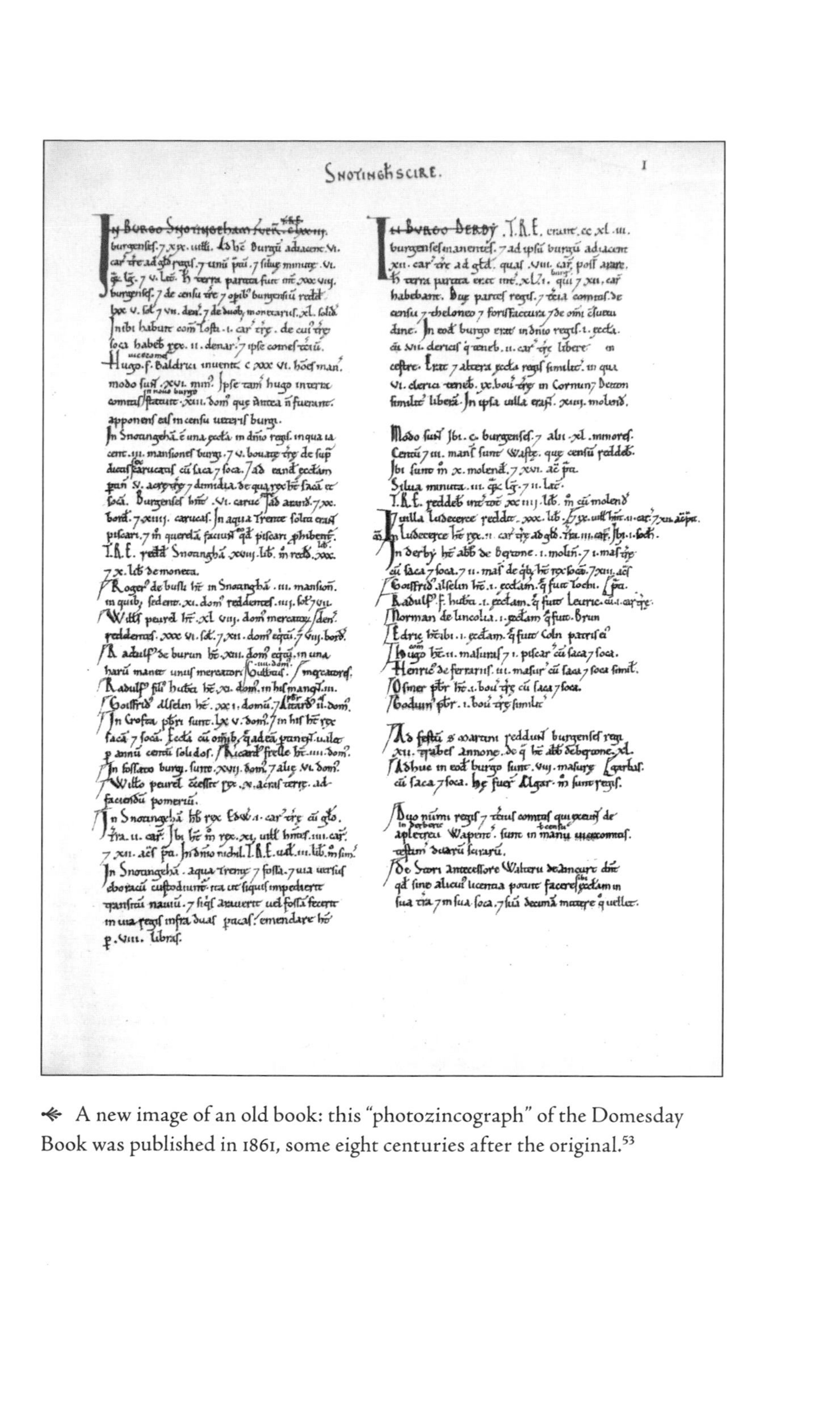

SNOTINGHSCIRE. I

A new image of an old book: this "photozincograph" of the Domesday Book was published in 1861, some eight centuries after the original.[53]

extra impression, the one left by the rubber blanket, was sharper than the first.[54]

The discovery of what came to be called "offset lithography" was a happy accident indeed. Though Rubel died within a few years of that fateful incident, others adapted the principle of offset lithography to full rotary presses. These three-cylinder machines comprised an inked lithographic cylinder (surmounted by a cascade of smaller rollers that transferred ink and water to it); a "blanket" or offset cylinder below it that received the inked image; and lastly an impression cylinder at the bottom to press the paper against the blanket. The soft rubber blanket was kinder to metal litho plates than a direct impression on paper and so prolonged the plates' useful lives, and it conformed to almost any moderately flat printing medium so that cheap, rough cardboard was as tractable as glossy photographic paper. And of course, as Ira Rubel had realized, the resulting printed image was sharper to boot.[55] There was almost no aspect of lithographic printing that was not improved.

By the 1960s, web-fed offset lithographic presses had united with photolithography to be crowned as the undisputed champions of mass-produced printing. The combined process was versatile, cheap, and adaptable to almost any kind of printing. First, the contents of the book, magazine, or newspaper to be printed were laid out however its makers desired—text might be set using movable type, a Linotype or Monotype machine, or the "cold type" of their phototypesetting replacements; images could be woodcut prints, paintings, drawings, or photographs—the methods employed made no difference. Once each page had been laid out in its "camera-ready" form and its components pasted onto a backing board, each page was captured as a photographic negative that in turn was exposed onto a photosensitized metal plate. Finally, these ready-made lithographic plates were wrapped around the cylinder of a rotary press, ready to be printed.[56]

It is part of the enduring appeal of lithography that it weathered the move to computer-designed books with little fuss. Each of the pages in the printed edition of this book is essentially a single illustration—a combination of text and imagery broken down into pixels too small for the eye to see—that has been etched onto an aluminum plate with preternatural precision by a computer-guided laser and printed in an offset lithographic press. Thanks to Alois Senefelder, William Henry Fox Talbot, and their successors, when we read a book's text, we are looking at a picture too.[57]

Part 4

FORM

12

Books Before the Book: papyrus scrolls and wax tablets

When we left ancient Egypt for China and Europe, the Egyptians had for millennia been writing hieroglyphic texts with brush and ink on papyrus. Of necessity, we skirted around the next step up in their hierarchy of writing needs: once you have something to write about, something to write with, and something to write on, what comes next? For the Egyptians, it was the papyrus scroll, the ancestor of the book.

About five thousand years ago, in the twilight of prehistory, the antagonistic kingdoms of Lower and Upper Egypt were united by a mythical king named Menes. Attacked by his own hunting dogs, Menes was said to have surfed to safety on the back of a friendly crocodile, founding the city of Crocodilopolis where his reptilian rescuer deposited him on the shore of Lake Moeris. Another story had him diverting the mighty Nile to make room for his new capital city of

Memphis. But Menes was not just a swashbuckling man of action; he was cultured too, as demonstrated by his invention of the concept of restaurant-style table service, and for pioneering the practice of eating in a reclining posture that later became emblematic of Roman decadence.

As befitted such a legendary figure, Menes had flair even in death. Said to have been Egypt's first human rather than divine, ruler, he met a sticky end when the now-unemployed gods sent an enraged hippopotamus from the waters of the Nile to kill their mortal successor.[1] Menes remains today a source of much debate among Egyptologists: Was he a real person, or a conflation of several figures? When precisely did he reign? Did he establish the "dynastic" era of the pharaohs, or was he the last of the predynastic kings?[2] Most important of all, is it really possible to ride a crocodile?

The reality, most likely, is that Menes was a fictionalized representation of a real king named Narmer, who took the throne of a unified Egypt around 3000 BCE.[3] Narmer's reign is considerably better attested to in the archaeological record than that of his legendary counterpart, and his reputation as a shrewd ruler survives today. He and his heirs brought together the disjointed bureaucratic machinery of the "Two Lands" to function as an integrated whole; they instituted censuses of people, livestock, and land; and they sought out efficiencies of scale including centralized grain stocks.[4]

All this caused a dramatic increase in the flow of information among ancient Egypt's inhabitants and institutions. Whether in the form of religious instructions, tax codes, or the everyday records of government business, human knowledge was growing too unwieldy to be held solely in one's head or to be passed along via oral storytelling. The Mesopotamians had already transformed clay counting tokens into cuneiform writing a century or two before Narmer took the throne, and hieroglyphics were not long to follow. Over the space of a century or less, straddling the transition from the predynastic period to Narmer's newly united Egypt, the Egyptians conjured up a full-fledged writing system, developed brushes and ink with which to write it, and invented sheets of papyrus on which to set it down.[5] In hindsight, it is little wonder that Thoth got the credit.

The Egyptians invented something else, too, during that frantic period at the dawn of writing. To borrow the *Oxford English Dictionary*'s words on the subject, Egypt's scribes had figured out how to combine individual sheets of papyrus to make "portable volume[s] consisting of a series of written, printed, or illustrated pages bound together for ease of reading"; they had invented the book, in other words, in the form of the papyrus scroll.[6] As evidenced by the papyri preserved by Egypt's arid climate, and as described in Pliny's second-century buyer's guide, the books of the ancient world were made from long series of papyrus sheets trimmed to matching heights and pasted together, to be rolled up for storage and unrolled for reading. What we do not know, however, is why the scroll ever came about in the first place.

Most theories revolve around papyrus's physical properties. The fibrous pith of the papyrus reed is prone to fraying, and a single sheet of papyrus has four exposed edges ready to unravel upon careless handling. Pasted into a scroll, however, a sheet presents only two edges to the reader's mercy.[7] Papyrus is relatively brittle too—folding and refolding a sheet will eventually cause it to crack and fray—but scrolls were gently rolled so as to avoid this. And yet, neither explanation is entirely plausible. Ancient scrolls are often found with their lower edges rubbed away by their readers' clothing; and when, much later, the paged book made its entrance, early bookmakers found that sheets of papyrus were robust enough to be folded into pages.[8]

In the end, it may simply be that the scroll was the easiest way to keep writing once a single sheet of papyrus was full. Having mixed a little flour and water into a paste, trimmed a new sheet to match the first, and then glued the two together, a scribe could continue writing, adding as many sheets as needed.[9] This easy extensibility, coupled with scrolls' inbuilt protection against fraying and folding, meant that scrolls were both more convenient and more durable than single sheets of papyrus.

The apparent simplicity of the scroll belied a sophisticated finished article. Joins between pages were always arranged so that each sheet overlapped the one to its left—the Egyptians' hieroglyphic and demotic scripts ran from right to left and so a scribe's pen would slip easily over a joint rather than catch on an exposed edge.[10] (The Greeks and Romans, who wrote from left to right, rotated their scrolls by 180 degrees to achieve the same effect.)[11] Some scroll makers "dovetailed" their joints to further improve the writing experience: each of the two overlapping sheets at a join was composed of two crosswise layers of papyrus pith, and by carefully delaminating and cutting away one of the interior layers, joins could be reduced to a manageable three plies thick, not four. Additionally, a scroll's sheets were always aligned so that the fibers on its writing surface ran horizontally, which made for a smoother writing experience and saved the horizontal fibers from being stretched too tightly around the scroll as it was rolled up.[12]

Thus the book was born, at least as far as the Egyptians, Greeks, and Romans would have recognized it, and thus it would live on for more than three thousand years to come.

The earliest known papyrus scroll was found—where else?—in an Egyptian tomb. In 1937, excavations at the opulent tomb of Hemaka, an adviser to King Narmer's great-great-grandson Den, turned up a single papyrus scroll, flattened a little and ensconced in a circular wooden box.[13] The chronology of Egypt's early history is a little rickety, and so guesses as to when Hemaka was buried are necessarily vague, though Den's coronation as pharaoh is thought to have occurred around 2970 BCE.[14] Whenever it was that Hemaka died, the fact that a scroll went with him to the afterlife demonstrates that the Egyptians had taken to pasting together sheets of papyrus no more than a few generations after the invention of hieroglyphics.[15]

Hemaka's roll of papyrus is blank. This is a perplexing state of affairs, since hieroglyphs were found on a host of other grave offerings found alongside the scroll (including Hemaka's name and title inscribed on an alabaster vase), but the one artifact dedicated solely to writing was untouched.[16] To the degree that scholars are willing to venture an opinion on all this, the consensus seems to be that Hemaka's scroll must have been some kind of funerary offering, a simulacrum of a book that was as accurate as it had to be in the circumstances, but that is as far as it goes.[17] The first written Books of the Dead were still more than a thousand years away, and evidently Hemaka had not been expected to need any reading material in the afterlife.[18]

The written papyrus bookroll is absent from the archaeological record for many centuries after Hemaka's death. In 2010, for example, a few tantalizing but illegible scraps of papyrus were retrieved from the ruins of an ancient harbor on the shores of the Red Sea. The harbor was dated to around 2600 BCE, but it is not clear if the papyrus fragments came from larger scrolls.[19] Later, from 2400 BCE or so, scrolls begin to taunt Egyptologists from the walls of tombs, inscribed as the hieroglyphs 𓏛 and 𓏜 (the first is sealed with a dab of clay, the second with clay and twine), but many of the tombs decorated with these carvings of scrolls are devoid of any actual scrolls.[20]

Gradually, however, archaeologists have pushed the date of the earliest known scrolls further into the past. The frontier now extends back to around 1900 BCE in the form of the so-called Prisse Papyrus, held in the vaults of the Bibliothèque nationale de France and widely acknowledged to be the oldest book in the world.[21]

The Prisse Papyrus was spirited out of Egypt in the mid-nineteenth century by Achille-Constant-Théodore Émile Prisse d'Avennes, a French engineer with a buccaneering streak. In 1827, at the age of nineteen, Prisse d'Avennes set out for Greece to help fight against the occupying Ottoman Turks. He later traveled on to India, where he served as secretary to the governor-general, then returned to Egypt, where he was happy to bend his loyalties in order to work for the Turkish regime

Statue of a scribe from Egypt's eighteenth dynasty, circa 1426–1400 BCE. Statues like this have been dated to a thousand years earlier, around the same time as the earliest written papyri.[22]

as a civil engineer.[23] But in 1836 the headstrong Prisse was summarily ejected from government employ. Dubbing himself "Idris Effendi" and donning the garb of a sheikh, he set out into Egypt's monument-strewn deserts as the self-declared guardian of its tombs, temples, and pyramids. By 1839 he had settled down in a suite of rooms in the temple of Karnak at Thebes, Egypt's ancient capital, where he copied down hieroglyphic inscriptions and took papier-mâché molds of the carvings that tourists chipped off as souvenirs and locals dismantled for building materials.[24] The most persistent tomb raiders were chased off with the aid of Prisse's rifle and a French tricolor that he planted in the ground like a battle standard.[25]

In May 1843, in the face of increasing vandalism and tomb robbery, Prisse attempted a more audacious form of "conservation." Under cover of darkness, he and a few workmen entered the "Hall of Ancestors," a room at Karnak dating to the fifteenth century BCE, and relieved it of sixty-one stone panels commemorating the bloodline of the pharaoh Thutmose III.[26] It took a year of subterfuge, bribery, and bravery to get the panels as far as Alexandria, where Prisse begged the French vice consul for help in shipping them to France. The official demurred, aware of the illegality of Prisse's enterprise, but reassured him that "You have succeeded so well up to the present in an operation I would have considered impossible that you cannot fail at the port."[27] A harried Prisse d'Avennes managed to get the panels aboard ship without the vice consul's help and fled with them to France as the Egyptian government raged at his back. It would be fourteen years before he was allowed to return.[28]

Prisse had escaped with more than the Karnak panels. Amid his jamboree of careful looting, the archaeologist had taken the time to purchase an ancient papyrus scroll from a workman who claimed to be holding it for a friend. Prisse suspected, though never proved, that the workman had excavated and concealed the scroll while on Prisse's payroll, and the Frenchman bristled at having to pay twice for the same artifact.[29] By the time Prisse got back to France he had recovered his composure, and in 1847 Prisse published the contents of the scroll to amazement from the archaeological community.[30]

The text of Prisse's find contained the collected wisdom of an official named Ptahhotep, the head of government, or vizier, under Djedkare Isesi of Egypt's fifth dynasty of pharaohs. Early guesses at the scroll's age and that of its text placed both at a staggering 5,500 years old; today's more measured consensus dates the text to between the late twenty-fourth and the early twenty-third centuries BCE, and Prisse's copy is thought to have been made around 1900 BCE. However one chooses to count, the Prisse Papyrus is at least 4,000 years old.[31]

Ptahhotep's pithy maxims were all about life and how to live it, exhorting his readers to be humble, quiet, and honorable. Humility was chief above all: "be not proud because thou art learned," he wrote, "but discourse with the ignorant man as with the sage," adding that "silence is more profitable unto thee than abundance of speech."[32] The sanctity of marriage came in a close second: "if thou desire to continue friendship in any abode wherein thou enterest, be it as a master, as brother, or as friend; wheresoever thou goest, beware of consorting with women." If a man succeeded in marrying a woman without offending her male relatives, he was encouraged to "fill her stomach, clothe her back [and] gladden her heart during thy lifetime."[33]

But while Ptahhotep focused on earthly matters, his fellow literati were a morbid lot. One scroll, copied soon after the Prisse Papyrus, was written from the point of view of the pharaoh Amenemhat I, assassinated in the middle of the eighteenth century BCE by a cabal of concubines and eunuchs.[34] Other, more practical, books were equally in thrall to death and dying: two medical scrolls, one a gynecological treatise and the other a veterinary book, have been dated to around the same time as the Prisse Papyrus, and both are consumed with the avoidance of illness and death. The passing away of a prized cow or bull could affect a family as much as, if not more than, the death of a newborn child, and hence the need to plan for both eventualities.[35] And of course, in addition to books written for living Egyptians were the manifold versions of the "Book of Going Forth by Day"—*das Todtenbuch*, or the Book of the Dead—that were taken by the thousand into the underworld.

Yet Egyptians could not escape the mundane realities of life. The apparatus of the Egyptian state continued to grow after the unification of Lower and Upper Egypt, and papyrus scrolls were used to record an increasing variety of censuses, mercantile matters, government expenses, and, of course, taxes. Taxation was ubiquitous: harvests, herds of livestock, land, handicrafts, fishing, and hunting were all subject to taxes levied in labor and goods.[36] One of the grandest of all surviving papyrus rolls, the 133-foot "Great Harris Papyrus" dated to around 1200 BCE and currently pinned to a frame in the British Museum like a butterfly in a glass drawer, is in large part a record of taxes collected for pharaoh Rameses III.[37]

Rameses III's reign was the high-water mark for the unified kingdom of Egypt. His descendants proved to be ineffective rulers, and by the eleventh century BCE the country had become two separate kingdoms in all but name, quarreling incessantly until the armies of Alexander the Great arrived in 332 BCE to put the ailing country out of its misery. Less than two decades later a new dynasty of pharaohs had been established by Ptolemy, Alexander's general, and a new capital established at Alexandria on the Nile delta.[38] Egypt's dependence on the papyrus scroll was about to blossom into a love affair.

Sometime early in the third century BCE, the Ptolemies erected a temple in Alexandria dedicated to the daughters of Zeus and Mnemosyne known as the Muses. Collectively, Calliope, Clio, Euterpe, Terpsichore, Erato, Melpomene, Thalia, Polyhymnia, and Urania were the source of all divine inspiration, believed by poets, actors, astronomers, and philosophers to be the wellspring of their creativity and talents.[39] Fittingly, the *Mouseion*, as their temple was known (we call its successors "museums"), was dedicated to the study of the natural world and the heavens above it.[40]

The Ptolemies attracted scholars with tax breaks and free accommodation, and encouraged them to spend their days in discussion, contemplation, reading, and writing.[41] Euclid wrote *Elements*, his groundbreaking book on mathematics, at the Mouseion; it was there that an astronomer named Aristarchus surmised that the Earth orbited the sun and not the other way around, while his colleague Eratosthenes calculated the diameter of the Earth to a scarcely believable accuracy of fifty miles. And it was here that Archimedes, a Sicilian engineer who had grown up by the sea and who must have felt at home in the mighty port of Alexandria, was inspired to invent a screw-shaped pump later given his name.[42]

The Mouseion's crown jewel was the fabled Library of Alexandria, reputed to contain some 700,000 scrolls.[43] And just as a visit to any modern library reveals shelf after shelf of nigh-identical books, each one a variation on the same basic design, a visiting scholar at Alexandria would have been greeted by endless rows and cubbyholes of scrolls all produced according to a common standard.

Named after the *biblos*, or papyrus, from which it was made, a typical *biblion*, or scroll, was between seven and thirteen inches in height and measured anywhere from twenty to a hundred feet in length.[44] A scroll's height was governed by the size of its constituent sheets—a scrupulous scroll maker would use top-of-the-range sheets of *hieratica*, if they could get it, which Pliny described as thirteen "digits" (around ten inches) on a side—while its length was dependent on the number of sheets from which it was made.[45] Rolls of twenty sheets were standard; rolls of fifty or even seventy sheets were exceptional but not unknown.[46]

The way in which scrolls were written was largely standardized too. With the rolled-up scroll held in their right hand, the scribe would roll it gradually into their left hand, writing on the exposed inner surface in narrow, newspaper-style columns as they went. (Ptolemaic Egypt was a

Hellenic outpost, where most of the literate populace wrote in Greek, and as such both the lines of their texts and their documents were read from left to right.)[47] Columns were a few inches wide, depending on the scribe's preference, and they were constrained by the scroll's height to a few tens of lines each.[48] Another point of standardization was the treatment of the so-called *protokollon*, the first of a scroll's constituent *kollemata*, or sheets.[49] A scroll was usually rolled up for storage so that its *protokollon* formed the outermost surface; as such, it received the brunt of any rough treatment at the hands of its readers, and early Greek scribes habitually left it blank.[50] Later, however, this wasted space began to gnaw at the sensibilities of efficiency-minded bureaucrats, and the *protokollon* became a place to record a scroll's official provenance and its date of manufacture. In time, the officious Greek *protokollon* became the English "protocol."[51]

Having completed his work, a scribe might decide to cut an especially long book into shorter "tomes," after the Greek *tomos*, "to cut"; and, with this done, each individual scroll would be rolled into what the Romans would later call a *volumen*, from the Latin *evolvere*, "to roll out," ready for storage.[52] Scrolls, writing, and the common language that surrounded them were constants for the scribes and scholars who populated Alexandria's Mouseion.

Intellectual property rights were subject to rather less agreement. Ptolemy III Euergetes, or "Benefactor," the third of his line to take the Alexandrian throne, was determined to be as beneficent as possible to the Mouseion's library, no matter the cost.[53] Having borrowed a number of classic works from Athens in exchange for a hefty deposit—fifteen "talents" of silver, totaling around more than 850 pounds in weight—he had the Mouseion's scribes copy the originals before sending the new versions (with a few new errors among their words, no doubt, an unavoidable product of copying by hand) back to the shocked Athenians.[54] His accompanying message was blunt: you're welcome, he told them, and you can always return the silver if you're dissatisfied. The Athenians kept the silver, and the Mouseion kept the books. Euergetes extended his new-for-old scheme to the ships that plied Alexandria's harbor, directing his customs officers to relieve visiting passengers of their books. Once again, the original books were deposited in the Mouseion's library while the ships departed with freshly minted copies.[55] And if this zero-sum piracy could not procure a desired book, Euergetes would send an emissary to the book fairs held in Athens and Rhodes to buy it.[56]

Euergetes's bibliomania positively stuffed the Library of Alexandria with books. Its purported 700,000 volumes were split between stone and wooden jars, or *bibliotheke*, and shelves divided up like office pigeonholes. A multivolume book might warrant its own cubby or jar, while single-volume works shared storage space with one another.[57] Rolled-up scrolls were stored vertically in jars and horizontally on shelves, with protruding tags affixed to one end so they could be identified without having to be unrolled. The Greeks called these labels *sittybos*—a misreading later transformed this into the Latin *sillybus*, and ultimately the English "syllabus"—whereas the Romans preferred *titulus*, or "title."[58]

Not all of the ancient world's scholars were as convinced of the scroll's usefulness as Ptolemy Euergetes was. Three millennia before, the mythical Egyptian king Thamus had worried about the effects of writing on the human memory; much later, two centuries before the founding of the Library of Alexandria, the Greek philosopher Socrates articulated what might be termed philosophical objections to books and writing. As Socrates explained to his student Phaedrus:

> *Writing, Phaedrus, has this strange quality, and is very like painting; for the creatures of painting stand like living beings, but if one asks them a question, they preserve a solemn silence. And so it is with written words; you might think they spoke as if they had intelligence, but if you question them, wishing to know about their sayings, they always say only one and the same thing. And every word [is] alike among those who understand and those who have no interest in it, and it knows not to whom to speak or not to speak; when ill-treated or unjustly reviled it always needs its father to help it; for it has no power to protect or help itself.*[59]

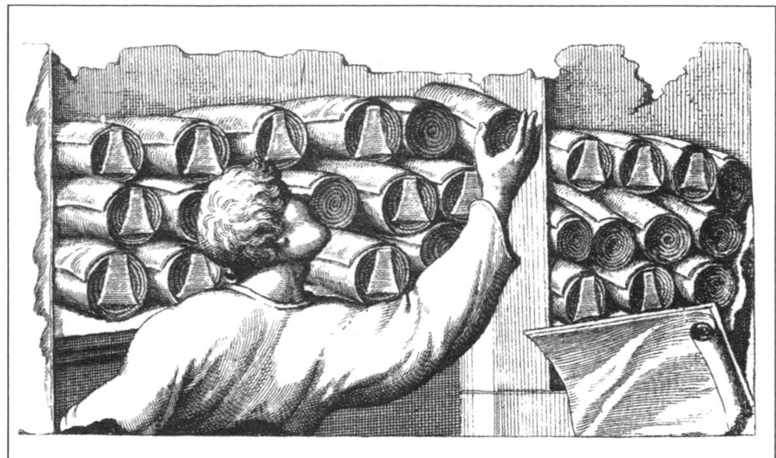

⇐ This image of scrolls stored in the classical equivalent of bookshelves comes from a drawing made in the seventeenth century of a Roman grave decoration, now destroyed. Triangular title tags—*sittybos* in Greek, *titulus* in Latin—are shown at the ends of the scrolls.[60]

For Socrates, scrolls were dead things, stony witnesses that could "speak" only the words that their author had given them, He did have one thing right, though: Greeks and Romans often read aloud as they worked their way through written works, and so a given scroll would invariably "say only one and the same thing" as it passed through the hands of different readers.[61] Unlike today's hushed reading rooms, the chambers of the Library of Alexandria and others like it would have been noisy places.

Socrates's philosophical quibbles were not the only questions that hung over the scroll as a medium for the storage and retrieval of information. The problems started on the bookshelves: there is a lot of empty space in the middle of a rolled-up scroll, and that means a lot of wasted space. Consider this book. The hardback edition is 8¼ inches high by 5½ wide and it contains 203 leaves of double-sided paper to yield 406 pages in total, not counting the frontmatter or the index. Ignoring margins, which were usually more generous in scrolls than they are in printed books, there are a little more than 128 square feet of usable paper between its covers. Its ancient equivalent, a single-sided bookroll perhaps 12 inches high and 20 feet long, would occupy a similar volume of shelf space, but the book holds *upward of seven times* more information. Little wonder, then, that archaeologists are skeptical about ancient boasts that the Library of Alexandria held some 700,000 scrolls—no building remotely large enough to house such a collection has yet been found in old Alexandria, and current guesses place the library's holdings at 35,000 to 40,000 volumes.[62]

With all the rolling and unrolling demanded while reading a scroll, with no page numbers to guide the reader to their desired location, and with no pages to riffle through in the first place, many book historians claim that finding information in a bookroll must have been frustrating.[63] But then, there is a suspicion among others that we are too far removed from the daily use of scrolls to be entirely sure about this. It *is* slower to access a particular part of a scroll, but many of the same intangible factors are at work as when flipping through a book: the visual appearance and the physical weight of the scroll's rolled-up ends guide one to the approximate location, and even without page numbers, chapter titles, and the other textual furniture found on the pages of a modern book, an unadorned column of characters does become familiar after a while. The act of scrolling through an electronic document is named by analogy with the ancient experience of shuffling through a bookroll, and we adapted quickly to that particular change in the reading experience.[64]

Whether a reader was searching for a favorite passage or reading through an unfamiliar work, "scrolling" through a scroll demanded their full attention. It takes two hands to simultaneously unfurl a bookroll at one end and roll it up at the other; there is no way to casually prop open a scroll in one hand while sipping from a glass of wine held in the other. (I have tried.) Perhaps because of this, the oenophile Romans accessorized some of their scrolls with a pair of sticks, or *umbilici*, one attached to each end of a scroll to facilitate rolling and unrolling. They made furniture to match too, in the form of reading desks sporting pegs behind which a scroll's *umbilici* could be lodged to keep it open at a desired location.[65] Shorter scrolls equipped with *umbilici* could be unrolled and their ends left to dangle off the end of a table; failing that, a pair of stones would serve well enough as paperweights.[66] And

⇜ A painting, found in Pompeii at the house of a baker named Terentius Neo, of a Roman couple holding the two main writing media of their time. Terentius Neo holds a scroll, a *titulus* dangling from its top, while his wife pensively clutches a wax writing tablet and prepares to write in it with a stylus.[67]

the dangers of a springy papyrus bookroll should not be underestimated: in the first century CE, an aging Roman senator named Lucius Verginius Rufus died after trying to retrieve a scroll that had sprung out of his grasp; he slipped on the marble floor, fracturing his hip, and never recovered.[68]

The Library of Alexandria suffered a catastrophic fire in 48 BCE, a victim of Julius Caesar's civil war to seize control of the Roman Republic, but the destruction of tens of thousands of bookrolls did not dent the scroll's popularity, or its ubiquity.[69] In spite of all its shortcomings—its flammability, unwieldiness, and comparative fragility—for the denizens of ancient Greece and Rome, the papyrus scroll was the obvious choice for recording texts of any great length. But the scroll had a not-so-secret accomplice: for everyday writing, when a scroll was too clumsy or too expensive, scribes, housewives, and slaves alike turned to a more practical medium.

In 1982, a few miles off the Turkish coast at a place called Uluburun and 150 feet beneath the waves, a sponge diver named Mehmet Çakir came across what he described as "metal biscuits with ears" on the seabed. The captain of Çakir's sponge boat had seen these "metal biscuits" before, in a drawing distributed among local sailors and fishermen by an American archaeologist named Don Frey, and he dutifully called Turkey's Museum of Underwater Archaeology to report the find. When Frey returned to survey the site, his suspicions were confirmed: Çakir's "metal biscuits with ears" were copper ingots, cast in imitation of an ox's hide and nestling in the remains of an ancient cargo ship—and they were kept company on the seafloor by an unprecedented haul of other objects.[70] Over the course of the next eleven years, Frey and others recovered hundreds of oxhide ingots; giant storage jars containing elaborate pottery items; colored glass beads; gold tableware; elephant and hippopotamus tusks; valuable *murex* snail shells for dye-making; swords and other weapons; and much more.[71]

The cargo of the Uluburun ship was drawn from all over the ancient world, from Sicily to Mesopotamia via Egypt, Cyprus, Greece, and Canaan, making it difficult to discern much about her nationality or intended route. Pinpointing the date of her demise, however, was easier. Archaeologists examined the growth rings in the ship's timbers and matched them to known fluctuations in the ancient climate to place her construction around the late fourteenth century BCE and her sinking not much later than that.[72] The freighter and its cargo had gone down off the Turkish coast more than three thousand years ago.

Among the riches scattered about the skeleton of the old ship, one particular find, a pair of wooden boards hidden inside one of the giant earthenware *pithoi*, or storage jars, was a revelation. Although fragmented and worn by their three-millennium slumber at the bottom of the sea, the boards were clearly a matching pair: they were about the size of smartphones, less than four inches long and two and a half wide; they were symmetrically "hollowed out," as if to form shallow trays; and each one sported a fileted edge designed to fit snugly against a pole or dowel. That missing cylinder was found in the form of two carved pieces of ivory, and, when laid out together, these fragments of wood and ivory formed an object immediately recognizable to any student of ancient Greece or Rome. It was a *diptych*, or twofold writing tablet, and it was the oldest one ever found.[73]

Except in Egypt, which was firmly wedded to papyrus scrolls, writing tablets were the everyday notebooks of the ancient world.[74] At their most basic they comprised a pair of wooden or ivory boards around a quarter of an inch thick, tied together with a thong or cord, the surface of each one hollowed out and filled with beeswax on which a scribe wrote with a pointed stylus. Portable and reusable, wax tablets were ideal for bookkeeping, correspondence, and drafting literary pieces, although they were occasionally called upon for more important duties.[75] The ancient Roman historian Herodotus tells the story

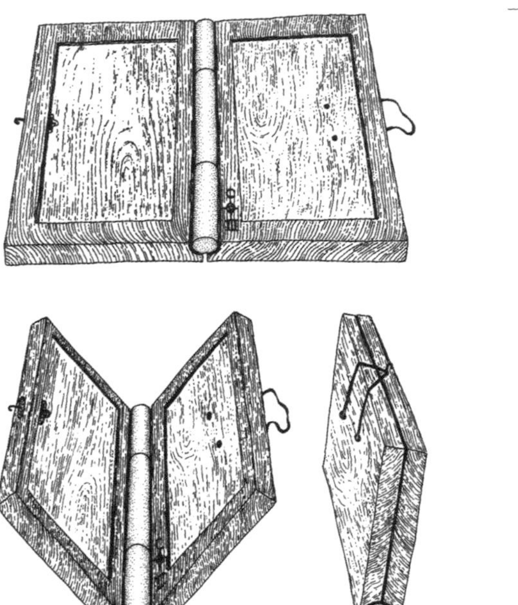

➻ The writing board set, or diptych, found at Uluburun. Despite being the oldest known diptych, it is considerably more elaborate than many later examples. The cylindrical ivory pieces at the top and bottom of the hinge were nailed to the right-hand board and the central piece to the board on the left. The central piece was held in place by dowels protruding from the top and bottom pieces so that the two boards rotated about their shared axis.[76]

of Demaratus, an exiled Spartan leader who learned of Xerxes's plan to invade Greece. Concerned for the welfare of his people—as well he might be, given Xerxes's reputation for excessive violence—Demaratus searched for some way to warn Sparta of the attack without also alerting Xerxes's forces, who patrolled the roads. Finally he melted the wax off a diptych, scratched out his warning on the naked wooden boards, and reapplied the wax so that a messenger could deliver the missive without fear of discovery. His plan was almost too cunning: Sparta's assembled grandees failed to make heads or tails of the blank diptych until Gorgo, the Spartan queen, guessed at the ruse.[77]

If the wax Demaratus used to hide his message was anything like the usual concoction applied to writing tablets, one hopes he washed his hands afterward. Greek writers often adulterated their wax with poisonous yellow "orpiment," or arsenic sulfide (the Romans preferred equally toxic "verdigris," or green copper acetate), both to dye it and to keep it soft so that mistakes could be erased with a flat implement or the entire surface smoothed over for reuse.[78] As such, most wax-tablet styli were pointed at one end and flattened, spatula-like, at the other.[79] This ease of correction made diptychs popular even when grander writing materials were available: Quintilian, a Roman writer of the first century CE, told his students that "It is best to write on wax owing to the facility which it offers for erasure [. . . parchment] delays the hand and interrupts the stream of thought owing to the frequency with which the pen has to be supplied with ink."[80] Erasure put wax writing tablets millennia ahead of their time. It was not until the invention of the graphite pencil in the sixteenth century, whose marks could be rubbed out with a piece of bread, that there was there an equally convenient way to selectively emend one's writing.[81]

A diptych's two boards were hinged together, usually along one of the long edges, so that they could be closed to protect the soft writing surfaces; but whereas a modern reader presented with a diptych would automatically hold it vertically, with its hinged edge running top-to-bottom like a book's spine, ancient illustrations show scribes grasping them horizontally with a "top" page and a "bottom" page, like a laptop computer.[82] Beyond the humble diptych, many *polyptychs*—collections of three tablets or more—were bound in the same way, with holes drilled along one edge of each tablet and the lot of them tied together with leather thongs. Threefold *triptychs*, fourfold *quadriptychs*, and even grander versions consisting of up to twenty boards were made in exactly the same fashion.[83]

Without wanting to spoil the ending to this particular story, neither the papyrus scroll nor the wax writing tablet was destined to live forever. But if the outcome of the tussle between scrolls, diptychs, and paged books is plain enough to see, it is not so easy to detect precisely why, when, and where battle was joined in the first place. The origins of the codex are every bit as obscure as those of its ancestors.

13

Joining the Folds: the invention of the codex

Franz Boas, the father of modern American anthropology, reportedly said, "Man never lies to his garbage heap," and he was right: a large part of what is known about humanity's past has been divined from contents of the piles and pits of refuse that surrounded our settlements.[1] History, it turns out, is written not by the strongest but by the messiest, and the history of books is no exception. The few tantalizing glimpses that we have into the formative years of the paged book are due to one particular episode of archaeological dumpster-diving, the heroically dogged excavation of many centuries' worth of one town's refuse that massively expanded our understanding of the literary cultures of ancient Egypt, Greece, and Rome.

Late in 1896, two English archaeologists made the trek from the leafy environs of their alma mater in Oxford to the Egyptian village of El-Bahnasa, a few days south of the ancient capital of Memphis and sited on a branch of the Nile called the Bahr Yusuf, or "Joseph's Canal."[2] Though adorned here and there with classical ruins, El-Bahnasa had been largely ignored by the many itinerant academics then combing

Egypt's ancient landscape, and so Bernard P. Grenfell and Arthur S. Hunt were presented with an untouched archaeological sandpit in which to play. They focused their attention on the "tells," or mounds, that surrounded the present village, and that had once encircled the ancient city of Oxyrhynchus (pronounced "oxy-*rink*-us") on whose ruins the modern settlement had been built.[3]

Named for the peculiar "elephant-nosed" fish that swam in the Bahr Yusuf, Oxyrhynchus had been Egypt's third-largest city in its heyday after the Alexandrian invasion, a thriving provincial capital with a population of perhaps 20,000.[4] Then, as now, a city of that size produced a correspondingly sizeable amount of trash, much of it in the form of discarded documents, scrolls, and other texts, and it all had to go somewhere. In the case of Oxyrhynchus, that somewhere was an uncultivated strip of desert that lay between the city and the irrigated farms that surrounded it: for centuries the city's inhabitants hauled their baskets of rubbish out to this literal wasteland and dumped them there, safe in the knowledge that the desert's shifting sands would cover up their leavings.[5] The resultant mounds grew and grew over the centuries, and the scene that greeted Grenfell, Hunt, and their small army of workers was a landscape littered with tells reaching tens of feet in height.[6] They set to work.

Eleven months after Grenfell and Hunt had returned to Britain, the pair published their findings in a substantial volume entitled *The Oxyrhynchus Papyri*.[7] Or rather, they published a tiny fraction of their findings: almost as soon as the first spade had bit into the sandy soil, they had pulled out scrolls, sheets, and fragments by the fistful.[8] In their first season of digging alone they discovered a hitherto-unseen verse by the poet Sappho; the earliest known copy of the Gospel of Matthew; a fragment of an unknown book of the New Testament entitled "The Acts of Paul and Thecla" relating the intertwined tales of the Apostle and a virginal devotee; and hundreds more.[9] This rich seam of documents stretched thirty feet down into the earth, preserved there by the protective sands and the arid climate.[10] And though the very oldest materials had been lost—scrolls from the time of the Ptolemies and before lay below the water table and had since rotted away—there were still almost two millennia of documents to extract, record, and pack into biscuit tins for transportation back to England.[11]

After a few years spent excavating elsewhere, Grenfell and Hunt returned to Oxyrhynchus in the winter of 1903–1904 and would visit again every year until 1907.[12] In the end they recovered half a million separate pieces of papyrus (and, crucially, a few scraps of parchment too), publishing them in yearly volumes until persistent ill health brought Grenfell's career to an end in 1920.[13] Hunt carried on alone until 1934, and a host of other scholars have succeeded him since then: the seventy-ninth volume of *The Oxyrhynchus Papyri* was published in 2014, and the current stewards of Grenfell and Hunt's trove expect that the series will number more than one hundred before the last biscuit tin is opened.[14]

The Oxyrhynchus hoard is the elephant in the room for papyrologists, and not just because of its name. More than half of all the papyrus scrolls that have survived from the first through the fourth centuries came out of the rubbish heaps around El-Bahnasa, and the sheer weight of evidence continues to exert a powerful pull on those who study ancient writing, literature, and culture.[15] But as intriguing as were the contents of the lost poems, religious tracts, and personal letters that Grenfell and Hunt discovered, their physical forms were just as important. For as long as anyone had cared about the development of the paged book, historians had placed its arrival sometime during the fourth century CE, and, given that the handful of surviving books from that time were all made of parchment, it was assumed that the invention of the paged book had accompanied the decline of the papyrus scroll.[16] It was all very tidy and very plausible, in the way that historical theories usually are before they stumble out into the unobliging messiness of the real world.

⤜ • ⤛

Grenfell and Hunt could not resist showing off their handiwork. In 1897, a full year before the first volume of *The Oxyrhynchus Papyri* was due to be published, the pair coauthored an essay describing a fragment of papyrus they called the *Logia Iesu*, or "The Sayings of Jesus."[17] Later catalogued as Papyrus Oxyrhynchus I 1, or P. Oxy. I 1, the *Logia* was not much to look at; it consisted of a rectangular sheet of papyrus about 5¾ by 3¾ inches in size, a little frayed around the edges, and, at first glance, steadfastly conventional.[18] Adapting the terminology used in the study of papyrus scrolls, the two scholars labeled the side on which the fibers ran horizontally as the *recto* (the same term was used to mean the inner surface of a scroll on which scribes wrote) and, by a similar analogy, referred to the back side as the *verso*.[19] But this was no ordinary papyrus.

First, there were no seams. Either P. Oxy. I 1 had never been part of a bookroll or the overlapping joins characteristic of pasted-together scrolls had been purposely cut off. Curiously, however, the right-hand edge of the sheet had a thin strip of papyrus pasted along it, as if to reinforce an exposed edge.[20] Second, both sides of the sheet had been written upon. Writing on the back of old scrolls was unusual but not unknown, especially when papyrus was scarce, but here the text continued seamlessly from *recto* to *verso*: after having completed one side, the scribe had flipped the sheet over to carry on writing.[21] The layout of the text also hinted at some kind of commonality between the two sides of the sheet. The scribe had neatened up the right-hand edge of the *recto*'s text, padding lines of uneven length with decorative marks to produce a consistent margin, while on the other side of the papyrus the left-hand edge of the text had been aligned to match. The reinforced edge; the continuation of the text from *recto* to *verso*; the visual symmetry—all this was strikingly suggestive of a page taken from a deliberately constructed book, not a hastily reused scroll.[22]

The final proof that P. Oxy. I 1 was a remnant of a paged book was almost absurdly plain to see. At the top right corner of the *recto* (they increasingly thought of it as the "front" side of the page, hinged to a long-disintegrated spine at the left), two Greek letters, iota (ι) and alpha (α), were set apart from the rest of the text.[23] Comparing the letters to similar examples found in later books, the two scholars decided that this could only be a page number, and, taking numerical values from their position in the Greek alphabet so that ι = 10 and α = 1, Grenfell and Hunt figured out that they had uncovered the eleventh and twelfth pages of the earliest known paged book.[24]

Certain features of the handwriting in the *Logia*, along with clues from the text itself, implied that it could not have been written after 140 CE and yet in dating it Grenfell and Hunt added a caveat: "the fact that the papyrus was in book, not roll, form, put[s] the first century out of the question, and make[s] the first half of the second unlikely." Content to ignore the resultant logical paradox, the *Logia*, they decided, "was probably written not much later than the year 200."[25] They may have lacked conviction, but nevertheless the two archaeologists had pushed back the birth of the codex by at least two hundred years—and undermined the conventional narrative of the parchment book as the first example of the form.

In the century since Grenfell and Hunt's excited account of the *Logia Iesu*, many other papyrus books have reinforced their findings. In the mid-1930s, an American mining magnate named A. Chester Beatty publicized his extensive collection of second-, third-, and fourth-century papyrus books in the *Times* of London; later, in 1945, a library of esoteric Christian tracts came to light at Nag Hammadi in Upper Egypt, all of them written in the form of papyrus books. Meanwhile, examination of the Oxyrhynchus Papyri continues to bring to light new examples of the very earliest books.[26] No papyrus codex has yet been dated earlier than the first century, but as the respected papyrologist Eric Turner said of one of the Oxyrhynchus books, "its mere existence is evidence that this book form had a prehistory."[27] What, then, had happened in that murky prehistory, and what was it that bridged the gap between the papyrus scroll and the paged book?

➻ • ➻

Speculation about a missing link between the scroll and the codex first arose toward the end of the nineteenth century. Its subject was the *orihon*, or concertina-folded book, a mythical scroll-codex hybrid that seemed to present believable if not definitive proof that the one had evolved into the other. Buoyed, perhaps, by new archaeological discoveries in the East, stories of the orihon have persisted even as the physical evidence remains stubbornly equivocal.[28]

The basic premise goes like this: faced with the monotonous task of rolling and unrolling a papyrus scroll, some exasperated ancient reader decided to remake their book in a more convenient form. It was thought that, using the gaps between the written columns of the text as guides, they had folded their scroll into a concertina shape, alternating between peaked "mountain folds" and concave "valley folds" as they moved along the scroll.[29] With the resultant folded block of papyrus held flat, they then pierced holes along the "back" edge of the block, formed by the valley folds, and tied them together with string. The result, the alleged orihon, was a proto-book whose pages consisted of two layers of papyrus, folded over at the outer edge and sewn together at the spine. A codex, in other words, that had been made from a scroll.[30]

In 1907, Cyril Davenport, one of the historians who first invoked the orihon as missing link, assured his reader that this form of the book was "well known in the East and also among primitive nations."[31] Era-appropriate chauvinism aside, the word "*orihon*" (折本) was taken from Japanese, meaning "folded book," and concertina-style books had long been common in China, Korea, and Japan.[32] Davenport must have felt his position considerably strengthened by the recent discovery of Dunhuang's famed "library cave" in China, where, among the tens of thousands of documents found there, were more than a hundred concertina-folded books, each one folded back on itself and glued together at the spine.[33] Nor were the Dunhuang orihons alone:

⤙ The opening pages of a handwritten paper orihon found at Dunhuang in China. Although it is undated, it must have been written in or before the eleventh century.

⇜ The "Codex Peresianus," or "Paris Codex," one of four surviving Mayan books. Each page is around 10 inches tall and 5 inches wide. All four codices are thought to have been made between 1250 and 1520.[34]

bolstering Davenport's case, another variety of concertina-folded book had arisen independently on the other side of the world. The orihon, it seemed, was as natural a form for books as the scroll or the codex.

When Spanish explorers arrived in Central America in the sixteenth century, they found literate Aztec and Mayan peoples who had been making books from *āmatl*, a papyruslike material derived from tree bark, for more than a millennium.[35] *Āmatl* had much in common with both papyrus and paper: the inner bark of fig or mulberry trees was dried, washed, boiled, and finally peeled into strips before those strips were beaten together to make finished sheets.[36] The end product was central to Mesoamerican culture: *āmatl* was used for calendars, almanacs, maps, and record-keeping; and for more esoteric purposes besides,

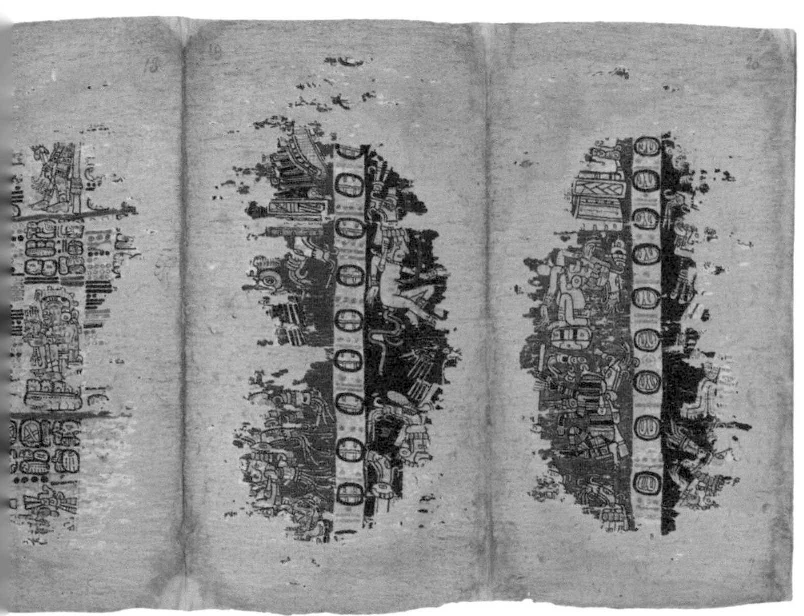

in the form of crowns, plumes, and bracelets employed in priestly rituals.[37] Most important of all were the *āmoxtli,* or books, made from sheets of *āmatl* pasted together in sequence and folded into the distinctive accordion form of the orihon.[38]

The arrival of the conquistadores spelled the end for this ancient literate culture. Spanish missionaries burned great piles of *āmoxtli* in a relentless drive to eradicate the indigenous beliefs of their new colonies. The history, scriptures, and everyday records of an entire culture were systematically reduced to ashes and the use of *āmatl* driven almost to extinction.[39] Barely a handful of Mayan books have survived.

But in spite of the awful spectacle of "civilizing" Europeans doing their best to stamp out a culture no less civilized than their own, and despite the seductive intrigue of walled-up desert libraries, the orihon's place in book history is not assured. Chinese concertina books first appeared during the Tang dynasty, between the seventh and tenth centuries, and, conspiracy theories aside, there is no evidence of transatlantic contact prior to the Vikings' eleventh-century voyages to Canada.[40] The Chinese and the Mayans invented their concertina books independently, and if the orihon ever existed in ancient Egypt then it lived and died there without a trace. In Egypt at least, the distinctive paged form of the codex had come about with nary an orihon in sight.

With the orihon's part in book history unproven at best, the other main theory as to how the papyrus scroll mutated into the paged book approaches the problem from an entirely different angle. The first paged books may not have had anything to do with books at all.

Whether in Egypt, Greece, or Rome, the smooth running of the ancient world was predicated on the exchange of letters. Politics, business, and family matters were managed by correspondence between friends, allies, patrons, and clients. Depending upon the context, a letter might be read privately, shared with friends and family, or broadcast publicly as the writer specified—or, equally, copied, plagiarized, or ignored as the recipient desired. A well-written epistle was treasured; a caustic put-down from a superior dreaded.[41] It is the interplay between the content and the physical form of these letters that some academics think explains the creation of the paged book.[42]

From 1906 to 1908, a German archaeologist named Eduard Sachau excavated a clutch of papyrus texts and ostraca on the island of Elephantine, the Nile's largest.[43] Today, the island is part of the city of Aswan, downriver from the giant Aswan Dam; in the fifth century BCE, when Sachau's texts were written, it was a Jewish colony sited on the edge of the Persian Empire, a swirl of languages and cultures.[44] In 1980, a theologian named Bezalel Porten focused his attention on a collection of letters from Sachau's Elephantine dig that had been written in the ancient Persian language of Aramaic and had suffered from a kind of uniform degradation over the intervening centuries. Many of the letters had broken apart into regular strips, separated along arrow-straight seams, and Porten wanted to understand why.[45]

The letter writers of ancient Elephantine had started out with scrolls; that much is certain. Porten found that each letter had been cut from a papyrus roll so that one or more pasted joins ran across each of the resulting sheets, and they had all been written in "landscape" orientation with lines of text running horizontally across the page.[46] Evidently the standard twenty-sheet scroll was so firmly entrenched in the mind of the average consumer (and perhaps in the papyrus market itself) that the purchase of individual sheets was not an option. To protect the letters as they traveled to their recipients, they were folded up like road maps, as one academic put it: starting at the bottom, the sender folded over a flap of papyrus about an inch in height, then repeated this until the letter had been "rolled up" all the way to the top.[47] Next, the letter was folded in half, from left to right, and finally tied with a piece of twine or cord. This folding was the cause of the letters' disintegration.[48]

How does this relate to the paged book? By the time of the Roman Empire, the exchange of letters had grown into its own literary genre: philosophers laid out their ideas in letters, and politicians disseminated their best speeches; and the adherents of religious movements, like the Christians, built entire books around the letters of their most trusted disciples.[49] Perhaps these groups of like-minded people, who regularly exchanged collections of letters, turned those conceptual collections into physical ones in the form of the paged book, and found that the pre-folded, road map–style letter was a natural fit when sewing a pile of them together to form a spine halfway across the pages. In this reading, the codex was not a single bookroll that had been folded up and sewn together but instead a bundle of dismembered scrolls reassembled into a new form.[50]

This is not exactly a watertight theory. When the writers of Porten's Aramaic letters reached the end of their first page, they took hold of the sheet at both sides and flipped it over so that their first new line of text on the back was directly opposite the *last* line on the front.[51] Trying to read a book bound from a stack of these back-to-front letters must have been an exercise in frustration; and what about the single column of text on each side, rudely cut in half by the spine of the book? Confusing matters further, the earliest complete papyrus codices were all made so that the joins inherited from their parent scrolls run parallel to their spines, and the text perpendicular to both—but a stack of Porten's letters, whose text was written parallel to their joins, would have produced a book whose text ran vertically, not horizontally.[52] No such books have been found.

Now, none of these issues are insurmountable. The earliest codex makers were, by definition, forward thinkers, and a few simple tweaks to their writing practices would have solved all these problems. It would have been easy enough to write across the joins, rather than parallel to them, and to write their letters in columns so that each column would lie on a separate leaf of the resultant book; and of course, all of this was already common practice for scrolls. Aside from this, it would have been simple to flip their sheets horizontally, not vertically, so that the text was the right way up on both sides. The hypothesized transformation of papyrus letters into the papyrus book is not farfetched.

The difficulty that modern historians are left with, however, is that no physical evidence exists; if any of this happened at all, it happened in the uncooperative prehistory of the codex. And even worse for the prospects of the papyrus codex, the hoary old idea that the *parchment* codex had been first all along steadfastly refused to admit defeat.

Parchment, so the story goes, was introduced to Rome in the second century BCE by Crates of Mallus, the clumsy Pergamene scholar for whom the phrase "break a leg" could have been invented.[53] Its impact was not immediate—in all the classical texts that have survived, *membrana*, or "skin," is not mentioned as a writing material until a hundred years after Crater's sewer tumble—but the seed had been planted, and great things awaited.[54]

One of the earliest hints of a new kind of parchment book appears in the writings of Gaius Suetonius Tranquillus, a biographer born in the first century CE whose *Lives of the Twelve Caesars* (that is, the first twelve rulers of the Roman Empire) has remained in print, so to speak, ever since it was written.[55] Suetonius was a diligent biographer, thorough to the point of indiscretion: it is because of his appetite for vulgar gossip that we know about the latter half of the reign of the emperor Tiberius, conducted from his pleasure villa on the island of Capri, where he was rumored to swim with young boys trained to nibble at his privates. Equally, however, it is because of him that Julius Caesar's immortal words, "*veni, vidi, vici*" (I came, I saw, I conquered) have survived until today.[56] It was with his usual compulsive thoroughness that Suetonius delved into the writing habits of Rome's most famous general:

> *There are extant some letters of [Caesar's] to the senate, written in a manner never practised by any before him; for they are distinguished into pages in the form of a memorandum book: whereas the consuls and commanders till then, used constantly in their letters to continue the line quite across the sheet, without any folding or distinction of pages.*[57]

Book historians were giddy at the prospect that Julius Caesar might have invented the paged book. Suetonius's account of Caesar's *memorialis libri*, usually translated as a "memorandum book" or "notebook," comprised of *paginas*, or "leaves," has been endlessly discussed, but never agreed upon.[58] There is no mention of how Caesar's notebook was constructed except in how it differed from those employed by others around him: Caesar folded his "leaves," whatever they were made of, and apparently broke up his text as necessary to fit them, but that is all. Was Suetonius describing a codex made of papyrus, or even parchment?[59] It remains a mystery, but it seems that someone, even if not Caesar himself, had been thinking outside of the scroll case a century or more before the first paged books were cast into the rubbish heaps outside Oxyrhynchus.

In the centuries after Caesar's time, Roman writers increasingly drew a distinction between the small, portable writing tablets known as *pugillares*—"belonging to the fist" or "capable of being held in the hand," as epitomized by the tiny diptych found at Uluburun—and larger tablets they called *tabellae*.[60] Pliny's nephew described how his uncle gave dictation to an attendant equipped with a *pugillar* whenever the urge took him: while being rubbed down after a bath; as he rode in his chariot; or as he commuted on his sedan chair.[61] "Stenographer wanted," the job description might have read, "must enjoy nudity and vigorous exercise."

In addition to differentiating between tablets of different sizes, Roman writers were mindful of their source materials. Specifically, the use of *membranae*, or "skins," as a robust and reusable writing surface (the Romans' watery ink washed right off) was mentioned by a number of authors.[62] But there was more to parchment than its utility as a writing surface. Poring over these accounts, some modern scholars think that the word "skins" had another connotation: it seems to have been used to refer to some kind of composite vehicle for writing, the same way that the word "papers" suggests a collection of documents rather than a pile of blank sheets, but the specific meaning behind it was never made clear.[63] The Greeks also attached a special meaning to the Latin term *membranae*: the old Greek word *difthérai*, or "animal skins," was well understood to refer to parchment, and yet the Latin *membranae* was often transliterated into Greek characters to imply some kind of standalone writing medium.[64]

Whatever *membranae* had meant in the past, in the first century CE any lingering doubts were firmly dispelled when Martial, a poet whose pithy couplets delighted Rome's book-buying elite, effusively praised parchment and the books that were made out of it. In penning the foreword to a collected edition of his epigrams, published between

84 and 86 CE, Martial enthused about a new, compact format in which buyers might purchase his books:[65]

> *You who long for my little books to be with you everywhere and want to have companions for a long journey, buy these ones which parchment confines within small pages: give your scroll-cases to the great authors—one hand can hold me. So that you are not ignorant of where I am on sale, and don't wander aimlessly through the whole city, I will be your guide and you will be certain: look for Secundus, the freedman of learned Lucensis, behind the threshold of the Temple of Peace and the Forum of Pallas.*[66]

Music lovers who have made the transition from vinyl to CD, movie buffs from DVD to Blu-ray, or readers from book to e-book will shudder at Martial's marketing tactics. In a few lines, the poet introduces a new media format, "which parchment confines within small pages," encourages his readers to buy a copy of his works in this new medium, and tells them precisely where to find his favored bookshop. Perhaps Martial had schemed with Secundus, the slave turned bookseller, to receive a higher percentage of the profits in exchange for encouraging readers to visit his shop on the edge of the Forum.[67]

Though Martial did not explicitly call his parchment edition a book, it very likely *was* one: parchment begs to be bound into a paged codex or similar form, and historians are convinced that Martial's poems mark the first mainstream appearance of the medium.[68] His collection of bite-size poems, intended to be a "companion for a long journey," would have been a perfect candidate to benefit from the fundamental advantages of the paged book—higher information density; ease of reference; one-handed operation—especially when allied to robust leaves of parchment that were immune to the rigors of an arduous trek.

Martial was unstinting in his admiration for parchment and parchment books. Later in *Epigrams*, in a guide to gift-giving during the annual Roman festival of Saturnalia, he listed a series of gifts that reflected changing attitudes to writing materials. Up first were waxed writing tablets of wood and ivory, followed by *pugillares membranae*—that is, parchment notebooks—that Martial explained were readily erased and reused. Papyrus sheets, in his opinion, were to be reserved for letter writing.[69] The compactness of the parchment codex was again invoked in a couplet that urged wealthy gift-givers to splurge on the complete works of Titus Livius Patavinus, or Livy, whose 142-book oeuvre was prohibitively large when copied out on unwieldy scrolls. "Narrowed into scanty skins is bulky Livy," wrote Martial, "the whole of whom my library does not contain."[70]

As if to confirm that Martial's enthusiasm for the paged parchment book had spread across the classical world, in 1898, a year after their publication of the papyrus *Logia Iesu*, the Oxyrhynchus team of Bernard Grenfell and Arthur Hunt announced that they had since found a leaf from a parchment book to go with it. The scribe of this previously unknown history book had copied it in the "rustic capitals" typical of documents from the city of Herculaneum, buried in 79 CE by the same Vesuvian eruption that spelled doom for Pompeii and for Pliny the Elder; but among those old-style capitals were a few "uncial," or "inch-high," letters more commonly found from the third century onward. As with the *Logia Iesu* before it, the two Englishmen struggled to reconcile these conflicting points of evidence; and again, they considered it "impossible to refer the fragment to a period earlier than the third century."[71]

This, in a nutshell, is the problem in declaring a victor in the race for the first paged books. The physical evidence is sparse and self-contradictory, the written evidence disappointingly vague. It may be that papyrus books were created by letter writers in Egypt, and spread northward from there to Greece and Rome; alternatively, the parchment codex may have been invented by the Greeks or Romans, closer to that material's spiritual home in Pergamon, and later adapted to use the plentiful local papyrus of Ptolemaic Egypt.[72] Even T. C. Roberts and

C. R. Skeat, coauthors of *The Birth of the Codex*, the seminal academic work on the subject, admit that no one can claim to know how, when, or where the paged book was born.[73]

Though the early years of the paged book are cloaked in mystery, its adolescence and adulthood played out in full view. Working with the vast body of books housed in the world's libraries, museums, and private collections, codicologists, or those who study the history of the paged book, have built up a minutely detailed timeline of every change in material, binding technique, and design from the fourth century onward.

For codicology, the moment at which the prehistory of the book resolves into honest-to-goodness *history* lies in a collection of leather-covered papyrus books known as the Nag Hammadi codices. This library of fourth-century books first burst into view in the late 1940s, garnering worldwide attention for Jean Doresse, the young French archaeologist who realized their provenance upon viewing them in the Coptic Museum of Cairo. The real credit for the discovery, however, fell to the two Egyptian camel drivers who unearthed the books in the first place, and whose discovery was marred by a series of bloody incidents that have colored the story ever since.[74] The circumstances of the brothers' find remained unclear until 1979, when an American scholar, one James M. Robinson, tracked them down in person and extracted their grisly tale.

One day late in 1945, near the town of Nag Hammadi in Upper Egypt, some eighty miles north of Luxor, brothers Muhammad 'Ali al-Sammam and Abu al-Majd were digging out nutrient-rich soil, or *sabakh*, in order to fertilize the harder earth of their nearby grain fields. Abu's mattock struck something solid under the soil, and together the two dug out a large earthenware jar topped with a ceramic bowl and sealed with some kind of tarry substance. At first afraid to open the jar in case it harbored a genie, Muhammad, the elder brother, worked up the courage to smash it open with his mattock. In place of the expected supernatural being, they found twelve leather-bound papyrus books, along with a smattering of loose papyrus sheets, which they gathered up and brought home to be deposited on the ground beside their mother's bread oven. ('Umm Ahmad, their mother, later admitted that she had thrown some of the loose leaves into the oven as fuel.)[75]

Some six months before the discovery, Muhammad's father, 'Ali, had caught, killed, and beheaded a presumed thief from a neighboring village, only to be found shot to death the next morning, his body lying next to that of decapitated thief. This was important, Muhammad explained to Robinson, because it had happened around the time of the harvest festival of Sham al-Nasim—Easter Monday, for the Copts of the Egyptian Orthodox Church—and he and his brother had discovered the hoard of books some six months later, placing it in December 1945. A month *after* they had found the codices, Muhammad and Abu were told that their father's alleged murderer, a member of a rival family, had been seen napping at the side of the road near their home; at their mother's urging, the boys attacked the sleeping man with their sharpened mattocks, killing and dismembering him before cutting out and eating his heart. The feud escalated, culminating in a massacre at a funeral procession in which twenty-seven members of Muhammad's family were shot, many of them fatally.[76] The brothers found it prudent to make themselves scarce, and so the story of the books' discovery remained unknown until some two decades after the fact, when Robinson induced them to reveal their story by means of persuasion, flattery, and outright bribery.[77]

Against the backdrop of a police investigation into the killing of 'Ali's supposed murderer, the brothers moved to rid themselves of the leather-bound papyrus codices. A local Coptic priest identified them as very old Christian texts but declined to buy them, and Muhammad and Abu resorted to parceling out the books for nominal sums to whoever would take them. Gradually, the scattered collection took on a life of its own: at first, the books changed hands for payments of tea, sugar, oranges, or a desultory few *piasters* (Egyptian cents), but as rumors of their importance circulated among Egypt's dealers in antiquities, their asking price rose. By 1947, a dealer from Cairo named Phocion J. Tano had acquired all but one of the books, but as offers rolled in from foreign buyers he heard that the Egyptian government was planning to purchase the library from him for a nonnegotiable sum. He conspired with Maria Dattari, an Italian antiquities dealer, who tried to take the books out of the country under the pretense that she was delivering them to the pope, but she was turned back at Cairo airport and a fuming Tano was forced to settle for the government's offer of 5,000 Egyptian pounds (about $15,000), scarcely one-twentieth of the books' true value.[78] The collection was deposited with the Coptic Museum of Cairo, but before anyone could examine them in detail Egypt found itself embroiled in a series of full-scale international incidents. The Suez crisis in 1956 and the Arab-Israeli wars of 1967 and 1973 meant that the facsimiles of the last of the Nag Hammadi books did not see the light of day until 1977, more than three decades after they had been dug out of the soft, loamy soil north of Luxor.[79]

For biblical scholars, the text of the codices provided new insight into the world of the "Gnostic" Christians, a heretical sect who believed that they could achieve a kind of enlightenment through the acquisition of esoteric *gnosis*, or "knowledge."[80] For book historians, though, the Nag Hammadi codices were of paramount importance: they were a *gnosis* of sorts in and of themselves, a time capsule that had preserved a small part of the lost world of ancient bookmaking for posterity.

The construction of the Nag Hammadi codices, the world's earliest complete bound and covered books, is simple. Each one was made from a sheaf of papyrus sheets—cut as usual from a series of scrolls—that had been folded in half and then bound to a single-ply sheepskin or goatskin cover by a pair of leather thongs. Around a foot in length along the spine, each codex opened to about eighteen inches wide, though many sported covers extending farther out into flaps that could be

➸ A modern model of a Nag Hammadi codex made by Irina Gorstein of the Frances Loeb Library's Conservation Lab. Reinforcing tabs of papyrus can be seen at the spine, along with the wraparound leather cover and thongs with which to tie the book closed.[81]

wrapped around the closed book. All of them had attached leather thongs with which they could be fastened shut.[82]

To bind the pages and cover together, the assembled stack of leather and papyrus was first pierced clean through by four slots, or holes, with two near the top of the spine and two near the bottom. Placing yourself in the role of ancient bookbinder, then, and with the unbound book spread flat in front of you, the whole thing was tied together with two leather thongs, one for each pair of slots: each thong passes through one slot from the outside of the book to the inside, through the cover and then the "text block," as bookbinders call it, before crossing over to and exiting via the other slot.[83] The loose ends of each cord are tied off outside the cover. In some of the Nag Hammadi books, the spine is reinforced by a separate strip of leather placed between the text block and the cover; in others, as seen above, small pieces of leather or papyrus, pierced to match the binding holes, have been placed atop the text block to stop the binding thongs from tearing the pages.[84]

The Nag Hammadi codices display certain self-evident truths about how books should be made. Most basic of all is their fundamental shape: each page is taller than it is wide, by a factor of around four to three, making them almost exactly the same size and aspect ratio as a sheet of letter paper. (European A4 paper is a little more elongated, though not by much.) Historians have never agreed on why papyrus books were rectangular: one theory is that pages were bound along a longer edge because it produced a more robust text block; another is that the columnar layout commonly used in scrolls naturally translated to pages that were taller than they were wide.[85] Whatever the reason, the Nag Hammadi codices are strikingly manageable in size and entirely conventional in format.

Other familiar touches abound. Each sheet of papyrus was cut successively narrower so that the completed book closed to present a flat edge, a finishing touch common to modern books. (Nowadays, handmade books are clamped in place and trimmed with a circular knife called a plough, while mass-produced books are squared off with a blow from a power-driven guillotine.)[86] And despite their great age, the covers that enwrapped those text blocks hold no surprises for the modern observer. The leather covers were reinforced by waste sheets of papyrus, and a leather flap, or "turn-in," was left at each edge of the cover to be folded over and pasted onto the papyrus inside.[87] Sixteen hundred years later, this basic recipe is still in use: if you relieve a hardcover book of its dust jacket, you will see turn-ins where the cover's cloth or paper wrapping has been folded over and pasted onto a pair of reinforcing boards.

In one very particular way, the papyrus waste hiding under the covers of the Nag Hammadi books has turned out to be more important than the pages they were intended to protect. Just as archaeologists have a weakness for rooting around in ancient trash heaps, so codicologists prey upon the scraps of papyrus, parchment, and paper that were used to stiffen ancient book bindings. (They call it cartonnage, like the layered, fibrous material the ancient Egyptians used to make death masks and sarcophagi.) In the case of the Nag Hammadi codices, those bindings were gently prized apart to yield discarded contracts, letters, and accounts that carried handwritten dates in the years 333, 341, 346, and 348.[88] The history of the paged book as we know it started in 333 CE, almost seventeen centuries ago.

14

Ties That Bind: binding the paged book

If you were to make a replica of a Nag Hammadi codex today (and many bookmakers, both amateurs and professionals, have done so), you might make a few changes. It is easier to obtain cardboard and paper than it is to find papyrus, and you would be forgiven for buying premade leather in preference to raising, slaughtering, and skinning a goat. With your raw materials assembled, you fold your sheaf of paper in half and cut the leather to match; you trim the closed pages to a flat edge; you pierce the lot with an awl; and you string it all together with leather thongs. The materials may have changed, but the basic design will be a faithful echo of the original. Yet if you then compare it to *this* book—or, better, one of those hand-me-down leather-covered, gold-lettered tomes that gather dust on bookshelves the world over—it will quickly become apparent that we no longer simply make books; now we bind them.

The little red-brown book shown opposite is known as the St Cuthbert Gospel. It is more than a thousand years old, and is said to have been the personal property of England's most famous native saint. It changed hands in 2012 for more than $14 million, making it the second most expensive book in the world (as of 2015, only the "Codex Leicester," one of Leonardo da Vinci's notebooks, is more valuable), and yet, despite its immense age and its exorbitant price tag, in most other ways that count the St Cuthbert Gospel is a direct ancestor of this and every other modern book.[1] It is the earliest surviving example of the craft of European (and later, Western) bookbinding.

Cuthbert, the bishop of the holy island of Lindisfarne off the Northumbrian coast, died on March 20, 687.[2] He was fifty years of age or thereabouts, and had led a pious life punctuated by miracles. Unable to sleep one night, Cuthbert witnessed the soul of Bishop Aidan, one of his predecessors at Lindisfarne, being carried to heaven; he was said to converse regularly with angels and to receive food from them; and less dramatically, he staved off a dose of the plague that had claimed the life of a superior, the prior of Melrose Abbey in the Scottish Borders.[3] Installed as the prior's replacement and later promoted to the bishopric of Lindisfarne, Cuthbert earned a reputation as an ascetic, pious man deserving of the veneration of his flock. When he died at his retreat on Inner Farne, a small island a few miles from Lindisfarne itself, his body was returned to the abbey and placed reverently in a stone sarcophagus beside the altar, there to be entreated for holy inspiration and guidance.[4]

The Vikings who raided Lindisfarne a century later had no time for dead bishops or live monks, and in 793 the island's religious community, Cuthbert's corpse and all, was relocated to the mainland. Thus began Cuthbert's posthumous pilgrimage: it was not until 995 that his remains finally came to rest at Durham, in the north of England, where his coffin was installed first in a church of wood, then one of stone, and

⭠ The St Cuthbert Gospel, made in England at end of the seventh century.

finally in Durham Cathedral itself.[5] And it was there, in 1104, that his little red book was found.

Just as the monks at Lindisfarne had done three centuries before, the cathedral authorities decided to place Cuthbert's body in a grand public shrine so that it might become a sort of tourist attraction. When they levered open his wooden travel coffin they found that Cuthbert's body was miraculously intact—proof of his holy nature, whispered those in attendance; proof that the monks at Lindisfarne had embalmed his corpse, say modern experts—and Cuthbert was elevated to the ranks of the "incorruptibles," those religious figures whose bodies are said to resist the decaying forces of death.[6]

The myth of Cuthbert's incorruptibility was amplified when his personal effects were found to be in near-perfect condition, although his reputation for poverty and abstemiousness took a knock. As prior of Melrose Abbey and bishop of Lindisfarne, Cuthbert had lived in a pastor's paradise, banqueting with royalty and receiving sumptuous gifts from his fellow churchmen. A few of these gifts followed him to the grave, including a silken funerary garment, an ivory comb, and an ostentatious jeweled gold cross.[7] Of more lasting importance, however, was the small red codex found with his body. This book was the saint's personal copy of the Gospel of John, placed in his coffin upon his burial on Lindisfarne and seemingly blessed with the same incorruptibility as Cuthbert himself. [8]

Known as the Stonyhurst Gospel for many years, after the Jesuit college where it had resided since 1769, after buying it at auction in 2011 the British Library rebranded Cuthbert's little red book as the "St Cuthbert Gospel."[9] Even so, the lack of a possessive apostrophe in the title reveals that historians are no longer sure that the book ever physically belonged to Saint Cuthbert himself. The handwriting of the scribe who copied the book, the selection of Latin abbreviations used in it, and comparisons with other manuscripts made during same period all suggest that the book was written and bound in or around 698 CE, more than a decade after Cuthbert's death.[10] But if the St Cuthbert Gospel was never owned by its eponymous saint, what is the fuss about?

On the face of it, the St Cuthbert Gospel is not a striking book. It is small, 5.4 by 3.6 inches in size, and is bound in plain crimson leather relieved by a few indented lines and a raised design at the center of the front cover.[11] With its parchment pages loosened a little by the passage of time, it looks more like a leather-covered Filofax than a milestone of history. Under the cover's leather are two wooden boards cut to the same size as the pages and sewn together with ninety-three leaves of vellum and one of paper.[12] And unlike the great communal Gospel books (not least the sumptuous Lindisfarne Gospels commissioned by Cuthbert's successor Eadfrith), the text of the St Cuthbert Gospel is restrained, laid out in a single column per page, and broken up only by a few modestly decorated capital letters.[13]

It is the sheer ordinariness of the St Cuthbert Gospel that makes it so valuable. It was almost certainly produced at Wearmouth-Jarrow, a celebrated monastery and bookmaking center in the north of England; and it is modest but well made, suggesting that the scribe who copied out its text and the bookbinder who sewed it together were confident in their process. And, crucially, it is in preternaturally good condition: when it was exhibited at the Society of Antiquaries in London in 1806, it was thought that the binding must have been replaced during the Elizabethan era—that is, the second half of the sixteenth century.[14] The St Cuthbert Gospel is as fine an example of the early medieval bookmaker's art as is ever likely to be found. Though Cuthbert himself is long gone (on inspection in 1899, his body was no more than a skeleton), his book is every bit as incorruptible as the man himself was not. Through it, we are granted a rare, unfiltered glimpse into the past.[15]

Bookmaking had advanced far from the Nag Hammadi codices of the fourth century when the monks at Wearmouth-Jarrow applied themselves to the book that would become known as the St Cuthbert Gospel. Perhaps the biggest change since ancient times was that parchment was no longer a novelty: Egyptian papyrus had been eclipsed long ago, thanks to a combination of economic forces and religious conservatism, as Europe's Christian majority rejected anything with a whiff of polytheism about it.[16] But more subtle than this change in writing material—and, from a mechanical point of view, more important—was the way in which pages were composed into a completed book.

If you were to pick up and open the St Cuthbert Gospel as if to read it, then tilted it toward you so that the top of its spine is visible, you would see that its pages are gathered into a series of individual groups, each one composed of a pile of stacked sheets folded down the middle and stitched together at the spine.[17] The same is not true of the Nag Hammadi codices, and, for their makers and their readers, that was a problem.

The old saw that a single sheet of paper cannot be folded more than seven times may be demonstrably false, but a stack of thick, fibrous papyrus offers more resistance. As they put together their proto-books the Nag Hammadi bookmakers would have struggled to fold more than a few sheets of thick, fibrous papyrus at a time, and codicologists studying the surviving books think that they folded each sheet individually, between eighteen and thirty-nine of them per book, before assembling them into stacks.[18]

With that task complete, the ancient bookmakers would have had to acknowledge that papyrus is not an especially accommodating material for books—or at least, not for books comprising a single gathering. The amount of papyrus packed into each of the Nag Hammadi codices would have made it difficult to read pages at either end of a book: to read the second and third pages in a booklet of thirty sheets, one must hold down fifty-nine layers of stiff, inflexible papyrus. The chunky central fold is awkward too: the farther out from the middle of the book one travels, the wider the radius of the fold; by degrees, the valleys between facing pages vanish into darkness and the usable text area on each page is diminished.[19]

And there was yet another problem, albeit one that would have become obvious only after using a book for some time. If you read straight through a book whose gatherings are composed of, say, four sheets each, only an average of two sheets are unfolded at any given time. (You can see this in action right now: if you look at the end of this book, you will see that all gatherings except the one at which you are reading are closed, and they remain closed except when you turn the page into a new gathering.) On the other hand, if you read straight through a book with, say, *thirty-nine* sheets per gathering, an average of nineteen and a half of them will be unfolded at any given time, and this is bad news when those sheets are prone to cracking after repeated folding and unfolding. This was mitigated to a degree by the arrival of resilient, flexible parchment, but the basic unwieldiness and fragility of single-gathering books remained.

It is possible that one of the Nag Hammadi bookmakers realized this. Of all the Nag Hammadi books, the one known as the Eid Codex, the Jung Codex, or, formally, Codex I, is simultaneously the most intriguing and the most mysterious of them all.

Forty-one papyrus leaves from Nag Hammadi eluded the grasp of Phocion J. Tano, the antiquities dealer who amassed the rest of the collection, to be snapped up by a competing dealer named Albert Eid. In defiance of stern warnings from the director of Cairo's Coptic Museum that exportation was absolutely prohibited, Eid, the son of the Belgian consul in Cairo, quietly circulated photographs of the manuscript among likely buyers. But then, his prospective clients were not above a little skullduggery of their own: when Jean Doresse reported his impressions of the forty-one leaves of the "Eid Codex" to his superiors at the Bibliothèque nationale de France, they instructed him to play down its importance to lower the price.[20]

Unfortunately, Doresse was not a good liar. The price stayed where it was, the BnF declared that it could not afford the codex, and Eid traveled to the United States to solicit other offers. Somehow, he managed to bring the codex with him. It has never been entirely clear how: some players in the drama claim that he hid the book at the bottom of a crate of more mundane antiquities; others say that it was smuggled out in a Belgian diplomatic pouch. (The eventual buyers asserted that it had come out of Egypt "by legal means," though they were vague as to exactly what that meant.) Having failed to secure an American buyer,

Eid returned to Brussels, where he deposited the codex in a safety-deposit box. He died in 1950, the book still unsold.[21]

The codex was eventually acquired in 1952 by the Jung Institute of Zürich, a society of psychoanalysts founded by Carl Jung, whose members hoped that the book's esoteric contents would help prove Jung's theories of psychological archetypes. The institute had tracked down Eid's widow in Cairo and opened a correspondence with her with the aim of buying the book. Simone Eid was eager to leave Egypt, then in the grip of a revolution against an ongoing British military presence, and she used the codex as a bargaining chip to secure her exit. An obliging Jung Institute deposited 35,000 Swiss francs ($8,100) in a Swiss bank account in April 1952 and agreed to keep the purchase a secret until Simone was safely out of the country.[22] The Jung Institute got its book, and the book got its name.

Publication of the Jung Codex was every bit as drawn out, if not more so, as that of the other Nag Hammadi codices. But when facsimiles of its pages were finally made available in 1975, codicologists found a book that was fundamentally different from the rest of the Nag Hammadi library. The Jung Codex, as far as they could tell, had been composed of multiple gatherings.

(Before diving into the details of the Jung Codex, it is worth explaining a few words that have taken on specific meaning in the bookbinding trade. Firstly, each of the single sheets in a book, folded in half and attached to the spine, is called a folio, from the Latin *folium*, or "leaf."[23] Secondly—and confusingly—the two halves of each folded folio are known as leaves, though for bookbinders, collectors, and codicologists the distinction between "folio" and "leaf" is an old and robust one.[24] Finally, each of the two sides of a leaf is a single page.[25] As a mnemonic, consider that you *leaf* through a book, turning over leaves as you go, on the way to find a particular *page*.)

After careful examination of the codex's contents, scholars were able to arrange its constituent folios in order to reveal that Codex I had been split into three gatherings of twenty-two, eight, and six sheets respectively for a total of thirty-six sheets or 144 pages.[26] The asymmetry of the arrangement aside, this would have been a far wieldier book than most of its counterparts, and more durable too. What is *not* clear, however, is whether the use of multiple gatherings was intentional. Separated from the pages themselves, the leather cover of Codex I endured its own long journey to publication: lost, found, and finally sold to a private collector, it remains divorced from its contents and even now its exact binding mechanism is unknown.[27] Were the two shorter gatherings added later, as addenda to the main one, or were all three bound at the same time? No one knows for sure. If the Jung Codex does mark the point at which the book emerged as a new species, book experts remain loath to declare it as such.[28]

The makers of the St Cuthbert Gospel, one of the Jung Codex's spiritual successors, were well acquainted with the advantages of multiple gatherings. Though the Gospel is still remarkably intact, at some point in the past its first gathering came loose and was sewn directly inside the front cover in order to keep the whole thing together. Because of this, codicologists can see the workings of the book without having to further dismantle it: down to the smallest of details, we know exactly how the St Cuthbert Gospel was made.[29]

The parchment folios for the St Cuthbert Gospel were arranged into eleven gatherings of four folios each, along with a single extra leaf at the very front of the book and a final gathering of just two folios.[30] This mostly symmetrical arrangement may be partially explained by the pinholes pierced through the fold of each gathering: it appears that each one was temporarily bound with a length of thread, in the manner of the old Nag Hammadi codices, so that the scribe could copy his text into it without having to worry about getting the pages in the right order. (He seems to have ruled only two pages of each gathering, relying on a firm hand to carry the imprint of the back of his penknife through to those behind.) Then, as the end of the book neared, the scribe must have realized that a gathering of two folios would be sufficient to complete it.[31]

With the text copied and the gatherings collated into the correct order, the real work of the binding began. The bookbinder (who may or may not have also been the scribe) removed the temporary threads and cut four *V*-shaped notches into the fold of each gathering at roughly equal intervals, so that when a gathering was opened flat the notches would reveal themselves as holes spaced equidistantly along its spine.[32] A pair of thin wooden boards, each one around a tenth of an inch thick, were cut to match the pages and drilled with holes near their edges to match the notches in the gatherings. Next, the bookbinder threaded two needles with fine flaxen thread and sewed the whole thing together.

This was not a job for the impatient or the clumsy.

Imagine, for a moment, the stack of folded parchment gatherings, sandwiched between wooden boards, that would have lain before the maker of the St Cuthbert Gospel. Each of the boards and gatherings has four holes, or notches, that we will label from top to bottom as *A*, *B*, *C*, and *D*. With a needle in hand, the bookmaker began by sewing the front board onto the first gathering, passing his needle into the gathering to run along its center fold from *A* to *B* and out again. Next, the needle passed into the second gathering, running this time from *B* to *A*, where it passed out of the gathering to be knotted to the first by means of a "chain" or "kettle" stitch.[33] This continued all the way to the back of the book, the thread diving into the interior of each folded parchment gathering and then out again to be consolidated in twin rows of chain stitches.

All this was repeated until all the gatherings had been sewn together at *A* and *B*, and the back board had been sewn onto the final gathering. Having done this, the bookbinder took up the second needle and thread and repeated the entire process at *C* and *D* so that the whole book was fastened together by four lines of chain stitches running across the exposed spines of the gatherings.[34] This is a simplified

↞ A sixteenth-century Ethiopian book bound using Coptic stitching. The boards are approximately 10 by 12 inches in size. Each of the six braids of thread that cross the spine pass into and out of each successive gathering, so that each gathering is sewn only to its neighbors.[35]

description of what was a complex process, and it is much easier to envisage with an example of the finished product at hand. Denuded of its leather cover, the eleventh-century Ethiopian book shown above is a fine example of that finished product, albeit with six notches per gathering rather than the four of the St Cuthbert Gospel. Each row of chain stiches crosses the spine from front board to the back, the thread passing into and out of each gathering in turn, and creating characteristic rows of plaited thread as it goes.

In this way, each of the components of the finished book—the front board, each of the gatherings, and the back board—was sewn only to its neighboring components. The front board was sewn to the first gathering, the first gathering to the second gathering, the second to the third, and so on. The product was a book that opened entirely flat: the stitching between gatherings acted as a flexible hinge, allowing each gathering to be opened without competing against all the others. It was a small innovation but a crucial one, and today this style of binding is called Coptic stitching in honor of the Egyptian Copts who pioneered it between the second and fourth centuries CE.[36] But though the Copts of Egypt presaged the modern book, somehow the Romans contrived to have the last word. That word was "codex," and it has survived even as every other aspect of books and bookmaking has been overhauled and updated over the centuries.

Wherever the idea for the paged book had come from, it seems that the simple wooden writing tablet was an important source of inspiration when it came to the construction of this new medium. Wax diptychs in a remarkable state of preservation have been found in the choked ruins of Herculaneum, each tablet drilled with holes and fastened with cords laid into grooves so that they did not protrude above the surface of the wood, and their simple binding mechanism has been touted as the ancestor of the Coptic binding of the St Cuthbert Gospel and other books like it.[37] And therein lies the clue: for centuries before the arrival of the paged book, Roman writers had referred to writing tablets as *caudices*, and later *codices*. Meaning "tree trunk" or "block of wood," at first the word "*codex*" was reserved for wooden writing tablets alone, though gradually it came to mean any tablet, whatever it was made of.[38] In the end the word transcended its physical origins altogether: tablets were so often used to record legal matters that "*codex*" came to mean a collection of laws—a code, in other words, from which the English word is taken—and so, when a new vehicle for the written word arrived sometime during the first or second century CE, an odd hybrid of sliced-up scrolls and wooden boards, the Romans had a name waiting for it.[39] The codex had arrived.

The St Cuthbert Gospel was finished with a leather cover pasted over its wooden boards, as would be customary for more than a thousand years. The raised designs on its cover are startlingly protuberant to modern eyes—this is not a book that would play well with others on a modern bookshelf—but illustrations reveal that as late as the seventeenth century books were most often laid flat on their bookshelves with the front cover facing upward, rather than stored vertically. Many medieval bookcases were almost like lecterns, their shelves angled downward so that books could proudly display their decorated covers.[40]

Conceptually at least, the raised Celtic swirls and borders of the St Cuthbert Gospel were simple to achieve. Straight lines were laid out by stringing cords between holes drilled in the cover, while the raised design at the center was most likely built up from leather scraps or the same thick, chalky gesso used to make raised illuminations. After this endoskeleton had been fixed in place, a sheet of crimson-dyed sheepskin or goatskin was cut into a rectangle slightly larger than the fully opened book, moistened, and then pasted into place. Working quickly, before the leather dried out and the paste hardened, the bookbinder worked the leather around the raised decorations and incised the indented lines with some kind of flat, pointed tool. (A bookbinder's "folder"—a flattened, polished sliver of bone the size and shape of a tongue depressor used for creasing folios and sundry other tasks—would have done the job admirably.)[41] Finally, like the Nag Hammadi codices, and like the hardcover edition of this book, the protruding edges of the cover were mitered at the corners, folded over, and pasted to the inside of the boards.[42] It was a skilled task, but one at which the maker of the St Cuthbert Gospel seems to have been well practiced, and which went unchanged for centuries afterward.

There was one last innovation to come. The chain stitching that allowed the St Cuthbert Gospel to be opened completely flat had to sustain all the stresses and strains of its daily use, and, as one particular owner of the book found to their cost, those stresses could not be borne forever. At some point the stitching that held the first gathering to the second gathering—and, in turn, to all the others—came loose, necessitating a clumsy repair.[43]

Around the eighth century, perhaps in one of the countless monasteries where monks busied themselves with the making of books, someone decided to fix the problem. Too many books were breaking apart, their Coptic stitching overpowered by repeated opening and closing. Perhaps this nameless bookmaker knelt at the altar of his church and gazed heavenward to beg for inspiration; and perhaps, up there in the ribbed trusses of the church's roof, he saw it.

What arose in the eighth century was a new style of stitching that gave books a backbone where earlier, Coptic-stitched books had none. The difference here was that rather than sew each component to its neighbor—the front board to the first gathering, the first gathering to the second, and so on—each component was attached *separately* to a series of paired hempen cords that ran across the spine of the book like rafters along a roof. (The figure opposite shows such a book before its cover has been applied.) First, the front board was drilled and laced onto the cords; next, the folded gatherings were pierced with notches to match and sewn onto the cords, one by one; and finally, the back board was laced and knotted onto the dangling cords to finish the job.[44] This new way of doing things was called double-cord binding, and it meant that each gathering had to support only its own weight, rather than that of the entire book.[45]

That double-cord binding was stronger than Coptic stitching was made evident by the so-called Ragyndrudis Codex, a book made during the eighth century using the double-cord method that was said to have been owned, up to the moment of his untimely death, by Saint Boniface.[46] Boniface was one of Christian Europe's founding saints, an Anglo-Saxon who traveled to the Continent first as a missionary bishop

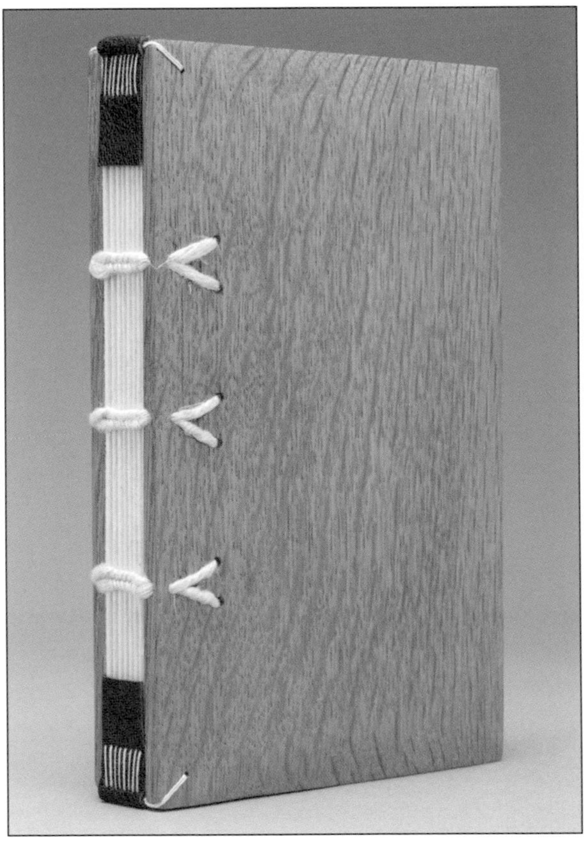

⇜ An uncovered model of a double-cord-bound codex, made by Irina Gorstein of the Frances Loeb Library's Conservation Lab. This style of binding is typical of books made during the seventh to twelfth centuries. Gatherings are sewn onto and supported by the cords that run across the spine, and elaborate but unfinished endbands can be seen at the top and bottom of the spine.[47]

and later as archbishop of Mainz.[48] In 752, according to legend, Boniface was ambushed in windswept Frisia on Europe's North Sea coast (now part of Holland and Germany) by heathen guerillas who fell upon his party with great fury. Boniface is said to have held up a holy book as the mob drew near—not to ward off his attackers' blows, his hagiographers hasten to add, but to receive spiritual protection at the instant of his martyrdom—and as their blows fell, the book in Boniface's hands bore the brunt of the fatal attack.

That fateful book, so goes the tale, was the Ragyndrudis Codex that now resides in Germany's Fulda Cathedral.[49] As a test of the newly invented technique of double-cord binding, the assault of a pagan mob must surely have been hard to beat. J.R.R. Tolkien, at least, was sufficiently impressed to sneak a doppelgänger of Boniface's book into *The Fellowship of the Ring*: his fictional "Book of Mazarbul" is found by Frodo, Gandalf, and company in the Mines of Moria, its cover mutilated by Orcish axes and its pages stained with Dwarvish blood.[50]

Like papermaking, movable type, and woodcut printing, bookbinding was not a craft disposed to great inventive leaps. Occasionally, a bookbinder was moved to experiment with some radical alteration to the basic formula of the book—two books bound to a single wooden covering board, for instance, or a series of books concertinaed together like an unholy orihon—but with the adoption of double-cord binding, the form of the book was effectively standardized. From the time of the St Cuthbert Gospel, the Ragyndrudis Codex, and their medieval ilk, through to the encyclopedias Britannica and Webster's dictionaries that lined nineteenth-century bookshelves, the evolution of the book was a gentle one, borne onward on a tide of tinkering, refinements, and changes in material.

↞ Jost Amman's 1568 woodcut depicting a bookbinder's workshop. In the background a worker sews a pile of gatherings onto cords stretched on a sewing frame; in the foreground another worker is planing the fore edge of a book held in a "lying press," a general-purpose press used to hold a book in place during a variety of operations.[51]

Some of the biggest changes to this formula, such as they were, happened early on. During the Carolingian era, when Charlemagne exhorted his dissolute clergy to focus on the production and study of religious books, the cords of hemp used in the earliest bindings gave way to twisted strips of leather and flat leather tapes, the better to provide books with a robust but supple backbone.[52] A clutch of related innovations arose: some bookmakers experimented with different sewing stitches; others recessed their cords or tapes into slots cut into their gatherings, across the spine; and later, in the eleventh century, the act of sewing books together was made easier by the invention of the "sewing frame," a pair of parallel wooden bars between which cords or tapes could be stretched taut.[53]

Gradually, what are now called endpapers evolved into a distinct (and often distinctive) component of the book. Endpapers are any leaves at the front and back of a book that are pasted to the inside of the boards: in some books, such as the St Cuthbert Gospel, these were no more than first and last of the regular leaves in the text block; in others, the text block was arranged so that its first and last gatherings comprised only a single folio each, which then formed the endpapers; and later, as bookmakers sought to streamline their craft, loose endpapers were simply pasted directly to the inside of the boards and their facing pages.[54] Endpapers have always served a practical purpose in anchoring the text block to the cover, and when marbled papers, decorated with swirls of color, became available in the seventeenth century, they became a way for bookbinders to inject some personality into their products.[55]

Similarly, the band of colored thread at the top of a hardback's spine was a practical feature before it became an ornamental one. In Coptic-bound books such as the St Cuthbert Gospel, the "headband" (if there is one at the bottom of the spine, it is called a tailband; together they are endbands) was a straightforward affair, made by piercing holes near the top of each gathering and stitching them through the leather of the cover.[56] In later books they were considerably more elaborate, made from multicolored silken cord sewn onto the gatherings at the top of the book and then laced into the boards or tacked through the covering leather. In some cases, endbands were recessed into notches cut into the text block so that they sat flush with the top and bottom of the spine.[57]

The most cited reason for the presence of a headband is that it helps protect a book's spine as it is removed from the shelf. If you have a bookcase nearby, reach up and take out a book; you will instinctively pull it out a fraction with your forefinger before doing anything else, and a headband, so it is said, resists the force of this gesture.[58] It is a neat explanation, but it is misleading. Endbands were already a thousand years old when books went from being shelved horizontally to vertically.[59] They were, simply, integral parts of a book's binding, an evolutionary midpoint between the chain stitching of Coptic bindings and the sewn cords of later books that helped keep boards, gatherings, and leather in one piece.[60]

When Johannes Gutenberg's movable type arrived in the middle of the fifteenth century, the endband was one of the first casualties. Adding them had always been a fiddly, labor-intensive process, and as unbound books stacked up, bookmakers were driven to reduce complexity wherever they could. Endbands were sewn onto alternate gatherings rather than every single one; they were placed on top of the text block rather than recessed into it; they were no longer sewn through the cover; and so forth. By the end of the sixteenth century, the average bookbinder sewed a book's gatherings at the top and bottom of the spine with a simple chain stitch and then glued on ersatz endbands to assuage their wounded sense of aesthetics.[61] The headband at the top of this book is the bibliographic equivalent of a vestigial limb, hanging around only because evolution has not yet caught up with it.

Other advancements were less obvious. If you look again at the headband of this book, it will be apparent that it has a slight curve to it, arcing outward from the book, and if you close the book, its "fore edge" (that is, the edge of the book opposite the spine) will display a corresponding concave arc.[62] Early in the sixteenth century, bookbinders discovered that shaping a book like this helped to reduce the strain on its stitching, and from that point on more and more books were "rounded" by coating the spine with glue, shaping the text block to the desired curve, and then fixing the book in a small wooden "lying press" until the glue was dry.[63]

A related discovery was made soon after. Again, by looking closely at the spine of this book you will see that the text block has "shoulders" where the gatherings at the front and back of the book spread outward a little, giving the spine a subtle mushroomlike shape. This second process is called backing, and it was done as the rounded book was still fixed in the lying press. With a few millimeters of the spine left protruding for this very purpose, the bookmaker gently tapped the spine with a hammer until its edges spread out a little. All this allowed for the boards to be attached flush with the spine, helped maintain the rounded shape of the text block, and, by adding a kink along each page near the spine, made the book more flexible.[64]

Finally, in addition to all these other modifications, the materials and methods used to make boards and covers changed over time. At first, Western bookmakers preferred stiff, wooden boards that could be fastened or even locked shut to stop parchment pages from curling; in the East, on the other hand, Coptic and Islamic bookmakers, whose

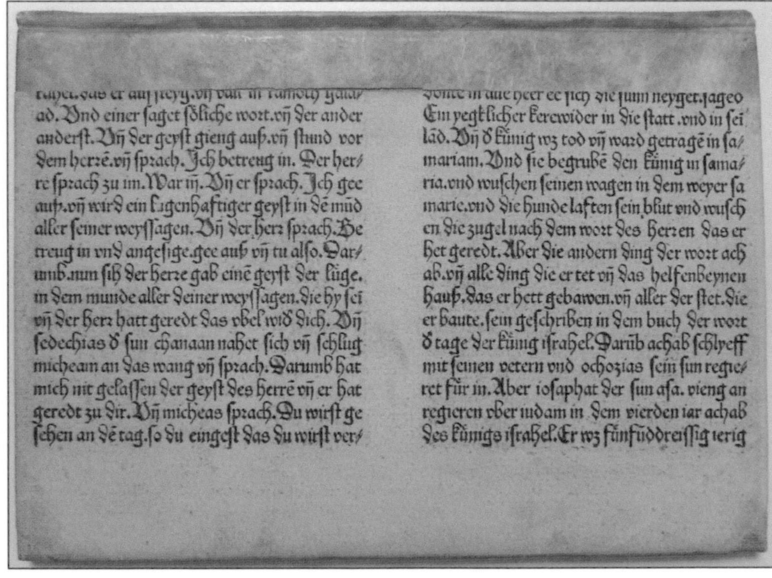
ad. Vnd einer saget söliche wort. vñ der ander
anderst. Vñ der geyst gieng auß. vñ stund vor
dem herrē. vñ sprach. Ich betreug in. Der herre sprach zu im. War iñ. Vñ er sprach. Ich gee
auß. vñ wird ein lugenhaftiger geyst in dē mūd
aller seiner weyssagen. Vñ der herr sprach. Be
treug in vnd angesige. gee auß vñ tu also. Darumb. nun sih der herre gab einē geyst der lüge.
in dem munde aller seiner weyssagen. die hy sei
vñ der herr hatt geredt das vbel wid dich. Vñ
sedechias d sun chanaan nahet sich vñ schlug
micheam an das wang vñ sprach. Darumb hat
mich nit gelassen der geyst des herrē vñ er hat
geredt zu dir. Vñ micheas sprach. Du wirst ge
sehen an dē tag. so du eingest das du wirst ver-

Ein yegklicher kerewider in die statt. vnd in sei
lād. Vñ d künig wz tod vñ ward getragē in sa-
mariam. Vnd sie begrubē den künig in sama-
ria. vnd wuschen seinen wagen in dem weyer sa
marie. vnd die hunde lasten sein blut vnd wusch
en die zugel nach dem wort des herren das er
het geredt. Aber die andern ding der wort ach
ab. vñ alle ding die er tet vñ das helfenbeynen
hauß. das er hett gebawen. vñ aller der stet. die
er baute. sein geschriben in dem buch der wort
d tage der künig israhel. Darūb achab schlyeff
mit seinen vetern vnd ochozias sein sun regie-
ret für in. Aber iosaphat der sun asa. vieng an
regieren vber iudam in dem vierden iar achab
des künigs israhel. Er wz fünfūddreissig ierig

⇚ An unapologetic reuse of an old book in the binding of a new one. The boards of this early fifteenth-century book are covered with leaves from an early printed German Bible. The book itself is called *Panegyris ad duces Bavariae*, or "Panegyrics to the dukes of Bavaria"; someone, at some point, felt that a book praising the dukes of Bavaria was worth the sacrifice of a Holy Bible.[65]

papyrus and paper folios were less unruly, pasted together waste material to make "pasteboard" bindings.[66] Europe's bookmakers followed suit as paper percolated in from the Islamic lands to the east, but the bookshelf, too, figured into the switch to pasteboard: as readers began to shelve their books into tightly packed, vertically aligned rows, there was less of a need for lockable, rigid boards to hold their parchment pages in place.[67] Pasteboard's rise has had the happy side effect of preserving all kinds of documents that would otherwise have been thrown out with the trash. One of the earliest surviving woodcut prints, the "Buxheim Saint Christopher" dated to 1423, was peeled out of the pasteboard cover of a book written in 1417 but re-bound sometime later, while fragments of a lost Roman law code were discovered as reinforcements in the spine of a medieval book.[68]

Of all the things that books are and have been made of, the material of a book's cover, the first thing to meet your eyes and greet your touch as you pluck a book off the shelf, has remained most constant. From the fourth century right down to the present day is an unbroken stream of books that have been bound in practical, long-lived leather.[69]

Leather lends itself to being decorated by "blind tooling," a process where heated metal tools are applied to moistened leather to leave a permanent indentation. Covers were decorated this way as far back as the days of the St Cuthbert Gospel, and designs grew only more elaborate from there: bookmakers fashioned tools ranging from simple straightedges to wheels, spiked rollers, repeating designs, and monolithic whole-page stamps.[70] Really, the only things missing from the average book's cover were letters and numbers: it was not until the sixteenth century, when books began to be shelved vertically, with their spines facing out, that titles and authors' names finally began to appear on their covers.[71]

Tooled designs grew more extravagant in the fifteenth century, when Venetian bookbinders experimented with the application of gold to tooled cover designs, mixing flecks of gold into paint or sticking on gold leaf with a mixture of vinegar and egg white called glair.[72] From Venice the practice spread across Europe.[73] By the nineteenth century, gilt-tooled book covers of delicate leather had become so exquisite—and so easily damaged—that they themselves needed protection: the earliest surviving dust jacket, a plain paper wrapper sealed with wax, dates to 1830.[74]

Quite apart from any cover designs, the animal from which a book's covering leather is made can reveal a book's provenance. The holy trinity of calfskin, goatskin, and sheepskin has, at times, and depending upon the available fauna, been joined by alligator leather; "Russian leather," or horsehide; deerskin; pigskin; kangaroo skin; sealskin; and walrus hide.[75] Sometimes, though, the origins of a book's cover can shock.

Over the winter of 1829–1830, the citizens of Edinburgh, Scotland, were gripped by a grisly murder trial. William Burke, an immigrant Irish soldier, stood accused with his accomplice William Hare of three killings (it emerged later that they were responsible for twelve more) in which the pair had got their victims drunk, then suffocated them. The bodies were taken to the home of Professor Robert Knox, a renowned anatomist at the University of Edinburgh, who paid Burke and Hare between £8 and £14 per cadaver. Hare turned king's evidence at the trial, blaming Burke for the murders and swearing that Knox had not been involved, thus leaving his accomplice alone to the mercy of the law. Burke was sent first to the gallows near Edinburgh Castle, where he was hanged on January 28, 1829, and then to the medical school; as was common practice in the case of an executed criminal, Burke's cadaver was to be dissected at the university's medical faculty the day after his hanging.[76] When a public viewing was announced, some 30,000 people came to gawp at the murderer's dismembered corpse. His preserved skeleton was put on show as a warning to others.[77]

But this was not the end for William Burke. Someone among the great and the good of Edinburgh's medical establishment acquired a piece of Burke's dissected skin, not more than a foot square, and had it tanned and bound into a pocket-sized notebook that resides today in Edinburgh's Surgeons' Hall. "Burke's Skin Pocket Book" reads the tooled title on the cover of this otherwise anonymous little book, its leather still as flexible as Burke's morals after almost two hundred years.[78]

Burke's incongruous little book is the most notorious example of "anthropodermic bibliopegy," or the binding of books in human skin, but it is far from the only one.[79] Harvard University's Houghton Library has its own chilling example in the form of a copy of *Des destinées de l'âme* (The destinies of the soul), a book written by a nineteenth-century French novelist named Arsène Houssaye and gifted by the author to his friend Dr. Ludovic Bouland. Like Robert Knox, Bouland was a man with ready access to corpses and so, when a mental patient of his succumbed to a stroke, he decided to cover the book in her skin. Bouland added a note to the book describing its provenance:

> *This book is bound in human skin parchment on which no ornament has been stamped to preserve its elegance. By looking carefully you easily distinguish the pores of the skin. A book about the human soul deserved to have a human covering: I had kept this piece of human skin taken from the back of a woman. It is interesting to see the different aspects that change this skin according to the method of preparation to which it is subjected. Compare for example with the small volume I have in my library, Sever. Pinaeus de Virginitatis notis which is also bound in human skin but tanned with sumac.*[80]

Evidently Ludovic Bouland was an anthropodermic bibliopegy aficionado. Of the other "small volume" in his library, a book called *De integritatis et corruptionis virginum notis* (Thoughts on the integrity and corruption of virgins) now held in the Wellcome Library in London, he wrote in 1865:

> *This curious little book on virginity and the female reproductive functions seems to me worth of* [sic] *a binding appropriate to the subject and covered by a portion of female skin, tanned by myself with sumac.*[81]

Whereas Bouland had kept the cover of *Des destinées de l'âme* plain, explaining that "no ornament has been stamped to preserve its elegance," his second effort was more elaborate. His copy of *De integritatis et corruptionis virginum notis* is a disconcerting monument to bookbinding, a perfectly preserved example both of the state of bookbinding and of the aesthetics of his day. Tanned a rich brown with sumac (a wild plant whose leaves are rich in tannic acid), with raised bands across the spine where its reinforcing cords run under the skin of the cover, and decorated with intricate and extensive gold tooling, it is the kind of book that under normal circumstances would beg to be picked up, leafed through, and marveled at.[82] But then this is not a normal book. "Permission is required to view this item," the Wellcome Library's catalogue entry notes dryly, and perhaps a little emotional detachment is required to view it too.[83]

Some books are still made in the mold of the St Cuthbert Gospel, the Ragyndrudis Codex and the like. If you yearn for a Coptic-stitched book, simply spend a few dollars on a Moleskine notebook, which is stitched together without a reinforced spine so that it opens flat.[84] And a few select books, the hardcover edition of this one included, are still sewn together using the double-cord method, but they are a dying breed: most of the books made in Europe and the United States, paperbacks and hardbacks alike, have long since stopped being sewn together in any way at all.

For all the steampunk gadgets, clattering machinery, and belching smokestacks that confronted the public during the Industrial

Ludovic Bouland's copy of *De integritatis et corruptionis virginum notis*, bound in the mid-nineteenth century in "a portion of female skin, tanned by myself with sumac."[85]

Revolution, for the book the biggest changes happened behind the scenes. Quietly, and by degrees, the making of books was taken out of human hands and entrusted to machines: in 1850, a paper-folding machine was invented by an Edinburgher named William Black; a year later, the "roller backer" appeared, a machine that could back a book's spine to a carefully predetermined form; and, in 1879, an Irish-American inventor named David M. Smyth patented the first in a long line of devices that could sew a book's gatherings without its operator having to so much as thread a needle.[86] All these contraptions, allied to Fourdrinier machines, Linotypes and Monotypes, and powered rotary presses, helped drag the bookmaking industry into the modern world.

But before all this, in 1837, an Englishman named William Hancock filed a patent that doomed more than a millennium of bookmaking tradition. In his description of US Patent 444 A, the innocuously titled "Improvement in Book-Binding," Hancock set out how bookmakers might transcend the fiddly lacing and sewing then required to bind any book more than a few pages long. First, he said, having printed, folded, collated, and trimmed a book's gatherings, but *before* they had been sewn together, they were to be locked in a lying press as if ready to be rounded and backed. Next, the spine of the text block was shorn clean off with a plough or guillotine, removing the folds between the pages, and then roughened with sandpaper. Over the course of a day or two, a series of coats of "caoutchouc," or rubber, dissolved in a solution of turpentine, were painted over the spine so that they seeped into the microscopic crevices between the pages and bound the whole thing together as they dried.

The spine was finished with a strip of cloth stuck to the final coat of caoutchouc and the completed text block was pasted into a separate cover, or "case," by its endpapers.[87] ("Case binding" was another recent innovation, having appeared in Britain a decade or two before Hancock's time. Most hardback books, this one included, are "cased in" to a separate cover of cloth- or paper-covered boards.)[88] This produced books that, in Hancock's words, "open perfectly flat or more nearly so than books bound by any other method," and one contemporary account of Hancock's method spoke glowingly of flexible, robust volumes whose exotic caoutchouc spines were "repulsive to insects, and not effected [*sic*] by humidity."[89]

Parallel to Hancock's invention of glued bookbinding, in the middle of the nineteenth century, a British publisher named George Routledge began selling cut-price novels at railway stations, hoping to capture the attention of travelers bored with magazines and newspapers. Routledge's "yellow-back" railway novels were sewn together as usual, but they were finished with lurid paper covers pasted onto boards made from straw pulp, making them far cheaper than leather- or cloth-bound books. They were enormously popular.[90] It was the start of a movement toward cheap, populist books, as epitomized by the serialized dime novel. And, bolstered by new adhesives, Hancock's glued binding was the perfect complement. It was so perfect, in fact, that today's characteristic paperback binding, where a book's spine is trimmed, roughened, glued, and pressed into a single-ply cover, is known as "perfect binding."[91] And unlike many industries, where new developments are applied first to the most expensive products, trickling down to cheaper equivalents as time goes by, for books the opposite has happened: Hancock's glued spines have trickled *up* from paperbacks to hardbacks. Overwhelmingly, the books on the shelves of a modern bookshop are glued together, not sewn.[92]

15

Size Matters: the invention of the modern book

For much of the book's history, the basic techniques of bookbinding were remarkably static. Bookmakers fiddled around the edges of their craft, refining methods, materials, and tools by degrees, but the basics remained the same. What changed instead was whom books were for, and what they were supposed to look like. The Industrial Revolution may have changed the machinery with which books were made, and William Hancock's caoutchouc bindings streamlined how they were put together, but the *idea* of the modern book, the fact that handy, affordable books such as this one exist at all is a direct result of a pattern established in the intellectual, mercantile, and artistic crucible of Renaissance Venice—and it all hinges on the size of a sheet of paper.

In 1974, a codicologist named Eric Turner published a catalogue of all surviving books made before the seventh century CE. His *Typology of the Early Codex* lists 892 separate books made between the first and sixth centuries, including copies of the same works, and as he analyzed his findings he came to the conclusion that the size of papyrus books depended on two factors.[1] The first was the height of the scrolls from which they had been made, and the second was ancient bookmakers' dislike for the overlapping joins between the pasted-together sheets of those scrolls.[2] The resulting papyrus books were of a remarkably familiar size and shape: the Nag Hammadi codices, for instance, average out at around 5½ by 10½ inches in size, with the largest and smallest of them deviating only an inch or so in either dimension. The oldest books in the world are almost exactly the same width as this one, and a scant couple of inches taller.[3]

It was clear that early bookmakers were aware of how their customers interacted with their products. Very few ancient books were wider than they were tall, helping keep the stresses and strains on their spines to a reasonable level; the vast majority had short, readable lines of text, broken into columns if need be; and few, in general, strayed far beyond the comfortable dimensions established by the Nag Hammadi library.[4, 5] Literary tastes may have changed since then, but the reach of our arms, the span of our hands, and the workings of our brains are still much the same as they were in the fourth century. Where early books did differ, however, was in how their folios were gathered.[6] Each bookmaker cut their sheets from a roll and assembled them as they saw fit, and though most of the Nag Hammadi codices were made from a single, unwieldy gathering, other bookmakers experimented with everything between one and fifty-six folios per gathering.[7] Eventually, a tacit agreement emerged that gatherings of four or five sheets represented the optimal balance between the labor required to collate and bind the gatherings and the usability of the finished product.[8]

When parchment arrived, things changed. If books had started out rectangular because human ergonomics and papyrus scrolls conspired to make them that way, parchment gave them a reason to *stay* rectangular.[9] After slaughtering a calf, lamb, or kid; after skinning it, soaking its pelt in a noxious vat, and then unhairing it; after stretching that pelt on a frame and finally trimming off the unhelpful organic curves around its perimeter, what you have is a rectangular sheet of parchment. From here, bookmakers found that they could produce a four-folio gathering by folding the sheet in half along its short axis, repeating this on the folded sheet, and then repeating it a final time on the doubly folded sheet. This creates a rectangular booklet whose leaves are conjoined along a fold at their top edge, and that can be opened up with a knife to make a *quaternio*, or "quire"—the eponymous four-folio gathering from which the majority of medieval books were made and from which many books are still made today.[10] Books are rectangular because cows, goats, and sheep are rectangular too.[11]

Folding a rectangular sheet of parchment this way had the added bonus of producing a quire whose facing pages were either both hair side or both flesh side, with hair and flesh sides alternating as a reader leafed through a medieval book.[12] (It is easy to see this in action: if you make a quire from a piece of origami paper that is colored on one side and white on the other, you will find that all facing pages have the same color.) If the historical evidence is any guide, bookmakers were wedded to the folded, four-folio quire from the very earliest days of their trade: parchment was sold in "in *quaternio* a foot in size" as early as 301 CE, and the parchment quire maintained its supremacy until paper came into mainstream use in the fifteenth century. (Having elbowed parchment aside, paper, too, was often sold in four-folio gatherings whose watermarks showed that they had been folded from a single large sheet in the same way as their parchment counterparts.)[13] Even those few medieval books whose gatherings were made from five, six, seven, eight, or nine folios were carefully arranged so that their extra leaves adhered to the standard hair-side-to-hair-side, flesh-side-to-flesh-side configuration.[14] The folded quire was so common that for a codicologist, any pair of facing pages that do *not* match is a sign that a leaf is missing.[15]

Curiously, papyrus codices were often constructed in the same way as parchment books. Papyrus does not have a hair side or a flesh side, of course, but it does have fibers running perpendicularly on the opposing sides of each sheet. It seems that the earliest bookmakers were fond of arranging their gatherings so that horizontal fibers matched horizontal fibers and vice versa: they did not merely chop a papyrus roll into sheets and then stack those together to make books; instead, they methodically flipped over or rotated every other sheet in order to achieve this harmony of horizontal and vertical fibers.[16] If, as some codicologists believe, bookmakers working with papyrus were mimicking others who used parchment, this is the closest we have to proof that the parchment codex was the original codex.

By the time printing and papermaking arrived in force in the latter part of the fifteenth century, bookmakers had converged on a hierarchy of book sizes derived from the four-folio quire. The largest books were called *folios*: each pair of leaves was made from a single sheet of paper folded in half, then gathered into quires of anywhere between two and five folios each.[17] *Quarto* books, on the other hand, were more regimented. Each gathering was made by folding a single sheet of paper in half and then in half again to produce four leaves—hence *quarto*—exactly half the size of those in a folio book.[18] After quartos came *octavos*, where a quarto gathering was folded one more time to yield a quire of four individual sheets, eight leaves, or sixteen pages, in exactly the same manner as the traditional parchment quire.[19]

Buyers of all books smaller than folios ran the risk of encountering unopened pages—that is, quires that had been sewn into a book but not opened up during the bookbinding process. The solution was to run a dull knife gently under the "bolt," or fold, that joined leaves together (or, more apocryphally, to use the edge of a playing card to do the same), leaving a more or less ragged edge where the leaves had separated.[20] It is rare to find a modern book with unopened edges—they are almost all trimmed off during the binding process—but you may yet come across books whose pages are ragged at the edges for a quite different reason.

Before the Fourdrinier machine came along, individual sheets of paper were made on laid molds consisting of a supporting frame, a mesh screen to sieve out the fibers, and a removable wooden "deckle," or rim, that corralled the pulp as the papermaker withdrew the mold from the vat.[21] An ill-fitting deckle allowed pulp to seep underneath so that sheets of handmade paper were often bounded by a ragged fringe of fibers. At first, these unkempt "deckle edges" were trimmed off, bemoaned as the shortcomings of an imperfect manufacturing process, but in the seventeenth century, as book collecting came into vogue, book buyers changed their minds. A neat, trimmed edge was often a sign a book had been rebound, and perhaps trimmed a little too zealously as a result. The deckle edge became a reassuring sign of a sympathetic, professional binding.[22]

When machine-made paper came along, the deckle edge was consigned to history: the endless webs of paper produced by Fourdrinier machines eliminated two deckle edges per sheet, and machines were often set up to trim off the vestigial deckle edge from the sides of the web for symmetry's sake.[23] And yet today, when the average mass-produced book is more likely to be thrown away than re-bound, demand for the deckle edge persists. It has become a pastiche of itself: when you find a modern book with a deckle edge you can be almost certain that it was added mechanically to arrow-straight paper edges by means of sandblasting, sawing, or tearing.[24]

To the bookmakers of the fifteenth century, unopened pages and deckle edges were the facts of doing business. Buyers of quartos and octavos were resigned to taking up their paper knives and opening up their pages. And yet, there were fewer printed octavos than might have been expected. For all its cozy familiarity from older times, early printers deliberately shied away from the octavo book. Gutenberg printed his 42-line Bible in a lavish folio format to mimic the grandest handwritten texts then available; twenty years later, Colard Mansion, whose book of

➻ (*Opposite*) The folds required to make a folio, quarto, or octavo gathering from a watermarked and countermarked sheet of paper. Cut out and experiment at your own risk.

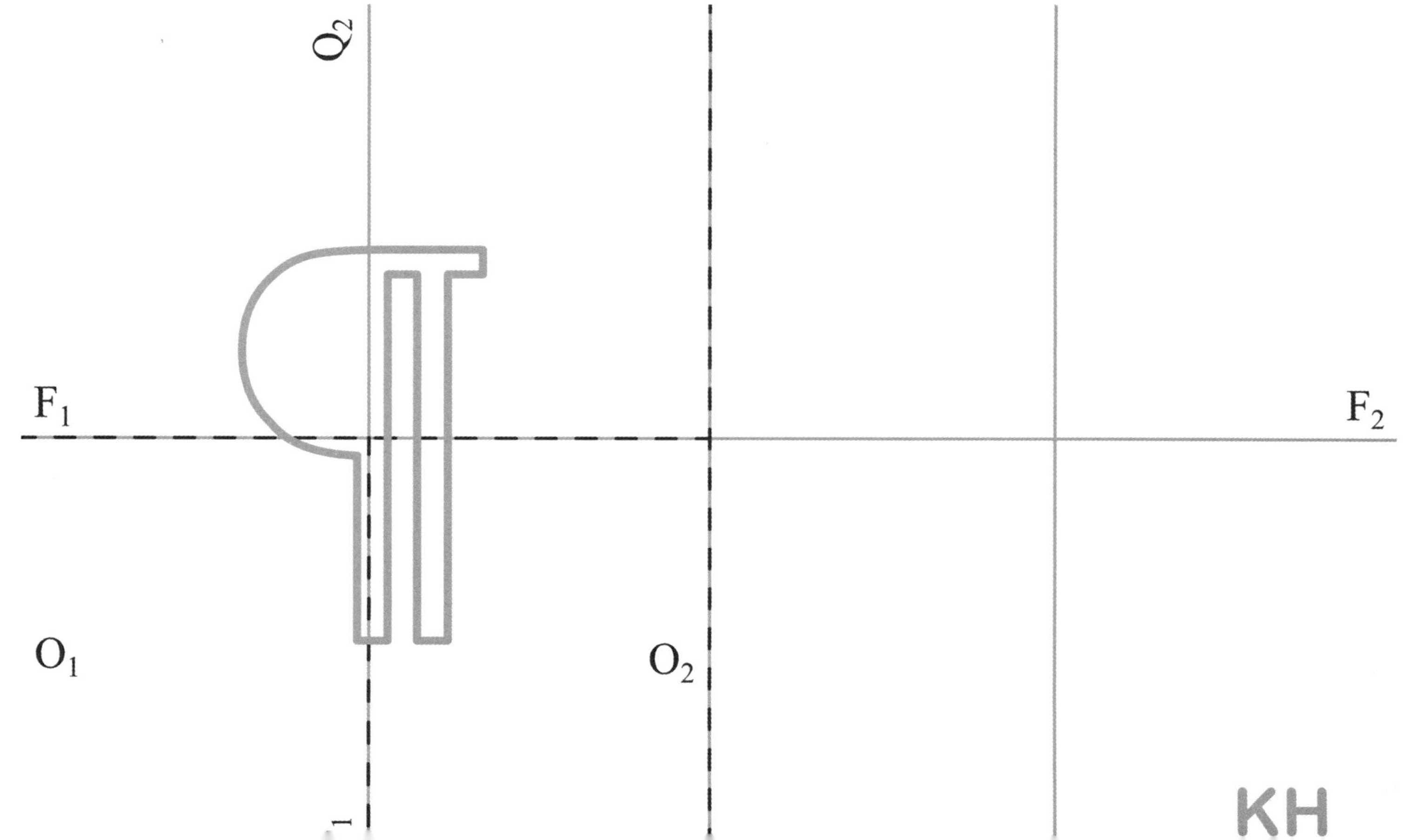

Q2
F1
F2
O1
O2
KH

cautionary tales was the first to be illustrated with copperplate engravings, did the same.[25] Fully half of all books printed before 1500 were quartos, and more than half of the rest were folios.[26] The first printed books, like the first automobiles, were luxury items.

The man who democratized books was a latecomer. In Venice, Italy, four decades after Gutenberg's movable type had burst out of Mainz in Germany, a scholar calling himself Aldus Manutius debuted as a printer with a new edition of an old Greek textbook called *Erotemata*, or "Questions."[27] Known to his friends as plain old Aldo Manuzio, and to us as Aldus, Manutius's *Erotemata* promised much but delivered rather less: it was not, as he wrote in the introduction, a completely new edition; rather, he had copied the text from a version published some years earlier, while the purportedly new Latin translation provided along with it was a lightly massaged copy of another old edition.[28] Aldus was a man of low cunning and questionable ethics, but his economy of manufacture could not be argued.

Very little is known of Aldus's life before he set himself up as a printer. It seems that he muddled along as a scholar and teacher until his forties, writing a modest Latin grammar and tutoring two young princes from the city-state of Carpi, where he inveigled himself into the graces of their family, the Pios. When Aldus moved to Venice in the late 1480s, a city brimming with enthusiasm for the printing press, he called in favors and founded a printer's workshop. Andrea Torresani, who had printed Aldus's Latin grammar, was tapped to provide technical know-how, while Pierfranceso Barbarigo, son and nephew to a succession of Venice's doges, and Alberto Pio, one of the grown-up princes of Carpi, were induced to provide financial backing.[29]

As an ardent student of Greek texts, Aldus knew that the language presented typographical challenges. Greek scribes often combined letters, and many letters and combinations of letters were further accessorized with accents and breathing marks. In 1900, for instance, an English librarian named Robert Proctor counted more than twelve hundred individually cast characters in a Greek book, and lamented that the printer had not used more; the Gutenberg Bible, by contrast, got by with 290, including letters, combinations of letters, abbreviations, and marks of punctuation.[30] But Aldus pushed on, hoping to tap into a market starved for Greek books, and together with his letter-cutter, Francesco Griffo, he managed to eke out a usable, if aesthetically challenged, typeface in 330 characters.[31] And so it was in Venice, in 1495, that Aldus published his bootlegged edition of the *Erotemata*, a twice-pirated chimera thrown together from unacknowledged sources and typeset in a distinctly ungainly Greek typeface—an edition that presaged the mass-produced book as we know it.

It was odd, then, that Aldus's next publication was a five-volume edition of the works of Aristotle, printed in folio, and for which he charged eleven ducats—roughly three months' wages for a skilled worker.[32] For the next four years the output of the Aldine press grew ever grander, culminating in 1499 with a 700-page Latin thesaurus and a handsomely illustrated dream-romance called the *Hypnerotomachia Poliphili* (Poliphilo's battle of love in a dream). Both were imposing folio books and both were eye-wateringly expensive, but when sales of the *Hypnerotomachia* failed to recoup the hundreds of ducats Aldus had invested in its production, he had to change his plans.[33] In 1501 the Aldine press issued a book that heralded a return of its founder's instincts for thrift and simplicity. The text was taken from the works of the ancient Roman poet Publius Vergilius Maro, better known as Virgil, an entirely conventional choice of source material for the time, but everything else about the book was a challenge to the status quo.

First of all, it was tiny. In an uncharacteristically brief introduction Manutius called his Virgil an *enchiridion*, or "handbook" (he later referred to these compact editions as *libri portatiles*, or "portable books"), and handy it was at little more than 6 inches tall and 4½ wide.[34] Second, as betrayed by the position of the watermarks on its pages, it was clear that his Virgil was an octavo—the first printed octavo, no less. At the time, paper was made in rectangular molds bisected by a notional line where the center fold of a folio book would lie: the left half of the mold carried a watermark while the right half of some molds bore a simpler "countermark," often the initials of the papermaker, at the bottom-right corner. Folio books made from molds like this display a watermark on one leaf of each folio and a countermark, if present, on its counterpart; in quartos, by dint of their extra fold, the watermark is split horizontally across every other pair of leaves; and in octavos the watermark is quartered, with quadrants appearing in a predictable pattern at the topmost corners of certain pages.[35] By examining the position and orientation of these marks on bound-up books, then, codicologists can determine how each quire was folded.[36] Thus Aldus Manutius's Virgil was determined to be an octavo made from diminutive 18-by-12-inch folios, each one printed with eight pages to a side and then folded, gathered, sewn, and cut to create quires of sixteen pages each.

Aldus's second major departure from convention was the typeface in which his "handbook" was set. Just as Johannes Gutenberg's 42-line Bible had echoed Germany's dense, gothic blackletter script, so Italian printers had turned to the handwriting of their peers.[37] In the case of sixteenth-century Venice, that handwriting was called "roman" script and it was based on the elegant handwriting of ancient Rome's finest scribes. Roman handwriting had become gradually debased over the years since the fall of the Roman Empire, mutating first into the rounded uncial letters of the early Middle Ages and later into the stately but illegible fence posts of Germany's blackletter. Fired by the Renaissance mania for all things classical, Italian scholars revived the noble lettering of old Rome, merging the stern, square capitals of monumental inscriptions with rounded, lowercase handwritten letters to create a pairing that has endured. The story, however, was only half correct. In their eagerness to resurrect the writing of the Roman Empire, the Italian humanists of Florence and Venice had mistakenly seized upon the handwriting of the *Holy* Roman Empire, Charlemagne's eighth-century imitation of the long-vanished original. What we call "roman" type (the lowercase *r* distinguishes the script from the capital-*R* Romans who inspired it) is a mix of Roman and Carolingian letters. It might better be called "(holy) roman."[38]

Oi; ch'aſcoltate in rime ſparſe il ſuono
Di quei ſoſpiri, ond'io nudriua il core
In ſul mio primo giouenile errore,
Quand'era in parte altr'huom da quel, ch'i ſono;
Del uario ſtile, in ch'io piango et ragiono
Fra le uane ſperanze e'l uan dolore;
Oue ſia, chi per proua intenda amore,
Spero trouar pieta, non che perdono.
Ma ben ueggi'hor, ſi come al popol tutto
Fauola fui gran tempo: onde ſouente
Di me medeſmo meco mi uergogno:
Et del mio uaneggiar uergogna è'l frutto,
E'l pentirſi, e'l conoſcer chiaramente
Che quanto piace al mondo è breue ſogno.

Per far una leggiadra ſua uendetta,
Et punir in un di ben mille offeſe,
Celatamente amor l'arco ripreſe,
Com'huom, ch'a nocer luogo et tempo aſpetta.
Era la mia uirtute al cor riſtretta;
Per far iui et ne gliocchi ſue difeſe,
Quando'l colpo mortal la giu diſceſe,
Oue ſolea ſpuntarſi ogni ſaetta.
Pero turbata nel primiero aſſalto
Non hebbe tanto ne uigor ne ſpatio,
Che poteſſe al biſogno prender larme;
Ouero al poggio faticoſo et alto
Ritrarmi accortamente da lo ſtratio;
Del qual hoggi uorrebbe, et non po aitarme.

a ii

↞ The opening page of Aldus's 1501 edition of Francesco Petrarcha's poems. As minimal as Aldus's books were, he knew that many of his customers would have their books illustrated to their tastes, and so the isolated capital letter at the top left of the page provides space for a hand-painted versal to be added later.

Francesco Griffo, Aldus's punchcutter, had already cut a handsome roman typeface for an essay by a writer named Bernardo Bembo (modern versions of that same typeface are called Bembo in memory of their first outing at the Aldine press) but Aldus had something different in mind for his pocket Virgil.[39] Of late, a slanting, graceful variant of roman script had become fashionable among certain scholars, and Manutius directed Griffo to cut a new typeface based on the handwriting of Niccolò de Niccoli, one of its most accomplished practitioners.[40]

Aldus's contemporaries called the new typeface "Aldino" after the printer who pioneered it, but today we call it "italic" after its Italian origins. It was both more flamboyant and more compact than its roman equivalent and so, apparently unwilling to dilute the impact of this new typeface, Aldus set his Virgil in italics in its entirety, with the sole exception of the C*apitals* T*hat* I*ntroduced* E*ach* L*ine* in deference to Niccolò de Niccoli's preference for doing so.[41] Italics allowed Aldus to squeeze in more letters per line *and* grabbed the attention of any reader fortunate enough to lay their eyes on this compact, groundbreaking book; and though printers have since retreated from Aldus's italics-heavy approach, both his portable format and his new typeface are still with us.[42]

Finally, Aldus was a ruthless editor. Whether they had been written or printed, Renaissance editions of classical works were invariably suffocated by reams of commentary. Readers filled the margins of their books with musings and translations, called out by little pointing hands or "manicules"; and later, with printing in the ascendant, authors and editors commandeered the white space of the page, providing preemptive footnotes lest an innocent reader be tempted to think for themselves.[43] Aldus, on the other hand, printed only the unadulterated words of Virgil himself, creating a sparse, clean book whose lack of visual frippery let the content do the talking. There was a single introductory page, then the text itself, and finally a "colophon," or explanatory note, describing the genesis of the book. Chapters began on new pages, and each page was given over entirely to the text at hand.

Aldus's austere Virgil, avant-garde, approachable, and portable all at once, was a hit. He printed and sold thousands of copies of it at a time when print runs rarely exceeded the low hundreds, and proceeded to replicate the feat with a series of old classics issued every two months thereafter.[44] The intertwined dolphin-and-anchor logo of the Aldine press became synonymous with well-made, compact books, and its proprietor was granted the ultimate in double-edged accolades when his emblem began to appear on the pages of pirated copies printed by competitors across France and Italy.[45]

Aldus's octavo Virgil ushered in the era of portable books—an era that continues today, where the majority of books have sixteen-page octavo gatherings, and the dimensions of Kindles and iPad minis still invoke Aldus's sixteenth-century paper prototype—and even smaller books followed. The *duodecimo,* for instance, from the Latin for "twelfth," added a new wrinkle to the manufacturing process: each quire was made by printing folios twelve pages to a side, the pages arranged in a three-by-four or two-by-six grid, then by cutting off a contiguous group of four pages and folding the two pieces into separate gatherings. The smaller two-leaf gathering was "insetted" into the larger four-leaf gathering to produce a quire of six leaves.[46] As complex as this sounds (and looks, as shown on page 322), the duodecimo became an important format in its own right, joining the list of folio, quarto, and octavo standards known to readers and collectors alike.

In *Moby-Dick,* Herman Melville invoked the language of book sizes when presenting his self-made taxonomy of whales, safe in the knowledge that his audience would understand. Melville classed the sperm whale, right whale, humpback whale, and fin whale as "folio whales"; the smaller pilot whale, orca, and narwhal were "octavo whales"; and the comparatively tiny dolphin and porpoise were "duodecimo whales."[47] Melville avoided the term "quarto" for reasons that will become clear,

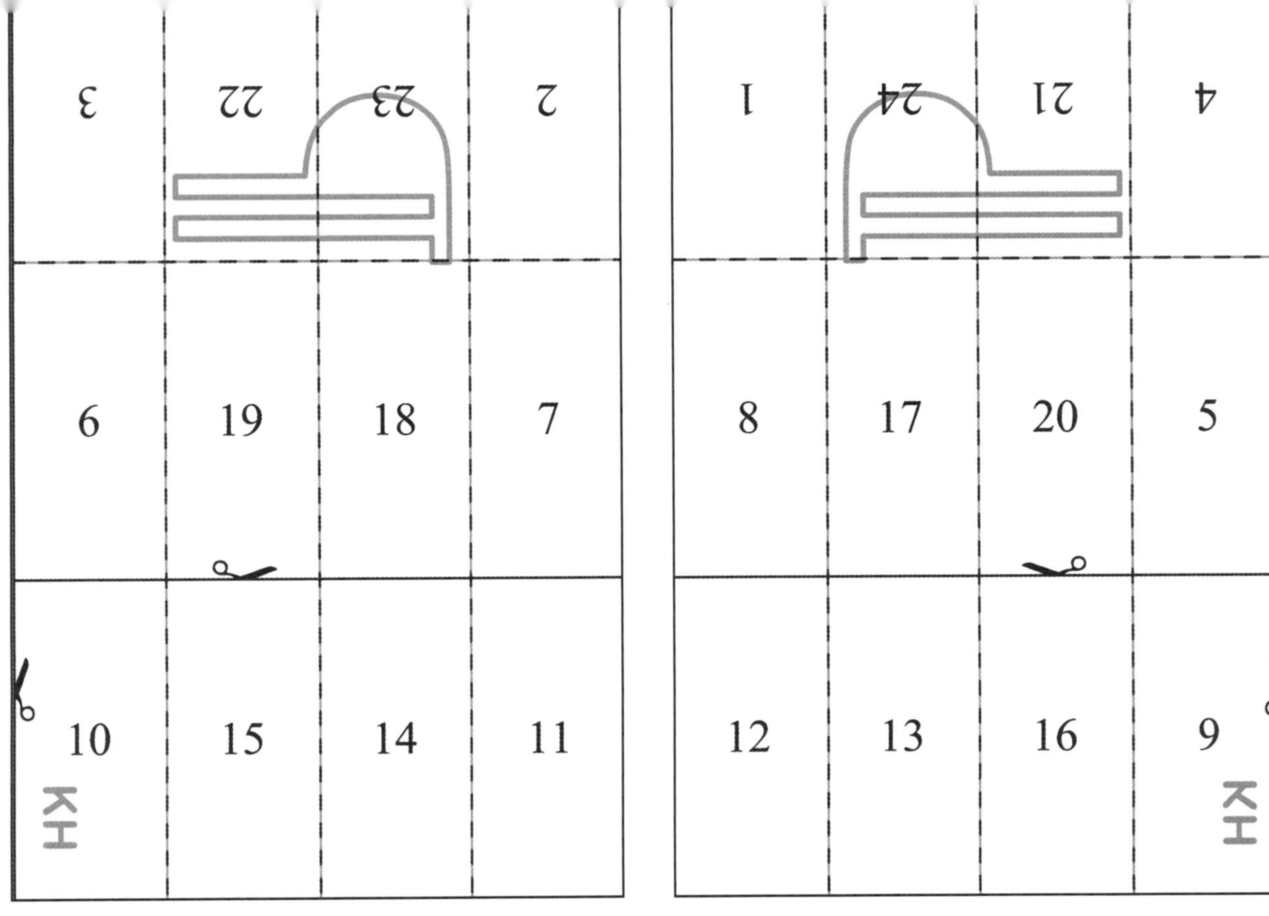

3
22
23
2
1
24
21
4
6
19
18
7
8
17
20
5
10
15
14
11
12
13
16
9
KH
KH

but he also made a more fundamental omission: when it comes to determining the size of a book, the size of the paper from which it is made is paramount. A folio book made from Post-it notes will be a lot smaller than an octavo folded from a sheet of giftwrap, not to mention a lot harder to open.

For as long as paper books have existed, bookmakers have had a bewildering menu of paper sizes from which to make them. As long ago as 1398 the authorities of the city of Bologna, Italy, erected a marble slab inscribed with a series of standard paper sizes ranging from *recute*, or "small," sheets measuring 12.4 by 17.7 inches to the more evocative *realle* (royal) and *imperialle* (imperial), the largest of which reached 19.7 by 29.1 inches.[48] (Aldus's Virgil was printed on sheets close in size to the diminutive *recute*.) British papermakers, too, embraced the opportunity to name their products in keeping with the prevailing themes of monarchy and empire: "crown" paper was 15 inches by 20, "royal" 20 by 25, and "imperial" 22 by 30.[49] The best known of all British paper sizes, however, had less to do with celebrating Britain's royal family than mocking it.

Charles I, king of Great Britain and Ireland from 1625 until he was deposed during the English Civil War more than two decades later, possessed a preternatural ability to infuriate the elected members of his government.[50] Among the many affronts the king visited upon his parliamentarians was the dispensation of royal privileges—monopolies by another name—for a variety of industries and crafts. Papermaking was one of these controlled industries, and all English paper was watermarked with the royal coat of arms.[51] But with Charles dead in 1649, his royalist militia defeated by the republican soldiers of the New Model Army, and parliament purged of its remaining royalists by an ambitious officer named Oliver Cromwell, the privileges granted by the erstwhile king were dismantled.[52] Cromwell's "Rump Parliament" is said to have decreed that the paper on which parliamentary

↞ (*Opposite*) The folding and page-numbering scheme for the opposing sides of a single duodecimo gathering. The smaller, four-sheet gathering is "insetted" into the middle of the larger, eight-sheet gathering.

proceedings were recorded should be freed from the indignity of bearing the king's arms, and a mocking jester's cap complete with jangling bells was substituted.[53] Cromwell himself put paid to this raucous stunt in 1653, dissolving the Rump Parliament by force of arms when it proved insufficiently compliant, but the association of the "fool's cap" with the 13½-by-17-inch sheets from which parliamentary journals were made was indelible.[54] Today's "foolscap" paper is still the same size.

Things have changed a little since then, and modern European paper names are less grandiose than their predecessors. Moreover, they have been subject to a process of ruthless rationalization since the fragmented days of *realle*, crown, *imperialle*, and foolscap. Printers and bookmakers have always been in thrall to "magic numbers," certain mathematical constants that exert a kind of aesthetic gravity on artists and designers; the grande dame of these is the so-called Golden Ratio* of 1.618 to 1, and it has been a feature of book design for almost as long as there have been books to be designed. The geometric decorations on the cover of the St Cuthbert Gospel, for instance, are laid out to conform to the Golden Section, while the pages of Gutenberg's Bible are 1.618 times as tall as they are wide. More recently, the iconic orange-banded paperbacks of Britain's Penguin Books (and the German Albatross Verlag paperbacks they mimicked) were sized according to the same ratio.[55]

Modern papermakers have found a different magic number to be equally useful. Pythagoras's constant—the square root of two, or approximately 1.414—turns out to have a very useful property in relation to paper sizes. In 1786, a German physics professor named Georg Lichtenberg wrote to a friend that any sheet of paper whose long edge was 1.414 times longer than its short edge could be cut or folded in half, parallel to its short edge, to yield a sheet with exactly the same

*The Golden Ratio, also known as the Golden Section or the Golden Mean, is calculated such that the ratio of the lengths of two sections of a straight line, one long and one short, is the same as the ratio of the length of the long portion to the line itself. Or, for the mathematically inclined, $\frac{a+b}{a} = \frac{a}{b} = \varphi$, where φ is the Golden Ratio.

proportions as the original. This could be repeated over and over again to create smaller and smaller sheets.[56]

In 1798, the French government seized upon Lichtenberg's discovery to help promote its new "metric" units of measurement: a sheet of *grand registre* paper, defined to be 420 millimeters wide by 594 millimeters tall, or approximately 16.55 by 23.39 inches, was exactly one-quarter of a square meter in area; folding a sheet of it in half yielded *moyen papier* one-eighth of a square meter in area with the same proportions as *grand registre*; and so on.[57] The French system never caught on, but when Germany standardized paper sizes in the early twentieth century it, too, heeded Lichtenberg's magical ratio to create the ubiquitous "A" series of paper sizes.[58] A sheet of A1 paper is 594 by 841 millimeters in size and half a square meter in area; folding or cutting it in half creates two sheets of A2, each a quarter-meter square, like the old French *grand registre*; A4 paper, the closest that the European system comes to American letter-size paper, is a sixteenth of a square meter in area; and so on down to A10, a tiny, business card–sized rectangle barely an inch by an inch and a half. It is a system that appeals to math professors, visual designers, and office managers alike (a sheet of A-series paper can be magnified or reduced on a photocopier to fit any other A-series sheet with no waste); it informs the size of books, passports, and even toilet paper; and it rules from Austria to New Zealand.[59]

American readers may be forgiven for feeling nonplussed.

Until the early decades of the twentieth century, any American bibliophile who saw a book referred to as a folio, quarto, or octavo could be reasonably sure that this meant a book folded from single-sheet folios measuring 19 by 25 inches—that is, exactly half of what passed for a standard American paper mold, at 25 by 38 inches. Whereas empire-obsessed European papermakers had given their paper sizes imposing titles such as "crown" and "imperial," their American counterparts called their uncut sheets "bible," "book," "offset," or "text" according to the uses for which they were destined.[60] This stumbled-upon paper size was resolutely unmagical: a folio book made from "bible," "book," or "text" paper measured 12½ by

19 inches, or around two-thirds as wide as it was tall; a quarto was squarer by comparison at 9½ by 12½ inches, while an octavo at 6¼ by 9½ inches returned to the proportions of a folio book.[61] This is why Herman Melville had ignored quarto books when creating his taxonomy of whales:

> *Why [the Octavo whales are] not denominated the Quarto is very plain. Because, while the whales of this order, though smaller than those of the former order, nevertheless retain a proportionate likeness to them in figure, yet the bookbinder's Quarto volume in its diminished form does not preserve the shape of the Folio volume, but the Octavo volume does."*[62]

(In reality, duodecimo books made from standard sheets of 19 by 25 inches do not have exactly the same proportions as folios and octavos, but they were close enough for Melville, who used "duodecimo" to denote the smallest of the whales.)[63]

Until the twentieth century, the quartet of folio, quarto, octavo, and duodecimo books made from 19-by-25-inch paper was as close as the Americas came to a standard set of book sizes. There were a host of other paper sizes available, but none was any more grounded in science than those normally used for books—and still none of them had uniquely identifying names. A printer talking about "book" paper could be referring to compact 17½-by-22-inch or giant 35-by-45-inch sheets as easily as the "standard" size of 19 by 25 inches.[64] There was nothing inherently wrong with this ad-hoc hierarchy of book and paper sizes, but nevertheless, in the early years of the twentieth century the American government felt it had to do something about the competing standards.

In 1921 Woodrow Wilson's government established two committees dedicated to standardizing paper sizes. Created independently, the Kafkaesque duo of the "Permanent Conference on Printing" and the "Committee on the Simplification of Paper Sizes" proceeded to define standard letter sizes of 8 by 10½ inches and 8½ by 11 inches respectively. At the time neither body deigned to explain how they had arrived at their respective standards—there was no clever Lichtenberg ratio in evidence, no study of ergonomics or economics to support their conclusions—and it later emerged that the Permanent Conference on Printing had slyly copied the dimensions of Secretary of State Herbert Hoover's personal letter paper and adjourned.

For its part, the Committee on the Simplification of Paper Sizes, a body made up largely of members of the pulp and paper industries, settled on what it thought was *already* a standard size of paper, even if it was a standard only by the loosest definition of the term.[65] The American Forest and Paper Association, the modern paper industry trade body, has this to say about the 8½-by-11-inch letter paper selected by their predecessors:

> *Back in the late 1600s, the Dutch invented the two-sheet mold. The average maximum stretch of an experienced vatman's arms was 44″. Many molds at that time were around 17″ front to back because the laid lines and watermarks had to run from left to right. [...] To maximize the efficiency of paper making, a sheet this big was made, and then quartered, forming four 8.5″ × 11″ pieces.*[66]

If this is to be believed, letter paper exists because seventeenth-century Dutch papermakers' molds, 44 inches wide and 17 inches deep, produced two sheets at a time that could be further quartered into familiar 8½-by-11-inch pieces. And to be fair, at one time 17-by-22-inch paper was relatively common, referred to as "bond," "ledger," "mimeograph," or "writing" paper according to its eventual usage, and letter paper is a quarter of its size.[67] The Committee on the Simplification of Paper Sizes had tradition on its side, even if the advent of the Fourdrinier machine, with its continuous web of paper, had rendered hand molds obsolete some hundred years earlier.

When the two committees were introduced to each other in 1923, they found the half-inch gap between their respective standards a gulf too wide to cross. The paper industry duly adopted 8½ by 11 inches while the government plumped for 8 by 10½ inches, and the two led parallel lives until the Reagan administration adopted the industry's standard some six decades later.[68] Finally, in 1995, America's de facto standards body, the nonprofit American National Standards Institute, ratified the standard 8½-by-11-inch sheet of letter paper as the starting point for a hierarchical series of paper sizes. Rechristened as "ANSI A," letter paper is doubled in size to yield ANSI B, or "ledger" paper (confusingly, this is half the size of traditional ledger paper); doubled again to make ANSI C; and so on.[69] It may lack the geometric elegance of Europe's A series, but the American system is here to stay: the pages of this book and many others like it are half the size of a sheet of letter paper; its folios are letter paper–sized and the ANSI C octavo quires from which they are folded are four times larger again. Five centuries on, Aldus Manutius's experiment is alive and well.

Colophon

backmatter head

The natural finish line for a book is an epilogue or a conclusion. An enthusiastic reader might carry on to find an appendix or two, some notes, a bibliography, or an index. In the early days of printing, however, before epilogues and appendices and bibliographies and indices, the last thing a reader saw was the "colophon," a single page at the back of the book named after the Greek word for "summit," or "finishing touch." The colophon was a place for the printer to record the details of the book's manufacture—the name of its firm; its coat of arms, perhaps; and the place and date of its production. (The colophons at the back of Fust and Schöffer's Psalters of 1457 and 1459 are thought to have been the first of their kind.)[1]

All of which brings us to *this* book. For a book about the book, a colophon is more apt than an epilogue; and so, here are the facts of its production.

To start at the beginning, it is printed on acid-free, pH-neutral freesheet paper made by the Yuen Foong Yu Group of Taiwan, produced according to the PREPS sustainability standard and weighing in at eighty-one pounds per ream of 500 sheets at the more-or-less standard size of 25 by 38 inches. This, though, is a hypothetical ream of paper; like all paper made on a Fourdrinier machine, the paper in this book was created (and sold) as a long, continuous web. It would be more accurate to say that it weighs 120 grams per square meter.[2]

The Book was produced in one single factory, at Asia Pacific Offset's bookmaking plant in Heyuan City, Guangdong Province, China.[3] There, a continuous web of paper 25 inches across is fed through an offset color lithographic press (a Komori LSP440, to be precise) that imposes sixteen pages at time on both sides of the paper. As picturesque as it is that *The Book* was made in paper's homeland, the practical truth of the matter is that Chinese printers can produce sewn books like this one—a rarity in today's bookshops—much more economically than those in the West.

The text on *The Book*'s pages is set in 11 point Adobe Jenson Pro Light, designed by Robert Slimbach between 1995 and 2000 in emulation of type cut in the fifteenth century by the French printer Nicolas Jenson. Jenson's letters, and Slimbach's modern interpretation of them, are direct descendants of the "roman" script cobbled together by the Italian scholars of the Renaissance in an attempt to honor their ancient Roman counterparts. Each page, whether composed from text, images, or both, starts life as a single, unified digital image that is separated into cyan, magenta, yellow, and black components (CMYK for short) for printing by laser-etched aluminum plates mounted in four successive offset lithographic print units.[4] What appear to be smoothly varying gradients of color are composed of overlaid patterns of tiny halftone dots, so that the combination of the four separate inks fools the eye into perceiving a rainbow of colors from across the spectrum.

As the web emerges from the press it is cut into 17-inch-long folios, each one bearing sixteen printed pages per side, and the opposing edges are trimmed down so that each folio is 22 inches wide. Thus, the continuous web of paper becomes a series of ANSI C folios, where each 17-by-22-inch sheet is precisely four times larger than a single sheet of letter paper. Next, each folio is machine-folded three times to create an octavo quire and the resultant quire's edges are guillotined off to open it up. The end result is a gathering of four folios, eight leaves, and sixteen pages, each of which is approximately 5½ by 8¼ inches in size—a hair smaller than half a sheet of ANSI A, the survivor of the two competing letter paper sizes established back in 1921.[5]

The printed, folded, trimmed, and collated quires are sewn together in the traditional double-cord manner, though once again a machine (this time a Müller Martini 3215 thread sewer, a cousin many times removed of David M. Smyth's sewing devices of the nineteenth century) does a tricky job that was once performed by hand. Endpapers are glued onto the text block near the spine—if you open the very first leaf of the book, made from heavy paper stock, you will find that it pulls the second, regular leaf along with it. Decorative endbands are glued to the top and bottom of the spine.[6]

Separately from the printing of the book, the case, or cover, is machine-made from paper glued over heavy cardboard. The lettering on the cover is applied by the modern equivalent of the blind tooling process used on leather covers: a heated brass mold in the form of the cover's lettering stamps a plastic-backed metallic foil onto the cover, causing the foil to separate from the plastic and fixing it to the cover. Finally, the book is "cased-in": glue is rolled onto the outer leaves of the text block—the endpapers—which are then spread open and pressed onto the inside surfaces of the front and back covers, all by machine. A copy of *The Book* is complete.

The Book, along with the millions of others like it produced each year, is the solution to an equation that takes in more than two thousand years of human history. It is rectangular because cows, goats, and sheep are rectangular too. It is a handy, right-sized volume like the Nag Hammadi codices because humans *like* books to be this size; it is an affordable octavo in the style of Aldus Manutius's groundbreaking pocket books, catering to the average wallet; and, in the interests of standardization and automation, its folios are letter paper–sized, a format that exists partly because of the reach of a vatman's arms, and partly because of the inventory concerns of an interwar government. Its letters, if not its language, would be as readable to a Carolingian monk as to a Renaissance scholar. It is protected by rigid boards, like the St Cuthbert Gospel; it is covered in a paper-wrapped cardboard case like George Routledge's populist "railway novels"; and it is sewn together in a way that echoes both medieval bookmakers and the Industrial Revolution.

Welcome to *The Book*.

Acknowledgments

Many people helped make this book happen. Here are some of them; I have almost certainly missed more than a few people, and I must apologize in advance for having done so.

David High, who designed the cover, Judith Stagnitto Abbate, who designed the interior of the book, and Brad Walrod, who typeset it, are responsible for turning a very plain manuscript into the beautiful book you hold in your hands.

Chrissie Heughan helped educate me about papermaking, and Jonathan Bloom was a great help in understanding paper's spread through Islamic lands. Johan de Zoete, curator of the Museum Enschedé, answered questions about early type molds. Harry McIntosh of the Chepman & Myllar Press, Edinburgh, demonstrated his Monotype caster for me and educated me in the ways of the Monotype system in general, as did Phil Abel and Nick Gill of Hand & Eye Letterpress, London. Nick Sherman, Doug Wilson, and Frank Romano helped put Linotype and Monotype machines into context. Rowena O'Connor and Liz Miller explained the ins and outs of woodcut printing, and Liz encouraged me to make my first woodcut print. Brooke Palmieri filled my head with many intriguing stories of books. Derek Guthrie at Tullis Russell in Markinch, Scotland, showed me around a modern paper mill (now closed, sadly) and answered endless questions about it, while Anna Oler at W. W. Norton provided a wealth of detail about the book production process. Michelle Gamble helped with photographs, and together, Sami Beese, Bianca Berning, Lorraine Gehring, Michael Gora, Thomas Guignard, Jonathan Hsy, Magdalena Moretti, Christoph Nahr, and Manuel Strehl translated a pair of tricky German and Latin book titles. Claire M. L. Bourne and Caroline Wood, along with many others mentioned above, helped review the book and caught some of my worst errors before they went to print.

My agent, Laurie Abkemeier; my editor, Brendan Curry; my copy-editor, Rachelle Mandik; and Sophie Duvernoy and Mitchell Kohles of W. W. Norton all provided much-needed help and support in writing and editing the book.

Last, but not least, my wife, Leigh, helped me and encouraged me throughout the whole process of writing the book. She read, reread, and edited chapter after chapter, and helped me keep body and soul together.

Thank you all!

Further Reading

There are many, many books on bookmaking and book history. Here are some of the best:

⇚ Avrin, Leila. *Scribes, Script, and Books: The Book Arts from Antiquity to the Renaissance*. ALA Classics. Chicago: American Library Association, 2010.

⇚ Bagnall, Roger. *The Oxford Handbook of Papyrology*. Oxford: Oxford University Press, 2009.

⇚ Bland, David. *A History of Book Illustration: The Illuminated Manuscript and the Printed Book*. 2nd ed. Berkeley: University of California Press, 1969.

⇚ Bloom, Jonathan M. *Paper before Print: The History and Impact of Paper in the Islamic World*. New Haven: Yale University Press, 2001.

⇚ Carter, Thomas. *The Invention of Printing in China and Its Spread Westward*. New York: Columbia University Press, 1931.

⇚ De Hamel, Christopher. *Scribes and Illuminators*. Toronto; Buffalo: University of Toronto Press, 1992.

⇚ Griffiths, Antony. *Prints and Printmaking: An Introduction to the History and Techniques*. Berkeley: University of California Press, 1996.

⇚ Henderson, George. *From Durrow to Kells: The Insular Gospel-Books, 650–800*. New York: Thames and Hudson, 1987.

⇚ Hind, Arthur. *An Introduction to a History of Woodcut: With a Detailed Survey of Work Done in the Fifteenth Century*. Vol. 1. New York: Dover Publications, 1963.

⇚ Hunter, Dard. *Papermaking: The History and Technique of an Ancient Craft*. Dover Books Explaining Science. New York: Dover Publications, 1978.

⟪ Jennett, Seán. *Pioneers in Printing: Johann Gutenberg, William Caxton, William Caslon, John Baskerville, Alois Senefelder, Frederick Koenig, Ottmar Mergenthaler, Tolbert Lanston.* London: Routledge & Kegan Paul, 1958.

⟪ Johnson, Malcolm. *The Nature and Making of Papyrus.* Barkston Ash, UK: Elmete Press, 1973.

⟪ Kapr, Albert. *Johann Gutenberg: The Man and His Invention.* Translated by Douglas Martin. Brookfield, VT: Scolar Press, 1996.

⟪ Kilgour, Frederick. *The Evolution of the Book.* Oxford: Oxford University Press, 1998.

⟪ Man, John. *The Gutenberg Revolution: How Printing Changed the Course of History.* London: Transworld Publishers, 2010.

⟪ Meggs, Philip. *Meggs' History of Graphic Design.* Hoboken, NJ: John Wiley & Sons, 2012.

⟪ Parkinson, Richard. *Cracking Codes: The Rosetta Stone and Decipherment.* London: British Museum Press, 1999.

⟪ Reed, Ronald. *The Nature and Making of Parchment.* Leeds, UK: Elmete Press, 1975.

⟪ Roberts, Colin, and T. C. Skeat. *The Birth of the Codex.* London: Published for the British Academy by the Oxford University Press, 1983.

⟪ Robinson, Andrew. *The Story of Writing: Alphabets, Hieroglyphs & Pictograms.* London: Thames & Hudson, 2001.

⟪ Schmandt-Besserat, Denise. "How Writing Came About." *Zeitschrift Für Papyrologie Und Epigraphik* 47 (1982): 1–5.

⟪ Senefelder, Alois. *The Invention of Lithography.* Translated by J. W. Muller. New York: Fuchs & Lang Manufacturing Co., 1911.

⟪ Tsien, Tsuen-Hsuin. *Chemistry and Chemical Technology, Part 1: Paper and Printing.* Edited by Joseph Needham. Science and Civilisation in China 5. Cambridge: Cambridge University Press, 1985.

↞ ———. *Written on Bamboo & Silk: The Beginnings of Chinese Books & Inscriptions*. Chicago: University of Chicago Press, 2004.

↞ Turner, E. *Greek Papyri: An Introduction*. Princeton, NJ: Princeton University Press, 1968.

↞ Vrettos, Theodore. *Alexandria: City of the Western Mind*. New York: Free Press, 2001.

The following websites are also very much worth a look:

↞ The British Library's Catalogue of Illuminated Manuscripts (http://www.bl.uk/catalogues/illuminatedmanuscripts/) contains both an incredible selection of medieval manuscripts and an informative glossary of related terms.

↞ David M. MacMillan and Rollande Krandall's Circuitous Root (http://www.circuitousroot.com/) is an enormous resource dedicated to "antiquarian technology and other matters" that includes a great deal of material on early letterpress printing.

↞ The International Dunhuang Project (http://idp.bl.uk/) provides an illustrated catalogue of all documents found at the library cave at Dunhuang.

↞ Jesse Hurlbut's Manuscript Art blog (http://jessehurlbut.net/wp/mssart/) and the Sexy Codicology website (http://sexycodicology.net/) are both excellent windows onto the huge number of illustrated and illuminated manuscripts that exist in libraries across the world.

↞ Letterpress Commons (https://letterpresscommons.com/) is a handy repository of information on all kinds of letterpress printing.

Visit http://keithhouston.co.uk/ for addenda, errata, Creative Commons–licensed images, and more on the history of the book.

Notes

INTRODUCTION

1. J. Stewart, "Jacobellis v. Ohio," Legal Information Institute, Cornell University Law School, accessed November 3, 2014, http://www.law.cornell.edu/supremecourt/text/378/184#writing-USSC_CR_0378_0184_ZC1.
2. Brad Stone, "Amazon Erases Orwell Books from Kindle," *New York Times*, July 17, 2009, http://www.nytimes.com/2009/07/18/technology/companies/18amazon.html; "Fikk Amazon-Konto Slettet Og Mistet Alle Bøkene Hun Hadde Kjøpt" (NRK, October 22, 2012), http://www.nrk.no/kultur/1.8367977.
3. Malcolm Johnson, *The Nature and Making of Papyrus* (Barkston Ash, UK: Elmete Press, 1973); Ronald Reed, *The Nature and Making of Parchment* (Leeds, UK: Elmete Press, 1975).

CHAPTER 1 A CLEAN SHEET: THE INVENTION OF PAPYRUS

1. "Face of Pharaoh Finally Exposed," *New York Times*, November 20, 1925; Arthur Weigall, *The Life and Times of Cleopatra, Queen of Egypt a Study in the Origin of the Roman Empire* (Edinburgh: W. Blackwood, 1914); Theodore Vrettos, *Alexandria: City of the Western Mind* (New York: Free Press, 2001); Kate Spence, "Ancient Egyptian Chronology and the Astronomical Orientation of Pyramids," *Nature* 408, no. 6810 (November 16, 2000): 320–24.
2. "Cyperus Papyrus AGM" (Royal Horticultural Society), accessed November 3, 2013, http://apps.rhs.org.uk/plantselector/plant?plantid=4429; Malcolm Johnson, *The Nature and Making of Papyrus* (Barkston Ash, UK: Elmete Press, 1973), 3–11.
3. Johnson, *The Nature and Making of Papyrus*, 3–11; Naphtali Lewis, *Papyrus in Classical Antiquity* (Oxford: Clarendon Press, 1974), 3–6; National Academy of Sciences (U.S.). Ad Hoc Panel on Utilization of Aquatic Weeds, *Making Aquatic Weeds Useful: Some Perspectives for Developing Countries* (National Academies, 1976), 102–4.
4. Lewis, *Papyrus in Classical Antiquity*, 3–5, 21–32.
5. Lewis, *Papyrus in Classical Antiquity*, 21; R. J. Forbes, *Metallurgy in Antiquity, Part 1*, vol. 8, Studies in Ancient Technology (Leiden: E. J. Brill, 1971), 106–7.
6. James G. Keenan, "The History of the Discipline," in *The Oxford Handbook of Papyrology*, ed. Roger Bagnall (Oxford: Oxford University Press, 2009), 59.
7. Frederic G. Kenyon, *The Palaeography of Greek Papyri* (Oxford: Clarendon Press, 1899), 4.
8. Domenico Cirillo, *Cyperus Papyrus.* (Parma: Typis Bodonianis, 1796).
9. Kenyon, *The Palaeography of Greek Papyri*, 4; Keenan, "The History of the

Discipline," 59; Bernard P. Grenfell, Arthur S. Hunt, and David G. Hogarth, *Fayûm Towns and Their Papyri* (London: 1900), 17–18.

10. Grenfell, Hunt, and Hogarth, *Fayûm Towns*, 17.

11. Donald P. Ryan, "Papyrus," *The Biblical Archaeologist* 51, no. 3 (1988): 133.

12. E. A. W. Budge, *The Book of the Dead: The Papyrus of Ani in the British Museum* (London: British Museum, 1895), li.

13. Ryan, "Papyrus," 133–34, 138; Thor Heyerdahl, *The Ra Expeditions* (London: Flamingo, 1993), 18–21.

14. Emily Teeter, "Techniques and Terminology of Rope-Making in Ancient Egypt," *The Journal of Egyptian Archaeology* 73 (1987): 71–77; Willeke Wendrich, "Rope and Knots in Ancient Egypt," in *Encyclopaedia of the History of Science, Technology, and Medicine in Non-Western Cultures*, ed. Helaine Selin (Springer Netherlands, 2008), 1908–10, doi:10.1007/978-1-4020-4425-0_8686; Ryan, "Papyrus," 134.

15. Norman Davies, *The Tomb of Puyemrê at Thebes*, vol. 1 (New York, 1922), xvii; Margaret Stefana Drower, "Thutmose III," *Encyclopaedia Britannica*, accessed February 5, 2013, http://www.britannica.com/EBchecked/topic/594493/Thutmose-III.

16. Jean-Louis Huot, "Xerxes I," *Encyclopaedia Britannica*, accessed November 4, 2013, http://www.britannica.com/EBchecked/topic/650720/Xerxes-I; Frank Miller, *300* (Milwaukie, OR: Dark Horse Comics, 1998); Herodotus, *The Histories*, trans. A. Godley (Cambridge, MA: Harvard University Press, 1920), sec. 7.34–36, http://www.perseus.tufts.edu/hopper/text?doc=urn:cts:greekLit:tlg0016.tlg001.perseus-eng1.

17. Herodotus, *The Histories*, sec. 2.92.

18. Ryan, "Papyrus," 134–35.

19. Lewis, *Papyrus in Classical Antiquity*, 31–32, 97.

20. Ibid., 25–26.

21. Jaroslav Cerny, *Paper and Books in Ancient Egypt* (London: Lewis, 1947), 4; Lewis, *Papyrus in Classical Antiquity*, 113–22.

22. Ryan, "Papyrus," 135–36; Jean-Louis Cenival, "The Main Evolutionary Lines of Egyptian Architecture," in *Egypt*, ed. Henri Stierlin (Cologne: Benedikt Taschen, 1994), 179–82.

23. William Davies, *Egyptian Hieroglyphs*, Reading the Past (London: British Museum Publications, 1987), 10.

24. Plato, *Phaedrus*, trans. Harold N. Fowler, in *Plato in Twelve Volumes* (Cambridge, MA: Harvard University Press, 1925), sec. 274de, http://data.perseus.org/texts/urn:cts:greekLit:tlg0059.tlg012.perseus-eng1.

25. John D. Ray, "The Emergence of Writing in Egypt," *World Archaeology* 17, no. 3 (1986): 307–16; J. T. Hooker, *Reading the Past: Ancient Writing from Cuneiform to the Alphabet* (Berkeley: University of California Press, 1990), 207–9.

26. Frederick Kilgour, *The Evolution of the Book* (Oxford: Oxford University Press, 1998), 28–29.

27. Cerny, *Paper and Books in Ancient Egypt*, 11; Bridget Leach and John Tait, "Papyrus," in *Ancient Egyptian Materials and Technology*, ed. Paul Nicholson and Ian Shaw (Cambridge: Cambridge University Press, 2000), 277.

28. Miriam Lichtheim, *Ancient Egyptian Literature: A Book of Readings*, vol. 2 (Berkeley:

University of California Press, 2006), 224–30; A. Egberts, "The Chronology of 'The Report of Wenamun,'" *The Journal of Egyptian Archaeology* 77 (1991): 57–67.

29. Homer, *Odyssey*, trans. A. T. Murray (Cambridge, MA: Harvard University Press, 1919), 21.10, http://data.perseus.org/texts/urn:cts:greekLit:tlg0012.tlg002.perseus-grc1; Lewis, *Papyrus in Classical Antiquity*, 86–88.

30. "Roman Republic," *Encyclopaedia Britannica*, accessed November 6, 2013, http://www.britannica.com/EBchecked/topic/857952/Roman-Republic; Lewis, *Papyrus in Classical Antiquity*, 88–89.

31. Heinz Heinen, "Ptolemy II Philadelphus," *Encyclopaedia Britannica*, accessed November 6, 2013, http://www.britannica.com/EBchecked/topic/482146/Ptolemy-II-Philadelphus; Lewis, *Papyrus in Classical Antiquity*, 88–89.

32. John Roberts, ed., "Pliny the Elder," *Oxford Dictionary of the Classical World*, accessed November 7, 2013, http://www.oxfordreference.com/10.1093/acref/9780192801463.001.0001/acref-9780192801463-e-1749.

33. Ibid.; Jacob Bigelow, "Death of Pliny the Elder," in ed. Eliakim Littell, *Living Age*, vol. LXI (Boston: Littell, 1859), 123–25.

34. Roberts, "Pliny the Elder."

35. Alia Hanafi, "In Memoriam Hassan Ragab, 1911–2004," l'Assemblée Générale de Association Internationale de Papyrologues (Association Internationale de Papyrologues), August 7, 2004, http://www.ulb.ac.be/assoc/aip/ragab.htm.

36. Pliny the Elder, *The Natural History*, trans. John Bostock and B. A. Riley (Red Lion Court, Fleet Street: Taylor and Francis, 1855), sec. 13.21, http://data.perseus.org/texts/urn:cts:latinLit:phi0978.phi001.perseus-eng1.

37. Ibid., sec. 7.2.

38. Ibid., sec. 13.23.

39. Ibid.; Lewis, *Papyrus in Classical Antiquity*, 34–40.

40. A. Owen, "History and Treatment of the Papyrus Collection at the Brooklyn Museum," in *The Book & Paper Group Annual*, vol. 12 (American Institute for Conservation, 1993), 36–43; A. Wallert, "The Reconstruction of Papyrus Manufacture: A Preliminary Investigation," *Studies in Conservation* 34, no. 1 (1989): 1–8.

41. Ignace H. M. Hendriks, "Pliny, Historia Naturalis XIII, 74–82 and the Manufacture of Papyrus," *Zeitschrift Für Papyrologie Und Epigraphik* 37 (1980): 121–36.

42. Wallert, "The Reconstruction of Papyrus Manufacture: A Preliminary Investigation."

43. Pliny the Elder, *The Natural History*, sec. 13.23.

44. Andrew D. Dimarogonas, "Pliny the Elder on the Making of Papyrus Paper," *The Classical Quarterly (New Series)* 45, no. 2 (1995): 588–90, doi:10.1017/S0009838800043718; Peter E. Scora and Rainer W. Scora, "Some Observations on the Nature of Papyrus Bonding," *Journal of Ethnobiology* 11 (1991): 193–202.

45. F. N. Hepper and T. Reynolds, "Papyrus and the Adhesive Properties of Its Cell Sap in Relation to Paper-Making," *The Journal of Egyptian Archaeology* 53 (1967): 156–57; Hassan Ragab, "A New Theory Brought Forward About the Adhesion of Papyrus Strips," *IPH Yearbook of Paper History* 1 (1980): 113–30.

46. Owen, "History and Treatment"; Scora and Scora, "Some Observations."

47. Corrado Basile, "A Method of Making Papyrus and Fixing and Preserving It by Means of a Chemical Treatment," in *Conservation of Paintings and the Graphic Arts, Lisbon Congress 1972* (London: IIC, 1972), 901–6.

48. Ibid.; Adam Bülow-Jacobsen, "Principatus Medio. Pliny, N. H. XIII, 72 Sqq.," *Zeitschrift Für Papyrologie Und Epigraphik* 20 (1976): 113–16.

49. Dimarogonas, "Pliny the Elder on the Making of Papyrus Paper."

50. Pliny the Elder, *The Natural History*, sec. 13.23.

51. Kenyon, *The Palaeography of Greek Papyri*, 15–19.

52. Pliny the Elder, *The Natural History*, sec. 13.21.

53. Strabo, *Geography*, trans. H. C. Hamilton and W. Falconer (London: George Bell & Sons, 1903), sec. 13.1.54, http://data.perseus.org/texts/urn:cts:greekLit:tlg0099.tlg001.perseus-eng2; Lewis, *Papyrus in Classical Antiquity*, 60–61; Anthony J. P. Kenney, "Aristotle," *Encyclopaedia Britannica*, accessed November 12, 2013, http://www.britannica.com/EBchecked/topic/34560/Aristotle.

54. Kenyon, *The Palaeography of Greek Papyri*, 6–7.

55. Owen, "History and Treatment."

56. David Magie, trans. "Tacitus X," in *The Scriptores Historiae Augustae*, vol. 3 (Cambridge, MA: Harvard University Press, 1921), 313–15; Henry Petroski, *The Book on the Bookshelf*, 1st ed. (New York: Alfred A. Knopf, 1999), 32–33.

57. William G. Urry, "Paleography," *Encyclopaedia Britannica*, accessed November 12, 2013, http://www.britannica.com/EBchecked/topic/439491/paleography.

58. Pliny the Elder, *The Natural History*; Adam Bülow-Jacobsen, "Writing Materials in the Ancient World," in *The Oxford Handbook of Papyrology*, ed. Roger Bagnall (Oxford: Oxford University Press, 2009), 8–10.

59. Leach and Tait, "Papyrus."

60. Pliny the Elder, *The Natural History*, sec. 13.23.

61. Lewis, *Papyrus in Classical Antiquity*, 39.

CHAPTER 2 ❧ HIDEBOUND: THE GRISLY INVENTION OF PARCHMENT

1. Esther Hansen, *The Attalids of Pergamon* (Ithaca: Cornell University Press, 1971), 1–3, 70–129.

2. Strabo, *Geography*, trans. H. C. Hamilton and W. Falconer (London: George Bell & Sons, 1903), sec. 13.4.2, http://data.perseus.org/texts/urn:cts:greekLit:tlg0099.tlg001.perseus-eng2; Plutarch, *Antony*, in *Plutarch's Lives*, ed. Bernadotte Perrin (Cambridge, MA: Harvard University Press, 1920), chap. 58, http://data.perseus.org/texts/urn:cts:greekLit:tlg0007.tlg058.perseus-eng1.

3. Strabo, *Geography*, sec. 13.1.54.

4. Frederic G. Kenyon, *Books and Readers in Ancient Greece and Rome* (Oxford: Clarendon Press, 1889), 87–88.

5. Jerry Stannard, "Pliny the Elder," *Encyclopaedia Britannica*, accessed July 17, 2013, http://www.britannica.com/EBchecked/topic/464822/Pliny-the-Elder; Ignace H. M. Hendriks, "Pliny, Historia Naturalis XIII, 74–82 and the Manufacture of Papyrus," *Zeitschrift Für Papyrologie Und Epigraphik* 37 (1980): 121–36.

6. Herodotus, *The Histories*, trans. A. Godley (Cambridge, MA: Harvard University Press, 1920), sec. 5.1.58, http://www.perseus.tufts.edu/hopper/text?doc=urn:cts:greekLit:tlg0016.tlg001.perseus-eng1.

7. David Diringer, "From Leather to Parchment," in *The Book Before Printing: Ancient, Medieval, and Oriental* (Mineola, NY: Courier Dover Publications, 1953), 170–227.

8. Ronald Reed, *The Nature and Making of Parchment* (Leeds: Elmete Press, 1975), 39.

9. "Astringent," *Encyclopaedia Britannica*, accessed July 18, 2013, http://www.britannica.com/EBchecked/topic/39937/astringent; William M. Ciesla, "Gall Nuts," in *Non-Wood Forest Products from Temperate Broad-Leaved Trees* (Rome: Food & Agriculture Org., 2002), 98–100; Reed, *Nature and Making of Parchment*, 25–26.

10. Reed, *Nature and Making of Parchment*, 26–29.

11. Ibid., 38.

12. Richard R. Johnson, "Ancient and Medieval Accounts of the 'Invention' of Parchment," *California Studies in Classical Antiquity* 3 (January 1, 1970): 115–22, doi:10.2307/25010602; "Seleucid Kingdom," *Encyclopaedia Britannica*, accessed July 19, 2013, http://www.britannica.com/EBchecked/topic/533278/Seleucid-kingdom.

13. Johnson, "Ancient and Medieval Accounts."

14. Polybius, *Histories*, trans. Evelyn S. Shuckburgh (London: Macmillan, 1889), sec. 27.19, http://data.perseus.org/texts/urn:cts:greekLit:tlg0543.tlg001.perseus-eng1.

15. Ibid., sec. 28.18–22.

16. "Ptolemy VII Neos Philopator," *Encyclopaedia Britannica*, accessed August 1, 2013, http://www.britannica.com/EBchecked/topic/482182/Ptolemy-VII-Neos-Philopator.

17. "Ptolemy VI Philometor," *Encyclopaedia Britannica*, accessed July 19, 2013, http://www.britannica.com/EBchecked/topic/482179/Ptolemy-VI-Philometor; "Ptolemy III Euergetes," *Encyclopaedia Britannica*, accessed April 11, 2014, http://www.britannica.com/EBchecked/topic/482183/Ptolemy-VIII-Euergetes-II; Johnson, "Ancient and Medieval Accounts."

18. Livy, *History of Rome*, trans. Rev. Canon Roberts (New York: E. P. Dutton, 1912), sec. 44.19, 45.11–12, http://data.perseus.org/texts/urn:cts:latinLit:phi0914.phi0011.perseus-eng3.

19. Ibid., sec. 45.11–12.

20. Ibid.

21. John D. Grainger, *The Syrian Wars* (Leiden: Brill Academic Publishers, 2010), 6–7.

22. William Safire, "Draw a Line in the Sand," in *Safire's Political Dictionary* (Oxford University Press, 2008), 200–201.

23. Johnson, "Ancient and Medieval Accounts."

24. Ibid.

25. Ibid.

26. E. A. Andrews et al., "Membrāna," *A Latin Dictionary*, http://www.perseus.tufts.edu/hopper/text?doc=Perseus:text:1999.04.0059:entry=membrana.

27. Nicole Howard, "Writing Surfaces: Papyrus to Parchment," in *The Book: The Life Story of a Technology* (Baltimore: Johns Hopkins University Press, 2009), 2–5.

28. Reed, *Nature and Making of Parchment*, 43–44.

29. Ronald Reed, *Ancient Skins, Parchments and Leathers* (London: Seminar Press, 1972), 16–19, 29.

30. Reed, *Nature and Making of Parchment*, 44–45.
31. Ibid., 46; Howard, *The Book*, 2–5.
32. Reed, *Nature and Making of Parchment*, 60; Raymond Clemens, *Introduction to Manuscript Studies* (Ithaca: Cornell University Press, 2007), 13.
33. Christopher S. Woods, "The Conservation of Parchment," in *Conservation of Leather and Related Materials*, ed. Marion Kite and Roy Thomson (London: Routledge, 2012), 200–224.
34. Reed, "Parchment in the Medieval Period," in *Nature and Making of Parchment*, 71–96.
35. Elizabeth Owen, "4QDeutn: A Pre-Samaritan Text?," *Dead Sea Discoveries* 4, no. 2 (1997): 162–78.
36. Devorah Dimant, "Qumran—Written Material," in ed. Lawrence Schiffman, *Encyclopedia of the Dead Sea Scrolls* (New York: Oxford University Press, 2000).
37. J. B. Poole and R. Reed, "The Preparation of Leather and Parchment by the Dead Sea Scrolls Community," *Technology and Culture* 3, no. 1 (1962): 1–26.
38. "'Shochet," *OED Online*, accessed August 4, 2013, http://www.oed.com/view/Entry/178398; David Bridger and Samuel Wolk, eds., "Maimonides, Moses," in *The New Jewish Encyclopedia* (Springfield, NJ: Behrman House, 1976); Eliyahu Touger, trans., "The Laws [Concerning] Torah Scrolls, Tefillin, and Mezuzut, 1.6-9, 11," *Mishneh Torah*, accessed July 24, 2013, http://www.chabad.org/library/article_cdo/aid/925417/jewish/Chapter-One.htm; Poole and Reed, "The Preparation of Leather."
39. Poole and Reed, "The Preparation of Leather."
40. W. Clarysse et al., "Graph of Papyrus and Parchment Use in Christian Documents from 3rd Century BC to 8th Century AD," *Leuven Database of Ancient Books*, accessed July 2013, available at trismegistos.org. Visit http://bit.ly/1foltnQ.
41. Reginald Poole, "Papal Documents from Hadrian I," in *Lectures on the History of the Papal Chancery Down to the Time of Innocent III* (Cambridge: Cambridge University Press, 1915), 37.
42. Revelation 2:12–13 (21st Century King James Version).
43. Daniel V. Thompson, "Medieval Parchment-Making," *The Library* s4–XVI, no. 1 (1935): 113–15, doi:10.1093/library/s4-XVI.1.113.
44. Daniel V. Thompson Jr., "The Schedula of Theophilus Presbyter," *Speculum* 7, no. 2 (1932): 199–20.
45. "Ad Faciendas Cartas de Pellibus Caprinis More Bononiense," in *BL Harley MS 3915*, n.d., f148v; Theophilus and Charles Reginald Dodwell, "The Author of the Treatise," in *The Various Arts* (Oxford: Clarendon Press, 1986), xxxiii–xliv.
46. Reed, *Nature and Making of Parchment*, 74–75.
47. Thompson, "Medieval Parchment-Making."
48. Michelle P. Brown, "Parchmenter," in *Understanding Illuminated Manuscripts: A Guide to Technical Terms* (J. Paul Getty Museum, 1994), 95.
49. Thompson, "Medieval Parchment-Making"; Raymond Clemens, "Parchment," in *Introduction to Manuscript Studies* (Ithaca: Cornell University Press, 2007), 9–17; Michelle P. Brown, "Pounce," in *Understanding Illuminated Manuscripts: A Guide to Technical Terms*

(J. Paul Getty Museum, 1994), 99; Michelle P. Brown, "Pumice," in *Understanding Illuminated Manuscripts: A Guide to Technical Terms* (J. Paul Getty Museum, 1994), 104.

50. Bernhard Bischoff, *Latin Palaeography: Antiquity and the Middle Ages* (Cambridge: Cambridge University Press, 1995), 8–11; Reed, *Nature and Making of Parchment*, 87–92.

51. Reed, *Nature and Making of Parchment*, 85–87; Michael Clarke and Deborah Clarke, "Gum Arabic," *The Concise Oxford Dictionary of Art Terms*, accessed July 27, 2013, http://www.oxfordreference.com/10.1093/acref/9780199569922.001.0001/acref-9780199569922-e-839.

52. Bischoff, *Latin Palaeography*, 8–11; Lloyd B. Jensen, "Royal Purple of Tyre," *Journal of Near Eastern Studies* 22, no. 2 (1963): 104–18.

53. "Parchment," *OED Online*, accessed August 23, 2013, http://www.oed.com/view/Entry/137746.

54. "Vellum," *OED Online*, accessed August 30, 2013, http://www.oed.com/view/Entry/221992; W. Lee Ustick, "'Parchment' and 'Vellum,'" *The Library* s4–XVI, no. 4 (1936): 439–43, doi:10.1093/library/s4-XVI.4.439.

55. Ustick, "'Parchment' and 'Vellum'"; Bischoff, *Latin Palaeography*, 8–11.

56. Clemens, "Parchment."

57. Bischoff, *Latin Palaeography*, 8–11.

58. Timothy Stinson, "Counting Sheep: Potential Applications of DNA Analysis to the Study of Medieval Parchment Production," in *Codicology and Palaeography in the Digital Age 2*, ed. F. Fischer, C. Fritze, and G. Vogeler, Kodikologie Und Paläographie Im Digitalen Zeitalter (Books on Demand, 2010), 191–207; Antonietta Buglione, "People and Animals in Northern Apulia from Late Antiquity to the Early Middle Ages: Some Considerations," in *Breaking and Shaping Beastly Bodies: Animals as Material Culture in the Middle Ages* (Oxford: Oxbow Books, 2007): 189–216.

59. Ustick, "'Parchment' and 'Vellum'"; Bischoff, *Latin Palaeography*, 8–11.

60. Reed, *Nature and Making of Parchment*, 77.

CHAPTER 3 ⇚ PULP FICTIONS: THE AMBIGUOUS ORIGINS OF PAPER IN CHINA

1. "I'm a Lumberjack," *The Economist*, April 3, 2012, http://www.economist.com/blogs/graphicdetail/2012/04/daily-chart-0.

2. Martial, *Epigrams*, trans. Walter A. C. Ker (London: W. Heinemann, 1919), v. 1.2.

3. A. F. Rudolf Hoernle, "Who Was the Inventor of Rag-Paper?," *Journal of the Royal Asiatic Society of Great Britain and Ireland* (1903): 663–84.

4. Edmund H. Fulling, "Botanical Aspects of the Paper-Pulp and Tanning Industries in the United States: An Economic and Historical Survey," *American Journal of Botany* 43, no. 8 (1956): 623–24.

5. Hoernle, "Who Was the Inventor of Rag-Paper?"; Tsuen-Hsuin Tsien, *Written on Bamboo & Silk: The Beginnings of Chinese Books & Inscriptions* (Chicago: University of Chicago Press, 2004), 159–61.

6. Tsuen-Hsuin Tsien, *Chemistry and Chemical Technology, Part 1: Paper and Printing*,

ed. Joseph Needham, Science and Civilisation in China 5 (Cambridge: Cambridge University Press, 1985), 35–38.

7. Tsien, *Written on Bamboo & Silk*, 1, 38–39, 69, 89.

8. Ibid., xxi; Endymion Porter Wilkinson, *Chinese History: A Manual* (Harvard University Asia Center, 2000), 444–47.

9. W. Y. Hsiung, "Bamboo in China: New Prospects for an Ancient Resource," *Unasylva* 39 (1987): 42–49.

10. Tsien, *Paper and Printing*, 23–25.

11. Wilkinson, *Chinese History*, 444–47; Tsien, *Written on Bamboo & Silk*, 97–98, 115–20.

12. Wilkinson, *Chinese History*, 444–47.

13. Tsien, *Written on Bamboo & Silk*, 130.

14. Ki Mae Heussner, "Get Out of Jail Free: Monopoly's Hidden Maps," ABC News, September 18, 2009, http://abcnews.go.com/Technology/monopolys-hidden-maps-wwii-pows-escape/story?id=8605905.

15. Tsien, *Paper and Printing*, 23–25.

16. Ibid.

17. Lois Mai Chan, "The Burning of the Books in China, 213 B.C.," *The Journal of Library History* 7, no. 2 (1972): 101–8; H. Ping, P. F. Williams, and Y. Wu, "From 'Killing a Chicken to Frighten the Monkeys' to 'Killing a Monkey to Frighten the Other Monkeys,'" in *The Thought Remolding Campaign of the Chinese Communist Party-State*, ICAS Publications Monographs (Amsterdam University Press, 2012), 37–39; "Han Dynasty," *Encyclopaedia Britannica*, accessed November 25, 2013, http://www.britannica.com/EBchecked/topic/253872/Han-dynasty.

18. Tsien, "Earthenware Types," in *Chemistry and Chemical Technology, Part 1*, 38–42; Dard Hunter, *Papermaking: The History and Technique of an Ancient Craft*, Dover Books Explaining Science (New York: Dover Publications, 1978), 50–53; Wilkinson, *Chinese History*, 501–7.

19. Mary Anderson, *Hidden Power: The Palace Eunuchs of Imperial China* (Buffalo, NY: Prometheus Books, 1990), 15–18.

20. B. B. Peterson, "Empress Dowager Dou," in *Notable Women of China: Shang Dynasty to the Early Twentieth Century*, East Gate Book (Armonk, NY: M.E. Sharpe, 2000), 103–8.

21. Ibid.; Hunter, *Papermaking*, 50–52.

22. Peterson, "Empress Dowager Dou"; Hunter, *Papermaking*, 50–52; K. McMahon, *Women Shall Not Rule: Imperial Wives and Concubines in China from Han to Liao* (Lanham, MD: Rowman & Littlefield Publishers, 2013), 102–5.

23. Hunter, *Papermaking*, 50–52; Tsien, *Paper and Printing*, 40; Joseph Needham and Wang Ling, *Physics and Physical Technology, Part 2: Mechanical Engineering*, Science and Civilisation in China 2 (Cambridge: Cambridge University Press, 1965), 31.

24. Hunter, *Papermaking*, 49–53; Jie Wu, *A Study of Group Compositions in Early Tang China (618–713)* (Seattle: University of Washington Press, 2008), 5–8.

25. Victor W. von Hagen, "Paper and Civilization," *The Scientific Monthly* 57, no. 4 (1943): 304.

26. Hunter, *Papermaking*, 52.
27. Charles Davis, "Materials Used for Paper," in *The Manufacture of Paper Being a Description of the Various Processes for the Fabrication, Coloring, and Finishing of Every Kind of Paper* (Philadelphia: H.C. Baird, 1886), 64–76.
28. Martyn Rix, Steve Davis, and Mark Nesbitt, "Broussonetia Papyrifera (paper Mulberry)," *Plants & Fungi* (Royal Botanic Gardens, Kew, 2013), http://www.kew.org/plants-fungi/Broussonetia-papyrifera.htm; Hsuan Keng, "Economic Plants of Ancient North China as Mentioned in 'Shih Ching' (Book of Poetry)," *Economic Botany* 28, no. 4 (1974): 405.
29. Tsien, *Paper and Printing*, 36–37, 41.
30. Hunter, *Papermaking*, 53; Hyejung Yum, "Traditional Korean Papermaking: Analytical Examination of Historic Korean Papers and Research into History, Materials and Techniques of Traditional Papermaking of Korea," (research paper, Getty Postgraduate Fellowship, 2003), accessed August 9, 2015, https://www.library.cornell.edu/preservation/publications/koreanpapermaking.html.
31. Chrissie Heughan, interview with the author, November 2013.
32. Hui-Lin Li, "An Archaeological and Historical Account of Cannabis in China," *Economic Botany* 28, no. 4 (1974): 437–48; Hunter, *Papermaking*, 50–53.
33. Yingxing Song, *Chinese Technology in the Seventeenth Century*, trans. E-tu Zen Sun and Shiou-chuan Sun (Mineola, NY: Courier Dover Publications, 1997), v.
34. Tsien, *Paper and Printing*, 35–38; Heughan interview.
35. Hunter, *Papermaking*, 78–84.
36. Ibid.
37. Ibid., 84–94.
38. Tsien, *Paper and Printing*, 35–38; Heughan interview.
39. Heughan interview; Tsuen-Hsuin Tsien, *Collected Writings on Chinese Culture* (Chinese University Press, 2011), 53–54.
40. Tsien, *Paper and Printing*, 40–41; Hunter, *Papermaking*, 51–53.
41. McMahon, *Imperial Wives and Concubines in China*, 102–5; Xingpei Yuan et al., "Late Eastern Han Politics," in *The History of Chinese Civilization: Qin, Han, Wei, Jin, and the Northern and Southern Dynasties*, trans. David R. Knechtges, vol. 2 (Cambridge: Cambridge University Press, 2012), 78–80.
42. Hunter, *Papermaking*, 52.
43. Ibid., 52–53.
44. Tsien, *Paper and Printing*, 48.
45. J. Edkins, *The Religious Condition of the Chinese: With Observations on the Prospects of Christian Conversion Amongst That People* (London: Routledge, Warnes & Routledge, 1859), 2.
46. Li, "An Archaeological and Historical Account"; Tsien, *Paper and Printing*, 38–40.
47. Tsien, *Written on Bamboo & Silk*, 145–47.
48. Tsien, *Paper and Printing*, 41; Tsien, *Written on Bamboo & Silk*, 148–50.

CHAPTER 4 ⇜ FROM SILK ROAD TO PAPER TRAIL: PAPER GOES GLOBAL

1. Dard Hunter, *Papermaking: The History and Technique of an Ancient Craft*, Dover Books Explaining Science (New York: Dover Publications, 1978), 52–60; "Silk (fibre)," *Encyclopaedia Britannica*, accessed December 12, 2013, http://www.britannica.com/EBchecked/topic/544449/silk; R. H. Cherry, "History of Sericulture," *Bulletin of the ESA* 33, no. 2 (1987): 83–85.
2. Tsuen-Hsuin Tsien, *Written on Bamboo & Silk: The Beginnings of Chinese Books & Inscriptions* (Chicago: University of Chicago Press, 2004), 161–66.
3. Hunter, *Papermaking*, 78–94.
4. Ibid., 183–94.
5. Ibid., 196.
6. Tsien, *Written on Bamboo & Silk*, 166.
7. Keith Story, *Approaches to Pest Management in Museums* (Suitland, VA: Conservation Analytical Laboratory, Smithsonian Institution, 1985), 13–16.
8. F. Smith and George Arthur Stuart, *Chinese Materia Medica Vegetable Kingdom* (Shanghai: American Presbyterian Mission Press, 1911), 316–17; Tsuen-Hsuin Tsien, *Chemistry and Chemical Technology, Part 1: Paper and Printing*, ed. Joseph Needham, Science and Civilisation in China 5 (Cambridge: Cambridge University Press, 1985), 74–46; Hunter, *Papermaking*, 468; Jonathan M. Bloom, *Paper Before Print: The History and Impact of Paper in the Islamic World* (New Haven: Yale University Press, 2001), 41.
9. Tsien, *Paper and Printing*, 84.
10. "Silk (fibre)"; Cherry, "History of Sericulture."
11. Bloom, *Paper Before Print*, 38–41; Tsien, *Written on Bamboo & Silk*, 150–52.
12. "Umayyad Dynasty," *Encyclopaedia Britannica*, accessed December 10, 2013, http://www.britannica.com/EBchecked/topic/613719/Umayyad-dynasty.
13. Ibid.; David Nicolle, "Introduction," in *Poitiers AD 732: Charles Martel Turns the Islamic Tide* (Oxford: Osprey Publishing, 2008), 7.
14. Bloom, "Umayyad Dynasty," in *Paper Before Print*, 42.
15. Ibid., 42–45.
16. Bloom, "The Introduction of Paper in the Islamic Lands," in *Paper Before Print*, 42–45; Bilal Orfali, "The Works of Abū Manṣūr Al-Thaʿālibī (350–429/961–1039)," *Journal of Arabic Literature* 40, no. 3 (2009): 273–75.
17. Bloom, "The Introduction of Paper in the Islamic Lands," 42–45; Jonathan M. Bloom, personal correspondence with the author, December 2013.
18. Jonathan M. Bloom, "Silk Road or Paper Road?," *The Silk Road Foundation Newsletter* 3, no. 2 (2005): 21–26.
19. Alfred Tennyson, "Recollections of the Arabian Nights," 1830; Bloom, *Paper Before Print*, 47–49.
20. Ibid., 48–49.
21. David J. Wasserstein, "Greek Science in Islam: Islamic Scholars as Successors to

the Greeks," *Hermathena*, no. 147 (1989): 62; Susan Douglass, "Suq Al-Warraqin," *Calliope* 10, no. 6 (2000): 38.

22. Adam Lucas, *Wind, Water, Work: Ancient and Medieval Milling Technology* (Leiden: Brill, 2006), 61–68; Bloom, *Paper Before Print*, 50–56; Karen Garlick, "A Brief Review of the History of Sizing and Resizing Practices," in *The Book & Paper Group Annual*, vol. 5 (American Institute for Conservation, 1986), 94–107.

23. Garlick, "A Brief Review."

24. J. L. Berggren, *Episodes in the Mathematics of Medieval Islam* (New York: Springer, 2003), 6–9, 31–32; Jonathan M. Bloom, "Paper: The Islamic Golden Age," *Essay*, BBC, November 28, 2013, http://www.bbc.co.uk/programmes/b03j9nhy.

25. Bloom, "Paper: The Islamic Golden Age."

26. "Reconquista," *Encyclopaedia Britannica*, accessed December 17, 2013, http://www.britannica.com/EBchecked/topic/493710/Reconquista; Catherine Delano Smith, "The Visigothic Kingdom," *Encyclopaedia Britannica*, accessed March 20, 2013, http://www.britannica.com/EBchecked/topic/557573/Spain/70358/The-Visigothic-kingdom.

27. Hunter, *Papermaking*, 473.

28. Ibid., 472; Victor W. von Hagen, "Paper and Civilization," *The Scientific Monthly* 57, no. 4 (1943): 313; Jim Wolf, "U.S. Lawmakers Seek to Block China Huawei, ZTE U.S. Inroads," Reuters, October 8, 2012, http://www.reuters.com/article/2012/10/08/us-usa-china-huawei-zte-idUSBRE8960NH20121008.

29. von Hagen, "Paper and Civilization," 313; Leor Halevi, "Christian Impurity versus Economic Necessity: A Fifteenth-Century Fatwa on European Paper," *Speculum* 83, no. 4 (2008): 917, doi:10.1017/S0038713400017073.

30. Hunter, *Papermaking*, 473.

31. "Koran 29:46 (Yusuf Ali Version)," n.d.; Hans J. Hillerbrand, "On Book Burnings and Book Burners: Reflections on the Power (and Powerlessness) of Ideas," *Journal of the American Academy of Religion* 74, no. 3 (2006): 602–3, doi:10.1093/jaarel/lfj117; "Reconquista."

32. Robert I. Burns, "The Paper Revolution in Europe: Crusader Valencia's Paper Industry: A Technological and Behavioral Breakthrough," *Pacific Historical Review* 50, no. 1 (1981): 1–30; "Alfonso X (king of Castile and Leon)," *Encyclopaedia Britannica*, accessed December 18, 2013, http://www.britannica.com/EBchecked/topic/14725/Alfonso-X.

33. Burns, "The Paper Revolution"; Bloom, *Paper Before Print*, 206–9.

34. Burns, "The Paper Revolution"; Halevi, "Christian Impurity," 918; Bloom, *Paper Before Print*, 206–9; Erik Kwakkel, "Choosing a Writing Support," *Quill: Books Before Print*, 2014, http://www.bookandbyte.org/quill/pages/choosing-a-writing-support.php.

35. Halevi, "Christian Impurity," 919.

36. Ibid., 924; Hunter, *Papermaking*, 260–61.

37. Halevi, "Christian Impurity," 918.

38. Hunter, *Papermaking*, 262–64.

39. Simon Barcham Green, "M207 Waterlow & Sons Ltd London—Ouroboros," *Simon Barcham Green's Papermaking Moulds*, 2011, http://papermoulds.typepad.com/

photos/m_207_waterlow_sons_ltd_l/m-207-c-waterlow-sons-ltd-london-ouroboros.html; Harold Bayley, *A New Light on the Renaissance Displayed in Contemporary Emblems* (London: J. M. Dent, 1909), 24.

40. Hunter, *Papermaking*, 258–59; "About Watermarks," Gravell Watermark Archive, 2013, http://www.gravell.org/watermarks.php.

41. Bayley, *A New Light*, 9–13.

42. N. Weber, "Cathari," in *The Catholic Encyclopedia* (New York: Appleton, 1908), http://www.newadvent.org/cathen/03435a.htm.

43. Thomas F. Madden, "Albigensian Crusade," *Encyclopaedia Britannica*, accessed December 19, 2013, http://www.britannica.com/EBchecked/topic/12976/Albigensian-Crusade.

44. Bayley, *A New Light*, 11.

45. Ibid., 214–31.

46. Ibid., 15–16, 70–77; Harold Bayley, *The Lost Language of Symbolism: An Inquiry into the Origin of Certain Letters, Words, Names, Fairy-Tales, Folk-Lore, and Mythologies* (London: J. M. Dent, 1912), 1–16.

47. E. Heawood, "The Use of Watermarks in Dating Old Maps and Documents," *The Geographical Journal* 63, no. 5 (1924): 394; Hunter, *Papermaking*, 258–59.

48. Ibid., 175; Edward Knight, "Ass (Paper-Making)," in *Knight's American Mechanical Dictionary: Being a Description of Tools, Instruments, Machines, Processes, and Engineering* (New York: Hard and Houghton, 1875), 170; "Glossary of Papermaking Terms," British Association of Paper Historians, accessed December 20, 2013, http://baph.org.uk/reference/glossary.html.

49. Hunter, *Papermaking*, 183–85, 194.

50. Ibid., 175–76.

51. Ibid., 173–75.

52. C. Marchetti, "A Postmortem Technology Assessment of the Spinning Wheel: The Last Thousand Years," *Technological Forecasting and Social Change* 13, no. 1 (1979): 91–93; Lynn White Jr., "Technology Assessment from the Stance of a Medieval Historian," *The American Historical Review* 79, no. 1 (1974): 12–13; von Hagen, "Paper and Civilization," 313.

53. "Cerecloth," *OED Online*, accessed December 21, 2013, http://www.oed.com/view/Entry/29893; von Hagen, "Paper and Civilization," 313.

54. Walter Endrei, "Changements dans la Productivité de L'industrie Lainière au Moyen Âge," *Annales. Histoire, Sciences Sociales* 26, no. 6 (1971): 1293; White Jr., "Technology Assessment," 12–13.

55. Marchetti, "A Postmortem"; White Jr., "Technology Assessment," 12–13.

56. James Rogers, *A History of Agriculture and Prices in England from the Year After the Oxford Parliament (1259) to the Commencement of the Continental War (1793)*, vol. 4 (Oxford: Oxford University Press, 1882), 590–608.

57. H. E. Bell, "The Price of Books in Medieval England," *The Library* s4–XVII, no. 3 (1936): 312–32, doi:10.1093/library/s4-XVII.3.312.

58. Kira L. S. Newman, "Shutt Up: Bubonic Plague and Quarantine in Early Modern

England," *Journal of Social History* 45, no. 3 (2012): 831, doi:10.1093/jsh/shr114; Hunter, *Papermaking*, 481–82.

59. Richard Daniel Smith, "Paper Impermanence as a Consequence of pH and Storage Conditions," *The Library Quarterly* 39, no. 2 (1969): 154.

60. Gary Bryan Magee, *Productivity and Performance in the Paper Industry: Labour, Capital and Technology in Britain and America, 1860–1914* (Cambridge: Cambridge University Press, 1997), 104–11.

61. Hunter, *Papermaking*, 538.

62. John Bidwell, *American Paper Mills, 1690–1832: A Directory of the Paper Trade, with Notes on Products, Watermarks, Distribution Methods, and Manufacturing Techniques* (Hanover, NH: Dartmouth College Press, 2013), xxvi, 1; John W. Maxson Jr., "Papermaking in America from Art to Industry, 1690 to 1860," *The Quarterly Journal of the Library of Congress* 25, no. 2 (1968): 121; Matt T. Roberts and Don Etherington, "Cartridge Paper," *Bookbinding and the Conservation of Books*, Foundation of the American Institute for Conservation, November 2011, http://cool.conservation-us.org/don/dt/dt0594.html.

63. Edmund H. Fulling, "Botanical Aspects of the Paper-Pulp and Tanning Industries in the United States: An Economic and Historical Survey," *American Journal of Botany* 43, no. 8 (1956): 622.

64. "French Revolution," *Encyclopaedia Britannica*, accessed December 27, 2013, http://www.britannica.com/EBchecked/topic/219315/French-Revolution; Hunter, *Papermaking*, 522.

65. Hunter, *Papermaking*, 341–44; Leonard N. Rosenband, "Comparing Combination Acts: French and English Papermaking in the Age of Revolution," *Social History* 29, no. 2 (2004): 165–78.

66. Hunter, *Papermaking*, 344–48.

67. Ibid., 348–49.

68. Ibid., 349, 532; Malcolm Thomis, *The Luddites: Machine-Breaking in Regency England* (Hamden, CT: Archon Books, 1970), 11–12.

69. Hunter, *Papermaking*, 349, 532.

70. Chrissie Heughan, interview with the author, November 2013; Hunter, *Papermaking*, 361, 401–6, 542, 546.

71. Fulling, "Botanical Aspects," 622.

72. Mark Twain, "Things I Shall Not Tell," in *The Innocents Abroad* (Velvet Element Books, 2008), 631–33; Ray Bradbury, *The Nefertiti-Tut Express: A Story in Screenplay* (Glendale, CA: The Ras Press, 2012).

73. Fulling, "Botanical Aspects," 622.

74. Charles Tomlinson, *Cyclopædia of Useful Arts, Mechanical and Chemical, Manufactures, Mining, and Engineering*, vol. 2 (London: G. Virtue, 1854), 364–65.

75. S. J. Wolfe, "Long Under Wraps, Cataloguing Puzzle Solved," *The Book: Newsletter of the Program of the History of the Book in American Culture*, no. 61 (2003): 4–5.

76. Bidwell, *American Paper Mills*, 171–76.

77. Fulling, "Botanical Aspects," 624.

78. "Asbestos (mineral)," *Encyclopaedia Britannica*, accessed December 31, 2013, http://www.britannica.com/EBchecked/topic/37756/asbestos.

79. Hunter, *Papermaking*, 311–12; Magee, *Productivity and Performance in the Paper Industry*, 104–11.

80. Thomas Jones, "Lhuyd, Edward (1660–1709)," *Welsh Biography Online* (National Library of Wales), accessed October 21, 2014, http://wbo.llgc.org.uk/en/s-LHUY-EDW-1660.html.

81. Fulling, "Botanical Aspects," 622; "Robert R. Livingston," *Encyclopaedia Britannica*, accessed December 29, 2013, http://www.britannica.com/EBchecked/topic/344865/Robert-R-Livingston.

82. Fulling, "Botanical Aspects," 622–23.

83. René Antoine Ferchault de Réaumer, "Histoire des Guêpes," *Mémoires de l'Académie Royale* (1719): 230–84; Fulling, "Botanical Aspects," 623.

84. "Friedrich Gottlob Keller," Paper Industry International Hall of Fame, 2013, http://www.paperhall.org/friedrichgottlobkeller/; Klaus Beneke, "Friedrich Gottlob Keller," *Mitteilungen Der Kolloid-Gesellschaft* (1998): 21–23; Peter Burger, *Charles Fenerty and His Paper Invention* (Toronto: P. Burger, 2007), 31–35.

85. Fulling, "Botanical Aspects," 624–25.

86. Chandru J. Shahani and William K. Wilson, "Preservation of Libraries and Archives," *American Scientist* 75, no. 3 (1987): 240.

87. Smith, "Paper Impermanence," 156; Garlick, "A Brief Review"; Shahani and Wilson, "Preservation of Libraries and Archives," 240.

88. Hunter, *Papermaking*, 526–27.

89. Smith, "Paper Impermanence," 153–54; Shahani and Wilson, "Preservation of Libraries and Archives," 240–41; John C. Williams, "Chemistry of the Deacidification of Paper," *Bulletin of the American Group. International Institute for Conservation of Historic and Artistic Works* 12, no. 1 (1971): 16–32.

90. Smith, "Paper Impermanence," 154; Shahani and Wilson, "Preservation of Libraries and Archives," 241; Lee E. Grove, "John Murray and Paper Deterioration," *Libri* 16 (1966): 194, doi:10.1515/libr.1966.16.3.194.

91. William Shakespeare, "Sonnet XVII," in *Sonnets*, ed. Thomas Tyler (London: D. Nutt, 1890), 174.

92. Smith, "Paper Impermanence," 155.

93. Ibid., 155–56; Shahani and Wilson, "Preservation of Libraries and Archives," 243.

94. Shahani and Wilson, "Preservation of Libraries and Archives," 243.

95. Marjorie Sun, "The Big Problem of Brittle Books," *Science* 240, no. 4852, New Series (1988): 598–600.

96. John W. Baty et al., "Deacidification for the Conservation and Preservation of Paper-Based Works: A Review," *BioResources* 5, no. 3 (2010): 1–3.

97. Sun, "The Big Problem of Brittle Books," 599–600.

98. Ibid.; Kenneth E. Harris et al., "Mass Deacidification: An Initiative to Refine the Diethyl Zinc Process" (1994): 6–7.

99. Sun, "The Big Problem of Brittle Books," 599–600.

100. "Using Gamma Rays to Save Old Books," *New York Times*, December 27, 1989; Baty et al., "Deacidification," 35–36.

101. "Mass Deacidification" (Washington, DC: Library of Congress), accessed January 5, 2014, http://www.loc.gov/preservation/about/deacid/index.html.

102. "ANSI/NISO Z39.48-1992 (R2009) Permanence of Paper for Publications and Documents in Libraries and Archives," National Information Standards Organization, 2010.

103. Fulling, "Botanical Aspects," 624.

104. Gerald W. Lundeen, "Preservation of Paper Based Materials: Present and Future Research and Developments in the Paper Industry," in *Conserving and Preserving Library Materials*, eds. Kathryn L. Henderson and William T. Henderson (Urbana-Champaign: University of Illinois Press, Graduate School of Library and Information Science, 1983): 80–81.

105. Anna Oler, personal correspondence with the author, November 2015.

CHAPTER 5 ⇚ STROKE OF GENIUS: THE ARRIVAL OF WRITING

1. George Edwin Fussell, "Origins of Agriculture: Sumer," *Encyclopaedia Britannica*, accessed July 14, 2015, http://www.britannica.com/EBchecked/topic/9647/origins-of-agriculture/10767/Sumer; Andrew Robinson, *The Story of Writing: Alphabets, Hieroglyphs & Pictograms* (London: Thames & Hudson, 2001), 71.

2. Dietz O. Edzard, "History of Mesopotamia," *Encyclopaedia Britannica*, accessed July 14, 2015, http://www.britannica.com/EBchecked/topic/376828/history-of-Mesopotamia; C. Walker, *Cuneiform*, Reading the Past series (Berkeley: University of California Press, 1987), 7–11.

3. Barbara Ann Kipfer, ed., *Encyclopedic Dictionary of Archaeology* (New York: Springer, 2000), 695.

4. Robinson, *The Story of Writing*, 72–73.

5. Hans J. Nissen, "The Archaic Texts from Uruk," *World Archaeology* 17, no. 3 (1986): 317.

6. Walker, *Cuneiform*, 9–11.

7. Naomi F. Miller and Wilma Wetterstrom, "The Beginnings of Agriculture: The Ancient Near East and North Africa," in *Cambridge World History of Food*, ed. K. F. Kiple and K. C. Ornelas (Cambridge: Cambridge University Press, 2000), 1123–39.

8. Denise Schmandt-Besserat, "How Writing Came About," *Zeitschrift Für Papyrologie Und Epigraphik* 47 (1982): 1–3.

9. "Cuneiform Tablet from an Assyrian Trading Post," *LACMA Collections*, Los Angeles County Museum of Art, accessed October 19, 2014, http://collections.lacma.org/node/248610.

10. Schmandt-Besserat, "How Writing Came About," 4–5; Barbara Ann Kipfer, "Bulla," in *Dictionary of Artifacts* (Hoboken, NJ: Wiley, 2008), 49–50.

11. Schmandt-Besserat, "How Writing Came About," 4–5.

12. Nissen, "The Archaic Texts from Uruk," 320.
13. Robinson, *The Story of Writing*, 42; Walker, *Cuneiform*, 11–13.
14. William Davies, *Egyptian Hieroglyphs*, Reading the Past series (London: British Museum Publications, 1987), 82.
15. Patrizia Piacentini, "Scribes," in *The Oxford Encyclopedia of Ancient Egypt*, accessed January 17, 2014, http://www.oxfordreference.com/10.1093/acref/9780195102345.001.0001/acref-9780195102345-e-0638.
16. "Ostracon," *OED Online*, accessed July 14, 2015, http://www.oed.com/view/Entry/133180.
17. Monica Tsuneishi, ed., "Ancient Writing Materials: Ostraka," Papyrology Collection, University of Michigan Library, accessed September 4, 2013, http://www.lib.umich.edu/papyrus-collection/ancient-writing-materials-ostraka; Jennifer Babcock, "Ancient Egyptian Ostraca: A Reevaluation," The Metropolitan Museum of Art, accessed October 10, 2012, http://www.metmuseum.org/about-the-museum/now-at-the-met/features/2012/ancient-egyptian-ostraca; Paul Roberts, "Egyptian Homosexuality," accessed February 5, 2014, https://www.academia.edu/3304010/Egyptian_Homosexuality; A. Maravelia, "Some Aspects of Ancient Egyptian Social Life from the Study of the Principal Love Poem's Ostraca from Deir Al-Medina," in *Egyptology at the Dawn of the 21st Century: Proceedings of the 8th International Conference of Egyptologists, Cairo 2000*, ed. Zahi Hawass and Lyla P. Brock, vol. 3 (Cairo: American University in Cairo Press, 2003), 281–82.
18. Tallet, "Ayn Sukhna and Wadi El-Jarf," 151–53.
19. Sara Forsdyke, *Exile, Ostracism, and Democracy: The Politics of Expulsion in Ancient Greece* (Princeton, NJ: Princeton University Press, 2005), 146–49.
20. Barbara Ann Kipfer, "Sherd," in *Dictionary of Artifacts*, 289.
21. Jaroslav Černý, *Paper and Books in Ancient Egypt* (Lewis, 1947), 11; P. Tallet, "Ayn Sukhna and Wadi El-Jarf: Two Newly Discovered Pharaonic Harbours on the Suez Gulf," *British Museum Studies in Ancient Egypt and Sudan*, no. 18 (2012): 151–53; John D. Ray, "The Emergence of Writing in Egypt," *World Archaeology* 17, no. 3 (1986): 310.
22. James Henry Breasted, "The Physical Processes of Writing in the Early Orient and Their Relation to the Origin of the Alphabet," *The American Journal of Semitic Languages and Literatures* 32, no. 4 (1916): 237–39.
23. Kathleen L. Sheppard, "Flinders Petrie and Eugenics," *Antiquity* (Durham: The Antiquity Trust, September 2008), http://antiquity.ac.uk/projgall/sheppard/; Margaret S. Drower, *Flinders Petrie: A Life in Archaeology* (Madison: University of Wisconsin Press, 1995), 424.
24. Lisa Mawdsley, "The Corpus of Potmarks from Tarkhan," *British Museum Studies in Ancient Egypt and the Sudan* 13 (2009): 198; W. Petrie, *Tarkhan I and Memphis V* (London: School of Archaeology in Egypt, University College; Bernard Quaritch, 1913), 1–5.
25. Breasted, "The Physical Processes," 237; Malcolm Johnson, *The Nature and Making of Papyrus* (Barkston Ash, UK: Elmete Press, 1973), 26–28; Michael Clarke and Deborah Clarke, "Gum Arabic," *The Concise Oxford Dictionary of Art Terms*, accessed July 27, 2013, http://www.oxfordreference.com/10.1093/acref/9780199569922.001.0001/acref-9780199569922-e-839.

26. Bridget Leach and John Tait, "Papyrus," in *Ancient Egyptian Materials and Technology*, ed. Paul Nicholson and Ian Shaw (Cambridge: Cambridge University Press, 2000), 238–39.
27. Breasted, "The Physical Processes," 231–34; G. A. Crüwell, "Contributions to Egyptian Penmanship," *The Library Quarterly* 2, no. 2 (1932): 135–37.
28. Araldo de Luca, Alessia Amenta, and Mathaf Al-Miṣrī, "Panels of Hesire," in *The Egyptian Museum in Cairo* (Cairo: The American University in Cairo Press, 2005), 63–69.
29. Janice Kamrin, *Ancient Egyptian Hieroglyphs: A Practical Guide* (New York: Harry N. Abrams, 2004), 126–27; Ahmed Shafik and Waseem R. Elseesy, "Medicine in Ancient Egypt," in *Medicine Across Cultures: History and Practice of Medicine in Non-Western Cultures*, ed. Helaine Selin, vol. 3, Science Across Cultures: The History of Non-Western Science (Dordrecht: Kluwer Academic Publishers, 2003), 35–36, doi:10.1007/0-306-48094-8.
30. Breasted, "The Physical Processes," 234–39; Alan H. Gardiner, "Y3," in *Egyptian Grammar: Being an Introduction to the Study of Hieroglyphs*, ed. A. H. Gardiner (London: Oxford University Press, 1957), 534.
31. Davies, *Egyptian Hieroglyphs*, 19–20.
32. Johnson, *Nature and Making of Papyrus*, 28.
33. Piacentini, "Scribes."
34. Johnson, *Nature and Making of Papyrus*, 26–30; Breasted, "The Physical Processes," 234–39; R. H. Hughes, J. S. Hughes, and G. M. Bernacsek, *A Directory of African Wetlands* (Gland, Switzerland: IUCN, 1992), 139–43.
35. W. J. Tait, "Rush and Reed: The Pens of Egyptian and Greek Scribes," in *Proceedings of the XVIII International Congress of Papyrology: Athens, 25–31 May 1986*, ed. Vasileios Mandēlaras, vol. 2 (Athens: Greek Papyrological Society, 1988), 477–80.
36. Aidan Dodson, "Third Intermediate Period," *The Oxford Encyclopedia of Ancient Egypt*, accessed February 5, 2014, http://www.oxfordreference.com/10.1093/acref/9780195102345.001.0001/acref-9780195102345-e-0717; John D. Ray et al., "Late Period," *The Oxford Encyclopedia of Ancient Egypt*, accessed February 5, 2014, http://www.oxfordreference.com/10.1093/acref/9780195102345.001.0001/acref-9780195102345-e-0401.
37. Alan Fildes and Joann Fletcher, *Alexander the Great: Son of the Gods* (Getty Publications, 2004), 52–55.
38. Joyce Tyldesley, "Cleopatra (Queen of Egypt)," *Encyclopaedia Britannica*, accessed July 14, 2015, http://www.britannica.com/EBchecked/topic/121230/Cleopatra.
39. Robinson, *The Story of Writing*, 21.
40. Diodorus of Sicily, *Diodorus of Sicily*, trans. C. H. Oldfather (Cambridge, MA: Harvard University Press, 1933), sec. 3.4.
41. Robinson, *The Story of Writing*, 21.
42. Ibid., 22–23; Charles George Herbermann, "Jörgen Zoega," in *The Catholic Encyclopedia: An International Work of Reference on the Constitution, Doctrine, Discipline, and History of the Catholic Church*, vol. 15 (New York: Appleton, 1912), 763; Tim Murray, *Milestones in Archaeology: A Chronological Encyclopedia* (Santa Barbara, CA: ABC-CLIO, 2007), 177.
43. Richard Parkinson, *Cracking Codes: The Rosetta Stone and Decipherment* (London: British Museum Press, 1999), 19–20.
44. Ibid., 21–23.

45. Ibid., 31–33.

46. Thomas Young, "Egypt," in *Supplement to Encyclopaedia Britannica, Vol. 4, Part 1* (Edinburgh: Chambers, 1819), 86–195; Parkinson, *Cracking Codes*, 31–32.

47. Parkinson, *Cracking Codes*, 32–36.

48. Ibid.; Alan H. Gardiner, "E23," in Gardiner, ed., *Egyptian Grammar*, 460.

49. A. R. Millard, "The Infancy of the Alphabet," *World Archaeology* 17, no. 3 (1986): 390.

50. Edward Maunde Thompson, *An Introduction to Greek and Latin Palaeography* (Oxford: Clarendon Press, 1912), 1–2; B. L. Ullman, "The Etruscan Origin of the Roman Alphabet and the Names of the Letters," *Classical Philology* 22, no. 4 (1927): 372–37.

51. Frank Simons, "Proto-Sinaitic—Progenitor of the Alphabet," *Rosetta*, no. 9 (2011): 16–17, 24–26.

52. Davies, *Egyptian Hieroglyphs*, 57–60.

53. R. S. Simpson, "Gardiner, Sir Alan Henderson (1879–1963)," *Oxford Dictionary of National Biography*, accessed February 2, 2014, http://www.oxforddnb.com/view/article/33322; Alan H. Gardiner, "The Egyptian Origin of the Semitic Alphabet," *The Journal of Egyptian Archaeology* 3, no. 1 (1916): 1–16.

54. Orly Goldwasser, "How the Alphabet Was Born from Hieroglyphs," *Biblical Archaeology Review*, 2010, http://members.bib-arch.org/publication.asp?PubID=BSBA&Volume=36&Issue=02&ArticleID=06.

55. David Testen, "Semitic Languages," *Encyclopaedia Britannica*, accessed November 2014, http://www.britannica.com/EBchecked/topic/534171/Semitic-languages.

56. Goldwasser, "How the Alphabet Was Born."

57. Ibid.; Robinson, *The Story of Writing*, 160–61.

58. Goldwasser, "How the Alphabet Was Born"; Millard, "The Infancy of the Alphabet," 394; Helmut Satzinger, "Syllabic and Alphabetic Script, or the Egyptian Origin of the Alphabet," *Aegyptus* 82, no. 1/2 (2002): 26.

59. A. Egberts, "The Chronology of 'The Report of Wenamun,'" *The Journal of Egyptian Archaeology* 77 (1991): 57–67; Miriam Lichtheim, "The Report of Wenamun," in *Ancient Egyptian Literature: A Book of Readings*, vol. 2 (Berkeley: University of California Press, 2006), 224–30.

60. Charlton Lewis and Charles Short, "Călămus," *A Latin Dictionary* (Oxford: Oxford University Press, 1879), accessed July 14, 2015, http://www.perseus.tufts.edu/hopper/text?doc=Perseus:text:1999.04.0059:entry=calamus.

61. David Diringer, *The Book Before Printing: Ancient, Medieval, and Oriental* (Mineola, NY: Courier Dover Publications, 1953), 556–59; Tait, "Rush and Reed," 478–79; Leila Avrin, *Scribes, Script, and Books: The Book Arts from Antiquity to the Renaissance*, ALA Classics (Chicago: American Library Association, 2010), 146; Giovanna Menci, "New Evidence for the Use of the Greek Reed Pen in the Hieratic Scripts of the Roman Period," in *Egyptology at the Dawn of the Twenty-First Century: Proceedings of the Eighth International Congress of Egyptologists, Cairo, 2000*, eds. Zahi A. Hawass and Lyla P. Brock (Cairo: American University in Cairo Press, 2003), 397–99.

62. Tait, "Rush and Reed," 478–79.

63. "P.Mich.inv. 4968; Recto," Advanced Papyrological Information System (Ann Arbor: University of Michigan Library), accessed October 20, 2014, http://quod.lib.umich.edu/a/apis/x-2359/4968R.TIF.

64. Frank Wiborg, *Printing Ink: A History with a Treatise on Modern Method of Manufacture and Use* (New York: Harper & Brothers, 1926), 70–76.

65. Naphtali Lewis, *Papyrus in Classical Antiquity* (Oxford: Clarendon Press, 1974), 88–89.

66. Vitruvius, *The Ten Books on Architecture*, ed. Morris Hicky Morgan (Cambridge, MA: Harvard University Press, 1914), sec. 7.10, http://data.perseus.org/texts/urn:cts:latinLit:phi1056.phi001.perseus-eng1; "Vitruvius," *Encyclopaedia Britannica*, accessed September 22, 2014, http://www.britannica.com/EBchecked/topic/631310/Vitruvius.

67. Pliny the Elder, *The Natural History*, trans. John Bostock and B. A. Riley (Red Lion Court, Fleet Street: Taylor and Francis, 1855), sec. 27.28, http://data.perseus.org/texts/urn:cts:latinLit:phi0978.phi001.perseus-eng1.

68. Martial, *Epigrams*, trans. Walter A. C. Ker (London: W. Heinemann, 1919), v. 4.10; John Roberts, ed., "Martial (Marcus Valerius Martiālis)," *Oxford Dictionary of the Classical World*, accessed August 25, 2014, http://www.oxfordreference.com/view/10.1093/acref/9780192801463.001.0001/acref-9780192801463-e-1369.

69. Rose Mary Sheldon, "Tradecraft in Ancient Greece," *Studies in Intelligence*, no. 9–102–2 (1986): 39–40, 45–46; John Roberts, ed., "Ovid (Publius Ovidius Nāsō, 43 BC–AD 17)," *Oxford Dictionary of the Classical World*, accessed October 20, 2014, http://www.oxfordreference.com/view/10.1093/acref/9780192801463.001.0001/acref-9780192801463-e-1578.

70. William Smith, William Wayte, and G. E. Marindin, "Atramentum," *A Dictionary of Greek and Roman Antiquities* (London: John Murray, 1890), http://www.perseus.tufts.edu/hopper/text?doc=Perseus:text:1999.04.0063:alphabetic letter=A:entry group=10.

71. Kristie Macrakis, *Prisoners, Lovers, & Spies: The Story of Invisible Ink from Herodotus to Al-Qaeda* (New Haven: Yale University Press, 2014), 11–12.

72. Ibid.; Smith, Wayte, and Marindin, "Atramentum"; Diringer, *The Book Before Printing*, 550.

73. Elmer Eusman, "How to Make Ink—Ingredients," The Iron Gall Ink Website, 1998, http://irongallink.org/igi_indexee73.html.

74. Elmer Eusman, "Iron Gall Ink—History," The Iron Gall Ink Website, 1998, http://irongallink.org/igi_index8a92.html; Diringer, *The Book Before Printing*, 551–53; Adam Bülow-Jacobsen, "Writing Materials in the Ancient World," in *The Oxford Handbook of Papyrology*, ed. Roger Bagnall (Oxford: Oxford University Press, 2009), 18.

75. Eusman, "Iron Gall Ink—History."

76. Bernhard Bischoff, *Latin Palaeography: Antiquity and the Middle Ages* (Cambridge: Cambridge University Press, 1995), 18–19.

77. "Palimpest," *Glossary for the British Library Catalogue of Illuminated Manuscripts*, British Library, accessed October 20, 2014, http://prodigi.bl.uk/illcat/GlossP.asp#palimpsest.

78. C. Wight, "Arundel 16," Catalogue of Illuminated Manuscripts, British Library, accessed October 29, 2014, http://www.bl.uk/catalogues/illuminatedmanuscripts/record.asp?MSID=1620&CollID=20&NStart=16; Michelle Brown, *A Guide to Western Historical Scripts from Antiquity to 1600* (London: British Library, 1990), 72–73.

79. "The History of the Archimedes Manuscript," *The Archimedes Palimpsest*, accessed October 20, 2014, http://archimedespalimpsest.org/about/history/index.php.

80. William M. Ciesla, *Non-Wood Forest Products from Temperate Broad-Leaved Trees* (Rome: Food and Agriculture Organization of the United Nations, 2002), 98–100; J. V. Thirgood, "The Historical Significance of Oak," in *Oak Symposium Proceedings* (Morganstown, WV, Upper Darby; USDA Forest Service, North Central Forest Experimental Station, 1971), 2.

81. Tim Allen, "The Forgotten Chemical Revolution," *British Archaeology*, no. 66 (2002): 14–19.

82. Elmer Eusman, "How to Make Ink—Recipes and Instructions," The Iron Gall Ink Website, 1998, accessed February 5, 2014, http://irongallink.org/igi_indexc33a.html; Elmer Eusman, "Iron Gall Ink—Manufacture of Ink," The Iron Gall Ink Website, 1998, accessed February 5, 2014, http://irongallink.org/igi_index048a.html; Eusman, "Ingredients"; Jack Thompson and Claes G. Lindblad, "Iron Gall Inks," in *Manuscript Inks: Being a Personal Exploration of the Materials and Modes of Production* (Portland, OR: Caber Press, 1996), 1–20.

83. Thompson and Lindblad, "Iron Gall Inks."

84. Elmer Eusman, "Iron Gall Ink—Chemistry," The Iron Gall Ink Website, 1998, accessed February 5, 2014, http://irongallink.org/igi_indexedde.html.

85. Ibid.; Gerald Smith, "The Chemistry of Historically Important Black Inks, Paints and Dyes," *Chemistry Education in New Zealand* (May 2009): 12–15.

CHAPTER 6 ⇺ THE PRINTS AND THE PAUPER: JOHANNES GUTENBERG AND THE INVENTION OF MOVABLE TYPE

1. John Man, *The Gutenberg Revolution: How Printing Changed the Course of History* (London: Transworld Publishers, 2010), 26, 143; Albert Kapr, *Johann Gutenberg: The Man and His Invention*, trans. Douglas Martin (Brookfield, VT: Scolar Press, 1996), 25–29.

2. Man, *The Gutenberg Revolution*, 143–49; Kapr, *Johann Gutenberg*, 142–45.

3. J. C. Russell, "Late Ancient and Medieval Population," *Transactions of the American Philosophical Society* 48, no. 3, New Series (1958): 62; Man, *The Gutenberg Revolution*, 21–25, 32–35.

4. Man, *The Gutenberg Revolution*, 36–53.

5. Ibid., 57–59.

6. "Burgomaster," *OED Online*, accessed February 12, 2014, http://www.oed.com/view/Entry/24959; Man, *The Gutenberg Revolution*, 60–65; Kapr, *Johann Gutenberg*, 65–69.

7. Man, *The Gutenberg Revolution*, 61; Kapr, *Johann Gutenberg*, 65–69.

8. Russell, "Late Ancient and Medieval Population," 62.

9. Man, *The Gutenberg Revolution*, 64–66; Kapr, *Johann Gutenberg*, 71–75.

10. "The Aachen Pilgrimage," *Heiligtumsfahrt 2014* (Kirche im Bistum Aachen),

accessed February 12, 2014, http://en.heiligtumsfahrt2014.de/wissenswertes/heiligtumsfahrt-aachen/.

11. Eva-Maria Hanebutt-Benz, "Gutenberg and Mainz," Gutenberg.de, accessed March 5, 2014, http://www.mainz.de/gutenberg/english/zeitgum.htm.

12. Man, *The Gutenberg Revolution*, 68–72; Kapr, *Johann Gutenberg*, 71–75.

13. Joel Mokyr, "Florin," in *The Oxford Encyclopedia of Economic History* (Oxford: Oxford University Press, 2003), 334–35.

14. Man, *The Gutenberg Revolution*, 53–54; Kapr, *Johann Gutenberg*, 47–52.

15. Otto Fuhrmann, *Gutenberg and the Strasbourg Documents of 1439* (New York: Press of the Woolly Whale, 1940), 228.

16. Harry Clark, "'Four Pieces in a Press': Gutenberg's Activities in Strasbourg," *The Library Quarterly* 49, no. 3 (1979): 303–9; Kapr, *Johann Gutenberg*, 74–82.

17. Man, *The Gutenberg Revolution*, 72–83; Kapr, *Johann Gutenberg*, 74–82.

18. E. Burke, "Fust (or Faust), John," *The Catholic Encyclopedia: An International Work of Reference on the Constitution, Doctrine, Discipline, and History of the Catholic Church* (New York: Appleton, 1909), http://www.newadvent.org/cathen/06326b.htm; "Helmasperger's Notarial Instrument," Gutenberg Digital (SUB Göttingen), accessed March 5, 2014, http://www.gutenbergdigital.de/gudi/eframes/helma/frmnot/frmnota.htm.

19. "Helmasperger's Notarial Instrument"; Man, *The Gutenberg Revolution*, 147–49; Kapr, *Johann Gutenberg*, 153–59.

20. "Helmasperger's Notarial Instrument"; Man, *The Gutenberg Revolution*, 147–49.

21. Jan Luiten Van Zanden, "Common Workmen, Philosophers and the Birth of the European Knowledge Economy: About the Price and the Production of Useful Knowledge in Europe 1350–1800," in *GEHN Conference on Useful Knowledge, Leiden* (London: LSE, 2004), 11.

22. Man, *The Gutenberg Revolution*, 145–47; H. R. Mead, "Fifteenth-Century Schoolbooks," *Huntington Library Quarterly* 3, no. 1 (1939): 37–42.

23. Mead, "Fifteenth-Century Schoolbooks."

24. "Ars Minor [fragment]," Princeton University Digital Library (The Trustees of Princeton University, 2010), http://arks.princeton.edu/ark:/88435/8c97kq49z.

25. Frederick Kilgour, *The Evolution of the Book* (Oxford: Oxford University Press, 1998), 90; Bernhard Bischoff and University of Cambridge, "Latin Handwriting in the Middle Ages," in *Latin Palaeography: Antiquity and the Middle Ages* (Cambridge: Cambridge University Press, 1995), 127–36.

26. Geoffrey A. Glaister, "Rubricator," in *Glossary of the Book* (George Allen and Unwin, 1960), 361; "Ars Minor [fragment]."

27. Man, *The Gutenberg Revolution*, 146.

28. Morimichi Watanabe, "An Appreciation," in *Introducing Nicholas of Cusa: A Guide to a Renaissance Man*, ed. C. M. Bellitto, T. M. Izbicki, and G. Christianson, 3rd ed. (New York: Paulist Press, 2004), 24; Morimichi Watanabe, "Cusanus' Legation Journey (1450–1452)," in *Nicholas of Cusa: A Companion to His Life and His Times* (Farnham, UK: Ashgate, 2011), 29–32.

29. Morimichi Watanabe, "Giovanni Andrea Bussi (1417–1475)," in *Nicholas of Cusa*, 89–91; Kapr, *Johann Gutenberg*, 61–64.
30. Watanabe, "An Appreciation"; Man, *The Gutenberg Revolution*, 95–96; Kapr, *Johann Gutenberg*, 61–64.
31. Man, *The Gutenberg Revolution*, 141–52; Kapr, *Johann Gutenberg*, 61–64.
32. Man, *The Gutenberg Revolution*, 154–56; Kapr, *Johann Gutenberg*, 61–64.
33. Janet Ing, "The Mainz-Indulgences of 1454/5: A Review of Recent Scholarship," *British Library Journal* 9, no. 1 (1983): 17.
34. "Helmasperger's Notarial Instrument"; Man, *The Gutenberg Revolution*, 159–62.
35. Mary E. Gekler, *Johannes Gutenberg, Father of Printing: Commemorating the Fifth Centenary of His Death, 1468–1968* (Franciscan Herald Press, 1968).
36. "Printing," *OED Online*, accessed February 12, 2014, http://www.oed.com/view/Entry/151491; Edith Porada, "Why Cylinder Seals? Engraved Cylindrical Seal Stones of the Ancient Near East, Fourth to First Millennium B.C.," *The Art Bulletin* 75, no. 4 (1993): 563.
37. Porada, "Why Cylinder Seals?," 563.
38. British Museum, Dept. of Egyptian Antiquities and George Long, *Egyptian Antiquities* (London: Charles Knight, 1836), 161; Jerome M. Eisenberg, "The Phaistos Disk: A One-Hundred-Year-Old Hoax?," *Minerva: The International Review of Ancient Art & Archaeology* (2008): 9–24; Herbert E. Brekle, "Das Typographische Prinzip. Versuch Einer Begriffsklärung," *Inschrift Und Material* (1997): 207–12.
39. Tsuen-Hsuin Tsien, *Chemistry and Chemical Technology, Part 1: Paper and Printing*, ed. Joseph Needham, Science and Civilisation in China 5 (Cambridge: Cambridge University Press, 1985), 201–5.
40. "Movable Type," *OED Online*, accessed July 14, 2015, http://www.oed.com/view/Entry/254203.
41. Arthur W. Hummel, "Movable Type Printing in China: A Brief Survey," *Quarterly Journal of Current Acquisitions* 1, no. 2 (1944): 18–24.
42. Thomas Carter, *The Invention of Printing in China and Its Spread Westward* (New York: Columbia University Press, 1931), 12–16, 23–32.
43. Ibid., 159–68; Tsien, *Paper and Printing*, 201–5.
44. Tsien, *Paper and Printing*, 201–5.
45. Carter, *Printing in China*, 23–32.
46. Ibid., 159–68; Tsien, *Paper and Printing*, 206–8.
47. Tsien, *Paper and Printing*, 205–11; Carter, *Printing in China*, 159–68.
48. Tsien, *Paper and Printing*, 205–11; Carter, *Printing in China*, 159–68.
49. Tsien, *Paper and Printing*, 205–11; Carter, *Printing in China*, 159–68.
50. Tsien, *Paper and Printing*, 205–11, 220–22; Carter, *Printing in China*, 159–68.
51. Yingxing Song, *Chinese Technology in the Seventeenth Century*, trans. E-tu Zen Sun and Shiou-chuan Sun (Mineola, NY: Courier Dover Publications, 1997), 286.
52. Ibid., 287; Tsien, *Paper and Printing*, 239–43.
53. Tsien, *Paper and Printing*, 246–52.
54. Pliny the Elder, *The Natural History*, trans. John Bostock and B. A. Riley (Red Lion Court, Fleet Street: Taylor and Francis, 1855), sec. 234–37, http://data.perseus.org/texts/

urn:cts:latinLit:phi0978.phi001.perseus-eng1; Louis Le Comte, *Memoirs and Observations Topographical, Physical, Mathematical, Mechanical, Natural, Civil, and Ecclesiastical* (London: B. Tooke, 1697), 192–93; Tsien, *Paper and Printing*, 234–37.

55. Tsien, *Paper and Printing*, 220–22.

56. Ibid.

57. Carter, *Printing in China*, 23–32.

58. Jerry Norman, *Chinese* (Cambridge: Cambridge University Press, 1988); Tsien, *Paper and Printing*, 220–22.

59. Carter, *Printing in China*, 159–68; Tsien, *Paper and Printing*, 220–22.

60. Kapr, *Johann Gutenberg*, 15–25.

61. Ibid., 123–30, 159–61.

62. L. A. Legros and J. C. Grant, *Typographical Printing-Surfaces: The Technology and Mechanism of Their Production* (Longmans Green, 1916), 11.

63. Kapr, *Johann Gutenberg*, 123–30, 159–61; Fred Smeijers, *Counterpunch: Making Type in the Sixteenth Century, Designing Typefaces Now* (London: Hyphen Press, 2011), 79–85; Theodore Rosendorf, "Counter," in *The Typographic Desk Reference* (New Castle, DE: Oak Knoll Press, 2009), 89.

64. Man, "The Bible," in *The Gutenberg Revolution*, 163–89; Smeijers, *Counterpunch*, 89.

65. Kapr, *Johann Gutenberg*, 123–30; Geoffrey A. Glaister, "Matrix," in *Glossary of the Book* (George Allen and Unwin, 1960), 252–53.

66. Phil Abel and Nick Gill, personal correspondence with the author, December 2013.

67. Kapr, *Johann Gutenberg*, 123–30.

68. Clark, "'Four Pieces in a Press'"; Kapr, *Johann Gutenberg*, 74–82.

69. Kapr, *Johann Gutenberg*, 74–82; Theodore De Vinne, *The Invention of Printing* (New York: F. Hart, 1876), 57.

70. Kapr, *Johann Gutenberg*, 123–30.

71. Legros and Grant, *Typographical Printing-Surfaces*, 11.

72. Kapr, *Johann Gutenberg*, 159–61; "Composition and Presses," *Gutenberg Bible*, British Library, accessed March 10, 2013, http://www.bl.uk/treasures/gutenberg/composition.html.

73. Kapr, *Johann Gutenberg*, 123–30.

74. Ibid.

75. B. W. Gonser and J. H. Winkler, "Type Metals," in *Metals Handbook*, ed. Taylor Lyman (Metals Park, OH: American Society for Metals, 1961), 1060–62.

76. Ibid.

77. Joseph Moxon, *Moxon's Mechanick Exercises, or The Doctrine of Handy-Works Applied to the Art of Printing: A Literal Reprint in Two Volumes of the First Edition Published in the Year 1683*, vol. 1 (New York: Typothetæ of the City of New York, 1896), 164–68.

78. "Typographus. Der Buchdrucker (The Printer) / Panoplia Omnium Illiberalium Mechanicarum . . . (Book of Trades)," *Collections Online* (British Museum), accessed March 5, 2014, http://www.britishmuseum.org/research/collection_online/collection_object_details.aspx?objectId=1504693&partId=1&people=134424.

79. Martin K. Speckter, *Disquisition on the Composing Stick*, Typophile Chap Books (New York: Typophiles, 1971), 19–24.
80. Daniel Berkeley Updike, *Printing Types, Their History, Forms, and Use: A Study in Survivals* (Cambridge, MA: Harvard University Press, 1927), 15–26.
81. Geoffrey A. Glaister, "Frisket," in *Encyclopedia of the Book* (New Castle, DE: Oak Knoll Press, 1996).
82. Speckter, *Disquisition*, 11–19.
83. Martin K. Speckter, "Making a New Point, or, How About That," *Type Talks*, March–April (1962).
84. Geoffrey A. Glaister, "Hand Composition," in *Encyclopedia of the Book*.
85. Clark, "'Four Pieces in a Press'"; Fuhrmann, *Gutenberg and the Strasbourg Documents of 1439*, 228.
86. "The Ink," *Gutenberg Bible*, British Library, accessed March 5, 2014, http://www.bl.uk/treasures/gutenberg/ink.html; Susan Jones, "Painting in Oil in the Low Countries and Its Spread to Southern Europe," *Heilbrunn Timeline of Art History*, The Metropolitan Museum of Art, October 2002, http://www.metmuseum.org/toah/hd/optg/hd_optg.htm.
87. Jones, "Painting in Oil"; Louis Andés, *Oil Colours and Printers' Inks: A Practical Handbook Treating of Linseed Oil, Boiled Oil, Paints, Artists' Colours, Lampblack and Printers' Inks, Black and Coloured* (London: Scott Greenwood, 1903), 1–2; C. Bloy, *A History of Printing Ink, Balls and Rollers, 1440–1850* (London: Wynkyn de Worde Society, 1972), 1–3.
88. Richard N. Schwab, Thomas A. Cahill, and Bruce H. Kusko, "Cyclotron Analysis of the Ink in the 42-Line Bible," *The Papers of the Bibliographical Society of America* 77 (1983): 283–315.
89. Man, *The Gutenberg Revolution*, 136.
90. Geoffrey A. Glaister, "Ink Ball," in *Encyclopedia of the Book*, 244.
91. James Moran, *Printing Presses: History and Development from the Fifteenth Century to Modern Times* (Berkeley: University of California Press, 1978), 23–24.
92. Ibid., 18–21.
93. Kapr, *Johann Gutenberg*, 159–61.
94. Kapr, *Johann Gutenberg*, 182; Man, *The Gutenberg Revolution*, 164; "The Paper," *Gutenberg Bible*, British Library, accessed April 28, 2015, http://www.bl.uk/treasures/gutenberg/paper.html.
95. Kapr, *Johann Gutenberg*, 162–65.
96. Peter Weidhaas, *A History of the Frankfurt Book Fair* (Toronto: Dundurn Press, 2007), 19–25.
97. "A Noble Fragment," Boston Public Library, accessed October 30, 2014, http://bpl.bibliocommons.com/item/show/1369106075_a_noble_fragment.
98. Kapr, *Johann Gutenberg*, 159–70.
99. "Helmasperger's Notarial Instrument"; Man, *The Gutenberg Revolution*, 184–87.
100. "Helmasperger's Notarial Instrument"; Kapr, *Johann Gutenberg*, 173–75.
101. Kapr, *Johann Gutenberg*, 202–21; Man, *The Gutenberg Revolution*, 188–89.

102. "Psalterium Benedictinum," *Peter Schoeffer: Printer of Mainz*, Southern Methodist University, accessed March 8, 2014, http://www.smu.edu/Bridwell/Collections/SpecialCollectionsandArchives/Exhibitions/PeterSchoefferPrinterofMainz/GUTENBERGFUSTANDSCHOEFFER/The 1459 Psalter; Kapr, *Johann Gutenberg*, 202–10.
103. Man, *The Gutenberg Revolution*, 191–211; B. A. Uhlendorf, "The Invention of Printing and Its Spread till 1470: With Special Reference to Social and Economic Factors," *The Library Quarterly: Information, Community, Policy* 2, no. 3 (1932): 200–201.

CHAPTER 7 ↞ OUT OF SORTS: TYPESETTING MEETS THE INDUSTRIAL REVOLUTION

1. "Incunabula," *Encyclopaedia Britannica*, accessed February 8, 2013, http://www.britannica.com/EBchecked/topic/284960/incunabula.
2. Filippo Strata, *Polemic against Printing*, ed. Martin Lowry, trans. Shelagh Grier (Birmingham: Hayloft, 1986), n.p.
3. Gustav Janouch and Francine Prose, *Conversations with Kafka*, trans. Goronwy Rees (New York: New Directions, 2012), 40.
4. Jeremy Atack, Fred Bateman, and Thomas Weiss, "The Regional Diffusion and Adoption of the Steam Engine in American Manufacturing," *The Journal of Economic History* 40, no. 2 (1980): 281–308; John Lord, *Capital and Steam-Power, 1750–1800* (London: P.S. King & Son, 1923), 147–80.
5. James Moran, *Printing Presses: History and Development from the Fifteenth Century to Modern Times* (Berkeley: University of California Press, 1978), 40–41.
6. G. M. Ditchfield, "Stanhope, Charles, Third Earl Stanhope (1753–1816)," *Oxford Dictionary of National Biography*, accessed March 13, 2014, http://www.oxforddnb.com/view/article/26241.
7. Moran, *Printing Presses*, 49–59.
8. J. Southward, *Practical Printing: A Handbook of the Art of Typography*, 4th ed. (J. M. Powell & Son, 1884), 365–74; Seán Jennett, *Pioneers in Printing: Johann Gutenberg, William Caxton, William Caslon, John Baskerville, Alois Senefelder, Frederick Koenig, Ottmar Mergenthaler, Tolbert Lanston* (London: Routledge & Kegan Paul, 1958), 107–8.
9. Jan Golinski, "Nicholson, William (1753–1815)," *Oxford Dictionary of National Biography*, accessed March 13, 2014, http://www.oxforddnb.com/view/article/20153; Bennet Woodcroft, "A.D. 1790, April 29.—№1748. Nicholson, William," in *Patents for Inventions. Abridgments of Specifications Relating to Bleaching, Dyeing and Printing Calico and Other Fabrics, and Yarns, Including the Manufacture of Rollers, Engraving, the Preparation* (London: Patent Office, 1859), 49–50.
10. A. A. Stewart, "Columbian Press," in *The Printer's Dictionary of Technical Terms: A Handbook of Definitions and Information About Processes of Printing; with a Brief Glossary of Terms Used in Book Binding* (School of Printing, North End Union, 1912); Briar Press, "Columbian," *Letterpress Commons*, accessed October 30, 2014, https://letterpresscommons.com/press/columbian/.
11. Jennett, *Pioneers in Printing*, 116–18.

12. Samuel Smiles, *Men of Invention and Industry* (London: J. Murray, 1890), 159.

13. Jennett, *Pioneers in Printing*, 118–24; Dennis Karwatka, "Friedrich Koenig and His Steam-Powered Printing Press," *Tech Directions* 66, no. 8 (2007): 10.

14. Jennett, *Pioneers in Printing*, 130–36; Moran, *Printing Presses*, 101–12.

15. Jennett, *Pioneers in Printing*, 130–36; Robert Lechêne, "Printing: Koenig's Mechanical Press (Early 19th Century)," *Encyclopaedia Britannica*, accessed March 12, 2014, http://www.britannica.com/EBchecked/topic/477017/printing/36841/Koenigs-mechanical-press-early-19th-century.

16. A. E. Musson, "Newspaper Printing in the Industrial Revolution," *The Economic History Review* 10, no. 3, New Series (1958): 411–26.

17. Jennett, *Pioneers in Printing*, 130–36; John Walter, "London, Tuesday, November 29, 1814," *The Times*, November 29, 1814.

18. Anita McConnell, "Cowper, Edward Shickle (1790–1852)," *Oxford Dictionary of National Biography*, accessed March 14, 2014, http://www.oxforddnb.com/view/article/6504?docPos=2.

19. William E. Loy, "David Bruce," *The Inland Printer* 22, no. 6 (1899): 701; Richard M. Hoe, "Improvement in Rotary Printing-Presses. U.S. Patent 5,199," United States Patent Office, 1847; "Richard March Hoe," *Encyclopaedia Britannica*, accessed June 24, 2013, http://www.britannica.com/EBchecked/topic/268638/Richard-March-Hoe.

20. W. Bullock, "Printing-Machine. U.S. Patent 38,200," United States Patent Office, 1863.

21. Lechêne, "Printing."

22. E. Burrows, "Ill-Fated Inventors," *Engineering Technology* 6, no. 10 (November 2011): 50–51; "William Bullock," Union Dale Cemetery, Pittsburgh, PA, 2009, http://uniondalecemetery.org/notables-detail.php?notableID=23.

23. Musson, "Newspaper Printing."

24. L. A. Legros and J. C. Grant, *Typographical Printing-Surfaces: The Technology and Mechanism of Their Production* (Longmans Green, 1916), 378–91; James W. Paige, "Improvement in Type-Setting Machines. U.S. Patent 157,694," US Patent and Trademark Office, 1874.

25. C. H. Gold, *"Hatching Ruin" or Mark Twain's Road to Bankruptcy*, Mark Twain and His Circle Series (University of Missouri Press, 2003), 1–12.

26. Bruce Michelson, *Printer's Devil: Mark Twain & the American Publishing Revolution* (Berkeley: University of California Press, 2006), 1–16.

27. Mark Twain et al., *Autobiography of Mark Twain*, vol. 1 (Berkeley: University of California Press, 2010), 101–6.

28. Legros and Grant, *Typographical Printing-Surfaces*, 378–91.

29. M. Twain, F. Anderson, and R. P. Browning, *Mark Twain's Notebooks & Journals*, vol. 3, Mark Twain Papers (Berkeley: University of California Press, 1980), 147.

30. Twain et al., *Autobiography of Mark Twain*, 1:101–6; Samuel H. Williamson, "Seven Ways to Compute the Relative Value of a U.S. Dollar Amount—1774 to Present," *Measuring Worth*, 2013, http://www.measuringworth.com/uscompare/index.php.

31. Legros and Grant, *Typographical Printing-Surfaces*, 378–91; History and Heritage Committee, "Paige Compositor," ASME, Asme.org, accessed December 2012, http://www.asme.org/about-asme/history/landmarks/topics-a-l/communications-and-data-processing/-11-paige-compositor-(1877).

32. J. S. Thompson, *History of Composing Machines* (The Inland Printer Company, 1904), 25; James W. Paige, "Machine for Setting, Distributing, and Justifying Type. U.S. Patent 547,859," US Patent and Trademark Office, 1882.

33. History and Heritage Committee, "Paige Compositor."

34. Gold, "*Hatching Ruin*," 1–12.

35. Twain et al., *Autobiography of Mark Twain*, 1:101–16.

36. "The Inventions of Dr. William Church," *Scientific American* 88, no. 7 (February 1903): 115–16.

37. David M. MacMillan and Rollande Krandall, "Dr. William Church's Typecaster," *Circuitous Root*, 2010, http://www.circuitousroot.com/artifice/letters/press/noncomptype/casters/pre-bruce/church/index.html.

38. Moran, *Printing Presses*, 175.

39. William Baxter, "The Evolution and Present Status of the Automobile," in *The Popular Science Monthly*, ed. J. McKeen Cattell (New York: Popular Science, 1900), 406–19; "Church's, for Imprs. in Steam Carriages," in *The London Journal of Arts and Sciences, and Repertory of Patent Inventions*, vol. 2, W. Newton, ed. (London: Sherwood, Gilbert, and Piper, 1833), 89–101.

40. MacMillan and Krandall, "Dr. William Church's Typecaster."

41. Jennett, *Pioneers in Printing*, 164.

42. Ibid., 164–65.

43. Charles T. Moore, "Improvement in Methods of Preparing Transfer-Sheets or Matrices for Printing. U.S. Patent 201,436," US Patent and Trademark Office, 1878.

44. George Iles, *Leading American Inventors* (New York: Holt, 1912), 404–6.

45. "JAMES O. CLEPHANE DEAD; Development of Linotype Machine Largely Due to His Efforts," *New York Times*, December 1, 1910; Iles, *Leading American Inventors*, 406.

46. Iles, *Leading American Inventors*, 317–30.

47. Douglas Wilson, dir., *Linotype, the Film: In Search of the Eighth Wonder of the World*, Onpaperwings Production, 2012.

48. Frank J. Romano, "Bridging the Gap," *Electronic Publishing* 27, no. 6 (2003): 48.

49. Ottmar Mergenthaler and Carl Schlesinger, *The Biography of Ottmar Mergenthaler, Inventor of the Linotype* (New Castle, DE: Oak Knoll Books, 1989), 4–7.

50. Jennett, *Pioneers in Printing*, 165–66.

51. Iles, *Leading American Inventors*, 408–9.

52. Jennett, *Pioneers in Printing*, 167–72; History and Heritage Committee, "Ottmar Mergenthaler's Square Base Linotype Machine," ASME, http://www.asme.org/about-asme/history/landmarks/topics-a-l/communications-and-data-processing/-235-ottmar-mergenthaler-s-square-base-linotype-ma.

53. Wilson, *Linotype*.

54. Jennett, *Pioneers in Printing*, 167–72; History and Heritage Committee, "Ottmar Mergenthaler's Square Base Linotype Machine."

55. J. R. Rogers and Mergenthaler Linotype Company, *Linotype Instruction Book: A Detailed Description of the Mechanism and Operation of the Linotype with Instructions for Its Erection, Maintenance, and Care* (Mergenthaler Linotype Company, 1925), 3–18.

56. Mergenthaler Linotype Company, *Linotype Machine Principles* (Mergenthaler Linotype Co., 1940), 250–63; "Etaoin Shrdlu," *OED Online*, accessed July 14, 2015, http://www.oed.com/viewdictionaryentry/Entry/64669.

57. Mergenthaler Linotype Company, *Linotype Machine Principles*, 123–32.

58. Jennett, *Pioneers in Printing*, 168–69.

59. Michelson, *Printer's Devil*, 6.

60. History and Heritage Committee, "Ottmar Mergenthaler's Square Base Linotype Machine"; John Southward, *Type-Composing Machines of the Past, the Present, and the Future. A Paper Read before the Balloon Society of Great Britain, at St. James' Hall, October 3rd, 1890* (Leicester: Raithby, 1891).

61. H. Zapf, "About Micro-Typography and the Hz-Program," *Electronic Publishing* 6, no. 3 (1993): 286.

62. Southward, *Type-Composing Machines*.

63. "Monotype (Typesetting Machine)," *Encyclopaedia Britannica*, accessed April 13, 2011, http://www.britannica.com/EBchecked/topic/390177/Monotype.

64. Leon E. Truesdell, *The Development of Punch Card Tabulation in the Bureau of the Census, 1890–1940: With Outlines of Actual Tabulation Programs* (Washington, DC: Government Printing Office, 1965), 17–24.

65. United States Census Bureau, "Directors 1865–1893," United States Census Bureau, November 2012, http://www.census.gov/history/www/census_then_now/director_biographies/directors_1865_-_1893.html#seaton; United States Census Bureau, "Early Census Processing and the Seaton Device," United States Census Bureau, October 2012, http://www.census.gov/history/www/innovations/technology/early_census_processing_and_the_seaton_device.html.

66. L. Heide, *Punched-Card Systems and the Early Information Explosion, 1880–1945*, Studies in Industry and Society (Baltimore: Johns Hopkins University Press, 2009), 27–33; United States Census Bureau, "Tabulation and Processing," United States Census Bureau, October 22, 2012, http://www.census.gov/history/www/innovations/technology/tabulation_and_processing.html; Truesdell, *The Development of Punch Card Tabulation*, 17–24.

67. Lanston Monotype Machine Company, "Death of Tolbert Lanston," *Monotype: A Journal of Composing Room Efficiency*, no. 1 (1913): 13.

68. Rich Hopkins, "A Brief History of Lanston Monotype," *ATF Newsletter* no. 10 (November 1984): 24–27; Lanston Monotype Machine Company, "Death of Tolbert Lanston."

69. Heide, *Punched-Card Systems*, 27–33.

70. Herman Hollerith, "The Electrical Tabulating Machine," *Journal of the Royal Statistical Society* 57, no. 4 (1894): 678.

71. Robert Sobel, *Thomas Watson, Sr.: IBM and the Computer Revolution* (BeardBooks,

2000), 14–15; United States Census Bureau, "John Shaw Billings," United States Census Bureau, November 2012, http://www.census.gov/history/www/census_then_now/notable_alumni/john_shaw_billings.html.

72. William R. Aul, "Herman Hollerith: Data Processing Pioneer," *Think* (November 1974): 22–24.

73. Virginia Hollerith and Herman Hollerith, "Biographical Sketch of Herman Hollerith," *Isis* 62, no. 1 (1971): 70.

74. Heide, *Punched-Card Systems*, 27–33.

75. Jennett, *Pioneers in Printing*, 178–79.

76. Heide, *Punched-Card Systems*, 27–33.

77. Jennett, *Pioneers in Printing*, 178–79.

78. United States Census Bureau, "Directors 1865–1893."

79. Hopkins, "A Brief History of Lanston Monotype."

80. Jennett, *Pioneers in Printing*, 181.

81. Lanston Monotype Machine Company, *The Monotype System: A Book for Owners & Operators of Monotypes* (Lanston Monotype Machine Company, 1912), 1–4.

82. Ibid.

83. Harry McIntosh, personal interview with the author, April 11, 2012.

84. Lanston Monotype Machine Company, *The Monotype System*, 30–32.

85. Jennett, *Pioneers in Printing*, 176–77.

86. Lanston Monotype Machine Company, "Death of Tolbert Lanston"; Hopkins, "A Brief History of Lanston Monotype."

87. Aul, "Herman Hollerith: Data Processing Pioneer."

CHAPTER 8 ⋘ SAINTS AND SCRIVENERS: THE RISE OF THE ILLUMINATED MANUSCRIPT

1. John Roberts, ed., "Diocletian," *Oxford Dictionary of the Classical World*, accessed October 13, 2014, http://www.oxfordreference.com/view/10.1093/acref/9780192801463.001.0001/acref-9780192801463-e-708.

2. Guy Halsall, "The Barbarian Invasions," in *The New Cambridge Medieval History*, ed. Fouracre and McKitterick, vol. 1, 35–55.

3. Ibid.

4. Claire Stancliffe, "Religion and Society in Ireland," in *The New Cambridge Medieval History*, ed. Fouracre and McKitterick, vol. 1, 397–425.

5. Clare Stancliffe, "Patrick [St Patrick, Pádraig] (fl. 5th Cent.)," *Oxford Dictionary of National Biography*, accessed April 7, 2014, http://www.oxforddnb.com/view/article/21562.

6. Philip Meggs, *Meggs' History of Graphic Design* (Hoboken, NJ: John Wiley & Sons, 2012), 48–50.

7. "Illuminate," *OED Online*, accessed March 2014, http://www.oed.com/view/Entry/91536.

8. Meggs, *History of Graphic Design*, 18–19; Richard Lepsius, *Das Todtenbuch Der Ägypter Nach Dem Hieroglyphischen Papyrus in Turin* (Leipzig: G. Wigand, 1842).

9. Meggs, *History of Graphic Design*, 19.

10. Ibid.; Raymond Faulkner and Carol Andrews, *The Ancient Egyptian Book of the Dead* (London: British Museum Press, 2010), 11–16.

11. "Page from the Book of the Dead of Hunefer," British Museum, accessed October 31, 2014, http://www.britishmuseum.org/explore/highlights/highlight_objects/aes/p/page_from_the_book_of_the_dead.aspx; "Papyrus from the Book of the Dead of Ani," British Museum, accessed October 31, 2014, http://www.britishmuseum.org/explore/highlights/highlight_objects/aes/p/book_of_the_dead_of_ani.aspx.

12. E. A. W. Budge, *Book of the Dead: Facsimiles of the Papyri of Hunifer, Anhai, Kerāsher and Netchemet, with Supplementary Text from the Papyrus of Nu, with a Transcript, Translation, Etc.* (London: British Museum, 1900), Hunefer 4; "Page from the Book of the Dead of Hunefer"; "Hunefer, an Ancient Egyptian Official," British Museum, accessed October 31, 2014, http://www.britishmuseum.org/explore/highlights/article_index/h/hunefer_an_ancient_egyptian_0.aspx.

13. Henry Petroski, *The Book on the Bookshelf*, 1st ed. (New York: Alfred A. Knopf, 1999), 32–33; Kurt Weitzmann, *Illustrations in Roll and Codex* (Princeton, NJ: Princeton University Press), 3–11.

14. "The Cathach / The Psalter of St Columba," Royal Irish Academy, 2010, https://www.ria.ie/library/special-collections/manuscripts/cathach.aspx; Máire Herbert, "Columba [St Columba, Colum Cille] (c.521–597)," *Oxford Dictionary of National Biography*, accessed April 7, 2014, http://www.oxforddnb.com/view/article/6001?docPos=2.

15. Herbert, "Columba [St Columba, Colum Cille] (c.521–597)."

16. Bernhard Bischoff, *Latin Palaeography: Antiquity and the Middle Ages* (Cambridge: Cambridge University Press, 1995), 181–89.

17. George Henderson, *From Durrow to Kells: The Insular Gospel-Books, 650–800* (New York: Thames and Hudson, 1987), 54–55; Bernard Meehan, *The Book of Durrow: A Medieval Masterpiece at Trinity College Dublin* (Dublin: Town House, 1996), 16.

18. "Lindisfarne Gospels," *Sacred Texts*, British Library, accessed October 31, 2014, http://www.bl.uk/onlinegallery/sacredtexts/lindisfarne.html.

19. Henderson, *From Durrow to Kells*, 131–51; Meggs, *History of Graphic Design*, 48–50.

20. Bischoff, *Latin Palaeography*, 190–201; Meggs, *History of Graphic Design*, 48–50.

21. "Insular Script," *Encyclopaedia Britannica*, accessed August 26, 2012, http://www.britannica.com/EBchecked/topic/289453/Insular-script; M. B. Parkes, *Pause and Effect: Punctuation in the West* (Berkeley: University of California Press, 1993), 20–29.

22. John Bowker, "Chi-Rho," *The Concise Oxford Dictionary of World Religions*, accessed October 31, 2014, http://www.oxfordreference.com/view/10.1093/acref/9780192800947.001.0001/acref-9780192800947-e-1528.

23. Paul Saenger, "Silent Reading: Its Impact on Late Medieval Script and Society," *Viator: Medieval and Renaissance Studies* no. 13 (1982): 367–414.

24. Andrew Pearson, "Piracy in Late Roman Britain: A Perspective from the Viking Age," *Britannia* 37 (2006): 337–53.

25. Ibid.; Paul Meyvaert, "The Book of Kells and Iona," *The Art Bulletin* 71, no. 1 (1989): 6–19.

26. Stancliffe, "Religion and Society in Ireland."
27. Helmut Koenigsberger, "The Barbarian Successor States," in *Medieval Europe: 400–1500* (Harlow: Longman, 1987), 40–42.
28. Bischoff, *Latin Palaeography*, 190–201.
29. Geoffrey Barraclough, "Holy Roman Empire," *Encyclopaedia Britannica*, accessed August 12, 2013, http://www.britannica.com/EBchecked/topic/269851/Holy-Roman-Empire.
30. G. W. Trompf, "The Concept of the Carolingian Renaissance," *Journal of the History of Ideas* 34, no. 1 (1973): 3–26; Barrie Dobson and Michael Lapidge, "Carolingian Renaissance," *Encyclopedia of the Middle Ages*, accessed August 26, 2012, http://www.oxfordreference.com/view/10.1093/acref/9780227679319.001.0001/acref-9780227679319-e-483.
31. Henri-Jean Martin, *The History and Power of Writing* (Chicago: University of Chicago Press, 1995), 121.
32. Hugh Ford, "St. Benedict of Nursia," *The Catholic Encyclopedia* (New York: Appleton, 1907), http://www.newadvent.org/cathen/02467b.htm.
33. Martin, *The History and Power of Writing*, 121.
34. Trompf, "The Concept of the Carolingian Renaissance," 3–26; Dobson and Lapidge, "Carolingian Renaissance"; Martin, *The History and Power of Writing*, 124, 127–28.
35. Frederick Kilgour, *The Evolution of the Book* (Oxford: Oxford University Press, 1998), 68–80.
36. Celia M. Chazelle, "Pictures, Books, and the Illiterate: Pope Gregory I's Letters to Serenus of Marseilles," *Word & Image* 6, no. 2 (1990): 138–53, doi:10.1080/02666286.1990.10435425; Ronald G. Witt, *The Two Latin Cultures and the Foundation of Renaissance Humanism in Medieval Italy* (Cambridge: Cambridge University Press, 2012), 51–52; Martin, *The History and Power of Writing*, 120.
37. C. U. Clark, "How Our Roman Type Came to Us," *The North American Review* 195, no. 677 (1912): 546–49.
38. G. C. Alston, "Rule of St. Benedict," *The Catholic Encyclopedia*, http://www.newadvent.org/cathen/02436a.htm.
39. Florence Edler de Roover, "The Scriptorium," in *The Medieval Library*, ed. James Thompson (New York: Hafner, 1957), 606–8.
40. Walter Horn and Ernest Born, "The Medieval Monastery as a Setting for the Production of Manuscripts," *The Journal of the Walters Art Gallery* 44 (1986): 17–20, 34.
41. Ibid., 21–22.
42. de Roover, "The Scriptorium," 606–8.
43. Ibid., 597.
44. Ibid., 595.
45. Saenger, "Silent Reading"; de Roover, "The Scriptorium," 606.
46. de Roover, "The Scriptorium," 606; D. R. Webster, "The Carthusian Order," *The Catholic Encyclopedia*, http://www.newadvent.org/cathen/03388a.htm.
47. Robert G. Calkins, "Stages of Execution: Procedures of Illumination as Revealed in an Unfinished Book of Hours," *Gesta* 17, no. 1 (1978): 61–70; Julie Somers, "Image Interrupted—The

Unfinished Medieval Manuscript," *Medievalfragments*, March 15, 2013, http://medievalfragments.wordpress.com/2013/03/15/image-interrupted-the-unfinished-medieval-manuscript/.

48. de Roover, "The Scriptorium," 601–2; Christopher De Hamel, *Scribes and Illuminators* (Toronto; Buffalo: University of Toronto Press, 1992), 20–26; "Hard Point," *Glossary for the British Library Catalogue of Illuminated Manuscripts*, British Library, accessed October 20, 2014, http://prodigi.bl.uk/illcat/GlossH.asp#hardpoint; "Lead Point," *Glossary for the British Library Catalogue of Illuminated Manuscripts*, British Library, accessed October 20, 2014, http://prodigi.bl.uk/illcat/GlossL.asp#leadpoint; "Ruling," *Glossary for the British Library Catalogue of Illuminated Manuscripts*, British Library, accessed October 20, 2014, http://prodigi.bl.uk/illcat/GlossR.asp#ruling.

49. De Hamel, *Scribes and Illuminators*, 20.

50. de Roover, "The Scriptorium," 601–2.

51. Horn and Born, "The Medieval Monastery," 34–35; de Roover, "The Scriptorium," 598–99.

52. Kilgour, *The Evolution of the Book*, 68–80.

53. Horn and Born, "The Medieval Monastery," 34–35; de Roover, "The Scriptorium," 598–99.

54. De Hamel, *Scribes and Illuminators*, 29; de Roover, "The Scriptorium," 601–2.

55. J. Alexander, *Medieval Illuminators and Their Methods of Work* (New Haven: Yale University Press, 1992), 10–18; Calkins, "Stages of Execution," 61–70; "Lead Point"; "Metal Point," *Glossary for the British Library Catalogue of Illuminated Manuscripts*, British Library, accessed October 20, 2014, http://prodigi.bl.uk/illcat/GlossM.asp#metalpoint.

56. Calkins, "Stages of Execution," 61–70; De Hamel, *Scribes and Illuminators*, 20–26.

57. Ibid., 57–58.

58. Cennino Cennini, *The Book of the Art of Cennino Cennini: A Contemporary Practical Treatise on Quattrocento Painting* (London: G. Allen & Unwin, 1922), 111–12; De Hamel, *Scribes and Illuminators*, 57; "Making Manuscripts," Getty Museum, 2014, https://www.youtube.com/watch?v=nuNfdHNTv90.

59. Cennini, *The Book of the Art of Cennino Cennini*, 111–12.

60. Jack C. Thompson, "Notes on the Manufacture of Goldbeater's Skin," in *The Book & Paper Group Annual*, vol. 2 (American Institute for Conservation, 1983), 119–21.

61. Matt T. Roberts and Don Etherington, "Goldbeating," *Bookbinding and the Conservation of Books*, Foundation of the American Institute for Conservation, November 2011, http://cool.conservation-us.org/don//dt/dt1576.html.

62. Mark Steadman, "The Goldbeater, the Cow and the Airship," Copenhagen: Post & Tele Museum, May 1, 2006, http://www.ptt-museum.dk/en/online_magazine/previous_articles/broadcasting/?id=74; Thompson, "Notes on the Manufacture of Goldbeater's Skin," 119–21.

63. Calkins, "Stages of Execution," 61–70.

64. "Pigment," *Glossary for the British Library Catalogue of Illuminated Manuscripts*, British Library, accessed October 20, 2014, http://prodigi.bl.uk/illcat/GlossP.asp#pigment; Michael Clarke and Deborah Clarke, "Tempera," *The Concise Oxford Dictionary of Art Terms*, accessed October 31, 2014, http://www.oxfordreference.com/view/10.1093/acref/9780199569922.001.0001/acref-9780199569922-e-1658.

65. "Pigment"; Amy Baker, "Common Medieval Pigments," *The Cochineal*, Kilgarlin Center for Preservation of the Cultural Record, 2004, https://www.ischool.utexas.edu/~cochinea/html-paper/a-baker-04-pigments.html; John Friedman and Kristen Mossler Figg, "Saffron," in *Trade, Travel, and Exploration in the Middle Ages: An Encyclopedia* (New York: Garland, 2000), 532–33.

66. Daniel Thompson, *The Materials and Techniques of Medieval Painting* (New York: Dover Publications, 1956), 100–102.

67. Ibid., 90–92.

68. "Rubric," *OED Online*, accessed April 18, 2014, http://www.oed.com/view/Entry/168394#eid24733102; de Roover, "The Scriptorium," 598–99; Thompson, *Materials and Techniques*, 102.

69. Leila Avrin, *Scribes, Script, and Books: The Book Arts from Antiquity to the Renaissance*, ALA Classics (Chicago: American Library Association, 2010), 224.

70. C. Wight, "Sloane 2435," *Catalogue of Illuminated Manuscripts*, British Library, accessed October 29, 2014, http://www.bl.uk/catalogues/illuminatedmanuscripts/record.asp?MSID=8573.

71. Edward J. Nell, "Economic Relationships in the Decline of Feudalism: An Examination of Economic Interdependence and Social Change," *History and Theory* 6, no. 3 (1967): 313–50.

72. Meggs, *History of Graphic Design*, 55–58.

73. Ibid., 61–63.

CHAPTER 9 ⇜ EX ORIENTE LUX: WOODCUT COMES TO THE WEST

1. Laurence Bergreen, *Marco Polo: From Venice to Xanadu* (London: Quercus, 2008), 3–5.

2. Ibid., 6–7.

3. Ibid., 7–8; Maryanne Kowaleski, ed., "Compilatione of Rustichello Da Pisa," *French of Italy*, Fordham University, accessed October 31, 2014, http://www.fordham.edu/academics/programs_at_fordham_/medieval_studies/french_of_italy/sources_by_community/northern_italian_wri/frenchlanguage_texts/compilatione_of_rust_80611.asp.

4. Fosco Maraini, "Marco Polo," *Encyclopaedia Britannica*, accessed October 31, 2014, http://www.britannica.com/EBchecked/topic/468139/Marco-Polo; Bergreen, *Marco Polo*, 53, 79.

5. Marco Polo, Henri Cordier, and Henry Yule, *The Book of Ser Marco Polo, the Venetian: Concerning the Kingdoms and Marvels of the East*, 3rd ed. (London: J. Murray, 1903), 1:423–26.

6. Ibid., 2:132–33.

7. Ibid., 1:423–26.

8. Douglas Harper, "Cathay," *Online Etymology Dictionary*, accessed April 28, 2014, http://www.etymonline.com/index.php?search=cathay.

9. Clifford Rogers, William Caferro, and Shelley Reid, "Gunpowder," in *The Oxford Encyclopedia of Medieval Warfare and Military Technology* (New York: Oxford University Press, 2010), 231–32; Peter Bernholz, *Monetary Regimes and Inflation: History,*

Economic and Political Relationships (Cheltenham: Edward Elgar, 2003), 52–54; John Black, Nigar Hashimzade, and Gareth Myles, "Fiat Money," *A Dictionary of Economics*, http://www.oxfordreference.com/view/10.1093/acref/9780199696321.001.0001/acref-9780199696321-e-1175; I.C.B. Dear and Peter Kemp, eds., "Magnetic Compass," *The Oxford Companion to Ships and the Sea*, http://www.oxfordreference.com/view/10.1093/acref/9780199205684.001.0001/acref-9780199205684-e-1544.

10. Dard Hunter, *Papermaking: The History and Technique of an Ancient Craft*, Dover Books Explaining Science (New York: Dover Publications, 1978), 48–63.

11. Tsuen-Hsuin Tsien, *Chemistry and Chemical Technology, Part 1: Paper and Printing*, ed. Joseph Needham, Science and Civilisation in China 5 (Cambridge: Cambridge University Press, 1985), 47–52; Polo, Cordier, and Yule, *The Book of Ser Marco Polo*, 2:36–37.

12. Thomas Carter, *The Invention of Printing in China and Its Spread Westward* (New York: Columbia University Press, 1931), 75.

13. Ibid., 7–9.

14. Ibid.

15. Claudius Cornelius Müller, "Shihuangdi," *Encyclopaedia Britannica*, accessed April 30, 2014, http://www.britannica.com/EBchecked/topic/540412/Shihuangdi/.

16. Ibid.; Zhengyuan Fu, *Autocratic Tradition and Chinese Politics* (Cambridge: Cambridge University Press, 1993), 111; Lois Mai Chan, "The Burning of the Books in China, 213 B.C.," *The Journal of Library History* 7, no. 2 (1972): 101–8.

17. Carter, *Printing in China*, 8–11; Tsien, *Paper and Printing*, 136–39.

18. Ibid.

19. "Dunhuang," *Encyclopaedia Britannica*, accessed May 12, 2014, http://www.britannica.com/EBchecked/topic/608871/Dunhuang.

20. Rong Xinjiang and Valerie Hansen, "The Nature of the Dunhuang Library Cave and the Reasons for Its Sealing," *Cahiers d'Extreme-Asie* 11, no. 1 (1999): 247–50.

21. Carter, *Printing in China*, 40.

22. Kenneth Starr, *Black Tigers: A Grammar of Chinese Rubbings* (Seattle: University of Washington Press, 2008), 13; Dennis C. Twitchett, "Taizong," *Encyclopaedia Britannica*, accessed January 2, 2013, http://www.britannica.com/EBchecked/topic/580608/Taizong.

23. "What Is a Rubbing?," *Chinese Stone Rubbings Collection*, Berkeley East Asian Library, September 23, 2004, http://www.lib.berkeley.edu/EAL/stone/rubbings.html.

24. Richard Sears, "Character: 拓," Chinese Etymology, http://www.chineseetymology.org. Visit http://bit.ly/1MuZq6q.

25. Carter, *Printing in China*, 12; Tsien, *Paper and Printing*, 143–46; "The Making of a Chinese Rubbing," The Field Museum, September 25, 2008, https://www.youtube.com/watch?v=ADfhgDRIhUk.

26. Tsien, *Paper and Printing*, 143–46; "Carved in Stone," *Art & Architecture Library*, accessed October 31, 2014, http://lib.stanford.edu/art/exhibitions/carved-in-stone.

27. Richard von Glahn, "The Origins of Paper Money in China," in *The Origins of Value: The Financial Innovations That Created Modern Capital Markets*, ed. William N. Goetzmann and K. Geert Rouwenhorst (Oxford: Oxford University Press, 2005), 79.

28. "Six Dynasties," *Encyclopaedia Britannica*, accessed October 31, 2014, http://www.britannica.com/EBchecked/topic/547040/Six-Dynasties.

29. Xinjiang Rong, "Land Route or Sea Route? Commentary on the Study of the Paths of Transmission and Areas in Which Buddhism Was Disseminated During the Han Period," ed. Victor H. Mair, *Sino-Platonic Papers*, no. 144 (2004): 1–31; Carter, *Printing in China*, 17–19.

30. Sonya S. Lee, "Transmitting Buddhism to a Future Age: The Leiyin Cave at Fangshan and Cave-Temples with Stone Scriptures in Sixth-Century China," *Archives of Asian Art* 60 (2010): 43–57.

31. "Dacang Jing," *Encyclopaedia Britannica*, accessed May 7, 2014, http://www.britannica.com/EBchecked/topic/579582/Dacang-Jing; "Xuanzang," *Encyclopaedia Britannica*, accessed May 24, 2013, http://www.britannica.com/EBchecked/topic/274015/Xuanzang.

32. Nigel Crowther, *Sport in Ancient Times* (Norman: University of Oklahoma Press, 2010), 4–5; Carter, *Printing in China*, 33–34.

33. Lucien Ellington, *Japan* (Santa Barbara, CA: ABC-CLIO, 2009), 28.

34. Arthur Wright, *Buddhism in Chinese History*, Stanford Studies in the Civilizations of Eastern Asia (Stanford, CA: Stanford University Press, 1959), 67–68.

35. Carter, *Printing in China*, 35; Ellington, *Japan*, 28.

36. "Kōken," *Encyclopaedia Britannica*, accessed May 7, 2014, http://www.britannica.com/EBchecked/topic/321233/Koken.

37. Ibid.; Delmer Brown, *The Cambridge History of Japan*, vol. 1 (Cambridge: Cambridge University Press, 1993), 262–63.

38. Carter, *Printing in China*, 35–38.

39. Tsien, *Paper and Printing*, 147–50.

40. "Kōken."

41. Tsien, *Paper and Printing*, 253–54; "Conserving the Diamond Sutra," International Dunhuang Project, 2013, https://www.youtube.com/watch?v=SgN5HQXTlMc.

42. Roderick Whitfield, *Cave Temples of Dunhuang: Art and History on the Silk Road* (London: British Library, 2000), 128.

43. Tsien, *Paper and Printing*, 146–51, 253–54.

44. Joyce Morgan and Conrad Walters, "Accruing Merit from Copying the Diamond Sutra," *IDP News Issue No. 38*, International Dunhuang Project, 2012, https://web.archive.org/web/20130405100701/http://idp.bl.uk/archives/news38/idpnews_38.a4d#3.

45. "Advanced Search for Free Text 'Woodblock,'" International Dunhuang Project, accessed October 31, 2014, http://idp.bl.uk/.

46. Xinjiang and Hansen, "The Nature of the Dunhuang Library Cave and the Reasons for Its Sealing," 272.

47. Xiu Ouyang, "Feng Dao," in *Historical Records of the Five Dynasties*, trans. Richard L. Davis (New York: Columbia University Press, 2004), 439–43.

48. Tsien, *Paper and Printing*, 156–57; Carter, *Printing in China*, 47–54.

49. Qinghua Guo, "Yingzao Fashi: Twelfth-Century Chinese Building Manual," *Architectural History* 41 (1998): 1–13; Ci Song, *The Washing Away of Wrongs: Forensic Medicine in*

Thirteenth-Century China (Ann Arbor: Center for Chinese Studies, University of Michigan Press, 1981); Joseph Needham and Ling Wang, *Mathematics and the Sciences of the Heavens and the Earth*, Science and Civilisation in China 3 (Cambridge: Cambridge University Press, 1959), 353; Tsien, *Paper and Printing*, 159–72.

50. Tsuen-Hsuin Tsien, *Collected Writings on Chinese Culture* (Chinese University Press, 2011), 129–44; Carter, *Printing in China*, 23–27.

51. Tsien, *Collected Writings*, 129–44; Carter, *Printing in China*, 23–27.

52. Hans Vogel, *Marco Polo Was in China: New Evidence from Currencies, Salts and Revenues* (Leiden: Brill, 2012), 128.

53. Joseph Needham and Ling Wang, *Introductory Orientations*, Science and Civilisation in China 1. (Cambridge: Cambridge University Press, 1954), 107; Carter, *Printing in China*, 7–71, 107.

54. Endymion Porter Wilkinson, *Chinese History: A Manual* (Harvard University Asia Center, 2000), 250–51; Carter, *Printing in China*, 70–71.

55. William N. Goetzmann and Elizabeth Köll, "Paying in Paper: A Government Voucher from the Southern Song," in *The Origins of Value*, ed. Goetzmann and Rouwenhorst, 97.

56. Polo, Cordier, and Yule, *The Book of Ser Marco Polo*, 1:424.

57. Neil Shafer, *Let's Collect Paper Money!: An Introduction to the Exciting Hobby of Collecting Paper Money of the World* (Racine, WI: Western Publishing Company, 1976).

58. Vogel, *Marco Polo Was in China*, 133; Goetzmann and Köll, "Paying in Paper," 92; von Glahn, "The Origins of Paper Money in China," 79.

59. Bergreen, *Marco Polo*, 331–43.

60. Ibid., 347–48.

61. Carl Lindahl, John Lindow, and John McNamara, *Medieval Folklore: An Encyclopedia of Myths, Legends, Tales, Beliefs, and Customs*, Volume A–K (Santa Barbara, CA: ABC-CLIO, 2000), 370.

62. Robert Curzon, "A Short Account of Some of the Most Celebrated Libraries in Italy," in *Miscellanies of the Philobiblon Society*, vol. 1 (London: Philobiblon Society, 1854), 3–59.

63. Stanley Lane-Poole and Elizabeth Baigent, "Curzon, Robert, Fourteenth Baron Zouche of Harringworth (1810–1873)," *Oxford Dictionary of National Biography*, accessed May 15, 2014, http://www.oxforddnb.com/view/article/6969; Curzon, "A Short Account," 3–9.

64. Curzon, "A Short Account," 6–9.

65. Carter, *Printing in China*, 119–20, 123–25; Tsien, *Paper and Printing*, 313–19.

66. Aldo Prinzivalli, "Jacopo Facen (1803–1886), Medico, Erudito E Letterato," *Biografie Mediche* no. 2 (2013): 16–18.

67. Jacopo Facen, *Le Ombre Feltresi: Visione* (Feltre: Marsura, 1843), 21–22.

68. Curzon, "A Short Account," 8.

69. Carter, *Printing in China*, 75–81.

70. Tsien, *Paper and Printing*, 313–19.

71. Polo, Cordier, and Yule, *The Book of Ser Marco Polo*, 1:180; Luigi Villari, "A British Scholar on Marco Polo," *East and West* 5, no. 3 (1954): 222–26.

72. Leslie Ross, "Andachtsbilder," in *Medieval Art: A Topical Dictionary* (Westport, CT: Greenwood Press, 1996), 12; Roberto Cobianchi, "The Use of Woodcuts in Fifteenth-Century Italy," *Print Quarterly* 23, no. 1 (2006): 47–54; Arthur Hind, *An Introduction to a History of Woodcut: With a Detailed Survey of Work Done in the Fifteenth Century*, vol. 1 (New York: Dover Publications, 1963), 94.

73. Frederick Kilgour, *The Evolution of the Book* (Oxford: Oxford University Press, 1998), 82–84.

74. Cobianchi, "The Use of Woodcuts," 47–54.

75. Ibid.

76. Hind, *History of Woodcut*, 1:110; Kilgour, *The Evolution of the Book*, 82–84.

77. Kilgour, *The Evolution of the Book*, 82–84.

78. Wendy Thomson, "The Printed Image in the West: History and Techniques," *Heilbrunn Timeline of Art History*, The Metropolitan Museum of Art, October 2003, http://www.metmuseum.org/toah/hd/prnt/hd_prnt.htm.

79. Kilgour, *The Evolution of the Book*, 82–84; Hind, *History of Woodcut*, 1:99; Antony Griffiths, *Prints and Printmaking: An Introduction to the History and Techniques* (Berkeley: University of California Press, 1996), 13.

80. Wendy Thomson, "The Printed Image in the West: Woodcut," *Heilbrunn Timeline of Art History*, The Metropolitan Museum of Art, October 2003, http://www.metmuseum.org/TOAH/hd/wdct/hd_wdct.htm; Hind, *History of Woodcut*, 1:125; Kilgour, *The Evolution of the Book*, 82–84.

81. George P. Burris, "Estienne's De Dissectione (1545), an Example of Sixteenth Century Anatomical Illustration," *Bios* 37, no. 4 (1966): 147–56; Hind, *History of Woodcut*, 1:14.

82. Jacob Wisse, "Albrecht Dürer (1471–1528)," *Heilbrunn Timeline of Art History*, The Metropolitan Museum of Art, October 2002, http://www.metmuseum.org/toah/hd/durr/hd_durr.htm; Suzanne Boorsch and Nadine Orenstein, "The Print in the North: The Age of Albrecht Dürer and Lucas van Leyden," *Metropolitan Museum of Art Bulletin* (New York: The Metropolitan Museum of Art, 1997), 6.

83. Thomson, "The Printed Image in the West: Woodcut"; Charles Nauert, "Desiderius Erasmus," ed. Edward N. Zalta, *Stanford Encyclopedia of Philosophy*, The Metaphysics Research Lab, Center for the Study of Language and Information, Stanford University, 2009, http://plato.stanford.edu/entries/erasmus/.

84. Richard K. Emmerson, "The Apocalypse in Medieval Culture," *The Apocalypse in the Middle Ages. Ithaca 1992b. S* (1992): 293–32.

85. Albrecht Dürer, *The Four Horsemen*, 1498, National Gallery of Art, Washington, DC.

86. Gerald Ward, "Chiaroscuro," in *The Grove Encyclopedia of Materials and Techniques in Art* (Oxford; New York: Oxford University Press, 2008), 104–6.

87. Hans Burgkmair, *The Lovers Surprised by Death*, n.d., National Gallery of Art, Washington, DC.

88. "Hans Burgkmair, *Lovers Surprised by Death*, a Woodcut," British Museum, accessed May 23, 2014, http://www.britishmuseum.org/explore/highlights/highlight_objects/pd/h/burgkmair,_lovers_surprised.aspx.
89. "Italian School, after Titian (Tiziano Vecellio): *Saint Jerome in the Wilderness* (22.73.3-119)," *Heilbrunn Timeline of Art History*, The Metropolitan Museum of Art, http://www.metmuseum.org/toah/works-of-art/22.73.3-119; Louise S. Richards, "The Titian Woodcut by Domenico Dalle Greche," *The Bulletin of the Cleveland Museum of Art* 43, no. 9 (1956): 197–201, 203; Tiziano Vecellio, *The Submersion of Pharaoh's Army in the Red Sea (block K)*, Harvard Art Museums, accessed October 31, 2014, http://www.harvardartmuseums.org/art/253297.
90. "Albrecht Dürer and Others, *The Triumphal Arch*, Woodcut," British Museum, accessed May 23, 2014, http://www.britishmuseum.org/explore/highlights/highlight_objects/pd/a/albrecht_dürer,_triumphal_arch.aspx.
91. "Albrecht Dürer: Portrait of the Artist as an Entrepreneur," *The Economist*, December 17, 2011, http://www.economist.com/node/21541710.
92. Hind, *History of Woodcut*, 1:140.
93. Paul Needham, "Prints in the Early Printing Shops," in *The Woodcut in Fifteenth-Century Europe*, ed. Peter Parshall (Washington, DC: National Gallery of Art, 2009), 45–46.
94. Ibid.
95. Philip Meggs, *Meggs' History of Graphic Design* (Hoboken, NJ: John Wiley & Sons, 2012), 69; Theodore De Vinne, *The Invention of Printing* (New York: F. Hart, 1876), 254–63.
96. Needham, "Prints in the Early Printing Shops," 45–46.
97. Ibid., 55; "Albrecht Pfister's Vier Historien: Joseph, Daniel, Judith, Esther," *First Impressions*, The University of Manchester Library, 2011, http://www.library.manchester.ac.uk/firstimpressions/assets/downloads/03-Albrecht-Pfisters-Vier-Historien—Joseph,-Daniel,-Judith,-Esther.pdf; "Ulrich Boner," *Encyclopaedia Britannica*, accessed May 7, 2014, http://www.britannica.com/EBchecked/topic/72987/Ulrich-Boner#ref230251.
98. J. Victor Scholderer, "Albrecht Pfister of Bamberg," *The Library* s3–III, no. 10 (1912): 230–36, doi:10.1093/library/s3-III.10.230.
99. Needham, "Prints in the Early Printing Shops," 58, 61.
100. John Corbett, "Biblia Pauperum," *The Catholic Encyclopedia*, http://www.newadvent.org/cathen/02547a.htm.
101. Needham, "Prints in the Early Printing Shops," 62; Thomson, "The Printed Image in the West: Woodcut"; Kilgour, "Block Printing," in *The Evolution of the Book*, 82–84.
102. William Ivins, *Prints and Visual Communication*. (Cambridge, MA: MIT Press, 1953), 163–64.

CHAPTER 10 ➺ ETCHING A SKETCH: COPPERPLATE PRINTING AND THE RENAISSANCE

1. "Albrecht Pfister," *First Impressions*, The University of Manchester Library, 2011, http://www.library.manchester.ac.uk/firstimpressions/Pioneers-of-Print/Albrecht-Pfister/; J. Victor Scholderer, "Albrecht Pfister of Bamberg," *The Library* s3–III, no. 10 (1912): 230–36, doi:10.1093/library/s3-III.10.230.

2. William Ivins, *Prints and Visual Communication* (Cambridge, MA: MIT Press, 1953), 165; Arthur Hind, *An Introduction to a History of Woodcut: With a Detailed Survey of Work Done in the Fifteenth Century*, vol. 1 (New York: Dover Publications, 1963), 14.

3. Tsuen-Hsuin Tsien, *Chemistry and Chemical Technology, Part 1: Paper and Printing*, ed. Joseph Needham, Science and Civilisation in China 5 (Cambridge: Cambridge University Press, 1985), 220–22; Phil Abel, Nick Gill, and Andy Taylor, personal correspondence with the author, June 2014.

4. Hind, *History of Woodcut*, 1:15–16.

5. Ivins, *Prints and Visual Communication*, 165.

6. Umberto Bosco, "Giovanni Boccaccio: Petrarch and Boccaccio's Mature Years," *Encyclopaedia Britannica*, accessed April 30, 2014, http://www.britannica.com/EBchecked/topic/70836/Giovanni-Boccaccio/756/Petrarch-and-Boccaccios-mature-years.

7. Filippo Strata, *Polemic Against Printing*, ed. Martin Lowry, trans. Shelagh Grier (Birmingham: Hayloft, 1986), n.p.

8. D. McKitterick, *Print, Manuscript and the Search for Order, 1450–1830* (Cambridge: Cambridge University Press, 2003), 84; Paul Saenger, "Colard Mansion and the Evolution of the Printed Book," *The Library Quarterly* 45, no. 4 (1975): 405–18.

9. "*De la Ruine des Nobles Hommes et Femmes* (Of the ruin of noble men and women)—Master of the Boccaccio Illustrations, Netherlandish, 1470–1490," Museum of Fine Arts, Boston, accessed June 6, 2014, https://www.mfa.org/collections/object/de-la-ruine-des-nobles-hommes-et-femmes-of-the-ruin-of-noble-men-and-women-155954.

10. Antony Griffiths, *Prints and Printmaking: An Introduction to the History and Techniques* (Berkeley: University of California Press, 1996), 31–34; "Intaglio," *Encyclopaedia Britannica*, accessed June 11, 2014, http://www.britannica.com/EBchecked/topic/289562/intaglio.

11. "Intaglio," *OED Online*, accessed June 6, 2014, http://www.oed.com/view/Entry/97322.

12. "Giorgio Vasari," *Encyclopaedia Britannica*, accessed June 7, 2014, http://www.britannica.com/EBchecked/topic/623661/Giorgio-Vasari; Griffiths, *Prints and Printmaking*, 42.

13. "Niello," *Encyclopaedia Britannica*, accessed October 2013, http://www.britannica.com/EBchecked/topic/414584/niello; "Maso Finiguerra," *Encyclopaedia Britannica*, accessed June 7, 2014, http://www.britannica.com/EBchecked/topic/207338/Maso-Finiguerra.

14. Griffiths, *Prints and Printmaking*, 42.

15. "*De La Ruine des Nobles Hommes et Femmes.*"

16. Griffiths, *Prints and Printmaking*, 39–42; "Maso Finiguerra."

17. Griffiths, *Prints and Printmaking*, 39.

18. Ibid.; Ivins, *Prints and Visual Communication*, 166.

19. Griffiths, *Prints and Printmaking*, 38; Arthur Hind, *A Short History of Engraving & Etching, for the Use of Collectors and Students with Full Bibliography, Classified List and Index of Engravers* (London: Constable and Co., 1911), 4.

20. Griffiths, *Prints and Printmaking*, 38.

21. "The *Book of Trades* (Das Ständebuch)," Victoria and Albert Museum, January 13, 2011, http://www.vam.ac.uk/content/articles/t/the-book-of-trades-das-standebuch/.

22. Griffiths, *Prints and Printmaking*, 31–34.

23. Ibid.; Hind, *A Short History of Engraving & Etching*, 14.

24. Griffiths, *Prints and Printmaking*, 31–34; "Identification: Engraving," *Graphics Atlas*, Image Permanence Institute, Rochester Institute of Technology, 2014, http://www.graphicsatlas.org/identification/?process_id=89.

25. Griffiths, *Prints and Printmaking*, 31–34.

26. FitzRoy Carrington, "Florentine Studies: I. The Illustrations to Landino's 'Dante,' 1481," *Art & Life* 11, no. 7 (1920): 372–77.

27. David Bland, *A History of Book Illustration: The Illuminated Manuscript and the Printed Book*, 2nd ed. (Berkeley: University of California Press, 1969), 119–20; Carrington, "The Illustrations to Landino's 'Dante,' 1481."

28. "Colard Mansion and Early Illustrations," *First Impressions*, The University of Manchester Library, 2011, http://www.library.manchester.ac.uk/firstimpressions/assets/downloads/08-Colard-Mansion-and-early-illustrations.pdf.

29. Bland, *A History of Book Illustration*, 117–19.

30. Robert Maclean, "Book Illustration: Engraving and Etching," *Special Collections*, University of Glasgow Library, August 28, 2012, http://universityofglasgowlibrary.wordpress.com/2012/08/28/book-illustration-engraving-and-etching/; Suzanne Boorsch and Nadine Orenstein, "The Print in the North: The Age of Albrecht Dürer and Lucas van Leyden," in *Metropolitan Museum of Art Bulletin* (New York: The Metropolitan Museum of Art, 1997), 3.

31. Boorsch and Orenstein, "The Print in the North," 12.

32. Bland, *A History of Book Illustration*, 119–20; Frederick Kilgour, "Title Pages, Pagination, and Illustration," in *The Evolution of the Book* (Oxford: Oxford University Press, 1998), 94–95; "Plate," *OED Online*, http://www.oed.com/view/Entry/145348.

33. William Henning, *An Elegant Hand: The Golden Age of American Penmanship and Calligraphy* (New Castle, DE: Oak Knoll Press, 2002), 292.

34. Peter Mansoor, "Armour: Premodern Armour," *Encyclopaedia Britannica*, accessed October 15, 2013, http://www.britannica.com/EBchecked/topic/35454/armour#ref1102676.

35. Stefan Krause, "The Etched Decoration of German Renaissance Armor," *Fellows Series*, The Metropolitan Museum of Art, November 18, 2011, http://www.metmuseum.org/about-the-museum/now-at-the-met/features/2011/the-etched-decoration-of-german-renaissance-armor.

36. R. Oakeshott, *European Weapons and Armour: From the Renaissance to the Industrial Revolution* (Woodbridge, UK: Boydell; Boydell & Brewer, 2012), 198–99.

37. Ivins, *Prints and Visual Communication*, 162; Dirk H. Breiding, "Techniques of Decoration on Arms and Armor," *Heilbrunn Timeline of Art History*, The Metropolitan Museum of Art, October 2003, http://www.metmuseum.org/toah/hd/dect/hd_dect.htm.

38. Ivins, *Prints and Visual Communication*, 162; Breiding, "Techniques of Decoration on Arms and Armor."

39. Krause, "The Etched Decoration of German Renaissance Armor"; "Acid-Etched Metal in Renaissance and Early Modern Europe," Victoria and Albert Museum, 2010, http://www.vam.ac.uk/content/articles/a/acid-etched-metal-in-renaissance-and-early-modern-europe/.

40. Breiding, "Techniques of Decoration on Arms and Armor."

41. Boorsch and Orenstein, "The Print in the North," 8, 10.
42. Basil Hunnisett, *Engraved on Steel: The History of Picture Production Using Steel Plates* (Aldershot; Brookfield, VT: Ashgate, 1998), 237.
43. Boorsch and Orenstein, "The Print in the North," 10, 31.
44. Griffiths, *Prints and Printmaking*, 56–58; Ivins, *Prints and Visual Communication*, 171.
45. "Etch," *OED Online*, accessed June 2013, http://www.oed.com/view/Entry/64677.
46. Griffiths, *Prints and Printmaking*, 56–58.
47. A. Palmer, *The Life and Letters of Samuel Palmer, Painter and Etcher* (London: Seeley, 1892), 337.
48. Bland, *A History of Book Illustration*, 118–19; Ivins, *Prints and Visual Communication*, 166.
49. Amy Meyers, "Audubon, John James," ed. Joan Marter, *The Grove Encyclopedia of American Art* (Oxford: Oxford University Press, 2011), 169–71.
50. Lee Vedder, *John James Audubon's The Birds of America: A Visionary Achievement in Ornithological Illustration* (San Marino, CA: Huntington Library, 2006), 5–6; Meyers, "Audubon, John James."
51. Audubon.org, "John James Audubon," National Audubon Society, accessed June 18, 2014, http://www.audubon.org/john-james-audubon.
52. Meyers, "Audubon, John James"; Audubon.org, "John James Audubon."
53. Ibid.; "Alexander Wilson," *Encyclopaedia Britannica*, accessed July 3, 2013, http://www.britannica.com/EBchecked/topic/644631/Alexander-Wilson.
54. Richard Rhodes, *John James Audubon: The Making of an American* (New York: Alfred A. Knopf, 2004), 214, 274.
55. Samuel H. Williamson and Laurence H. Officer, "Computing 'Real Value' Over Time with a Conversion Between U.K. Pounds and U.S. Dollars, 1774 to Present," *Measuring Worth*, 2013, http://www.measuringworth.com/exchange/; Rhodes, *John James Audubon*, 286.
56. Lois Bannon, *Handbook of Audubon Prints* (Gretna, LA: Pelican, 1985), 33.
57. Jeff Holt, *The Composite Plates of Audubon's Birds of America* (Philadelphia: Delaware Valley Ornithological Club, 2008), 10.
58. Vedder, *John James Audubon's The Birds of America*, 1–2; "Ornithological Biography: Or an Account of the Habits of the Birds of the United States of America," *Rare Books*, National Library of Scotland, October 19, 2012, http://www.nls.uk/collections/rarebooks/acquisitions/singlebook.cfm/idfind/880.
59. Bannon, *Handbook of Audubon Prints*, 33–34.
60. Colta Ives, "The Printed Image in the West: Aquatint," *Heilbrunn Timeline of Art History*, The Metropolitan Museum of Art, October 2002, http://www.metmuseum.org/toah/hd/aqtn/hd_aqtn.htm; "Aquafortis," *OED Online*, accessed March 2014, http://www.oed.com/view/Entry/10003; S. Prideaux, *Aquatint Engraving: A Chapter in the History of Book Illustration* (London: Duckworth & Co., 1909), 11–19.
61. Robert Havell and John James Audubon, "Columbia Jay," *The Birds of America*, 1830 National Gallery of Art, https://images.nga.gov/en/asset/show_zoom_window_popup.html?asset=100830.

62. Rhodes, *John James Audubon*, 289.

63. Finlo Rohrer, "Audubon's Birds of America: The World's Most Expensive Book," *BBC News Magazine*, http://www.bbc.co.uk/news/magazine-11937736; "The Birds of America; from Original Drawings by John James Audubon. London: Published by the Author, 1827-1838," *Magnificent Books, Manuscripts and Drawings from the Collection of Frederick 2nd Lord Hesketh*, Sotheby's, December 7, 2010, http://www.sothebys.com/en/auctions/ecatalogue/2010/magnificent-books-manuscripts-and-drawings-from-the-collection-of-frederick-2nd-lord-hesketh-l10413/lot.50.html; Williamson and Officer, "Computing 'Real Value.'"

CHAPTER 11 ⇺ BETTER IMAGING THROUGH CHEMISTRY: LITHOGRAPHY, PHOTOGRAPHY, AND MODERN BOOK PRINTING

1. Louis Prang, "Lithography," *Modern Art* 4, no. 3 (1896): 82–86.

2. Alois Senefelder, *The Invention of Lithography*, trans. J. W. Muller (New York: Fuchs & Lang Manufacturing Co., 1911), 1; Prang, "Lithography"; Seán Jennett, *Pioneers in Printing: Johann Gutenberg, William Caxton, William Caslon, John Baskerville, Alois Senefelder, Frederick Koenig, Ottmar Mergenthaler, Tolbert Lanston* (London: Routledge & Kegan Paul, 1958), 91.

3. Jennett, *Pioneers in Printing*, 91–92.

4. Ibid.

5. Ibid.; Senefelder, *The Invention of Lithography*, 2–3.

6. Jennett, *Pioneers in Printing*, 92; Senefelder, *The Invention of Lithography*, 3.

7. Jennett, *Pioneers in Printing*, 92–94; Senefelder, *The Invention of Lithography*, 3–5.

8. Senefelder, *The Invention of Lithography*, 7–9.

9. Ibid.; Jennett, *Pioneers in Printing*, 94–95; Prang, "Lithography."

10. Jennett, *Pioneers in Printing*, 95–97; Senefelder, *The Invention of Lithography*, 11–17.

11. Jennett, *Pioneers in Printing*, 96–97; Senefelder, *The Invention of Lithography*, 12.

12. Senefelder, *The Invention of Lithography*, 19–24.

13. Ibid., 25–26.

14. Ibid.

15. "Lithography," *OED Online*, accessed June 2012, http://www.oed.com/view/Entry/109158.

16. Antony Griffiths, *Prints and Printmaking: An Introduction to the History and Techniques* (Berkeley: University of California Press, 1996), 102.

17. Senefelder, *The Invention of Lithography*, 30.

18. Griffiths, *Prints and Printmaking*, 100, 139.

19. Senefelder, *The Invention of Lithography*, 138–42.

20. Griffiths, *Prints and Printmaking*, 102; "Toulouse-Lautrec and Montmartre—Lithography," Washington, DC: National Gallery of Art, 2005, https://www.nga.gov/exhibitions/2005/toulouse/lithography.shtm; Gaz Regan, "Absinthe Cocktails," *Imbibe Magazine*, December 18, 2012, http://imbibemagazine.com/Absinthe-Cocktails.

21. Senefelder, *The Invention of Lithography*, 138–42.

22. Ibid., 191–94.

23. Griffiths, *Prints and Printmaking*, 103.

24. Senefelder, *The Invention of Lithography*, 191–94.
25. Ibid., 28.
26. Jennett, *Pioneers in Printing*, 102–5; Felix Man, *150 Years of Artists' Lithographs, 1803–1953* (London: Heinemann, 1953), xv.
27. "Louis Prang," *Encyclopaedia Britannica*, accessed October 31, 2014, http://www.britannica.com/EBchecked/topic/857968/Louis-Prang.
28. Lee Vedder, *John James Audubon's The Birds of America: A Visionary Achievement in Ornithological Illustration* (San Marino, CA: Huntington Library, 2006), 3; Richard Godfrey, "Lithography," *The Oxford Companion to Western Art*, accessed June 26, 2014, http://www.oxfordreference.com/view/10.1093/acref/9780198662037.001.0001/acref-9780198662037-e-1493.
29. Griffiths, *Prints and Printmaking*, 120.
30. Ibid., 104–8; Liz Miller, personal interview with the author, August 2014.
31. David Bland, *A History of Book Illustration: The Illuminated Manuscript and the Printed Book*, 2nd ed. (Berkeley: University of California Press, 1969), 214, 222–23; Griffiths, *Prints and Printmaking*, 23–25.
32. Bland, *A History of Book Illustration*, 242–45.
33. Malcolm Daniel, "Daguerre (1787–1851) and the Invention of Photography," *Heilbrunn Timeline of Art History*, The Metropolitan Museum of Art, October 2004, http://www.metmuseum.org/toah/hd/dagu/hd_dagu.htm; Malcolm Daniel, "William Henry Fox Talbot (1800–1877) and the Invention of Photography," *Heilbrunn Timeline of Art History*, The Metropolitan Museum of Art, October 2004, http://www.metmuseum.org/toah/hd/tlbt/hd_tlbt.htm.
34. Daniel, "Daguerre"; Daniel, "William Henry Fox Talbot."
35. Donald D. Keyes, "The Daguerreotype's Popularity in America," *Art Journal* 36, no. 2 (1976): 116–22.
36. William Henry Fox Talbot, *The Boulevards of Paris*, May 1843, Getty Collection, J. Paul Getty Museum, http://www.getty.edu/art/gettyguide/artObjectDetails?artobj=46633.
37. Griffiths, *Prints and Printmaking*, 121; Ellen Sharp, "A Note on William Henry Fox Talbot and 'The Pencil of Nature,'" *Bulletin of the Detroit Institute of Arts* 66, no. 4 (1991): 42–46; Matt T. Roberts and Don Etherington, "Tipped In," *Bookbinding and the Conservation of Books*, Foundation of the American Institute for Conservation, November 2011, http://cool.conservation-us.org/don/dt/dt3522.html.
38. Griffiths, *Prints and Printmaking*, 121; Sharp, "A Note on William Henry Fox Talbot," 42–46; Daniel, "William Henry Fox Talbot."
39. Mike Ware, "Light-Sensitive Chemicals," ed. John Hannavy, in *Encyclopedia of Nineteenth-Century Photography* (London: Routledge, 2013), 857–59; John Hannavy, ed., "Ponton, Mongo (1801–1880)," in *Encyclopedia of Nineteenth-Century Photography*, 1146–47.
40. Dusan Stulik and Art Kaplan, "Carbon," in *The Atlas of Analytical Signatures of Photographic Processes* (Los Angeles: The Getty Conservation Institute, 2013), 4–5.
41. "A.D. 1852, October 29.—№ 565. Talbot, William Henry Fox," in *Patents for Inventions. Abridgments of Specifications Relating to Photography* (London: Patent Office, 1861), 17–18; Luis Nadeau, "Photoglyphic Engraving," ed. John Hannavy, in *Encyclopedia of Nineteenth-Century Photography*, 1080–81.

42. Ivins, *Prints and Visual Communication*, 126–27.
43. David Rudd Cycleback, "Half-Tone Printing," ed. John Hannavy, in *Encyclopedia of Nineteenth-Century Photography*, 632–33; Stulik and Kaplan, "Halftone," in *The Atlas of Analytical Signatures of Photographic Processes*, 5–8.
44. William Henry Fox Talbot, *Three Sheets of Gauze, Crossed Obliquely*, May 1852, Getty Collection, J. Paul Getty Museum, http://www.getty.edu/art/gettyguide/artObjectDetails?artobj=253662.
45. Griffiths, *Prints and Printmaking*, 122–23; Cycleback, "Half-Tone Printing."
46. Griffiths, *Prints and Printmaking*, 122–23.
47. Hans I. Bjelkhagen, "Poitevin, Alphonse-Louis (1819–1882)," ed. John Hannavy, in *Encyclopedia of Nineteenth-Century Photography*, 1139–40; Hope Kingsley, "Carbon Prints," ed. John Hannavy, in *Encyclopedia of Nineteenth-Century Photography*, 270–71.
48. The Earl de Grey and Ripon, "Address to the Royal Geographical Society of London," *Proceedings of the Royal Geographical Society of London* 4, no. 4 (1859): 160–61.
49. Anthony J. Hamber, "Lithography," ed. John Hannavy, *Encyclopedia of Nineteenth-Century Photography*, 864–65; "Domesday Book (English History)," *Encyclopaedia Britannica*, accessed May 9, 2012, http://www.britannica.com/EBchecked/topic/168528/Domesday-Book; *Domesday Book, or, The Great Survey of England of William the Conqueror A.D. MLXXXVI: Facsimile of the Part Relating to Cornwall* (Southampton: Ordinance Survey Office, 1861).
50. "Lithography (printing)," *Encyclopaedia Britannica*, accessed August 26, 2012, http://www.britannica.com/EBchecked/topic/343748/lithography.
51. "The History of Lithography," *DIGM 3350: Digital Media Materials and Processes*, University of Houston, accessed April 30, 2015, http://sites.tech.uh.edu/digitalmedia/materials/3350/History_of_Litho.pdf.
52. Ibid.
53. H. James, *Domesday Book: Facsimile of the Part Relating to Each County* (Southampton: Ordinance Survey Office, 1861); "Domesday Book (English History)."
54. Lorraine Ferguson and Douglass Scott, "A Time Line of American Typography," *Design Quarterly* no. 148 (1990): 39; "Offset Printing," *Encyclopaedia Britannica*, accessed October 31, 2014, http://www.britannica.com/EBchecked/topic/425722/offset-printing.
55. Ibid.
56. David Nord, Joan Shelley Rubin, and Michael Schudson, *A History of the Book in America*, vol. 5 (Chapel Hill: University of North Carolina Press, 2009), 63–66.
57. Helmut Kipphan, *Handbook of Print Media: Technologies and Production Methods* (New York: Springer, 2001), 583–84.

CHAPTER 12 ⪡ BOOKS BEFORE THE BOOK: PAPYRUS SCROLLS AND WAX TABLETS

1. G. Maspero, *The Dawn of Civilization: Egypt and Chaldæa*, ed. A. H. Sayce, trans. M. L. McClure (London: Society for Promoting Christian Knowledge, 1910), 235; William

Smith, "Menes," in *Dictionary of Greek and Roman Antiquities* (London: Walton and Maberly, 1853), 1040.

2. Toby A. H. Wilkinson, *Early Dynastic Egypt* (Taylor & Francis, 2002), 66–68.

3. Ibid., 66–70.

4. Ibid., 69, 111–12.

5. Jaroslav Cerny, *Paper and Books in Ancient Egypt* (London: Lewis, 1947); John D. Ray, "The Emergence of Writing in Egypt," *World Archaeology* 17, no. 3 (1986): 307–16; Wilkinson, *Early Dynastic Egypt*, 112.

6. "Book," *OED Online*, accessed July 14, 2015, http://www.oed.com/view/Entry/21412.

7. Adam Bülow-Jacobsen, "Writing Materials in the Ancient World," in *The Oxford Handbook of Papyrology*, ed. Roger Bagnall (Oxford: Oxford University Press, 2009), 19, 21.

8. Ibid.; Naphtali Lewis, *Papyrus in Classical Antiquity* (Oxford: Clarendon Press, 1974), 60–61.

9. Pliny the Elder, *The Natural History*, trans. John Bostock and B. A. Riley (Red Lion Court, Fleet Street: Taylor and Francis, 1855), 13.21, http://data.perseus.org/texts/urn:cts:latinLit:phi0978.phi001.perseus-eng1; Malcolm Johnson, *The Nature and Making of Papyrus* (Barkston Ash, UK: Elmete Press, 1973), 16–17; E. Turner, *Greek Papyri: An Introduction* (Princeton, NJ: Princeton University Press, 1968), 4.

10. Bülow-Jacobsen, "Writing Materials in the Ancient World," 19.

11. "Boustrophedon (Writing Style)," *Encyclopaedia Britannica*, accessed May 19, 2011, http://www.britannica.com/EBchecked/topic/75943/boustrophedon.

12. William A. Johnson, "The Ancient Book," in *The Oxford Handbook of Papyrology*, ed. Bagnall, 257; Bülow-Jacobsen, "Writing Materials in the Ancient World," 21; Turner, *Greek Papyri*, 4–5.

13. Cerny, *Paper and Books in Ancient Egypt*, 11; Bridget Leach and John Tait, "Papyrus," in *Ancient Egyptian Materials and Technology*, ed. Paul Nicholson and Ian Shaw (Cambridge: Cambridge University Press, 2000), 277.

14. Toby A. H. Wilkinson, *Royal Annals of Ancient Egypt: The Palermo Stone and Its Associated Fragments* (London: Kegan Paul International, 2000), 256.

15. Cerny, *Paper and Books in Ancient Egypt*, 11; Ray, "The Emergence of Writing in Egypt."

16. "Coupe Inscrite au Nom du Chancelier du Roi de Basse-Egypte, Hemaka," L'Agence Photo, Réunion des Musées Nationaux-Grand Palais, accessed October 31, 2014, http://www.photo.rmn.fr/C.aspx?VP3=SearchResult&IID=2C6NU04WADNW.

17. Cerny, *Paper and Books in Ancient Egypt*, 11; Leach and Tait, "Papyrus," 277.

18. Irmtraut Munro, "The Evolution of the Book of the Dead," in *Journey Through the Afterlife: Ancient Egyptian Book of the Dead*, ed. John Taylor (Cambridge, MA: Harvard University Press, 2010), 54–55.

19. P. Tallet, "Ayn Sukhna and Wadi El-Jarf: Two Newly Discovered Pharaonic Harbours on the Suez Gulf," *British Museum Studies in Ancient Egypt and Sudan*, no. 18 (2012): 147–68.

20. Alan H. Gardiner, "Y1, Y2," in *Egyptian Grammar: Being an Introduction to the Study*

of Hieroglyphs (London: Oxford University Press, 1957), 533; Margaret Murray, *Saqqara Mastabas, Pt 1: 1904* (London: Quaritch, 1905), 12.

21. Frederick Kilgour, *The Evolution of the Book* (Oxford: Oxford University Press, 1998), 30–33.

22. "Scribe Statue of Amunhotep, Son of Nebiry," Egyptian, Classical, Ancient Near Eastern Art, Brooklyn Museum, accessed October 31, 2014, https://www.brooklynmuseum.org/opencollection/objects/3940/Scribe_Statue_of_Amunhotep_Son_of_Nebiry/.

23. François Pouillon, "Prisse d'Avennes, Achille Constant Théodore Émile," in *Dictionnaire des Orientalistes de Langue Française* (Paris: IISMM, 2012), 830–31.

24. Achille-Constant-Théodore Émile Prisse d'Avennes and Olaf E. Kaper, *Atlas of Egyptian Art* (Cairo: American University in Cairo Press, 2000), v–x; Timothy Darvill, "Thebes, Egypt," *The Concise Oxford Dictionary of Archaeology*, accessed October 31, 2014, http://www.oxfordreference.com/view/10.1093/acref/9780199534043.001.0001/acref-9780199534043-e-4225?rskey=pXim6B&result=1.

25. Mary Norton, "Prisse: A Portrait," *Saudi Aramco World*, accessed July 30, 2014, https://www.saudiaramcoworld.com/issue/199006/prisse-a.portrait.htm.

26. "Akhmenu," *Digital Karnak*, University of California, 2008, http://dlib.etc.ucla.edu/projects/Karnak/feature/Akhmenu.

27. Norton, "Prisse: A Portrait"; Prisse d'Avennes and Kaper, *Atlas of Egyptian Art*, v–x.

28. Prisse d'Avennes and Kaper, *Atlas of Egyptian Art*, v–x.

29. Isaac Myers, *Oldest Books in the World: An Account of the Religion, Wisdom, Philosophy, Ethics, Psychology Manners, Proverbs, Sayings, Refinements Etc of the Ancient Egyptians* (New York: Edwin W. Dayton, 1900), 3–4.

30. Ptaḥ-ḥetep et al., *The Instruction of Ptah-Hotep: And, the Instruction of Ke'gemni: The Oldest Books in the World* (London: J. Murray, 1912), 24.

31. Ibid.; Kilgour, *The Evolution of the Book*, 30–33.

32. Ptaḥ-ḥetep et al., *The Instruction of Ptah-Hotep*, 42, 51.

33. Ibid., 49–50.

34. Kilgour, *The Evolution of the Book*, 30–33; Miriam Lichtheim, *Ancient Egyptian Literature: A Book of Readings*, vol. 1 (Berkeley: University of California Press, 2009), 136–39.

35. Kilgour, *The Evolution of the Book*, 30–33.

36. F. M. Heichelheim, "Recent Discoveries in Ancient Economic History," *Historia: Zeitschrift Für Alte Geschichte* 2, no. 2 (1953): 129–35.

37. Kilgour, *The Evolution of the Book*, 23–24; "The Great Harris Papyrus," British Museum, accessed July 30, 2014, http://www.britishmuseum.org/explore/highlights/highlight_objects/aes/t/the_great_harris_papyrus.aspx.

38. Aidan Dodson, "Third Intermediate Period," ed. Donald B. Redford, *The Oxford Encyclopedia of Ancient Egypt*, http://www.oxfordreference.com/10.1093/acref/9780195102345.001.0001/acref-9780195102345-e-0717; John D. Ray et al., "Late Period," ed. Donald B Redford, *The Oxford Encyclopedia of Ancient Egypt*, accessed February 5, 2014, http://www.oxfordreference.com/10.1093/acref/9780195102345.001.0001/acref-9780195102345-e-0401; Alan Fildes and Joann Fletcher, *Alexander the Great: Son of the Gods* (Los Angeles: Getty Publications, 2004), 52–55.

39. John Roberts, ed., "Muses," *Oxford Dictionary of the Classical World*, accessed July 28, 2014, http://www.oxfordreference.com/view/10.1093/acref/9780192801463.001.0001/acref-9780192801463-e-1464.
40. "Museum," *OED Online*, accessed July 28, 2014, http://www.oed.com/viewdictionaryentry/Entry/124079; Theodore Vrettos, *Alexandria: City of the Western Mind* (New York: Free Press, 2001), 34–35.
41. Vrettos, *Alexandria*, 34–35.
42. Ibid., 40–55.
43. Aulus Gellius, *The Attic Nights of Aulus Gellius*, ed. John C. Rolfe (Cambridge, MA: Harvard University Press, 1927), 7.17, http://data.perseus.org/texts/urn:cts:latinLit:phi1254.phi001.perseus-eng1.
44. Henry George Liddell and Robert Scott, "Βιβλίον Dim. of Βίβλος," *An Intermediate Greek-English Lexicon*, accessed July 27, 2014, http://www.perseus.tufts.edu/hopper/text?doc=Perseus:text:1999.04.0058:entry=bibli/on.
45. Johnson, "The Ancient Book," 257; Bülow-Jacobsen, "Writing Materials in the Ancient World," 15; Pliny the Elder, *The Natural History*, sec. 13.24; Carmelo Malacrino, *Constructing the Ancient World: Architectural Techniques of the Greeks and Romans* (Los Angeles: J. Paul Getty Museum, 2010), 110.
46. Johnson, "The Ancient Book," 257, 263; Johnson, *Nature and Making of Papyrus*, 16; Pliny the Elder, *The Natural History*, sec. 13.23.
47. Bülow-Jacobsen, "Writing Materials in the Ancient World," 19.
48. Johnson, "The Ancient Book," 257–59.
49. Henry George Liddell et al., "Πρωτό-Κολλον," *A Greek-English Lexicon*, accessed October 28, 2014, http://www.perseus.tufts.edu/hopper/text?doc=Perseus:text:1999.04.0057:entry=prwto/kollon; Henry George Liddell et al., "Κόλλ-Ημα," *A Greek-English Lexicon*, accessed October 28, 2014, http://www.perseus.tufts.edu/hopper/text?doc=Perseus:text:1999.04.0057:entry=ko/llhma.
50. Bülow-Jacobsen, "Writing Materials in the Ancient World," 19.
51. "Protocol," *OED Online*, accessed July 14, 2015, http://www.oed.com/view/Entry/153243.
52. Nicole Howard, *The Book: The Life Story of a Technology* (Baltimore: Johns Hopkins University Press, 2009), 3; E. A. Andrews et al., "Vŏlūmen," *A Latin Dictionary*, accessed August 29, 2014, http://www.perseus.tufts.edu/hopper/text?doc=Perseus:text:1999.04.0059:entry=volumen; E. A. Andrews et al., "Ē-Volvo," *A Latin Dictionary*, accessed August 29, 2014, http://www.perseus.tufts.edu/hopper/text?doc=Perseus:text:1999.04.0059:entry=evolvo.
53. "Ptolemy III Euergetes," *Encyclopaedia Britannica*, accessed April 11, 2014, http://www.britannica.com/EBchecked/topic/482183/Ptolemy-VIII-Euergetes-II.
54. M. C. Howatson, ed., "Weights," *The Oxford Companion to Classical Literature*, accessed October 31, 2014, http://www.oxfordreference.com/view/10.1093/acref/9780199548545.001.0001/acref-9780199548545-e-3102.
55. "Galen," *Extracts from Greek and Latin Writers in Translation*, accessed June 20, 2014, http://www.attalus.org/translate/extracts.html#galen.

56. Martyn Lyons, *Books: A Living History* (London: Thames & Hudson, 2011), 26–27.
57. Henry Petroski, *The Book on the Bookshelf*, 1st ed. (New York: Alfred A. Knopf, 1999), 26.
58. E. A. Andrews et al., "Tĭtŭlus," *A Latin Dictionary*, http://nlp.perseus.tufts.edu/hopper/text?doc=Perseus:text:1999.04.0059:entry=ti^tu^lus; Henry George Liddell and Robert Scott, "Σίλλυβος," *An Intermediate Greek-English Lexicon*, http://nlp.perseus.tufts.edu/hopper/text?doc=Perseus:text:1999.04.0058:entry=si/llubos; E. A. Andrews et al., "Sittybus," *A Latin Dictionary*, http://www.perseus.tufts.edu/hopper/text?doc=Perseus:text:1999.04.0059:entry=sittybus; Douglas Harper, "Syllabus," *Online Etymology Dictionary*, accessed July 30, 2014, http://www.etymonline.com/index.php?term=syllabus.
59. Plato, "Phaedrus," trans. Harold N. Fowler, in *Plato in Twelve Volumes* (Cambridge, MA: Harvard University Press, 1925), sec. 274de, available at http://data.perseus.org/texts/urn:cts:greekLit:tlg0059.tlg012.perseus-eng1.
60. John Clark, *The Care of Books: An Essay on the Development of Libraries and Their Fittings, from the Earliest Times to the End of the Eighteenth Century* (Cambridge: Cambridge University Press, 1909), 36–37.
61. Richard Kraut, "Socrates," *Encyclopaedia Britannica*, accessed June 5, 2014, http://www.britannica.com/EBchecked/topic/551948/Socrates; James Fenton, "Read My Lips," *The Guardian*, July 29, 2006.
62. Kilgour, *The Evolution of the Book*, 43–47; Gellius, *Attic Nights*, 7.17.
63. Kilgour, *The Evolution of the Book*, 52–54.
64. "Scroll," *OED Online*, accessed January 31, 2014, http://www.oed.com/view/Entry/173659.
65. Petroski, *The Book on the Bookshelf*, 25–26; Kilgour, *The Evolution of the Book*, 52–54.
66. John Clarke, *Art in the Lives of Ordinary Romans: Visual Representation and Non-Elite Viewers in Italy, 100 B.C.–A.D. 315* (Berkeley: University of California Press, 2003), 261–68.
67. Johnson, "The Ancient Book," 263–64.
68. Pliny the Younger, William Melmoth, and W.M.L. Hutchison, *Letters*, vol. 1 (London: W. Heinemann, 1915), 91.
69. Plutarch, "Caesar," ed. Bernadotte Perrin, in *Plutarch's Lives* (Cambridge, MA: Harvard University Press, 1920), chap. 49.6, available at http://data.perseus.org/texts/urn:cts:greekLit:tlg0007.tlg048.perseus-eng1; Vrettos, *Alexandria*, 93–94.
70. Cemal Pulak, "The Uluburun Shipwreck: An Overview," *International Journal of Nautical Archaeology* 27, no. 3 (1998): 188–224, doi:10.1111/j.1095-9270.1998.tb00803.x.
71. George F. Bass, "Oldest Known Shipwreck Reveals Splendors of the Bronze Age," *National Geographic* 172, no. 6 (1987): 692–733.
72. C. Pulak, "Dendrochronological Dating of the Uluburun Ship," *INA Quarterly* 23 (1996): 12–13.
73. Robert Payton, "The Ulu Burun Writing-Board Set," *Anatolian Studies* 41 (1991): 99–106.
74. Leila Avrin, *Scribes, Script, and Books: The Book Arts from Antiquity to the Renaissance*, ALA Classics (Chicago: American Library Association, 2010), 63, 173.

75. Bülow-Jacobsen, "Writing Materials in the Ancient World," 11–12.
76. Payton, "The Ulu Burun Writing-Board Set, 99–106"
77. Herodotus, *The Histories*, trans. A. Godley (Cambridge, MA: Harvard University Press, 1920), 7.239, available at http://www.perseus.tufts.edu/hopper/text?doc=urn:cts:greekLit:tlg0016.tlg001.perseus-eng1.
78. Franck Collard, *The Crime of Poison in the Middle Ages* (Westport, CT: Praeger Publishers, 2008), 275; Avrin, *Scribes, Script, and Books*, 68; Kilgour, *The Evolution of the Book*, 49–52; D. J. Wiseman, "Assyrian Writing-Boards," *Iraq* 17, no. 1 (1955): 3–13.
79. Bülow-Jacobsen, "Writing Materials in the Ancient World," 11–12.
80. Quintilian, *The Institutio Oratoria of Quintilian*, trans. Harold Edgeworth Butler (Cambridge, MA: Harvard University Press, 1922), sec. 10.3.31, available at http://data.perseus.org/citations/urn:cts:latinLit:phi1002.phi00110.perseus-eng1:3.
81. Henry Petroski, *The Pencil: A History* (London: Faber, 2003), 31, 36–38.
82. Bülow-Jacobsen, "Writing Materials in the Ancient World," 11–12.
83. Kilgour, *The Evolution of the Book*, 49–52; Bülow-Jacobsen, "Writing Materials in the Ancient World," 11–12.

CHAPTER 13 ⋞ JOINING THE FOLDS: THE INVENTION OF THE CODEX

1. I dearly wish that I could point to the source of this quotation but I have been unable to narrow it down beyond a handful of educational websites, none of which cites a source. Any pointers would be gratefully received.
2. Barbara G. Mertz, "Memphis," *Encyclopaedia Britannica*, accessed August 17, 2013, http://www.britannica.com/EBchecked/topic/374532/Memphis; P. J. Parsons and Gideon Nisbet, "Waste Paper City," *POxy: Oxyrhynchus Online*, Imaging Papyri Project, University of Oxford, 1997, accessed August 18, 2014, http://www.papyrology.ox.ac.uk/POxy/oxyrhynchus/parsons1.html; "Bahnasa: View North Along the Bahr Yusuf Canal: 1897," *Oxyrhynchus: A City and Its Texts*, Imaging Papyri Project, University of Oxford, 1998, accessed July 17, 2013, http://www.papyrology.ox.ac.uk/POxy/VExhibition/the_site/canal1897.html.
3. "Oxyrhynchus," *OED Online*, accessed August 17, 2014, http://www.oed.com/view/Entry/135694; "Tell," *OED Online*, accessed August 17, 2014, http://www.oed.com/view/Entry/198786; Bernard P. Grenfell and Arthur S. Hunt, "Excavations at Oxyrhynchus (1896–1907)," in *Oxyrhynchus: A City and Its Texts*, ed. Alan K Bowman et al. (London: Published for the Arts and Humanities Research Council by the Egypt Exploration Society, 2007), 345.
4. "Bronze Statuette of Oxyrhynchus Fish: Date Uncertain," *Oxyrhynchus: A City and Its Texts*, Imaging Papyri Project, University of Oxford, 1998, accessed August 17, 2014, http://www.papyrology.ox.ac.uk/POxy/VExhibition/introduction/fish_statuette.html; Richard Alston, *The City in Roman and Byzantine Egypt* (London: Routledge, 2002), 331; "Where Is Oxyrhynchus?," *POxy: Oxyrhynchus Online*, Imaging Papyri Project, University of Oxford, 1998, accessed August 17, 2014, http://www.papyrology.ox.ac.uk/POxy/oxyrhynchus/whereis.html.
5. Parsons and Nisbet, "Waste Paper City."

6. "Excavations at Oxyrhynchus 1: 1903?," *Oxyrhynchus: A City and Its Texts,* Imaging Papyri Project, University of Oxford, 1998, accessed August 17, 2014, http://www.papyrology.ox.ac.uk/POxy/VExhibition/the_site/excavations1903.html; "Conjectural Site Plans of Oxyrhynchus," *Oxyrhynchus: A City and Its Texts,* Imaging Papyri Project, University of Oxford, 1998, accessed August 17, 2014, http://www.papyrology.ox.ac.uk/POxy/VExhibition/the_site/site_plans.html.

7. Bernard P. Grenfell and Arthur S. Hunt, *The Oxyrhynchus Papyri,* vol. 1 (London: Egypt Exploration Fund, 1898), v–vi.

8. Parsons and Nisbet, "Waste Paper City."

9. Edgar Johnson Goodspeed, "The Acts of Paul and Thecla," *The Biblical World* 17, no. 3 (1901): 185–90; Grenfell and Hunt, "Excavations at Oxyrhynchus," 24, 315–16.

10. Parsons and Nisbet, "Waste Paper City."

11. Ibid.; John Roberts, ed., "Oxyrhynchus," *Oxford Dictionary of the Classical World,* accessed August 17, 2014, http://www.oxfordreference.com/view/10.1093/acref/9780192801463.001.0001/acref-9780192801463-e-1579.

12. "The Oxyrhynchus Papyri Collection," Egypt Exploration Society, accessed August 9, 2015, http://www.ees.ac.uk/research/Oxyrhynchus Papyri.html.

13. Parsons and Nisbet, "Waste Paper City."

14. W. Henry, *The Oxyrhynchus Papyri,* vol. LXXIX, Graeco-Roman Memoirs (London: Egypt Exploration Society, 2014); William Dalrymple, "Unearthing History," *New Statesman,* April 23, 2007, http://www.newstatesman.com/books/2007/04/egypt-greek-papyri-parsons.

15. W. Clarysse et al., "Graph of Oxyrhynchus Papyrus Scrolls from 3rd Century BC to 8th Century AD," Leuven Database of Ancient Books, July 2013, available at trismegistos.org. Visit http://bit.ly/1IvrJP2.

16. E. Turner, *Greek Papyri: An Introduction* (Princeton, NJ: Princeton University Press, 1968), 10.

17. Bernard Grenfell, *[Logia Iesu* (romanized form)*] Sayings of Our Lord from an Early Greek Papyrus Discovered and Edited, with Translation and Commentary* (London: Published for the Egypt Exploration Fund by H. Frowde, 1897).

18. Ibid., 6.

19. Monica Tsuneishi, "Papyrus Glossary," University of Michigan Library, accessed March 11, 2014, http://www.lib.umich.edu/papyrology-collection/papyrus-glossary.

20. Grenfell, *Logia Iesu,* 5–6.

21. Leila Avrin, *Scribes, Script, and Books: The Book Arts from Antiquity to the Renaissance,* ALA Classics (Chicago: American Library Association, 2010), 91.

22. Grenfell, *Logia Iesu,* 5–6.

23. Ibid., fig. verso.

24. Ibid., 5–6; E. Turner, *The Typology of the Early Codex* (Philadelphia: University of Pennsylvania Press, 1977), 74–77.

25. Grenfell, *Logia Iesu,* 5–6, 16; Grenfell and Hunt, "ΛΟΓΙΑ ΙΗΣΟΥ," in *The Oxyrhynchus Papyri,* vol. 1: 1–3.

26. Ronald Lindsay Prain and Anita McConnell, "Beatty, Sir (Alfred) Chester (1875–1968)," *Oxford Dictionary of National Biography*, accessed August 14, 2014, http://www.oxforddnb.com/view/article/30660; "Biblical," *Papyri—The Western Collection*, Chester Beatty Library, Dublin, accessed August 17, 2014, http://www.cbl.ie/Collections/The-Western-Collection/Papyri/Biblical.aspx; Christoph Markschies, *Gnosis: An Introduction* (London; New York: T & T Clark, 2003), 48–49.

27. Turner, *Typology*, 38.

28. "Orihon," *OED Online*, accessed August 15, 2014,, http://www.oed.com/view/Entry/132580; Turner, *Greek Papyri*, 173.

29. Gavin Ambrose and Paul Harris, *Pre-Press and Production* (Lausanne: Ava Publishing SA, 2010), 106.

30. Hugh Chisholm, ed., "Bookbinding," in *The Encyclopædia Britannica: A Dictionary of Arts, Sciences, Literature and General Information*. (New York: The Encyclopaedia Britannica Company, 1910), 216–21; Cyril Davenport, *The Book, Its History and Development*, The "Westminster" Series (New York: D. Van Nostrand, 1907), 27–29.

31. Davenport, *The Book*, 28.

32. Peter Kornicki, *The Book in Japan: A Cultural History from the Beginnings to the Nineteenth Century* (Honolulu: University of Hawai'i Press, 2001), 43.

33. "Advanced Search for Free Text 'Concertina,'" International Dunhuang Project, accessed August 17, 2014, http://idp.bl.uk/; Colin Chinnery and Li Yi, "Bookbinding," International Dunhuang Project, February 7, 2007, http://idp.bl.uk/education/bookbinding/bookbinding.a4d.

34. "Codex Peresianus," *Gallica*, Bibliothèque nationale de France, accessed October 29, 2014, http://gallica.bnf.fr/ark:/12148/btv1b8446947j.r=codex+peresianus.langEN; Gabrielle Vail, "The Maya Codices," *Annual Review of Anthropology* 35 (2006): 497.

35. Victor W. von Hagen, "Paper and Civilization," *The Scientific Monthly* 57, no. 4 (1943): 301–14.

36. Alan Sandstrom and Pamela Effrein Sandstrom, *Traditional Papermaking and Paper Cult Figures of Mexico* (Norman: University of Oklahoma Press, 1986), 27–31.

37. von Hagen, "Paper and Civilization"; Citlalli López Binnqüist, "The Endurance of Mexican Amate Paper: Exploring Additional Dimensions to the Sustainable Development Concept," diss., University of Twente, 2003, 84–88.

38. David Diringer, *The Book Before Printing: Ancient, Medieval, and Oriental* (Mineola, NY: Courier Dover Publications, 1953), 431.

39. Binnqüist, "The Endurance of Mexican Amate Paper," 89–91; Sandstrom and Sandstrom, *Traditional Papermaking and Paper Cult Figures of Mexico*, 15–18.

40. Simon Eliot and Jonathan Rose, *A Companion to the History of the Book* (Hoboken, NJ: John Wiley & Sons, 2011), 99–100; Helge Ingstad and Anne Stine Ingstad, *The Viking Discovery of America: The Excavation of a Norse Settlement in L'Anse Aux Meadows, Newfoundland* (St. John's, NF: Breakwater, 2000), iv–v.

41. Stanley Stowers, *Letter Writing in Greco-Roman Antiquity* (Philadelphia: Westminster Press, 1989), 27–31, 35.

42. Gary Frost, "Adoption of the Codex Book: Parable of a New Reading Mode," in *The Book & Paper Group Annual*, vol. 17 (American Institute for Conservation, 1998), 67–74.
43. Bezalel Porten, "Aramaic Letters: A Study in Papyrological Reconstruction," *Journal of the American Research Center in Egypt* 17 (1980): 3–7.
44. Jill Kamil, *Aswan and Abu Simbel: History and Guide* (Cairo: American University in Cairo Press, 1993), 1–3; Emil G. Kraeling, "New Light on the Elephantine Colony," *The Biblical Archaeologist* 15, no. 3 (1952): 49–67.
45. Bezalel Porten, *The Elephantine Papyri in English: Three Millennia of Cross-Cultural Continuity and Change*, Documenta et Monumenta Orientis Antiqui (Leiden: E. J. Brill, 1996), 110, 115, 139.
46. Porten, "Aramaic Letters," 3–7.
47. Frost, "Adoption of the Codex," 67–74.
48. Porten, "Aramaic Letters," 3–7.
49. Stowers, *Letter Writing in Greco-Roman Antiquity*, 27–35, 37–40; Anthony Maas, "Epistle (in Scripture)," *The Catholic Encyclopedia*, accessed August 19, 2014, http://www.newadvent.org/cathen/05509a.htm.
50. Frost, "Adoption of the Codex," 67–74.
51. Porten, "Aramaic Letters," 3–7.
52. Turner, *Greek Papyri*, 14; Frost, "Adoption of the Codex," 67–74; Adam Bülow-Jacobsen, "Writing Materials in the Ancient World," in *The Oxford Handbook of Papyrology*, ed. Roger Bagnall (Oxford: Oxford University Press, 2009), 24–25.
53. Suetonius, "Lives of Eminent Grammarians," in *The Lives of the Twelve Caesars*, ed. Alexander Thomson and Thomas Forester (G. Bell, 1893), chap. 2, 507–8.
54. Horace, "De Arte Poetica Liber," in *The Works of Horace*, ed. Christopher Smart (Philadelphia: J. Whetham, 1836), l. 389.
55. Gian Conte, *Latin Literature: A History* (Baltimore: Johns Hopkins University Press, 1999), l. 549–50.
56. Suetonius, "Julius Caesar," in *The Lives of the Twelve Caesars*, ed. Thomson and Forester, chap. 37, available at http://data.perseus.org/texts/urn:cts:latinLit:phi1348.abo011.perseus-eng1; Suetonius, "The Life of Tiberius," trans. J. C. Rolfe, *The Lives of the Caesars* (Loeb, 1913), chap. 43–45, available at http://penelope.uchicago.edu/Thayer/E/Roman/Texts/Suetonius/12Caesars/Tiberius*.html.
57. Suetonius, "Julius Caesar," chap. 56.
58. Suetonius, "Divus Julius," in *De Vita Caesarum*, ed. Max Ihm (Lipsiae: in aedibvs B. G. Tevbneri, 1908), chap. 56; E. A. Andrews et al., "Pāgĭna," *A Latin Dictionary*, accessed October 29, 2014, http://www.perseus.tufts.edu/hopper/text?doc=Perseus:text:1999.04.0059:entry=pagina.
59. Colin Roberts and T. C. Skeat, *The Birth of the Codex* (London: Published for the British Academy by the Oxford University Press, 1983), 18–20.
60. Frederic G. Kenyon, *Books and Readers in Ancient Greece and Rome* (Oxford: Clarendon Press, 1889), 91; Roberts and Skeat, *The Birth of the Codex*, 15; E. A. Andrews et al., "Pŭgillāris," *A Latin Dictionary*, accessed August 25, 2014, http://www.perseus.tufts.edu/hopper/text?doc=Perseus:text:1999.04.0059:entry=pugillaris; E. A. Andrews et al.,

"Tăbella," *A Latin Dictionary*, accessed August 25, 2014, http://www.perseus.tufts.edu/hopper/text?doc=Perseus:text:1999.04.0059:entry=tabella.

61. Pliny the Younger, William Melmoth, and W. M. L. Hutchison, *Letters*, vol. 1 (London: W. Heinemann, 1915), 201–3.

62. Kenyon, *Books and Readers*, 91; Roberts and Skeat, *The Birth of the Codex*, 20.

63. Roberts and Skeat, *The Birth of the Codex*, 20.

64. Ibid., 21–23.

65. Ibid., 26; John Roberts, ed., "Martial (Marcus Valerius Martiālis)," *Oxford Dictionary of the Classical World*, accessed August 25, 2014, http://www.oxfordreference.com/view/10.1093/acref/9780192801463.001.0001/acref-9780192801463-e-1369.

66. Martial, *Epigrams*, trans. Walter A. C. Ker (London: W. Heinemann, 1919), v. 1.2.

67. Luke Roman, "Martial and the City of Rome," *The Journal of Roman Studies* 100 (2010): 88–117, doi:10.1017/S0075435810000092.

68. Bülow-Jacobsen, "Writing Materials in the Ancient World," 23.

69. Martial, *Epigrams*, vv. 14.3–9; Roberts and Skeat, *The Birth of the Codex*, 25.

70. Martial, *Epigrams*, vv. 14.203, 14.214, 14.220; Roberts and Skeat, *The Birth of the Codex*, 25–27.

71. Grenfell and Hunt, "Historical Fragment," in *The Oxyrhynchus Papyri*, vol. 1: 59–61.

72. Bülow-Jacobsen, "Writing Materials in the Ancient World," 24.

73. Roberts and Skeat, *The Birth of the Codex*, 29; Turner, *Greek Papyri*, 40.

74. James M. Robinson, "The Discovery of the Nag Hammadi Codices," *The Biblical Archaeologist* 42, no. 4 (1979): 206–24; James M. Robinson, *The Nag Hammadi Story*, Nag Hammadi and Manichaean Studies (Leiden: Brill, 2014), 3–6.

75. Robinson, "The Discovery of the Nag Hammadi Codices," 3–6.

76. Ibid.

77. Ibid.

78. Robinson, *The Nag Hammadi Story*, 379.

79. Edwin M. Yamauchi, "The Nag Hammadi Library," *The Journal of Library History (1974–1987)* 22, no. 4 (1987): 425–41.

80. W.R.F. Browning, "Gnosticism," *A Dictionary of the Bible*, accessed August 30, 2014, http://www.oxfordreference.com/view/10.1093/acref/9780199543984.001.0001/acref-9780199543984-e-766?

81. "Irina Gorstein," Frances Loeb Library, Harvard Graduate School of Design, accessed October 31, 2014, http://www.gsd.harvard.edu/#/loeblibrary/collections/conservation-lab/irina-gorstein.html.

82. Linda K. Ogden, "The Binding of Codex II," in *Nag Hammadi Codex II, 2–7: Together with XIII, 2*, Brit. Lib. Or. 4926(1), and P. OXY. 1, 654, 655: With Contributions by Many Scholars*, ed. Bentley Layton (Leiden: E.J. Brill, 1988), 19–26; James M. Robinson, "Construction of the Nag Hammadi Codices," in *Essays on the Nag Hammadi Texts: In Honour of Pahor Labib*, ed. Martin Krause (Leiden: Brill, 1975), 170–90; Yamauchi, "The Nag Hammadi Library."

83. Matt T. Roberts and Don Etherington, "Text Block," *Bookbinding and the*

Conservation of Books, Foundation of the American Institute for Conservation, November 2011, http://cool.conservation-us.org/don/dt/dt3476.html.

84. Ogden, "The Binding of Codex II," 19–26; Robinson, "Construction of the Nag Hammadi Codices," 170–90.

85. Henry Petroski, *The Book on the Bookshelf*, 1st ed. (New York: Alfred A. Knopf, 1999), 33–34.

86. Ogden, "The Binding of Codex II," 19–26; Robinson, "Construction of the Nag Hammadi Codices," 170–90; Geoffrey A. Glaister, "Plough," in *Glossary of the Book* (George Allen and Unwin, 1960), 321; Geoffrey A. Glaister, "Guillotine," in *Glossary of the Book*, 162–63.

87. Ogden, "The Binding of Codex II," 19–26; Robinson, "Construction of the Nag Hammadi Codices," 170–90.

88. Yamauchi, "The Nag Hammadi Library," 428.

CHAPTER 14 ➳ TIES THAT BIND: BINDING THE PAGED BOOK

1. Miki Lentin, "British Library Acquires the St Cuthbert Gospel—the Earliest Intact European Book," Press and Policy Centre, British Library, 2012, http://pressandpolicy.bl.uk/Press-Releases/British-Library-acquires-the-St-Cuthbert-Gospel-the-earliest-intact-European-book-58c.aspx; Richard Davies, "Top 10 Most Expensive Books Ever Sold," *AbeBooks' Reading Copy*, September 25, 2013, http://www.abebooks.com/blog/index.php/2013/09/25/top-10-most-expensive-books-ever-sold.

2. David Rollason and R. B. Dobson, "Cuthbert [St Cuthbert] (c.635–687)," *Oxford Dictionary of National Biography*, accessed September 4, 2014, http://www.oxforddnb.com/view/article/6976.

3. Ibid.; Bede, "Life and Miracles of Saint Cuthbert," in *The Ecclesiastical History of the English Nation*, ed. Vida Dutton Scudder, Everyman's Library (London: J. M. Dent, 1910), 292–99.

4. Rollason and Dobson, "Cuthbert [St Cuthbert] (c.635–687)."

5. Ibid.

6. Ibid.; Heather Pringle, *The Mummy Congress: Science, Obsession, and the Everlasting Dead* (London: Fourth Estate, 2002), 247–49.

7. Rollason and Dobson, "Cuthbert [St Cuthbert] (c.635–687)"; David Wilson, *Anglo-Saxon Art: From the Seventh Century to the Norman Conquest* (Woodstock, NY: Overlook Press, 1984), 29.

8. Thomas Julian Brown et al., *The Stonyhurst Gospel of Saint John* (Oxford: The Roxburghe Club, 1969), 2–3.

9. Lentin, "British Library Acquires the St Cuthbert Gospel"; Brown et al., *The Stonyhurst Gospel*, 1.

10. Brown et al., *The Stonyhurst Gospel*, 22.

11. Ibid., 51–54.

12. Ibid., 46–47, 51, 56–57.

13. Rollason and Dobson, "Cuthbert [St Cuthbert] (c.635–687)"; Brown et al., *The Stonyhurst Gospel*, 7.

14. Brown et al., *The Stonyhurst Gospel*, 45; Patrick Collinson, "Elizabeth I (1533–1603)," *Oxford Dictionary of National Biography*, accessed September 10, 2014, http://www.oxforddnb.com/view/article/8636.

15. Chris Lloyd, "The Fascinating Tale of St Cuthbert and Those Who 'Dug' into His Past," *Durham Times*, July 26, 2013.

16. W. Clarysse et al., "Graph of Christian Documents with Documents of All Denominations from 3rd Century BC to 8th Century AD," Leuven Database of Ancient Books, accessed July 11, 2013, available at trismegistos.org. Visit http://bit.ly/1KXd148; W. Clarysse et al., "Graph of Papyrus and Parchment Use from 3rd Century BC to 8th Century AD," Leuven Database of Ancient Books, accessed July 11, 2013, via trismegistos.org. Visit http://bit.ly/1Egh3zN; Victor W. von Hagen, "Paper and Civilization," *The Scientific Monthly* 57, no. 4 (1943): 301–14.

17. Brown et al., *The Stonyhurst Gospel*, 56.

18. James M. Robinson, *The Facsimile Edition of the Nag Hammadi Codices* (Leiden: Brill, 1984), 39–40.

19. E. Turner, *Greek Papyri: An Introduction* (Princeton, NJ: Princeton University Press, 1968), 13.

20. James M. Robinson, *The Nag Hammadi Story*, Nag Hammadi and Manichaean Studies (Leiden: Brill, 2014), 351–62.

21. Ibid., 374–83.

22. Ibid., 383–426; Laurence H. Officer, "Switzerland, 1952–1952," *Measuring Worth*, http://www.measuringworth.com/datasets/exchangeglobal/result.php?year_source=1952&year_result=1952&countryE[]=Switzerland.

23. Matt T. Roberts and Don Etherington, "Folio," *Bookbinding and the Conservation of Books*, Foundation of the American Institute for Conservation, November 19, 2011, http://cool.conservation-us.org/don/dt/dt1404.html; "Folio," *OED Online*, accessed September 11, 2014, http://www.oed.com/view/Entry/72529.

24. Matt T. Roberts and Don Etherington, "Leaf," *Bookbinding and the Conservation of Books*, Foundation of the American Institute for Conservation, November 19, 2011, http://cool.conservation-us.org/don/dt/dt2018.html.

25. Matt T. Roberts and Don Etherington, "Page," *Bookbinding and the Conservation of Books*, Foundation of the American Institute for Conservation, November 19, 2011, http://cool.conservation-us.org/don/dt/dt2437.html.

26. Robinson, *The Facsimile Edition of the Nag Hammadi Codices*, 39–40.

27. Robinson, *The Nag Hammadi Story*, 384–89.

28. Robinson, *The Facsimile Edition of the Nag Hammadi Codices*, 39–40.

29. Brown et al., *The Stonyhurst Gospel*, 49.

30. Ibid., 56–57.

31. Ibid., 57–58.

32. Ibid., 46–47, 55.

33. Matt T. Roberts and Don Etherington, "Kettle Stitch," *Bookbinding and the Conservation of Books*, Foundation of the American Institute for Conservation, November 2011, http://cool.conservation-us.org/don/dt/dt1945.html.

34. Brown et al., *The Stonyhurst Gospel*, 46–47.

35. "Binding from Ethiopian Gospels (W.850.binding)," *The Works of Art*, The Walters Art Museum, accessed October 31, 2014, http://art.thewalters.org/detail/78137/binding-from-ethiopian-gospels/.

36. E. Turner, *The Typology of the Early Codex* (Philadelphia: University of Pennsylvania Press, 1977), 89–94.

37. Brown et al., *The Stonyhurst Gospel*, 47–48; Frederick Kilgour, *The Evolution of the Book* (Oxford: Oxford University Press, 1998), 51–53; Adam Bülow-Jacobsen, "Writing Materials in the Ancient World," in *The Oxford Handbook of Papyrology*, ed. Roger Bagnall (Oxford: Oxford University Press, 2009), 23.

38. E. A. Andrews et al., "Caudex," *A Latin Dictionary*, accessed September 15, 2014, http://www.perseus.tufts.edu/hopper/text?doc=Perseus:text:1999.04.0059:entry=caudex1; Colin Roberts and T. C. Skeat, *The Birth of the Codex* (London: Published for the British Academy by the Oxford University Press, 1983), 12–13.

39. Roberts and Skeat, *The Birth of the Codex*, 24; "Code," *OED Online*, accessed September 15, 2014, http://www.oed.com/view/Entry/35578.

40. Henry Petroski, *The Book on the Bookshelf*, 1st ed. (New York: Alfred A. Knopf, 1999), 117–19.

41. Matt T. Roberts and Don Etherington, "Folder," *Bookbinding and the Conservation of Books*, Foundation of the American Institute for Conservation, November 2011, http://cool.conservation-us.org/don/dt/dt1387.html.

42. Brown et al., *The Stonyhurst Gospel*, 51–54.

43. Ibid., 49.

44. Berthe Regemorter, *Binding Structures in the Middle Ages: A Selection of Studies*, trans. Jane Greenfield, Studia Bibliothecae Wittockianae (Brussels: Bibliotheca Wittockiana, 1992), 24.

45. Ibid., 23–41; Leila Avrin, *Scribes, Script, and Books: The Book Arts from Antiquity to the Renaissance*, ALA Classics (Chicago: American Library Association, 2010), 301–4.

46. Rosamond McKitterick, *The Carolingians and the Written Word* (Cambridge; New York: Cambridge University Press, 1989), 259; Regemorter, *Binding Structures in the Middle Ages*, 48–49.

47. "Irina Gorstein," Frances Loeb Library, Harvard Graduate School of Design, accessed October 31, 2014, http://www.gsd.harvard.edu/#/loeblibrary/collections/conservation-lab/irina-gorstein.html.

48. I. N. Wood, "Boniface [St Boniface] (672x5?–754)," *Oxford Dictionary of National Biography*, accessed September 4, 2014, http://www.oxforddnb.com/view/article/2843.

49. Michel Aaij, "Boniface's Booklife: How the Ragyndrudis Codex Came to Be a Vita Bonifatii," *The Heroic Age* 10 (2007), accessed September 16, 2014, http://www.heroicage.org/issues/10/aaij.html; Regemorter, *Binding Structures in the Middle Ages*, 48–49.

50. Michael Drout, *J.R.R. Tolkien Encyclopedia: Scholarship and Critical Assessment* (New York: Routledge, 2007), 404–5; J.R.R. Tolkien, *The Fellowship of the Ring: Being the First Part of The Lord of the Rings* (Boston: Mariner Books/Houghton Mifflin Harcourt, 2012), 313–14.

51. "Binding," *First Impressions*, The University of Manchester Library, 2011, http://www.library.manchester.ac.uk/firstimpressions/From-Manuscript-to-Print/Technology-of-the-Book/Binding/; Matt T. Roberts and Don Etherington, "Lying Press," *Bookbinding and the Conservation of Books: A Dictionary of Descriptive Terminology*, Foundation of the American Institute for Conservation of Historic and Artistic Works, November 2011, http://cool.conservation-us.org/don/dt/dt2131.html.

52. Regemorter, *Binding Structures in the Middle Ages*, 34.

53. Ibid., 33–35; Avrin, *Scribes, Script, and Books*, 301–4.

54. Avrin, *Scribes, Script, and Books*, 301–4.

55. Ibid.; Richard Wolfe, *Marbled Paper: Its History, Techniques, and Patterns: With Special Reference to the Relationship of Marbling to Bookbinding in Europe and the Western World*, Publication of the A.S.W. Rosenbach Fellowship in Bibliography (Philadelphia: University of Pennsylvania Press, 1990), 14.

56. Matt T. Roberts and Don Etherington, "Headband," *Bookbinding and the Conservation of Books*, Foundation of the American Institute for Conservation, November 2011, http://cool.conservation-us.org/don/dt/dt1721.html; Brown et al., *The Stonyhurst Gospel*, 51.

57. Roberts and Etherington, "Headband."

58. Avrin, *Scribes, Script, and Books*, 305–6.

59. Petroski, *The Book on the Bookshelf*, 117–19.

60. Roberts and Etherington, "Headband."

61. Ibid.

62. Matt T. Roberts and Don Etherington, "Rounding," *Bookbinding and the Conservation of Books*, Foundation of the American Institute for Conservation, November 2011, http://cool.conservation-us.org/don/dt/dt2916.html; Matt T. Roberts and Don Etherington, "Fore Edge," *Bookbinding and the Conservation of Books*, Foundation of the American Institute for Conservation, November 2011, http://cool.conservation-us.org/don/dt/dt1410.html; Avrin, *Scribes, Script, and Books*, 304.

63. Roberts and Etherington, "Rounding"; Avrin, *Scribes, Script, and Books*, 304.

64. Matt T. Roberts and Don Etherington, "Backing," *Bookbinding and the Conservation of Books*, Foundation of the American Institute for Conservation, November 2011, http://cool.conservation-us.org/don/dt/dt0198.html.

65. "Conradi Celtis Panegyris ad Duces Bauariae," *Incunable Collection* (University of Pennsylvania), accessed November 1, 2014, http://franklin.library.upenn.edu/record.html?id=FRANKLIN_3188699.

66. Matt T. Roberts and Don Etherington, "Pasteboard," *Bookbinding and the Conservation of Books*, Foundation of the American Institute for Conservation, November 2011, http://cool.conservation-us.org/don/dt/dt2500.html; Avrin, *Scribes, Script, and Books*, 304–05.

67. Douglas Cockerell and Noel Rooke, *Bookbinding and the Care of Books: A Text-Book for Bookbinders and Librarians* (London: Pitman, 1920), 259.

68. "St Christopher," John Rylands University Library Image Collections, July 2011, http://enriqueta.man.ac.uk/luna/servlet/detail/Manchester~91~1~4582~119395:St-Christopher; Rachel Kaufman, "Lost Roman Codex Fragments Found in Book Binding,"

National Geographic News, February 3, 2010, http://news.nationalgeographic.com/news/2010/02/100203-lost-codex-gregorianus-roman-law-book/; Mike Widener, "Medieval Manuscripts in Law Book Bindings, No. 19," *Yale Law School Library News*, February 16, 2010, http://library.law.yale.edu/news/medieval-manuscripts-law-book-bindings-no-19.

69. Avrin, *Scribes, Script, and Books*, 307–12.

70. Matt T. Roberts and Don Etherington, "Blind Tooling," *Bookbinding and the Conservation of Books*, Foundation of the American Institute for Conservation, November 2011, http://cool.conservation-us.org/don/dt/dt0366.html; "Blind Tooling," *Hand Bookbinding*, Princeton University Library, 2004, http://libweb5.princeton.edu/visual_materials/hb/cases/blindtooling/index.html.

71. Petroski, *The Book on the Bookshelf*, 123–24.

72. Matt T. Roberts and Don Etherington, "Glair (*Glaire*)," *Bookbinding and the Conservation of Books*, Foundation of the American Institute for Conservation, November 2011, http://cool.conservation-us.org/don/dt/dt1542.html; Matt T. Roberts and Don Etherington, "Gold Tooling," *Bookbinding and the Conservation of Books*, Foundation of the American Institute for Conservation, November 2011, http://cool.conservation-us.org/don/dt/dt1597.html.

73. Roberts and Etherington, "Blind Tooling."

74. "The History of the Dust Jacket," Victoria and Albert Museum, accessed November 1, 2014, http://www.vam.ac.uk/content/articles/h/history-of-the-dust-jacket/; Michelle Pauli, "Earliest-Known Book Jacket Discovered in Bodleian Library," *The Guardian*, April 24, 2009.

75. Matt T. Roberts and Don Etherington, "Leather," *Bookbinding and the Conservation of Books*, Foundation of the American Institute for Conservation, November 2011, http://www.cool.conservation-us.org/don/dt/dt2021.html.

76. J. Gilliland, "Burke, William (1792–1829)," *Oxford Dictionary of National Biography*, accessed September 4, 2014, http://www.oxforddnb.com/view/article/4031?docPos=3.

77. Ibid.; William Burke and John Macnee, *Trial of William Burke and Helen M'Dougal Before the High Court of Justiciary at Edinburgh on Wednesday, December 24, 1828: For the Murder of Margery Campbell or Docherty* (Edinburgh: Robert Buchanan, William Hunter, John Stevenson, Baldwin & Cradock, 1829), 50–51.

78. Erin Dean, "The Macabre World of Books Bound in Human Skin," *BBC News Magazine*, June 20, 2014, http://www.bbc.co.uk/news/magazine-27903742.

79. Ibid.; Gillian Fitzharris, "Holding a Book Bound in Human Skin," *Huffington Post*, August 19, 2013, http://www.huffingtonpost.co.uk/dr-lindsey-fitzharris/holding-a-book-bound-in-human-skin_b_3772196.html.

80. "Bound in Human Skin," *Houghton Library Blog*, May 24, 2013, http://blogs.law.harvard.edu/houghton/2013/05/24/bound-in-human-skin/.

81. Dean, "The Macabre World."

82. F. P. Veitch, R. W. Frey, and J. S. Rogers, *American Sumac: A Valuable Tanning Material and Dyestuff* (Washington, DC: US Government Printing Office, 1920), 1.

83. "I. Sever. Pinaei De Integritatis & Corruptionis Virginum Notis," *Library Catalogue*, Wellcome Library, accessed November 1, 2014, http://catalogue.wellcomelibrary.org/record=b1283248~S12.

84. Moleskine SpA, personal correspondence with the author, September 2014.
85. Dean, "The Macabre World."
86. "Our History," Smyth SrL, accessed November 1, 2014, http://www.smyth.it/en/about-us/our-history; Matt T. Roberts and Don Etherington, "Roller Backer," *Bookbinding and the Conservation of Books*, Foundation of the American Institute for Conservation, November 2011, http://cool.conservation-us.org/don/dt/dt2890.html; Geoffrey A. Glaister, "Folding Machine," in *Encyclopedia of the Book* (New Castle, DE: Oak Knoll Press, 1996), 180.
87. William Hancock, "Improvement in Book-Binding. U.S. Patent 444 A," United States Patent Office, October 1837.
88. Matt T. Roberts and Don Etherington, "Case Binding," *Bookbinding and the Conservation of Books*, Foundation of the American Institute for Conservation, November 2011, http://cool.conservation-us.org/don/dt/dt0596.html.
89. Hancock, "Improvement in Book-Binding"; *The Mechanics' Magazine, Museum, Register, Journal, and Gazette*, vol. 30 (London: M. Salmon, 1839), 110.
90. Elizabeth James, "Yellowbacks," *Aspects of the Victorian Book*, British Library, accessed November 2, 2014, http://www.bl.uk/collections/early/victorian/pu_yello.html; Richard Davies, "Cheap, Eye-Catching & Victorian: Discover Yellowbacks," AbeBooks, accessed November 2, 2014, http://www.abebooks.co.uk/books/rare-railway-library-routledge-london/victorian-yellowbacks.shtml; "Best-Sellers & Yellow-Backs: M. E. Braddon & Rhoda Broughton," *Victorian Writers Remembered & Forgotten*, University of South Carolina, December 6, 2006, http://library.sc.edu/zellatest/vicwriters/yellowbacks.htm.
91. Adrian Bullock, *Book Production* (Abingdon: Routledge, 2012), 162–64.
92. Matt T. Roberts and Don Etherington, "Caoutchouc Binding," *Bookbinding and the Conservation of Books*, Foundation of the American Institute for Conservation, November 2011, http://cool.conservation-us.org/don/dt/dt0574.html; Michael F. Suarez and H. R. Woudhuysen, *The Book: A Global History* (Oxford: Oxford University Press, 2013), 247.

CHAPTER 15 ⇷ SIZE MATTERS: THE INVENTION OF THE MODERN BOOK

1. "Books Statistics," Dadax, 2014, http://www.worldometers.info/books/; "US Publishing Industry Annual Survey Reports $27 Billion in Net Revenue, 2.6 Billion Units for 2013," Bookstats.org, June 26, 2014, http://bookstats.org/pdf/BOOKSTATS_2013_GENERAL_PUBLIC_WEBSITE_HIGHLIGHTS.pdf.
2. E. Turner, *The Typology of the Early Codex* (Philadelphia: University of Pennsylvania Press, 1977), 41–54.
3. Ibid., 140–41.
4. Ibid., 102–85.
5. Ibid., 14–22.
6. Geoffrey A. Glaister, "Gathering," in *Encyclopedia of the Book* (New Castle, DE: Oak Knoll Press, 1996), 192.
7. Turner, *Typology*, 58–59, 60–66.
8. Ibid., 62–63.

9. Henry Petroski, *The Book on the Bookshelf*, 1st ed. (New York: Alfred A. Knopf, 1999), 33–34.
10. Roger Bagnall, *The Oxford Handbook of Papyrology* (Oxford: Oxford University Press, 2009), 23–24; Leila Avrin, *Scribes, Script, and Books: The Book Arts from Antiquity to the Renaissance*, ALA Classics (Chicago: American Library Association, 2010), 218–19; Geoffrey A. Glaister, "Quaternion," in *Encyclopedia of the Book*, 406.
11. Christopher De Hamel, *Scribes and Illuminators* (Toronto; Buffalo: University of Toronto Press, 1992), 19–20.
12. Adam Bülow-Jacobsen, "Writing Materials in the Ancient World," in *The Oxford Handbook of Papyrology*, ed. Roger Bagnall (Oxford: Oxford University Press, 2009), 23–24.
13. De Hamel, *Scribes and Illuminators*, 20; Colin Roberts and T. C. Skeat, *The Birth of the Codex* (London: Published for the British Academy by the Oxford University Press, 1983), 7; Marcus Niebuhr Tod, "A New Fragment of the 'Edictum Diocletiani,'" *The Journal of Hellenic Studies* 24 (1904): 195–202, doi:10.2307/624027; E. Turner, *Greek Papyri: An Introduction* (Princeton, NJ: Princeton University Press, 1968), 19.
14. De Hamel, *Scribes and Illuminators*, 20; Turner, *Typology*, 62–64; Turner, *Greek Papyri*, 12.
15. De Hamel, *Scribes and Illuminators*, 19–20.
16. Frederic G. Kenyon, *Books and Readers in Ancient Greece and Rome* (Oxford: Clarendon Press, 1889), 106.
17. "Search for 'F°', '4°', and '8°,'" Incunabula Short Title Catalogue, British Library, accessed September 30, 2014, http://istc.bl.uk/.
18. Matt T. Roberts and Don Etherington, "Folio," *Bookbinding and the Conservation of Books*, Foundation of the American Institute for Conservation, November 19, 2011, http://cool.conservation-us.org/don/dt/dt1404.html; Matt T. Roberts and Don Etherington, "Quarto," *Bookbinding and the Conservation of Books*, Foundation of the American Institute for Conservation, November 2011, http://cool.conservation-us.org/don/dt/dt2759.html.
19. Matt T. Roberts and Don Etherington, "Octavo," *Bookbinding and the Conservation of Books*, Foundation of the American Institute for Conservation, November 2011, http://cool.conservation-us.org/don/dt/dt2355.html.
20. Matt T. Roberts and Don Etherington, "Uncut (*Uncut Edges*)," *Bookbinding and the Conservation of Books*, Foundation of the American Institute for Conservation, November 2011, http://cool.conservation-us.org/don/dt/dt3643.html; "Uncut Pages," *Rare, Old or Offbeat, LibraryThing*, September 13, 2009, http://www.librarything.com/topic/73028.
21. Dard Hunter, *Papermaking: The History and Technique of an Ancient Craft*, Dover Books Explaining Science (New York: Dover Publications, 1978), 84–94.
22. Matt T. Roberts and Don Etherington, "Deckle Edge," *Bookbinding and the Conservation of Books*, Foundation of the American Institute for Conservation, November 2011, http://cool.conservation-us.org/don/dt/dt0981.html.
23. "Deckle Detecting," *The Economist*, June 15, 2013, http://www.economist.com/blogs/babbage/2012/07/printed-books?fsrc=scn/tw/te/bl/deckledetecting.
24. Roberts and Etherington, "Deckle Edge"; *Economist*, "Deckle Detecting."
25. "Biblia Latina," Incunabula Short Title Catalogue, British Library, accessed September 30, 2014, http://istc.bl.uk/search/search.html?operation=record&rsid=131443&q=0;

"De Casibus Virorum Illustrium [French] *De la Ruine des Nobles Hommes et Femmes* (Tr: Laurent de Premierfait)," Incunabula Short Title Catalogue, British Library, accessed September 30, 2014, http://istc.bl.uk/search/search.html?operation=record&rsid=131443&q=0.

26. "Search for 'F°', '4°', and '8°.'"

27. Martin Davies, *Aldus Manutius: Printer and Publisher of Renaissance Venice* (London: British Library, 1995), 14–15.

28. Ibid., 18.

29. Ibid., 6, 9–10, 13.

30. Robert Proctor, *The Printing of Greek in the Fifteenth Century* (Oxford: The Bibliographical Society, 1900), 12–13; Stephan Füssel, "Bringing the Technical Inventions Together," in *Gutenberg and the Impact of Printing* (Farnham, UK: Ashgate Publishing, 2005), 15–18.

31. Davies, *Aldus Manutius*, 14–15.

32. Ibid., 20–26.

33. Ibid., 33–39; "Cornucopiae Linguae Latinae (Ed: Aldus Manutius). Add: Commentariolus in Prohemium Historiae Naturalis Plinii. Cornelius Vitellius: Epistola Parthenio Benacensi," Incunabula Short Title Catalogue, British Library, accessed November 1, 2014, http://istc.bl.uk/search/search.html?operation=record&rsid=131906&q=0; "Hypnerotomachia Poliphili. Add: Leonardus Crassus, Johannes Baptista Scytha and Andreas Maro," Incunabula Short Title Catalogue, British Library, accessed November 1, 2014, http://istc.bl.uk/search/search.html?operation=record&rsid=131907&q=0; N. Harris, "Hypnerotomachia Poliphili," ed. Michael F. Suarez and H. R. Woudhuysen, in *The Oxford Companion to the Book* (Oxford University Press, 2010), 807–8.

34. Davies, *Aldus Manutius*, 40–50.

35. "Watermarks and Chain Lines on Different Formats," Dawn of Western Printing, National Diet Library, Tokyo, 2004, http://www.ndl.go.jp/incunabula/e/chapter3/ori_example1.html.

36. Conor Fahy, "Notes on Centrifugal Octavo Imposition in Sixteenth-Century Italian Printing," *Transactions of the Cambridge Bibliographical Society* 10, no. 4 (1994): 488–504.

37. B. L. Ullman, "The Gothic Script of the Late Middle Ages" (Cooper Square Publishers, 1963), 118–30.

38. C. U. Clark, "How Our Roman Type Came to Us," *The North American Review* 195, no. 677 (1912): 546–49; Lane Wilkinson, *The Humanistic Minuscule and the Advent of Roman Type*, Paper (Chattanooga: University of Tennessee, 2009).

39. "Aldus Manutius, Scholar-Printer (c.1445–1515)," National Library of Scotland, May 14, 2012, http://www.nls.uk/collections/rare-books/collections/aldus-manutius.

40. B. L. Ullman, "A Rival System—Niccolò Niccoli," Storia e Letteratura (Ed. di storia e letteratura, 1974), 59–77; A. C. De La Mare, *The Handwriting of Italian Humanists: Francesco Petrarca, Giovani Boccacio, Coluccio Salutati, Niccolò Niccoli, Poggio Bracciolini, Bartolomeo Aragazzi of Montepulciano, Sozomo of Pistoia, Giorgio Antonio Vespucci* (Association Internationale de Bibliographilie, 1973).

41. Andy Hadel, "In Aedibus Aldi: Aldus & Co.," The Type Directors Club, 2012, https://www.tdc.org/articles/in-aedibus-aldi-aldus-co/.

42. Davies, *Aldus Manutius*, 42–46.

43. W.W.E. Slights, "The Edifying Margins of Renaissance English Books," in *Managing Readers*, Editorial Theory and Literary Criticism (Ann Arbor: University of Michigan Press, 2001), 19–60; H. J. Jackson, "History," in *Marginalia: Readers Writing in Books*, Nota Bene Series (New Haven: Yale University Press, 2002), 44–80; W. H. Sherman, "Towards a History of the Manicule," in *Used Books: Marking Readers in Renaissance England*, Material Texts (University of Pennsylvania Press, Incorporated, 2009), 28–52.

44. "Aldus Manutius," *First Impressions*, The University of Manchester Library, 2011, http://www.library.manchester.ac.uk/firstimpressions/Pioneers-of-Print/Aldus-Manutius/.

45. Davies, *Aldus Manutius*, 46–50.

46. Matt T. Roberts and Don Etherington, "Twelvemo," *Bookbinding and the Conservation of Books*, Foundation of the American Institute for Conservation, November 2011, http://cool.conservation-us.org/don/dt/dt3608.html; Matt T. Roberts and Don Etherington, "Inset," *Bookbinding and the Conservation of Books*, Foundation of the American Institute for Conservation, November 2011, http://cool.conservation-us.org/don/dt/dt1868.html.

47. Herman Melville, *Moby-Dick, Or, the Whale* (Harper & Bros.; Richard Bentley, 1851), 149–59.

48. Arthur D. Dunn, *Notes on the Standardization of Paper Sizes* (AD Dunn, 1972), 1–2.

49. Matt T. Roberts and Don Etherington, "Sizes of Paper," *Bookbinding and the Conservation of Books*, Foundation of the American Institute for Conservation, November 2011, http://cool.conservation-us.org/don/dt/dt3142.html.

50. Charles Jacobi, *Gesta Typographica: Or, A Medley for Printers and Others* (London: Elkin Mathews, 1897), 27–28; John Pym, "On Grievances in the Reign of Charles I," *The World's Famous Orations. Great Britain: I (710–1777)*, 1906, available at http://www.bartleby.com/268/3/8.html.

51. Maurice Ashley, "Charles I," *Encyclopaedia Britannica*, accessed November 1, 2014, http://www.britannica.com/EBchecked/topic/106686/Charles-I.

52. "Presbyterians, Independents and the New Model Army," *The Civil War*, UK Parliament, accessed November 1, 2014, http://www.parliament.uk/about/living-heritage/evolutionofparliament/parliamentaryauthority/civilwar/overview/presbyterians/; "Pride's Purge, 'The Rump' and Regicide," *The Civil War*, UK Parliament, accessed November 1, 2014, http://www.parliament.uk/about/living-heritage/evolutionofparliament/parliamentaryauthority/civilwar/overview/prides-purge/; Harold Bayley, *A New Light on the Renaissance Displayed in Contemporary Emblems* (London: J. M. Dent, 1909), 215.

53. Jacobi, *Gesta Typographica*, 27–28.

54. "The Rump Dissolved," *The Civil War*, UK Parliament, accessed November 1, 2014, http://www.parliament.uk/about/living-heritage/evolutionofparliament/parliamentaryauthority/civilwar/overview/rump-dissolved/; Jacobi, *Gesta Typographica*, 27–28; Roberts and Etherington, "Book Sizes."

55. Robert D. Stevick, "The St Cuthbert Gospel Binding and Insular Design," *Artibus et Historiae* 8, no. 15 (1987): 9–19; Markus Kuhn, "International Standard Paper Sizes," April 25, 2014, http://www.cl.cam.ac.uk/~mgk25/iso-paper.html; John Man, *The Gutenberg Revolution: How Printing Changed the Course of History* (London: Transworld Publishers,

2010), 166; Phil Baines, *Penguin by Design: A Cover Story, 1935–2005* (London: Allen Lane, 2005), 13.

56. Georg Lichtenberg, *Briefwechsel*, vol. 3 (München: Beck, 1990), 274–75; Markus Kuhn, "Lichtenberg's Letter to Johann Beckmann," February 7, 2006, http://www.cl.cam.ac.uk/~mgk25/lichtenberg-letter.html.

57. Markus Kuhn, "Loi sur le Timbre (No. 2136)," October 8, 2005, http://www.cl.cam.ac.uk/~mgk25/loi-timbre.html.

58. Kuhn, "International Standard Paper Sizes."

59. Ibid.

60. Roberts and Etherington, "Book Sizes"; Matt T. Roberts and Don Etherington, "Basic Size," *Bookbinding and the Conservation of Books*, Foundation of the American Institute for Conservation, November 2011, http://cool.conservation-us.org/don/dt/dt0246.html.

61. Roberts and Etherington, "Book Sizes"; Roberts and Etherington, "Sizes of Paper."

62. Melville, *Moby-Dick*, 154.

63. Roberts and Etherington, "Book Sizes."

64. Roberts and Etherington, "Sizes of Paper."

65. Dunn, *Notes on the Standardization of Paper Sizes*, 6–7.

66. "Why Is the Standard Paper Size in the U.S. 8½ x 11?," American Forest & Paper Association, accessed November 1, 2014, https://web.archive.org/web/20120220192919/http:/www.afandpa.org/paper.aspx?id=511.

67. Roberts and Etherington, "Basic Size."

68. Dunn, *Notes on the Standardization of Paper Sizes*, 6–7.

69. Gavin Ambrose and Paul Harris, *The Fundamentals of Typography* (Lausanne: AVA Academia, 2011), 73.

⇷ COLOPHON

1. Geoffrey A. Glaister, "Colophon," in *Encyclopedia of the Book* (New Castle, DE: Oak Knoll Press, 1996), 103; "Colophon," *OED Online*, accessed November 3, 2014, http://www.oed.com/view/Entry/36552.

2. Anna Oler, personal correspondence with the author, November 2015.

3. Ibid.

4. Ibid.

5. Ibid.

6. Adrian Bullock, *Book Production* (Abingdon: Routledge, 2012), 164–69.

Illustration Credits

Page 5: Domenico Cirillo. *Cyperus Papyrus*, 1796. Image courtesy of Álvaro Pérez Vilariño.

Page 7: Norman de Garis Davies. *The Tomb of Puyemrê at Thebes*, Volume I, Plate XV. Image courtesy of University of Glasgow Library.

Page 12: Image courtesy of Wikimedia Commons user "Aethralis." CC Attribution-ShareAlike 3.0 Unported. Original at http://commons.wikimedia.org/wiki/File:Papyrus_sheet.svg; published version at http://www.keithhouston.co.uk/?attachment_id=395.

Page 15: Author's collection.

Pages 26–27: Photo Shai Halevi. Full Spectrum Color Image. Courtesy of the Israel Antiquities Authority.

Page 29: Jost Amman, *Stände und Handwerker aus dem Jahre 1568* (Knorr & Hirth, 1923), 18. Public domain.

Page 32: Author's collection.

Pages 43, 44, and 45: Yingxing Song, *Chinese Technology in the Seventeenth Century* (Mineola, NY: Courier Dover Publications, 1997), 226, 228, 229. Public domain.

Page 46: Author's collection.

Page 57: Jost Amman, *Stände und Handwerker aus dem Jahre 1568* (Knorr & Hirth, 1923), 18. Public domain.

Page 59: © Simon Barcham Green 2015 (http://papermoulds.typepad.com/).

Page 67: ICV No 24186. Wellcome Library, London.

Page 73: Wisconsin Department of Natural Resources.

Page 81: Herbert R. Cole Collection (M.84.31.6), Los Angeles County Museum of Art (www.lacma.org). Public domain.

Page 83: © 2015 Pierre Tallet.

Page 86: James Quibell, Excavations at Saqqara, 1911–12: *The Tomb of Hesy* (Le Caire: Impr. de l'Institut français d'archéologie orientale, 1913), 299. Public domain.

Page 95: P.Mich.inv. 4968. Image digitally reproduced with the permission of the Papyrology Collection, Graduate Library, University of Michigan.

Pages 98 and 99: Arundel 16, f. 2. British Library Catalogue of Illuminated Manuscripts.

Pages 115 and 117: Theodore De Vinne, *The Invention of Printing* (New York: F. Hart, 1876), 25, 55, 57. Public domain.

Pages 119 and 120: Jost Amman, *Stände und Handwerker aus dem Jahre 1568* (Knorr & Hirth, 1923), 15, 19. Public domain.

Pages 124–25: Q450.5. A *Noble Fragment being a leaf of the Gutenberg Bible, 1450–1455*, verso and recto. Rare Books & Manuscripts Department, Boston Public Library.

Page 131: PGA - Anderson, H. —Columbian press . . . (A size) [P&P]. Library of Congress Prints and Photographs Division. Public domain.

Page 134: Source and © Koenig & Bauer AG.

Page 138: Image courtesy of David M. MacMillan and Rollande Krandall (http://www.circuitousroot.com/). CC Attribution-ShareAlike 3.0 Unported.

Pages 142 and 144: Mergenthaler Linotype Company, *Linotype Machine Principles* (Mergenthaler Linotype Co., 1940), 5, 2. Public domain.

Page 149: Image courtesy of David M. MacMillan and Rollande Krandall (http://www.circuitousroot.com/). CC Attribution-ShareAlike 3.0 Unported.

Page 159: E. A. W. Budge, *Book of the Dead: Facsimiles of the Papyri of Hunifer, Anhai, Kerāsher and Netchemet, with Supplementary Text from the Papyrus of Nu, with a Transcript, Translation, Etc.* (London: British Museum; Longman & Co., 1900), Hunefer 4. Image courtesy of Heidelberg University Library. CC Attribution-ShareAlike 3.0 Unported.

Page 160: Bayerische Staatsbibliothek, Pap.graec.mon. 128.

Page 163: Book of Kells (MS58), f. 34r. The Board of Trinity College Dublin.

Page 168: Evangelistary of Henry III, Staats- und Universitäsbibliothek Bremen, Signature: msb 0021, fol. 124v.

Page 173: Sloane 2435, f. 44v. British Library Catalogue of Illuminated Manuscripts.

Page 184: Or. 8210/P.2, frontispiece and text. British Library.

Page 188: © American Numismatic Association 2015.

Page 194: Theodore De Vinne, *The Invention of Printing* (New York: F. Hart, 1876), 70. Public domain.

Page 196: Albrecht Dürer, *The Four Horsemen*. Accession No. 2008.109.5. Patrons' Permanent Fund and Print Purchase Fund (Horace Gallatin and Lessing J. Rosenwald). Courtesy National Gallery of Art, Washington.

Page 197: Hans Burgkmair, *The Lovers Surprised by Death*. Accession No. 1948.11.15. Rosenwald Collection. Courtesy National Gallery of Art, Washington.

Page 200: Herzog August Bibliothek Wolfenbüttel: inkunabeln/16-1-eth-2f-1s.

Page 205: Boccaccio presenting his book to Cavalcanti, 1476. Master of the Boccaccio Illustrations, Netherlandish, 1470–1490. Maria Antoinette Evans Fund, 32.458. Photograph © 2016 Museum of Fine Arts, Boston.

Page 207: Jost Amman, *Stände und Handwerker aus dem Jahre 1568* (Knorr & Hirth, 1923), 16. Public domain.

Page 212: Daniel Hopfer, *Kunz von der Rosen*. Accession No. 1948.5.124. Rosenwald Collection. Courtesy National Gallery of Art, Washington.

Page 217: Robert Havell after John James Audubon, *Columbia Jay*. Accession No. 1945.8.96. Gift of Mrs. Walter B. James. Courtesy National Gallery of Art, Washington.

Page 226: Louis Prang, *Lithographer*. Accession No. 1964.8.2682. Rosenwald Collection. Courtesy National Gallery of Art, Washington.

Page 228: William Henry Fox Talbot, "The Boulevards of Paris" (May 1843). Digital image courtesy of the Getty's Open Content Program. J. Paul Getty Museum, Los Angeles.

Page 231: William Henry Fox Talbot, "Three Sheets of Gauze, Crossed Obliquely, about 1852–1857." Digital image courtesy of the Getty's Open Content Program. J. Paul Getty Museum, Los Angeles.

Page 232: Stephen Horgan, *Horgan's Half-Tone and Photomechanical Processes* (Chicago: Inland Printer, 1913), 101. Public domain.

Page 235: John J. N. Palmer, George Slater, and Anna Powell-Smith, "Nottinghamshire, Page 1," Open Domesday, accessed September 30, 2014, http://domesdaymap.co.uk/book/nottinghamshire/01/. Image courtesy of Professor J. J. N. Palmer, University of Hull.

Page 246: *Scribe Statue of Amunhotep, Son of Nebiry*, ca. 1426–1400 bce. Limestone, 26 x 13 3/16 x 14 13/16 in. (66 x 33.5 x 37.6 cm). Brooklyn Museum, Charles Edwin Wilbour Fund, 37.29E. Creative Commons-BY.

Page 253: John Clark, *The Care of Books: An Essay on the Development of Libraries and Their Fittings, from the Earliest Times to the End of the Eighteenth Century* (Cambridge: Cambridge University Press, 1909), fig. 11. Public domain.

Page 255: Roman civilization, 1st century ce Portrait of baker Terentius Neo and his wife in formal clothes, 55–79 ce, painting on plaster, 65 x 58 cm. From Pompeii. DEA Picture Library/De Agostini/Getty Images.

Page 258: Robert Payton, "The Ulu Burun Writing-Board Set," *Anatolian Studies* 41 (1991): fig. 4. © 2015 Robert Payton.

Page 267: Tang. 335/33 (ff. 1–2). Institute of Oriental Manuscripts, Russian Academy of Sciences.

Pages 268–69: Mexicain 386. Département des Manuscrits, Bibliothèque nationale de France.

Page 280: Irina Gorstein (book model), Adam Kellie (photography).

Page 285: © The British Library Board, ADD. 89000 (cover image).

Page 293: Binding from Ethiopian Gospels. Accession No. W.850.binding. Museum purchase with funds provided by the W. Alton Jones Foundation Acquisition Fund, 1998. The Walters Art Museum.

Page 297: Irina Gorstein (book model), Adam Kellie (photography).

Page 299: Jost Amman, *Stände und Handwerker aus dem Jahre 1568* (Knorr & Hirth, 1923), 21. Public domain.

Page 302: Leaf from a German translation of the Vulgate (ISTC ib00632000) used as binding waste. Penn Libraries call number: Inc C-372. Image courtesy of University of Pennsylvania Rare Book & Manuscript Library. CC Attribution 2.0 Generic.

Page 307: *De integritatis & corruptionis virginum notis*. Wellcome Library, London.

Page 315: Author's collection.

Page 319: *Le Cose Vulgari de Messer Francesco Petrarcha*, 1501, NLS shelf-mark Nha.T189. National Library of Scotland.

Page 322: Author's collection.

Index

Page numbers in *italics* refer to illustrations and examples.

Aachen Cathedral, 104–5
Abbasid dynasty, 53–54
Abu al-Majd, 277–78
Academy of Sciences, Bavaria, 222
acid-free paper, 73–74, *75*, 76
"Acts of Paul and Thecla, The," 262
ad card, *v*
adding machines, 146, *147*
    see also tabulating machines
Adobe Jenson Pro Light (typeface), 330
Adolf von Nassau, archbishop of Mainz, 127
Adventures of Tom Sawyer, The (Twain), 136
al-'Andalus, 56, 58
Albatross Verlag, 324
Albion press, 130
Aldine press, 317, 320
    dolphin-and-anchor logo of, 321
Aldus Manutius (Aldo Manuzio), 316–18, *319*, 320–21, 323, 328, 331
Aleppo, Syria, 100
Alexander the Great, 10, 249
    Egypt conquered by, 88
Alexandria, Egypt, 22, 249–50
    Library of, *see* Library of Alexandria
Alfonso X, king of Castile, 58
alphabets:
    Etruscan, 92
    Greek, 92
    Phoenician, 91–92
    Roman, 92
    Sinaitic, 92–93
aluminum sulfate, 14
    in papermaking, 69, 70, 74
āmatl (Mesoamerican writing surface), 268–69
Amazon, xvi
Amenemhat I, pharaoh, 248
American Forest and Paper Association, 327
American National Standards Institute, 328
American Revolution, 63–64
Amharic language, 93
Amman, Jost, *29*, *57*, 119, *119*, *120*, 122, *207*, *299*
Ammit, 158
āmoxtli (Mesoamerican books), 269
An, Han Chinese emperor, 47–48
Anatolia, *81*
Andachtsbilder, *see* devotional images
ankh, 87
ANSI paper sizes, 328, 330
anthropodermic bibliopegy, 305
antimony, 118

Antiochus IV, Seleucid king, 21–22
Egypt invaded by, 22–23
antiquarii, 169
Antony, Mark, 88
Anubis, 158, *159*
"A" paper sizes, 325
Apocalypse (Dürer), 195, *196*, 197
appendices, 329
Appolonia, Saint, 192
aquatint, 216, *217*, 218, 230
Arabian Peninsula, 93
Arabic language, 93
Arabs, paper used by, 54–56
cotton-based, 36
linen-based, 37
Aramaic, 270–72
Archimedes, 250
"Archimedes Palimpsest," 97, 100
Aristarchus, 23, 250
Aristophanes (librarian), 19, 23
Aristotle, 15, 19, 317
armor, etching on, 210–11
arsenic sulfide, 259
Ars grammatica (Donatus), 106–7, 199, 201
Asia Pacific Offset, 329
Aswan, Egypt, 270
Athens, 82–83, 251
Attalus, 23
Audubon, John James, 213–16, *217*, 218, 229
Augsburg, Germany, 211
author, *vii*
Aztecs, orihons (codices) of, 268

backmatter head, 329
Baghdad, 54, 55
Bahr Yusuf, 261–62
Balkans, 156
Bamberg, Germany, 199
bamboo:
uses of, 38
as writing surface, 37–39
Barbarigo, Pierfranceso, 316
Basile, Corrado, 14, 16
Bavaria, 225
Bavarian Academy of Sciences, 222
Bavarian army, 221
Bavarian limestone, 224
Bayley, Harold, 60–61
Bayt al-Hikma (House of Wisdom), 55
Beatty, A. Chester, 265
Belgium, 35
Bembo, Bernardo, 320
Bembo (typeface), 320
Benedict, Saint, 165
Benedict VIII, Pope, 28
Berbers, 53
Bewick, Thomas, 227
Bible, 106
Gutenberg edition of, 109, 114–23, *124–25*, 145, 199, 229, 314, 316–17, 318, 324
Biblia pauperum (Pfister), *200*, 201
bibliographies, 329
biblion (scroll), 250
Bibliotheca historica (Diodorus), 89
bibliotheke, 252
Bibliothèque nationale de France, 245, 289
biblos (papyrus), 250
Billings, John Shaw, 146–47
Birds of America, The (Audubon), 213, 215–16, *217*, 218, 225–26, 229
Birth of the Codex, The (Roberts and Skeat), 277

Bi Sheng, 110–11, 112
Black, William, 308
Black Death, 63
blackletter (Gothic textura), *99*, 107, 123, 318
black tigers (*hei laohu*), 180
blind tooling, 303–4, 331
blockbooks, 199
Boas, Franz, 261
boats, of papyrus, 6, *7*
Bologna, Italy, 323
Boner, Ulrich, 199
Boniface, Saint, 297–98
bookbinding, 283–309, *299*, 303
- backing process in, 301–2, 308
- case binding, 308, 331
- Coptic stitching in, 292–94, *293*, 300–301, 302–3, 306
- covers in, *see* covers
- double-cord, 296–98, *297*, 330–31
- dust jackets and, 304
- endpapers in, 300, 308
- glued, 308–9, 310, 331
- headbands (endbands) in, 300–301
- innovations in, 299–306, 308–9, 310
- Islamic, 302–3
- mechanization of, 308, 310
- multiple gatherings in, 290–95
- Nag Hammadi codices and, 279–81, 282
- paperbacks, 309
- paper sizes and, 323–28
- perfect binding, 309
- Ragyndrudis Codex and, 296–97
- St. Cuthbert Gospel and, 284–88, 291–93, 294, 295–96, 298, 300
- single gatherings in, 288–89

book industry, growth of, 69–70
book louse, 51*n*–52*n*
Book of Agriculture (Wang Zhen), 111
Book of Durrow, 161
Book of Kells, 161–64, *163*, 169–70
bookplate, *i*
books:
- burning of, 56, 58
- interdependence of paper and, 35–36, 50
- mass deacidification of, 71–72
- mass printing of, 128
- paged, *see* codex, codices

books, modern:
- trimmed edges of, 281

Books of Hours, 174
Books of the Dead, 20, 157–58, *159*, 245, 248–49
Botticelli, Sandro, 208
Bouchard, Pierre, 90
Bouland, Ludovic, 305–6, *307*
British Library, 28, 72, 286
British Museum, 90, 249
Bruce, David, 134–35
brushes, 84, 85, 88, 94, 180, 186, 242
Brussels, 35, 290
Brussels Madonna, 193
bubonic plague, 102, 105
Buchdrucker, Der (The Printer; Amman), 119
Buddhism:
- in China, 180–81, 183–84
- in Japan, 181–83

bullae, 80, 82
bullet, *14*
Bullock, William, 135
Burgkmair, Hans, 197–98, *197*
burins, 206–7

Burke, William, 304–5
"Burke's Skin Pocket Book," 305
Buxheim Saint Christopher, *194*, 303

Caesar, Julius, 256
  memorandum books of, 273–74
Cai Lun, 11, 39–49, *45*, 68, 83, 177, 178
  and invention of paper, 41–49, 50–51
  suicide of, 48
Cairo Museum, 20
Çakir, Mehmet, 256
calami (pens), 94
calfskin, xvii, 31, 123, 304
calligraphy, 113
Cambridge University, 62
Canaan, Canaanites, 92–93
caoutchouc (rubber), 308–9, 310
caption, *5*
carbon, in ink, 85, 95, 97, 122, 186
Carchemish, 20
Carpi, Italy, 316
cartonnage, 66, 282
case binding, 308, 331
Castaldi, Panfilo, 190, 191
Cathach, An, 160–61
Cathars, 59, 60
Catherine of Siena, Saint, 193
Catholic Church, woodblock printing and, 192–93
Census, US, 145–46, 152
chalk, 74
Champollion, Jean-François, 91
Chang'an, China, 181, 187
chapter number, *3*
chapter title, *3*
Charlemagne, 53, 165–66, 299, 318
Charles I, king of England, 323
Charles Martel, 53
chase, 121, 128, *200*
Chelsea Manufacturing Company, 67
Chen Sheng, 38
chiaroscuro, 197–98, *197*
Chicago Tribune, 144
China:
  Buddhism in, 180–81, 183–84
  copper coinage in, 176, 187
  ink in, 112–13
  invention of paper in, 36–37, 41–49, *43*, *44*, *45*, 50–51, 68, 113, 177, 178–79
  Japanese emulation of, 181
  Marco Polo in, 176–77
  movable type and, 109–14, 186
  orihons in, 266, *267*, 269–70
  paper money invented in, 176–77, 180, 187, *188*, 189, 191
  printing invented in, 177–81, 183–86
  rubbings in, 179–80
  woodblock printing in, 183–86
  writing surfaces used in, 37–38
chi rho, *163*
chlorine, in papermaking, 70
Christianity, Christians, 271
  book burning by, 56, 58
  in Ireland, 156–57
  papyrus linked to heathenism by, 287
  parchment adopted by, 27–28, 56
  spread of, 164–65
Christopher, Saint, 192, 193
chromolithograph, *226*
chu (*Broussonetia papyrifera*; paper mulberry), 47, 49
  in papermaking, 41–42, *46*, 68

Church, William, 139, 141
cinnabar, 172
clay tablets, xv*n*, xvi, 79–80
Clemens, Samuel (Mark Twain), 66, 151
  Paige Compositor and, 136–38, *138*, 148
Cleopatra VII, pharaoh, 88
Clephane, James O., 140–41
Clymer, George E., *131*
codex, codices, xv, xv*n*–xvi*n*, 260, *297*
  binding of, *see* bookbinding
  changing market for, 310–11
  collections of correspondence as origin of, 270–71
  deckle-edged, 314
  etymology of, 294–95
  Golden Ratio and, 324
  multiple-gathered, 311–12
  orihons and, 266
  of paper, 302–3, 312
  of papyrus, 261–65, 272, 276–82, 288–91, 302–3, 311, 312–13
  of parchment, 272–77, 284–88, 291–93, 311–12
  in Roman Egypt, 261–65, 270
  vs. scrolls, efficiency of, 253–54
  single-gathered, 311
  sizes of, 311–28, *314*, 331
  unopened edges in, 313–14
Codex Leicester, 284
Codex Peresianus, *268*
codicologists, 277, 281–82, 312, 318
Coele-Syria, 21, 23
coffee-table books, xv
colophons, 320, 329–31
Columba, Saint, 161, 164
Columbia Jay, *217*
Columbian press, 130, *131*
Committee on the Simplification of Paper Sizes, 326–27
composing stick, 120–21, 135, 136
compositors, 119–21, *120*, 135
computers, xv
  and lithography, 236–37
  typesetting and, 152
Confucianism, 185
Conrad von der Rosen, 211, *212*
Constantinople, 155
contents page, *xi*
copper, 118, 122
copper acetate, 259
copperas (ferrous sulfate), 97, 100–101
copperplate printing, xvii
  aquatint process and, 216, *217*, 218, 230
  engraving and, 203–5, *206*, 207–10, *207*, 215–16, 220
  etching and, 211–13, 216, 230
  Mansion and, *205*
copper sulfate, 97
Coptic language, 91
Coptic Museum, Cairo, 277, 279, 289
Coptic stitching, 292–94, *293*, 296, 300–301, 302–3, 306
Copts, 278, 294, 302–3
copyright, xvi
copyright page, 73–74
correctors, 170
correspondence, collections of, as origin of codices, 270–71
cotton, 36, 41, 63
couching, in papermaking, *44*, 46, 61, 64
counterpunch, 115*n*

covers, 295–96, 331
gold leaf on, 304
of human skin, 304–5
leather, 303–4
pasteboard, 302–3
reused leaves in, *302*
in St. Cuthbert Gospel, 295–96
tooled designs on, 303–4
Cowper, Edward, 134
Crates of Mallus, 23, 272–73
Crocodilopolis, Egypt, 241
crocuses, 172
Cromwell, Oliver, 323–24
Crusades, book burning in, 56, 58
cuneiform script, 9, 79–80, *81*, 82, 93–94, 242
Cusanus (Nicholas of Kues), 107–9
Cuthbert, Saint, 284–85

dabbers (ink balls), *120*, 122, 193
Daguerre, Louis-Jacques-Mandé, 227, 229
daguerreotypes, 227–28
Damascus, 54
Dandolo, Andrea, 175
Dante Alighieri, 208–9
Dark Ages, 164
Dattari, Maria, 279
Davenport, Cyril, 266, 268
Dazangjing (Great Treasury of Sutras), 181
deacidification, of books, 71–72
Dead Sea Scrolls, 26
De casibus virorum illustrium (On the Fates of Famous Men), 203, *205*
deckle edges, 314
deckles, 314
in papermaking, 45–46
dedication, *ix*
De dissectione partium corporis humani libri tres (On dissection of the human body; Estienne), 195
De diversis artibus (The Various Arts; Theophilus), 28–29
De integritatis et corruptionis virginum notis (Thoughts on the integrity and corruption of virgins), 305–6, *307*
Demaratus, 96, 258–59
demotic scripts, Egyptian, 90–91, 244
Den, pharaoh, 244
Deng, dowager empress of China, 47
Densmore, James, 140
dermis, 24
Des destinées de l'âme (The destinies of the soul; Houssaye), 305–6
Destruction of Pharaoh's Host in the Red Sea (Titian), 198
Deuteronomy, Book of, *26*
devotional images (*Andachtsbilder*), 192–93
as pilgrims' souvenirs, 192–93
woodblock printing of, 193
Diamond Sutra, oldest printed edition of, 183–84, *184*
dichromated gelatin, 230, 231, 233
Didot, Saint-Léger, 64–65
Diether von Isenburg, archbishop of Mainz, 127
diethyl zinc (DEZ), 72
difthérai, 274
diminuendo, 162
dingbat, *vii*
Diodorus of Sicily, 89
diptych (writing tablet), 257, *258*, 274
Disquisition on the Composing Stick (Speckter), 121

Divine Comedy (Dante), 208–9
Djedkare Isesi, pharaoh, 248
Dōkyō, 182
Domesday Book, 233, *235*
Dominican Order, 193
Donatus, Aelius, 106–7
Doresse, Jean, 277, 289
Dou, empress of China, 40–41, 47–48
double-cord binding, 296–98, *297*, 330–31
drop cap, 3
Dunhuang, China, 37, *179*, 183–85, 266, *267*
Dünne, Hans, 114–15, 116
duodecimo (book size), 321, *323*, 326
Dürer, Albrecht, 198, 203, 209, 212–13
  woodcuts of, 195, *196*, 197
Durham, England, 284–85
Durham Cathedral, 285
dust jackets, 304
duxustus parchment, 27

Eadfrith, 287
East Asia, papermaking in, 50, 53
e-books, xv–xvi
  publisher deletions of, xvi
Edelstein, Der (The Precious Stone; Boner), 199, 201
Edinburgh, Scotland, 214, 304–5
Edinburgh, University of, 304
Egypt:
  Copts in, 294
  linen-based paper in, 37
Egypt, ancient, 3–4, 6–10, 82–84, 89, 241–49, 270–71
  Alexander's conquest of, 88, 249
  Books of the Dead in, 20, 157–58, *159*, 245
  inks in, 84–85, 242
  papyrus scrolls in, 243–45, 247–56
  scribes in, 85, 87–88, *87*, *246*, 250–51
  taxation in, 249
  writing on leather in, 20
Egypt, Ptolemaic, 19–22, *22*, 88, 159, 249–52, 276
  Antiochus's invasion of, 22–23
  Roman conquest of, 88
Egypt, Roman, codices in, 261–65, 270
Egyptology, 3
Eid, Albert, 289–90
Eid Codex (Jung Codex; Codex I), 289–91
El-Bahnasa, Egypt, 262–63
electronic books, *see* e-books
electronic documents, as analogous to papyrus scrolls, 254
Elements (Euclid), 250
Elephantine Island, 270–71
enchiridion (handbook), 317
Encyclopedia Britannica, 90
endbands, 300–301, 331
endpapers, 300, 308, 331
England, 63
  see also Great Britain; United Kingdom
English Civil War, 323
engravings, 203–5, *206*, 207–10, *207*, 215–16, 220, 234
Epigrams (Martial), 274–76
epilogues, 329
Erasmus, 195
Eratosthenes, 250
Erotemata (Questions), 316, 317
Estienne, Charles, 195

etching:
- on armor, 210–11
- copperplate printing and, 211–13, 216, 230
- on iron plates, 211

Ethiopians, *293*
Etruscans, alphabet of, 92
Euclid, 250
Eumenes II, king of Pergamon, 19–20, 21, 23
Euphrates River, 79
Euripides, 15
Europe:
- illuminated manuscripts in, 165–66
- papermaking in, 56, *57*, 58–63
- spread of Christianity in, 164–65
- woodblock printing in, 190–201

extract, *13*
Eyck, Jan van, 121

Facen, Jacopo, 190–91
Fangshan, China, 181
feiqian (flying money), 187
Fellowship of the Ring, The (Tolkien), 298
Feltre, Italy, 190–91
Fenerty, Charles, 36
Feng Dao, 185
ferrous sulfate (copperas), 97, 100–101
Fifty Shades of Grey (James), 220
Filippo de Strata, 128–29
Finiguerra, Maso, 204, 206
First Folio (Shakespeare), 233
flying money (*feiqian*), 187
folio (book size), 313, 314, *314*, 317–18, 325–26, 330
folio (page number), *10, 11*
folios, 290, 291, 316
- gatherings of, 311–12

fonts, monospaced, 142
foolscap (paper size), 324
foot margin, *6*
footnotes, *xv*, 320
formes, 121, 122, 227, 230
four-color art, *307*
Fourdrinier, Henry and Sealy, 65
Fourdrinier papermaking machine, 64–66, *67*, 73, 76, 133, 135, 308, 314, 327, 329
Francesco Griffo, 317, 320
Frances Loeb Library, *280, 297*
Frankfurt Book Fair, 123
Franks, 156, 165
Frederick II, Holy Roman emperor, 56
freesheet paper, 74, *75*
French Revolution, 64
French Royal Academy, 68
Frey, Don, 256
Frisia, 298
frisket, *120*
Fritsch, Ahasverus, 71
frontmatter head, *xi, xv*
Fujiwara, Japan, 181
full-page art, *57*
Fust, Johann, 106, 109, 126–27
Fust & Schöffer, 127, 329

Gaels, 161
galley, 121
Gamble, John, 65
Gardiner, Alan H., 92–93
Gardiner, Maine, 66, 68
Gaul, 156
Genoa, 175, 189
Gentleman's Magazine, 70

Germanic tribes, 156, 164–65
Germany, 36, 63, 105, 107, 132, 139, 199, 206, 210–11, 225, 318, 325
  see also Mainz, Germany
gesso, 171
gewil parchment, 27
Gleissner, Franz, 221–22, 224
Gnostics, 279
goatskin, 20, 28, 30, 279, 295, 304
goldbeater's skin, 171
Golden Ratio, 324
gold leaf, 169, 171
  on covers, 304
Gorgo, queen of Sparta, 259
Gorstein, Irina, *280*, *297*
Gothic textura (blackletter) script, *99*, 107, 123, 318
Goths, 156
Graf Zeppelin, 171
graphite pencils, 259
Great Britain, 156
  illuminated manuscripts in, 161
  parliament of, 323–24
  Viking invasions of, 164, 284
  see also England; United Kingdom
Great Harris Papyrus, 249
Greece, ancient, 159
  alphabet of, 92
  papyrus in, 9–10, 94
  papyrus scrolls in, 10, 244, 250–56
  pen-and-ink writing in, 94–96
Greek, typefaces for, 316–17
Greeneville, Conn., 67
Gregory I, Pope, 166
Grenfell, Bernard P., 261–65, 276
grimoires, 34
guilds, medieval, 103
gum arabic, 30, 85, 94, 95, 100
  oleophobic quality of, 223, 224
gunpowder, Chinese invention of, 177
Gutenberg, Johannes, 62, 101, 102–3, 169, 177, 199, 225, 301, 316
  Ars grammatica of, 107, 199, 201
  background of, 105
  Bible of, 109, 114–23, *124–25*, 145, 199, 229, 314, 316–17, 318, 324
  holy mirror business of, 104–5
  ink and, 121–22
  movable type and, 106, 109, 114–23, 128
  papal indulgences printed by, 108–9
  presses of, 122–23
  in Strasbourg, 103–6
gutter, *6*

Haas, Wilhelm, 129
Hahl, August, 139–40
half title, *iii*
halftone printing, 230, *231*, 330
  movable type and, 230, *233*
Hancock, William, 308–9, 310
Han period, 39, 180
Hapi, 8
Hare, William, 304
Harun al-Rashid, 54
Havell, Robert, Jr., 216, *217*, 218
He, emperor of China (Liu Zhao), 40–41
headbands, 300–301
head margin, *6*
Hebrew language, 93
hei laohu (black tigers), 180
Hellespont, 6–7
Helmasperger, Ulrich, 126

Helmasperger Notarial Instrument, 126
Hemaka, 244–45
hemp, in papermaking, 37, 41, 42, 55
Hendriks, Ignace H. M., 12–13, *12*
Herculaneum, 10, 276, 294
Herodotus, 6–7, 11, 20, 257–58
herses (drying frames), *29*, 30
Hesire (Hesy-Ra), 85, 87, *87*
Heughan, Chrissie, *46*
hieratica, 250
hieroglyphics, 8–9, 82–88, 92, 241, 242, 244
  deciphering of, 89–91
Hispania, 55–56
Histiaeus, 96
Hittites, 20
Hoe, Richard M., 135
Hollerith, Herman, 146, 147
  tabulating machines of, 147, 148, 152
holy mirrors, 104–5
Holy Roman Empire, 109, 165, 174, 318
Homer, 9–10, *95*, *160*
Hoover, Herbert, 327
Hopfer, Daniel, 211, *212*, 213, 218
Houghton Library, 305
Hou Han Shu, 39, 40, 41
Houssaye, Arsène, 305
Hunefer, Book of the Dead of, *159*
Huns, 156
Hunt, Arthur S., 261–65, 276
Hunter, Dard, 60
Hypnerotomachia Poliphili (Poliphilo's battle of love in a dream), 317

ibn Salih, Ziyad, 53
Iliad (Homer), *95*, *160*
illuminated manuscripts, 155–57, 202
  in Britain, 161
  decline of, 174
  in Europe, 165–66
  gold and silver leaf in, 169, 171
  ground applied to, 170–71
  illustration of, 170–71
  inks for, 162, 169, 171–72
  in Ireland, 157, 160–62, 164
  monasteries and, 166
  parchment for, 169
  ruling of, 169
  text in, 169–70
  wealthy owners of, 174
illustrations, xvii
illustrators, of illuminated manuscripts, 170–71
imprint, *vii*
incunabula, 128
India, 35, 53
India ink, 186
indices, 329
Indochina, 53
indulgences, 108–9
Industrial Revolution, 71, 129, 306, 308, 310
information technology, papyrus scrolls as, 9
initial capitals, illuminated, 170, *173*
ink balls (dabbers), *120*, 122, 193
inks, 94
  in ancient Egypt, 84–85, 242
  in ancient Greece, 94–96
  in ancient Rome, 95–96
  carbon-based, 85, *95*, 97, 122, 186
  Chinese, 112–13
  Gutenberg and, 121–22

for illuminated manuscripts, 162, 169, 171–72
invisible, 96–97
iron gall, 97, *99*, 100–101, 170
lithographic, 140, 224, 225, 233
parchment and, 96–97
Innocent III, Pope, 60
insects, paper-eating, 51–52
Institut d'Égypte, Cairo, 90
insular script, 162
intaglio printing, *see* copperplate printing, engraving and
International Business Machines (IBM), 152
interrobang, 121
Iona, 161, 164
iPad minis, 321
Iraq, 9, 55, 82, 109
Ireland:
Christianity in, 156–57
illuminated manuscripts in, 157, 160–62, 164
iron gall ink, 97, *99*, 100–101, 170
iron plates, etching on, 211
Isis (goddess), 6
Islam, Islamic world:
bookbinding in, 302–3
and spread of papermaking, 53–56, 58
italic typefaces, *28*, 320

James, E. L., 220
James, Henry, 233–34
Japan, 53
Buddhism in, 181–83
China emulated by, 181
orihons in, 266
printing in, 183
Jenson, Nicolas, 330
Jews, parchment adopted by, 25–27
jian (bamboo slips), 38
jiance (bamboo scrolls), 38
Jia Sixie, 52
John, Gospel of, 161, 162, 286
Jung, Carl, 290
Jung Codex (Eid Codex; Codex I), 289–91
Jung Institute, 290
justification, in typesetting, *42*, 136–37, 143, 150

Kafka, Franz, 129
Karnak, 247
kelaf parchment, 27
Keller, Friedrich Gottlob, 36, 68–69
Kells, 161, 164
Kenyon, F. G., 4
Khwarizmi, al-, 55
Kindles, xvi, 220, 321
Knox, Robert, 304, 305
Koenig, Friedrich, 135
printing press of, 132–34, *134*
kollemata (papyrus sheets), 251
Komori LSP440 lithographic press, 329–30
Korea, 53
orihons in, 266
Kublai Khan, 176, 187

laid molds, in papermaking, 43, 45, 46, 51, *59*, 314
Lanston, Tolbert, 147
adding machine of, 146, 147
inventions of, 146
Monotype and, 151–52
Lanston Monotype Machine Company, 148

lapis lazuli, 172
Lata'if al-ma'arif (The Book of Curious and Entertaining Information; al-Tha'alibi), 54
lead, 118, 122
leather:
  on book covers, 303–4
  making of, 20–21, 24
  as writing surface, 20–21, 24
leaves, 290
Leo III, Pope, 165
Leonardo da Vinci, notebooks of, 284
Lepsius, Karl Richard, 157
letter (8½-by-11-inch) paper size, 326–28
letter punches, 114–16
Lhuyd, Edward, 68
Liang, Lady, 40
Library of Alexandria, 18, 19, 23, 250, 251–52, 253, 254
  fire at, 256
Library of Congress, 71, 72–73
libri portatiles (portable books), 317
Lichtenberg, Georg, 324–25
lignin, 71, 74
lime, 28, 30
Lindisfarne, 284, 286
Lindisfarne Gospels, 161, 164, 287
linen, 36, 37, 61–62
Linotypes, *138*, 141–45, *142*, *144*, 148, 151–52, , 236, 308
linseed oil, 121
lithography, xvii, 329–30
  artists and, 226
  color, 226
  computer-designed books and, 236–37
  ink, 140, 224, 225, 233
  modern applications of, 227
  offset, 236, 237
  Senefelder's invention of, 220–25
  typesetting with, 151
  versatility of, 225
  with zinc plates, 233–34
Liu Qing, 40, 47
Liu Zhao (Emperor He), 40–41
Lives of the Most Eminent Painters, Sculptors, and Architects (Vasari), 204
Lives of the Twelve Caesars (Suetonius), 273
Livingston, Robert R., 68
Livy, 276
Lizars, William Home, 214–15, 216
Logia Iesu, 264–65, 276
Louis XVI, king of France, 64
Lovers Surprised by Death (Burgkmair), 197–98, *197*
Lower Egypt, 8, 88
Luddite movement, 65
Luke, Gospel of, 161
lunellarium, *29*, 30
Luoyang, China, 39, 40, 181
lying presses, *299*, 301

Mädchenkenner, Die (The Connoisseurs of Girls; Senefelder), 219
magnesium oxide, 72–73
magnetic compass, Chinese invention of, 177
Maimonides, Moses, 26–27, 28
Mainz, Germany, 102–3, 127, 225, 298, 316
Mainz Psalters, 126–27, 329
Maltese language, 93

manicules, 320
Mansion, Colard, 203, *205*, 208, 209, 314, 316
Marie-Antoinette, queen of France, 64
Mark, Gospel of, 161, 162
Martial, 96, 274–76
Mason, Joseph, 214
Massachusetts, 63
matrix, matrices, *115*, 116, *117*, *142*, 143, *148*
Matthew, Gospel of, 161, 162, 262
Maximilian I, Holy Roman emperor, 198
Mayans, orihons (codices) of, 268, *268*, 270
medicine:
 Chinese ink in, 113
 papyrus plant in, 7
Melrose Abbey, 284, 286
Melville, Herman, 321, 326
membranae, 272–73, 274
memorialis libri, 273
Memphis, Egypt, 241–42
Menes (mythical first king of Egypt), 241–42
Menou, Jacques-François, 90
Mergenthaler, Ottmar, *138*, 139–40, 150
 Linotype and, 141–45, 148, 151–52
Mesoamerica, orihons (codices) in, 268–69, *268*, 270
Mesopotamia, Mesopotamians, 79, 82, 93, 109, 242, 257
Metamorphoses (Ovid), 209
mezuzah, 27
Middle Ages, 318
miniators, 172
miniatures, 172
minium (orange lead), 172
Mishneh Torah, 26–27
Moby-Dick (Melville), 321, 323
Moeris, Lake, 241
molds:
 in papermaking, *43*, 44–47, 51, 58, *59*
 for type, 116–18, *117*
Moleskine notebooks, 306
monasteries, 30, 157, 161, 164
 acquisition and copying of books by, 165–66
 illuminated manuscripts and, 166
 scriptoria of, 166–69, *168*
money:
 increasing importance of, 174
 see also paper money
Mongol Empire, 176, 192
Monotypes, 151–52, 308
 caster of, 148–49, *149*
 justification of, 150
 keyboard of, 148, *149*
Moore, Charles T., 140, 141
Moors, 55–56
Moses, 6
Mouseion, 249–50, 251–52
movable type, xv, 62, 199, 220, 234, 301, 316
 blockbooks displaced by, 199
 China and, 109–14, 186
 Gutenberg and, 106, 109, 114–23, 128
 halftone printing and, 230, *233*
 woodcuts combined with, 199, 201, 202–3, 227
Muhammad, prophet, 53
mummy paper, 66–67
murex, 30
Murray, John, 70–71

Museo del Papiro, 16
Muses, 249–50
Museum of Underwater Archaeology, Turkey, 256
Muslims, *see* Islam, Islamic world

Nag Hammadi, Egypt, 277
Nag Hammadi codices, 265, 277–78, 288–91, 311, 331
  construction of, 279–81, *280*, 282
Naples, Bay of, 10
Napoleon I, Emperor of France, 3
Nara, Japan, 181–82
Narmer, pharaoh, 242
NASA, 72
nationalism, rise of, 156
Natural History (Pliny), 11, 16, 19–20, 96
New Light on the Renaissance, A (Bayley), 60–61
New Testament, 262
Niccolò de Niccoli, 320
Nicholson, William, 130, 132, 133
Nicolas V, Pope, 108
Nicolò di Lorenzo della Magna, 208–9
Nile delta, 4, 8, 92, 249
Nile River, 3–4, 6, 14, 241–42, 261, 270
  annual flooding of, 8
1984 (Orwell), xvi
Northrop, 72
Norwich, Conn., 66

Octavian, emperor of Rome, 88
octavo (book size), 313, 314, *314*, 317, 318, 321, 325–26, 330, 331
Odoacer, 156
offset lithography, 236, 237
opener text, 3
orange lead (minium), 172
Ordnance Survey, 233
orihons:
  in China and Japan, 266, *267*, 269–70
  in Mesoamerica, 268–69, *268*, 270
  as supposed proto-books, 266
ornament, *xiii*
orpiment, 259
Orwell, George, xvi
Osiris, 6, 158
ostraca, 82, 270
ostracism, 82–83
ouroboros, *59*
Ovid, 96, 209
Oxford English Dictionary, 109, 243
Oxyrhynchus, Egypt, 95, 262–63
Oxyrhynchus Papyri, The (Grenfell and Hunt), 262, 263, 264

Paige, James W., 136, *138*, 139, 148, 151
Paige Compositor, 136–38, *138*, 148
Palazzo di San Giorgio, Genoa, 175, 189
Paleographers, 107, 179
palimpsests, 97–98, 100
Palladius, 156
Palmer, Samuel, 213
Panegyris ad duces Bavariae (Panegyrics to the dukes of Bavaria), *302*
pantograph, 224–25
papal bulls, 28
paper, papermaking, xv, xvii
  acid-free, 73–74, *75*, 76, 329
  Arab use of, 54–56
  Chinese invention of, 36–37, 41–49, *43*, *44*, *45*, 50–52, 68, 113, 177, 178–79, 191

Christians' distrust of, 56, 58
codices of, 302–3, 312
cost of, 76
in East Asia, 50, 53
in Europe, 56, *57*, 58–63
freesheet, 74, *75*
improvements in, 51, 55, 61, 69–76
insect damage and, 51–52
interdependence of books and, 35–36, 50
in Islamic world, 53–56, 58
as jealously guarded secret, 50, 52–53
linen-based (rag), 36, 37, 61–62, 66
mechanization of, 61, 64–66, 69–70
molds in, *43*, 44–47, 51, 58
parchment displaced by, 36
rag shortages and, 61–64, 66
rubbings on, 179–80
sizes of, 323–28
spinning wheel and, 62
in US, 63–64, 66
watermarks in, 58–59, *59*, 312, *313*, 317–18, 327
wood pulp-based, 68–76
world consumption of, 35
paperbacks, xv, xvii, 309
Papermaking (Hunter), 60
paper money:
in China, 180
Chinese invention of, 176–77, 187, *188*, 189
paper mulberry (*Broussonetia papyrifera; chu*), 47, 49
in papermaking, 41–42, *46*, 68
papyrologists, papyrology, 4, 13, 16, 263, 265
papyrus (*Cyperus papyrus*), 3–7, *5*
dividing of, 12–13, *12*
harvesting of, *7*
modern cultivation of, 16–17
symbolism of, 8
uses of, 4, 6, 7, *7*, 9–10
papyrus (writing surface), xvii, 3, 8–9, 10, *15*, 28, 55, 83–84, *83*, 93–94, 96, 242–43, 276
codices of, 261–65, 272, 276–82, 288–91, 302–3, 311, 312–13
eclipse of, 287
export of banned by Egypt, 19
grades of, 17
in Greco-Roman world, 15–16, 18, 23–24
illustrated, 157–59, *160*
making of, 11–14, *12*
modern production of, 16–17
parchment as superior to, 25, 31
Papyrus Oxyrhynchus I 1 (P. Oxy I 1), 264–65, 276
papyrus scrolls, xv, *xvn*, xvi, 10, 244, *253*, *255*, 260, 263, 311
accessories for, 254–55
Egyptian invention of, 243–45, 247–56
electronic documents as analogous to, 254
in Greco-Roman world, 244, 250–56
inefficiency of, 253–56
as information technology, 9
parchment, xv, 55, *99*, 101, 287
calfskin, xii, 31, 123, 304
Christian adoption of, 27–28, 56
codices of, 272–77, 284–88, 291–93, 311–12

parchment (*continued*)
 cost of, 62, 97
 etymology of, 31
 goatskin, 20, 28, 30
 for illuminated manuscripts, 169
 ink and, 96–97
 invention of, 18–21, 23–24
 Jewish adoption of, 25–27
 making of, 24–25, 27, 28–31, *29*, 33–34
 in making of gold and silver leaf, 171
 paper's displacement of, 36
 sheepskin, 31, 312
 shortcomings of, 25
 spread of, 24
 as superior to papyrus, 25, 31
 see also vellum
parchmenters, 30
Parliament, British, 323–24
part number, *1*
part title, *1*
pasteboard covers, 302–3
Patrick, Saint, 156–57
Pencil of Nature, The (Talbot), 228–29, *228*
pencils, 259
Penguin Books, 324
penknives, 169, 170
pens, 84, 85
 quill, 97, 101, 169, 170
 reed, 16, 47, 94, *95*
Pension Office, US, 146, 148
perfect binding, 309
Pergamon, 21, 23–24, 28, 276
 and invention of parchment, 19–21, 23–24
 library at, 19, 23
"Permanence of Paper for Publications and Documents in Libraries and Archives," 74
Permanent Conference on Printing, 326–27
Persian Empire, 270
Peter the Venerable, 56, 62
Petrarcha, Francesco, *319*
Petrie, Flinders, 15, 84, 92
Petticoat Lane, 63
Pfister, Albrecht, 199, *200*, 201, 202
 Biblia pauperum of, *200*, 201
Phaistos Disk, 109
Philadelphia, Pa., 214
Philo, 96–97
Philobiblon Society of Great Britain, 189
Philometor, *see* Ptolemy VI Philometor, pharaoh
Phoenicia, Phoenicians, 9
 alphabet of, 91–92
photography, 227
 in book and newspaper illustration, xvii, 228–29, 230–31, *233*
 halftone, 230–31, *231*, *233*
photogravure, *231*, *233*
photolithography, 233, 236
phototypesetting, 151
photozincography, 233, *235*
Picts, 161
Pio, Alberto, 316
pippins, 30
plague, bubonic, 102, 105
Plan of St. Gall, 167
platens, 122–23, 130, *131*, 132
plates (standalone illustrations), 210, 231

Plato, 8, 15
Pliny the Elder, 10–11, 15, 95, 96, 113, 243, 274, 276
on invention of parchment, 19–20
on making papyrus scrolls, 11–14
on papyrus-making, 17
Pliny the Younger, 28–29, 274
plummets, 10[illegible], 170
poetry extract, *71*
Poitevin, Alphonse-Louis, 23[illegible]
Poitiers, battle of (732), 53
Polo, Marco, 175–77, 187, 189, 190
polyptychs, 259
Pompeii, 10, *255*, 276
Ponton, Mungo, 229
Popilius Laenas, Gaius, 22–23
Porten, Bezalel, 270–72
potassium dichromate, 229
pouncing, 30, 97
Prague, 219
Prang, Louis, *226*
PREPS sustainability standard, *75*, 329
printer's devil, 144
printing:
Chinese invention of, 177–81, 183–86
Gutenberg and, 107–9
history of, 109
in Japan, 183
matrices in, *115*, 116
molds in, 116–18, *117*
punches in, 114–16
in Renaissance, 202–13
with wood blocks, *see* woodblock printing
printing presses, xvii, 174
Albion, 130
Columbian, 130, *131*
denunciations of, 128–29
of Gutenberg, 122–23
of iron, 129–30
Koenig's design for, 132–34, *134*
modernization of, 129–52
Nicholson's design for, 130, 132, 133
rotary, 130, 132, 133, 135
spread of, 126–27, 128
Stanhope, 130, 133
Prisse d'Avennes, Achille-Constant-Théodore Émile, 245, 247–48
Prisse Papyrus, 245, 247–48
Proctor, Robert, 316
prose extract, *89*
protocol, etymology of, 251
protokollon, 95, 251
Ptahhotep, Egyptian vizier, 248
Ptolemaic dynasty, 19–20, 23, 88, 159, 249–50
Ptolemy I, pharaoh, 249
Ptolemy III Euergetes, pharaoh, 251–52
Ptolemy VI Philometor, pharaoh, 21–22
Ptolemy VII, pharaoh, 22*n*
Ptolemy VIII Euergetes, pharaoh, 22
pugillares (writing tablets), 274
pugillares membranae, 276
pumice, 29, 30, 97
punches, 114–16, *115*
Puyemrê, *7*
Pythagoras's constant, 324–25

Qin dynasty, 38, 39, 178
Qin Shi Huang (First Emperor), 178
quarto (book size), 313, 314, *314*, 316, 318, 325–26

quaternio (quire), 312–13
Quintilian, 259
quire (*quaternio*), 312–13, 330
Qu'ran, 56, 58

Ra, 158
Ragab, Hassan, 11–12, 14, 16
rag and bone men, 63
rags, in papermaking, 36, 37, 42–43, 55, 61–64, 66
Ragyndrudis Codex, 296–98
railway novels, 309, 331
Rainer, Archduke of Austria, 37
Rameses III, pharaoh, 249
Rashid (Rosetta), Egypt, 90
Rath, Erich von, 209
Reagan administration, 328
Réaumur, René Antoine Ferchault de, 68–69
"Recollections of the Arabian Nights" (Tennyson), 54
recto, 264
recto running head, *11*
Red Sea, 245
Reid, Whitelaw, 144
Renaissance, 36, 60, 114, 318, 330
  printing in, 202–13
"Report of Wenamun," 9
Revelations, 28
Revolutionary War, 63–64
Riedel, Friedrich, 132
Robert, Louis-Nicolas, 64–65, 69, 135
Robert Havell and son, 215
Roberts, T. C., 276–77
Robinson, James M., 277–78
Roche, Saint, 192
roller backer, 308
Roman Empire, 60, 101, 106, 273
  correspondence in, 271
  decline of, 155–56, 318
  handwriting in, 318
Roman Republic, 10, 256
roman typefaces, 318, 320, 330
Rome, ancient, 21, 155, 159
  alphabet of, 92
  Egypt conquered by, 88
  Egyptian hieroglyphics and, 89
  papyrus in, 10, 96
  papyrus scrolls in, 244, 250–56
  pen-and-ink writing in, 95–96
  writing in, 162, 164
Rome, sack of (410), 156
Romulus Augustulus, emperor of Rome, 156
ropes, from papyrus, 6–7, *7*, 9–10
Rosetta Stone, 90–91
rosin (pine resin), 69
rotary (cylinder) presses, 132, 134–35, 234, 308
Routledge, George, 309, 331
Royal Geographical Society, 60
Royal Society of London, 68
rubbings, in China, 179–80
Rubel, Ira, 234, 236
rubrica, 172
rubricators, 107, 122, 172
rubrics, 172
Rump Parliament, 323–24
Russia, 190
Rustichello, 175–76, 177, 187, 189

Sachau, Eduard, 270
Saffah, Abu al-Abbas as-, 53
saffron yellow ink, 172
Safire, William, 23

St Cuthbert Gospel, 284–88, *285*, 291–93, 294, 295–96, 298, 300, 303, 324, 331
 cover of, 295–96
Samarqand, 53
Sammam, 'Ali al-, 278
Sammam, Muhammad 'Ali al-, 277–78
Sappho, 262
Saturnalia, 276
Saxons, 156
Scepsis, 19
Schmandt-Besserat, Denise, 80
Schöffer, Peter, 106, 127
Schow, Niels Iversen, 4
Schriftgiesser, Der (The Typecaster; Amman), *119*
Scotland, 161, 215, 304–5
scribes, xv
 in ancient Egypt, 85, 87–88, *87*, *246*, 250–51
 Chinese, 179
 in Egypt, 264
 medieval, 97, *99*, 100, 101, 128, 160–61, 166–72, *168*, 198–99, 286, 287, 291–92
scriptio continua, 162, 164
scriptores, 169
scriptoria, 166–69, *168*
seals, Chinese use of, 178–79
Seaton, Charles W., 145–48
Sebastian, Saint, 192
section break, *8*
Seleucid Empire, 21, 23
Semitic languages, 93
Senefelder, Alois, 219–26, 227, 237
 lithographic process patented by, 225
Senefelder, Peter, 219
Serabit el-Khadim, 92, 93
sewing frames, *299*, 300
Shakespeare, William, 71, 233
sheepskin, 31, 122, 279, 295, 304
Shen Kuo, 110–11
sherds, 83
Sholes, Christopher Latham, 140
Shōtoku, empress of Japan, 182–83
silhouetted art, *144*
silk:
 manufacture of, as jealously guarded secret, 50, 52–53
 World War II escape maps on, 38
 as writing surface, 37, 38–39, 178–79
Silk Road, 18[illegible]
silver leaf, 171
Sinai Peninsula, 92
Sinaitic script, 92–93
sittybos, 252, *253*
Sixth Syrian War, 21–23
sizing, in papermaking, 51, 55, 230
Skeat, C. R., 276–77
Slimbach, Robert, 330
Smeijers, Fred, 115
Smyth, David M., 308, 331
Society of Antiquaries, 287
Socrates, on books and writing, 252–53
Song, Lady, 40
Song dynasty, 48
sorts, *115*, *117*, 118, *120*, 121
Southward, James, 145
Spain, 56, 100
 papermaking in, 56, 58
Spanish conquistadores, 268–69
Sparta, Spartans, 96, 258–59
Speckter, Martin K., 121

spinning wheel, papermaking and, 62
Stanhope, Charles, 130
Stanhope presses, 130, 133
Stanwood and Tower mill, 66, 67–68
stereotype, 134, 135, 141, 220
Stewart, Potter, xv
Strabo, 11
Strasbourg, 103–6
Strata, Filippo de, 203
stylus, styli, *255*, 259
    silver-tipped, 170
Suavius, Lambert, 209
subtitle, *vii*
Suetonius, 273
sulfur dioxide, 71
Sulla, 15
Sumer, 9
Sumerians, 20, 79–80, 82, 84
suq al-warraqin (stationer's market), 55
Surgeons' Hall, Edinburgh, 305
"syllabus," etymology of, 252

ta (rubbing), 179
tabellae (writing tablets), 274
tabulating machines, 145–46, 152
Tacitus, Marcus Claudius, emperor of Rome, 16
Taizong, emperor of China, 179, 180, 181
Talas, battle of (751), 53, 54
Talbot, William Henry Fox, 227–29, *228*, 230, 231, *231*, 233, 237
talbotypes, 227–29, *228*
Tallet, Pierre, *83*
Talmud, 56
Tang dynasty, 48, 269–70
tannic acids, 20–21, 100, 101*n*
Tano, Phocion J., 279, 289
Tarkhan, Egypt, 84
taxes, taxation, in ancient Egypt, 249, 250
tefillin, 27
Ten Commandments, *26*
Tennyson, Alfred Lord, 54
Terentius Neo, *255*
textura (Gothic script), 107
Tha'alibi, Abu Mansur al-, 54, 191
Thamus (mythical Egyptian king), 8, 252
Thebes, Egypt, 247
Theophilus, 28–29
Thoth, 8, 87, 158, *159*, 243
Thutmose III, pharaoh, 247
Tian gong kai wu (The Creations of Nature and Man), *43*
Tiberius, emperor of Rome, 273
Tigris River, 79
Times (London), 265
    Koenig press at, 132–34, *134*
tin, 118
titanium oxide, 74
Titian, 198, 203
title, *vii*
titulus, 252, *253*, *255*
Tolkien, J. R. R., 298
tomes, 251
Tommaso d'Antonio, 193
Torah, 26–27
Torresani, Andrea, 316
Toulouse-Lautrec, Henri, 224
Travis, William B., 23
tree galls, 20–21, 97, 100–101
Tres riches heures du duc de Berry, les (Very rich hours of the Duke of Berry), 174
Triumphal Arch (Dürer), 198
Turkey, 6, 20, *81*, 176, 256
Turks, 53
Turner, Eric, 265, 310–11

Twain, Mark, *see* Clemens, Samuel
tympan, *120*, 122–23
type cases, 120, *120*
typesetting, 118
  Church's principle and, 139, 141
  composing stick and, 120–21, 135, 136
  computers and, 152
  justification in, 136–37, 143, 150
  Linotype and, *138*, 141–45, *142*, *144*, 148, 151–52
  lithographic, 151
  matrices in, 143, 148
  mechanization of, 136–52
  Monotype and, 148–49, 150, 151–52
  Paige Compositor and, 136–38, *138*
  photographic, 151
Typology of the Early Codex (Turner), 310–11

udjat (eye of Horus), 87
ultramarine ink, 172
Uluburun, Turkey, shipwreck at, 256–57, *258*, 274
Umayyad caliphate, 53
umbilici, 254–55
uncials, 276, 318
United Kingdom, 69
  see also England; Great Britain; Scotland
United States:
  paper consumption in, 35
  papermaking in, 63–64, 66
uterine (virgin) vellum, 33–34

Valle, Pietro della, 79–80
Vandals, 156
Van Leyden, Lucas, 212–13
Vasari, Giorgio, 204
Vatican, 28
vellum, xvii, 31, *33*, 123, 287, 304
  virgin (uterine), 33–34
Venice, 175, 189, 310, 316
verdigris, 259
vermilion ink, 172, 179
verso, 264
verso running head, *10*
Vesuvius, Mount, 10, 276
Victoria, Lake, 3–4
Vienna, University of, 37
Vikings, 164, 284
Virgil, 317
  Aldine press edition of, 318, 320–21, 323
Virgin Mary, devotional images of, 193
virgin (uterine) vellum, 33–34
Vitruvius, 95
Voelter, Heinrich, 69
volumen, 251

Wadi el-Jarf, Egpyt, *83*
Walter, John, 133–34
Wang Yuanlu, 179
Wang Zhen, 111–12, 113, 120, 186
watermarks, 58–59, *59*, 312, 317–18
wax writing tablets, xvi, 96, *255*, 256–60, 274, 276, 294
  diptychs, 284
  erasability of, 259
Wearmouth-Jarrow monastery, 287
Wellcome Library, London, 305–6
Wenquan ming (The Eulogy on the Hot Springs), 179
white lead, 172
White Nile, 3–4
Wilson, Alexander, 214
Wilson, Woodrow, 326

Wolfe, S. J., 66
woodblock printing, xvii, 111–12
  Bewick's improvement of, 227
  Catholic Church and, 192–93
  chiaroscuro, 197–98, *197*
  in China, 183–86
  of devotional images, 193
  Dürer and, 195, *196*, 197
  in Europe, 190–201
  in Japan, 183
  movable type combined with, 199, 201, 202–3, 227
  woods used in, 185–86
wood engraving, 227, 231, 234
wood pulp, in papermaking, 68–76
Wörrstadt, Niklaus von, 103–4
wove molds, in papermaking, 45, 46–47, 51
writing:
  in ancient Rome, 162, 164
  cuneiform, 79–80, *81*, 82
  history of, 79–101
  invention of, 8–9
  secret, 96–97
writing tablets, *see* wax writing tablets
Wu, Han Chinese emperor, 48

Xàtiva, Spain, 56, 58
Xerxes, King of Persia, 6–7, 96, 258

yin (printing), 177–79, 180, 184
Young, Thomas, 90–91
Yuen Foong Yu Group, 75, 329
Yule, Henry, 191–92

Zapf, Hermann, 145
Zhang, Hang emperor of China, 40
zhi (paper), 41, 47
zhu bo, 37, 39
zinc plates, lithography with, 233–34
Zoëga, Jørgen, 89–90
Zouche of Harringworth, Robert Curzon, baron, 189–90